FODOR'S
NEW ORLEANS

Area Editor: JOHN R. KEMP
Editorial Contributors: JEANIE BLAKE, THOMAS BONNER, JR., CHARLES
  R. CHAPPLE, THOMAS G. FITZMORRIS, VINCENT FUMAR, ROGER
  GREEN, D. CLIVE HARDY, ERROL LABORDE, JOHN POPE, ROULHAC
  TOLEDANO
Editor: LISA A. CHECCHI
Editorial Associate: ELENORE BODIE
Research: TOM SZENTGYORGYI
Illustrations: TED BURWELL
Maps and Plans: BURMAR TECHNICAL CORP., PICTOGRAPH

FODOR'S TRAVEL GUIDES
New York

All the following Guides are current (most of them also in
the Hodder and Stoughton British edition.)

CURRENT FODOR'S COUNTRY AND AREA TITLES:

AUSTRALIA, NEW ZEALAND AND SOUTH PACIFIC	ISRAEL
	ITALY
AUSTRIA	JAPAN
BELGIUM AND LUXEMBOURG	JORDAN AND HOLY LAND
	KOREA
BERMUDA	MEXICO
BRAZIL	NORTH AFRICA
CANADA	PEOPLE'S REPUBLIC OF CHINA
CARIBBEAN AND BAHAMAS	
CENTRAL AMERICA	PORTUGAL
EASTERN EUROPE	SCANDINAVIA
EGYPT	SCOTLAND
EUROPE	SOUTH AMERICA
FRANCE	SOUTHEAST ASIA
GERMANY	SOVIET UNION
GREAT BRITAIN	SPAIN
GREECE	SWITZERLAND
HOLLAND	TURKEY
INDIA	YUGOSLAVIA
IRELAND	

CITY GUIDES:

BEIJING, GUANGZHOU, SHANGHAI	PARIS
CHICAGO	ROME
DALLAS AND FORT WORTH	SAN DIEGO
HOUSTON	SAN FRANCISCO
LONDON	STOCKHOLM, COPENHAGEN, OSLO, HELSINKI, AND REYKJAVIK
LOS ANGELES	
MADRID	
MEXICO CITY AND ACAPULCO	TOKYO
NEW ORLEANS	WASHINGTON, D.C.
NEW YORK CITY	

FODOR'S BUDGET SERIES:

BUDGET BRITAIN	BUDGET ITALY
BUDGET CANADA	BUDGET JAPAN
BUDGET CARIBBEAN	BUDGET MEXICO
BUDGET EUROPE	BUDGET SCANDINAVIA
BUDGET FRANCE	BUDGET SPAIN
BUDGET GERMANY	BUDGET TRAVEL IN AMERICA
BUDGET HAWAII	

USA GUIDES:

ALASKA	HAWAII
CALIFORNIA	NEW ENGLAND
CAPE COD	PENNSYLVANIA
COLORADO	SOUTH
FAR WEST	TEXAS
FLORIDA	USA (in one volume)

CONTENTS

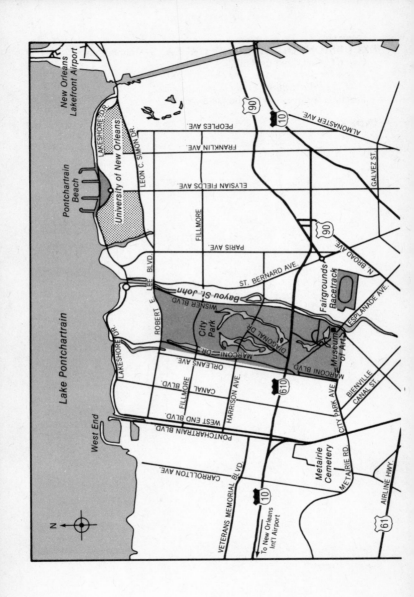

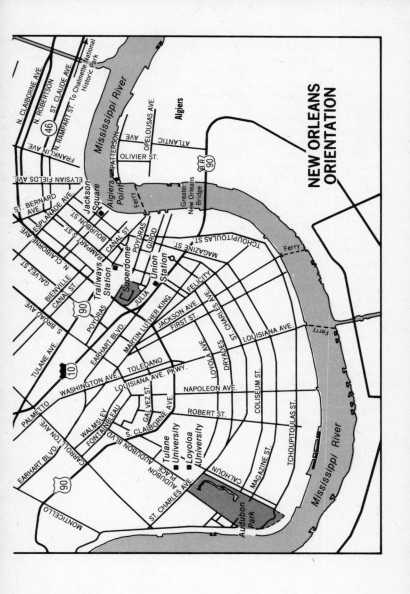

NEW ORLEANS
ORIENTATION

FOREWORD

We think New Orleans is a special city in that it is regarded as the least "American" of any in the United States. It is best known for its unique regional cuisine, remarkable amalgam of architectural styles, boisterous Mardi Gras festivities, and as the birthplace of jazz music. These attributes and more have made New Orleans one of this country's most popular destinations among visitors from all over the world. 1984 promises to be another exciting year in New Orleans as it hosts the 1984 Louisiana World Exposition—the city's second world's fair with the new theme "The World of Rivers—Fresh Water as a Source of Life."

Our New Orleans writers have put together information on the widest possible range of activities, and within that range present you with selections of events and places that will be safe, worthwhile, and of good value. The descriptions we provide are just enough for you to make your own informed choices from among our selections. As a special feature, we have added an insert on the 1984 Louisiana World Exposition to acquaint you with the pavilion layout and activities that will occur there.

All selections and comments in *Fodor's New Orleans* are based on the editors' and contributors' personal experiences. We feel that our first responsibility is to inform and protect you, the reader. Errors are bound to creep into any travel guide, however. We go to press in the middle of the year, and much change can and will occur in New Orleans even while we are on press and certainly also during the succeeding 12 months or so when this edition is on sale. We cannot, therefore, be responsible for the sudden closing of a restaurant, a change in a museum's days or hours, a shift of hotel ownership (for the worse), and so forth. We sincerely welcome letters from our readers on these changes, or from those whose opinions differ from ours, and we are ready to revise our entries for next year's edition when the facts warrant it.

Send your letters to the editors at **Fodor's Travel Guides,** 2 Park Avenue, New York, New York 10016. Continental or British Commonwealth readers may prefer to write to Fodor's Travel Guides, 9-10 Market Place, London W1N 7AG, England.

FACTS AT YOUR FINGERTIPS

PLANNING YOUR TRIP. If you don't want to bother with reservations on your own, a travel agent won't cost you a cent, except for specific charges like telegrams. He gets his fee from the hotel or carrier he books for you. A travel agent can also be of help for those who prefer to take their vacations on a "package tour"—thus keeping your own planning to a minimum. If you prefer the convenience of standardized accommodations, remember that the various hotel and motel chains publish free directories of their members that enable you to plan and reserve everything ahead of time.

If you're driving and you don't belong to an auto club, now is the time to join one. It can be very helpful about routings and providing emergency service on the road. If you plan to route yourself, make certain the map you get is dated for the current year (highways and thruways are appearing and being extended at an astonishingly rapid rate). Some of the major oil companies will send maps and mark preferred routes on them if you tell them what you have in mind. Try: *Exxon Touring Service,* Exxon Corporation, 1251 Avenue of the Americas, New York, NY 10020; *Texaco Travel Service,* P.O. Box 1459, Houston, TX 77001; or *Mobil Oil Corp. Touring Service,* P.O. Box 24, Versailles, KY 40383. In addition, most areas have their own maps, which pinpoint attractions, list historical sites, parks, etc. City chambers of commerce are also good sources of information. Specific addresses are given under *Visitor Information* and *Tourist Information.*

Plan to board the pets, discontinue paper and milk deliveries, and tell your local police and fire departments when you'll be leaving and when you expect to return. Ask a kindly neighbor to keep an eye on your house; fully protect your swimming pool against intruders. Have a friend keep your mail, or have it held at the post office. Look into the purchase of trip insurance (including baggage), and make certain your auto, fire and other policies are up-to-date. Today, most people who travel use credit cards for important expenses such as gas, repairs, lodgings and some meals. Consider converting the greater portion of your trip money into traveler's checks. Arrange to have your lawn mowed at the usual times, and leave that kindly neighbor your itinerary (insofar as is possible), car license number and a key to your home (and tell police and firemen he has it). Since some hotel and motel chains give discounts (10–25 percent) to senior citizens, be sure to have some sort of identification along if you qualify. Usually AARP or NRTA membership is best. (See below under *Accommodations.*)

VISITOR INFORMATION. The *Greater New Orleans Tourist and Convention Commission* (334 Royal St., New Orleans, LA 70130) and the *Louisiana Office of Tourism* (P.O. Box 44291, Baton Rouge, LA 70804) provide invaluable visitor information. The state Office of Tourism also main-

1

tains several impressive visitor centers along major highways entering the state. The New Orleans Tourist and Convention Commission staffs a visitors' information desk at the New Orleans International Airport.

 TIPS FOR BRITISH VISITORS. Passports. You will need a valid passport and a U.S. Visitor's Visa (which can only be put in a passport of the 10-year kind). You can obtain the visa either through your travel agent or airline, or directly from the *United States Embassy,* Visa and Immigration Department, 24 Grosvenor Sq., London W1 (tel. 01–499 7010/3443). Allow 4 weeks if applying to the Embassy by mail; if you apply in person, your visa can be obtained in about 3 hours.

No vaccinations are required for entry into the U.S.

Customs. If you are 21 or over, you can take into the U.S.: 200 cigarettes, or 50 cigars, or 2 kilos of tobacco; 1 U.S. liter of alcohol. Everyone is entitled to take into the U.S. duty-free gifts to a value of $100. Be careful not to try to take in meat or meat products, seeds, plants, fruits, etc. And avoid narcotics like the plague.

Insurance. We heartily recommend that you insure yourself to cover health and motoring mishaps, with *Europ Assistance,* 252 High St., Croydon CRO INF (tel. 01–680 1234). Their excellent service is all the more valuable when you consider the possible costs of health care in the U.S.

Tour Operators. The price battle that has raged over transatlantic fares has meant that most tour operators now offer excellent budget packages to the U.S. Among those you might consider as you plan your trip are—

American Express, 6 Haymarket, London SW1.

Thomas Cook Ltd., P.O. Box 36, Thorpe Wood, Peterborough, PE 3 6SB.

Cosmos, Cosmos House, 1 Bromley Common, Bromley, Kent BR2 9LX.

Cunard, 8 Berkeley St., London W1.

Jetsave, Sussex House, London Rd., East Grinstead RH19 1LD.

Page and Moy, 136–140 London Rd., Leicester LE2 1EN.

Speedbird, 152 King St., London W6 OQU.

Air Fares. We suggest that you explore the current scene for budget flight possibilities. All the main transatlantic carriers have stand-by tickets, available a short time before the flight only, as well as APEX and other fares at a considerable saving over the full price. Quite frankly, only business travelers who don't have to watch the price of their tickets fly full-price these days—and find themselves sitting right beside an APEX passenger!

Hotels. You may have need of a fast-booking service to find a hotel room. One of the very best ways to do this is to contact *HBI-HOTAC,* Globegate House, Pound Lane, London NW10 (tel. 01–451 2311). They book rooms for most of the large chains (Holiday Inns, Hilton, Ramada, etc.), so you can have a multiple choice with only one contact. HBI-HOTAC specializes in booking for business firms, but also deals with the general public.

WHEN TO GO. Visiting New Orleans can be fun year round. The summers are long, hot and humid, but winter is mild when comparing it to more northern climes. Perhaps the best time to visit the city and nearby plantations is in the early spring. The days are pleasant, except for the seasonal cloudbursts, and the nights are cool. The main avenues, parks, private gardens and plantations are alive with the beautiful spring flowers, especially the numerous varieties of azaleas that are so common and popular in the New Orleans area. The weather is intensely hot and humid from mid-June through August, but that is rather typical of the Deep South. If you can't avoid a visit to New Orleans during the summer, fear not, all hotels and restaurants are air-conditioned. Falls are generally pleasant with warm and balmy days and cool evenings.

Winter in New Orleans means the Sugar Bowl football classic and Mardi Gras. The Sugar Bowl is one of the oldest bowl games in the country. It features the top-ranked U.S. college teams. New Orleans is known the world over for its Mardi Gras celebration, which begins in February and ends Shrove Tuesday. *Spring* brings St. Patrick's Day and St. Joseph Day parades (March 15 and 17); the Spring Fiesta, and the Jazz and Heritage Festival (April); and the New Orleans PGA Open golf tournament (April). In recent years, the city has added two new festivals to the calendar to attract visitors to New Orleans during the hot and humid *summer*. La Fete and the New Orleans Food Festival are billed as an annual family summer festival, featuring special events in the French Market, fireworks and other attractions, beginning July 4 and ending on Bastille Day (July 14).

Fall brings the New Orleans Philharmonic Orchestra's new season (September); Festa d'Italia (October); and horse racing at the Fairgrounds (November–March).

PACKING. *What to take, what to wear.* Make a packing list for each member of the family, then check off items as you pack them. It will save time, reduce confusion. Time-savers to carry along include extra film (plenty), suntan lotion, insect repellent, toothpaste, soap, etc. Always carry an extra pair of glasses, including sunglasses, particularly if they're prescription ones. A travel iron is always a good tote-along, as are some plastic bags (small and large) for wet bathing suits and soiled clothing. They also are excellent for packing shoes, cosmetics and other easily damaged items. If you fly, remember that despite signs to the contrary, airport security X-ray machines do in fact damage film rolls in about 17 percent of the cases. Have them inspected separately or pack them in special protective bags. Fun extras to carry include binoculars, a compass, and a magnifying glass—to read fine-print maps.

All members of the family should have sturdy shoes with nonslip soles—sidewalks in the New Orleans French Quarter can be slippery when wet. Carry the family raingear in a separate bag and keep it in the back of the car (so no one will have to get out and hunt for it in a downpour en route).

Women will probably want to stick to one or two basic colors for their holiday wardrobes so they can manage with one set of accessories. If possible, include one knit or jersey dress or a pants suit that won't need ironing, and for the winter months take a *lightweight* coat. For dress-up evenings, take along a few "basic" dresses you can vary with a simple change of accessories. That way you can dress up or down to suit the occasion.

Be sure to check what temperatures will be like along the route. Depending upon where you are coming from, traveling in mountains can mean cool evenings—even in summer—and so can traveling through the desert. An extra sweater is always a safe thing to pack, even if just to protect yourself from the air conditioning.

Men will probably want to take a jacket and tie for dining out, especially for the better restaurants in New Orleans. T-shirts are now accepted almost everywhere during the daytime; in some resort areas, they're worn evenings as well. Don't forget extra slacks.

Pack lightly, but keep weather extremes in mind, expecially New Orleans' unpredictable winters.

Planning a lot of sun time? Don't forget something to wear en route to the pool, beach or lakefront and for those few days when you're getting reacquainted with the sun on tender skin.

 CLIMATE. New Orleans is noted for its subtropical climate. The city has an average annual temperature of about 70°F. The city also is noted for its unpredictable weather. During winter months, one could wear short-sleeved summer wear one day only to watch the temperature drop to freezing by nightfall. Although New Orleans rarely experiences extremely cold temperatures, the city's high humidity can make the weather uncomfortably chilly. Morning fog is particularly heavy beginning in October and lasting until mid-March. New Orleans also experiences heavy amounts of rainfall throughout the winter months and especially in the spring. Several inches of rain can fall within minutes. Summers are long, hot and humid. Hot weather can, and often does, run from March to October.

	Average Daily Temp.
January	57°F.
February	58
March	62
April	69
May	76
June	81
July	83
August	83
September	79
October	71
November	61
December	57

WHAT WILL IT COST? This is obviously a crucial question and one of the most difficult. The American Automobile Association (AAA) estimated that in 1983 expenses for a couple driving across the country would average around $48 per day for meals, $48 for lodging, and about $8 for each 100 miles for gasoline. We hope you can do it for less, and we have included a number of concrete and practical suggestions for cutting costs wherever you can. A couple can travel comfortably in New Orleans for about $144 a day (not counting gasoline or other transportation costs), as you can see in the table below. The costs were figured on a couple staying in the French Quarter where prices are somewhat higher than other parts of the city or suburbs.

In some areas, you can cut expenses by traveling off-season, when hotel rates are usually lower. Prices are higher in New Orleans during Mardi Gras and other major events. The budget-minded traveler can also find bargain accommodations at tourist homes or family-style YMCAs and YWCAs. Colleges offer dormitory accommodations to tourists during the summer vacations at single-room rates of $2–$10 per night, with meals from $.60–$3.50. A directory of some 200 such opportunities all over the U.S. is *Mort's Guide to Low-Cost Vacations and Lodgings on College Campuses, USA–Canada,* from CMG Publications Co., P.O. Box 630, Princeton, NJ 08540, $5 postpaid.

Another way to cut down on the cost of your trip is to look for out-of-the-way resorts. Travelers are frequently rewarded by discovering very attractive areas that haven't as yet begun to draw quantities of people.

If you are budgeting your trip (who isn't?), don't forget to set aside a realistic amount for the possible rental of sports equipment (perhaps including a boat or canoe), entrance fees to amusement and historical sites, etc. There are no tolls on the highways, but allow for modest tolls elsewhere, extra film for cameras and souvenirs.

Typical Expenses for Two People

Room at moderate hotel or motel (French Quarter)	$ 60
Breakfast at hotel or motel, including tip	10
Lunch at inexpensive restaurant, including tip	7
Dinner at moderate restaurant, including tip	35
Sightseeing bus tour	22
Evening drink	5
Admission to museum or historic site	5
Total	$144

After lodging, your next biggest expense will be food, and here you can make very substantial economies if you are willing to get along with only one meal a day (or less) in a restaurant. Plan to eat simply, and to picnic. It will save you time and money and will help you enjoy your trip more. That beautiful scenery does not have to whiz by at 55 miles per hour. There are picnic and rest areas, often well equipped in scenic spots, even on highways and thruways, so finding a pleasant place to stop is usually not difficult. Before you leave home put together a picnic kit.

Also, hotel restaurants, especially in the French Quarter, are much more expensive than neighborhood cafes. A considerable amount of money can be saved by eating breakfast and lunch in one of these smaller, inexpensive places. There are several such places in the French Quarter and Central Business District and they are easy to find.

If you like a drink before dinner or bed, bring your own bottle. Most hotels and motels supply ice free or charge very little for it, but the markup on alcoholic beverages in restaurants, bars, lounges and dining rooms is enormous. Bottles of alcoholic beverages may be purchased anytime—day or night—in liquor stores, groceries and drugstores in New Orleans, so it's easy to keep a bottle in your room if you want to. And in any case, a good dry domestic wine makes a fine aperitif and can be far cheaper than a cocktail.

 HINTS TO THE MOTORIST. Probably the first precaution you will take is to have your car thoroughly checked by your regular dealer or service station to make sure that everything is in good shape. Secondly, you may find it wise to join an auto club that can provide you with trip planning information, insurance coverage, and emergency and repair service along the way. Thirdly, if you must have your car serviced, look for a repair shop displaying the *National Institute for Automotive Service Excellence* seal. *NIASE* tests and certifies the competence of auto mechanics in about 10,000 repair shops nationwide.

Driving in New Orleans can be especially challenging. New Orleanians are not very good drivers. They dart in and out of traffic lanes as though they've never discovered the turn signal device on their steering column. Driving in the French Quarter is especially hectic as the streets are narrow and congested. The best thing to do is to park your car in some French Quarter parking lot and walk or take some form of public transportation. New Orleans' flat terrain shouldn't present problems to a reasonably cautious driver.

Whether you are traveling through an empty wilderness or a heavily populated, well-serviced area enroute to New Orleans, there are certain items of car equipment that you should have along: (1) spare tire, properly inflated; (2) an empty 1-gallon can and about 5 feet of hose for getting gas; (3) a tool kit that includes an adjustable wrench, a knife, pliers, screwdrivers and a tire pressure gauge; (4) extra spark plugs and a fan belt; (5) an extra can of oil; (6) jumper cables and gloves; (7) an extra set of keys (and a good place to hide them); (8) road flares and a flashlight; (9) a fire extinguisher; (10) the name and address of your car insurance agent and your car insurance number; and (11) a trash bag.

If you get stuck—on interstate, freeway, or country lane—use the universal rule of the road. Pull off the highway onto the shoulder, raise the hood, attach something white (a handkerchief, scarf, etc.) to the door handle on the driver's side, and sit inside and wait—with the doors locked. This is especially effective on limited-access highways, usually patrolled vigilantly by state highway officers. A special warning to women stalled at night: remain inside with the doors locked, and make sure the Good Samaritan is indeed what he seems. It is easier to find telephones along the major highways these days, since their locations are more frequently marked than they used to be. If you're an AAA member, call the nearest garage listed in your Emergency Road Service Directory. Or ask the operator for help.

Louisiana and New Orleans speed limits comply with federal law—55 mph. General speed limits for school zones range from 15 mph to 20 mph. The speed limit on most New Orleans streets is 35 mph, unless marked otherwise. Watch the signs: there is no state or city requirement for posting warning signs on radar, mechanical or electrical speed-checking devices.

Pulling a Trailer

Most states have special safety regulations for trailers, and these change frequently. If you plan to operate your trailer in several states, check with your motor club, the police or the state motor vehicle department about the rules. Also talk it over with the dealer from whom you buy or lease your trailer. Generally, speed limits for cars hauling trailers are lower, parking of trailers (and automobiles) is prohibited on expressways and freeways, and tunnels often bar trailers equipped with cooking units which use propane gas.

 WHAT TO DO WITH THE PETS. Traveling by car with your pet or cat? More and more motels and hotels accept them. Some turn them down, some want to look first, some offer special facilities. Check first before you register. If it's a first trip with your pet, accustom it to car travel by short trips in your neighborhood. And when you're packing, include its favorite food, bowls and toys. Discourage your dog from riding with its head out the window. Wind and dust particles can permanently damage its eyes. Dog are especially susceptible to heat stroke. Don't leave your dog or any pet in a parked car on a hot day while you dawdle over lunch. Keep your pet's bowl handy for water during stops for gas; gasoline attendants are usually very cooperative about this. Make sure your pet exercises periodically; this is a good way for you and the kids to unwind from unbroken traveling, too. Also make sure your pet is up-to-date with its shots and medication.

 ACCOMMODATIONS. *General Hints.* Don't take potluck for lodgings. You'll waste a lot of time hunting and often won't be happy with the accommodations you finally find. If you are without reservations, by all means begin looking early in the afternoon. If you have reservations, but expect to arrive later than 5:00 or 6:00 P.M., advise the hotel or motel in advance. Some places will not, unless advised, hold reservations after 6:00 P.M. And if you hope to get a room at the hotel's minimum rate, be sure to reserve ahead or arrive early.

In New Orleans, try to reserve well in advance, especially during Mardi Gras or other seasonal events. Include a deposit for all places except motels (and for motels too, if they request one). Many chain or associated motels and hotels will make advance reservations for you at affiliated hostelries of your choosing along your route.

A number of hotels and motels have one-day laundry and dry cleaning services, and many motels have coin laundries. Most motels, but not all, have telephones in the rooms. If you want to be sure of room service, however, better stay at a hotel. Many motels have swimming pools, and even beachfront motels along the nearby Mississippi Gulf Coast have pools. Even some motels in the heart of New Orleans have pools. An advantage at motels is the free parking. There's seldom a charge for parking at country and resort hotels.

Hotel and motel chains. In addition to the hundreds of excellent independent motels and hotels throughout the state, there are also many that belong to national or regional chains. A major advantage of the chains to many travelers is the ease of making reservations en route, or at one fell swoop in advance. If you are a guest at a member hotel or motel one night, the management will be delighted to secure a sure booking at one of its affiliated hotels at no cost to you. Chains usually have toll-free WATS (800) lines to assist you in making reservations on your own. This, of course, saves you time, money and worry. For directory information on (800) lines, dial (800) 555–1212 to see if there is an (800) number for the hotel you want to reach.

The main national motel chains are *Holiday Inn, Howard Johnson's, Quality Inns, Ramada Inns, Sheraton Motor Inns,* and *TraveLodge.* Other popular family-type motel chains include: *Best Western, Friendship Inn Hotels, Rodeway Inns, Vagabond Motor Hotels,* and *Motel 6.*

Since the single biggest expense of your whole trip is lodging, you may well be discouraged and angry at the prices of some hotel and motel rooms, particularly when you know you are paying for things you neither need or want, such as a heated swimming pool, wall-to-wall carpeting, a huge color TV set, two huge double beds for only two people, meeting rooms, a cocktail lounge, maybe even a putting green. Nationwide, lodging prices for two people now average $48 a night; hotels are more expensive. This explains the recent rapid spread of a number of budget motel chains whose rates are usually much lower.

Free parking is assumed at all motels and motor hotels; you must pay for parking at most city hotels, though certain establishments frequently have free parking for occupants of higher-than-minimum-rate rooms. *Babysitter* lists are always available in good hotels and motels, and *cribs* for the children are always on hand—sometimes at no cost, but more frequently at a cost of $1 or $2 per night. The cost of a *cot* in your room, supplementing the beds, will also be around $3 per night, but moving an *extra single bed* into a room will cost from $7 in better hotels and motels.

Senior citizens may in some cases receive special discounts on lodgings. The Days Inn chain offers various discounts to anyone 55 or older. Holidan Inns give a 10 percent discount year-round to members of the NRTA (write to National Retired Teachers Association, Membership Division, 215 Long Beach Blvd., Long Beach, CA 90802). Howard Johnson's Motor Lodges give 10 percent off to NRTA and AARP (Association of Retired Persons) members (call 800–654–2000); and the ITT Sheraton chain gives 25 percent off (call 325–3535) to members of the AARP, the NRTA, the National Association of Retired Persons, The Catholic Golden Age of United Societies of U.S.A., and the Old Age Security Pensioners of Canada.

Hotel and Motel Categories

Hotels and motels in all the Fodor's guidebooks to the U.S.A. are divided into five categories, arranged primarily by price but also taking into some consideration the degree of comfort, the amount of service, and the atmosphere that will surround you. Occasionally, an establishment with *deluxe* prices will offer only first-class service or atmosphere, or a hotel which charges only *moderate* prices may offer superior comfort and service, so we will list it as expensive. Be sure to read the listing to see that you are getting good values for your money. Our ratings are flexible and subject to change. Dollar amounts may overlap slightly from category to category because of the range of accommodations available in given hotels. In every case, however, the dollar ranges for each category are clearly stated with each establishment. We should also point out that many fine hotels and motels outside the New Orleans area had to be omitted for lack of space.

Deluxe. The minimum facilities must include bath and shower in all rooms, valet and laundry service, suites available, a well-appointed restaurant and a bar (where local law permits), room service, TV and telephone in room, air conditioning and heat (unless locale makes one or the other unnecessary), pleasing decor, and an atmosphere of luxury, calm and elegance. There should be ample and personalized service. In a deluxe *motel*, there may be less service rendered by employees and more by automatic machines (such as refrigerators and ice-making machines in your room), but there should be a minimum of do-it-yourself in a truly deluxe establishment.

Expensive. All rooms must have bath or shower, valet and laundry service, restaurant and bar (local law permitting), at least some room service, TV and telephone in room, attractive furnishings, heat and air conditioning (locale not precluding). Although decor may be as good as that in deluxe establishments, hotels and motels in this category are frequently designed for commercial travelers or for families in a hurry and are somewhat impersonal in terms of service. As for *motels* in this category, valet and laundry service will probably be lacking; the units will be outstanding primarily for their convenient location and functional character, not for their attractive or comfortable qualities.

Moderate. Each room should have an attached bath or shower, there should be a restaurant or coffee shop, TV available, telephone in room, heat and air conditioning (locale not precluding), relatively convenient location, clean and comfortable rooms, and public rooms. *Motels* in this category may not have attached bath or shower, may not have a restaurant or coffee shop (though one is usually nearby), and, of course, may have no public rooms to speak of.

Inexpensive. Nearby bath or shower, telephone available, clean rooms are the minimum.

BED-AND-BREAKFAST lodgings are a rather new approach to visitor accommodations. Like their European counterparts, most accommodations in the New Orleans area are relatively inexpensive and offer personalized service. Decors run the gamut from modern to high Victorian. All such accommodations are in private homes. Many of the fine old plantation homes along the Mississippi River north of Baton Rouge in the St. Francisville area offer overnight lodging and meals.

In many small towns across the country, small guest houses are excellent examples of the best a region has to offer of its own special atmosphere. Each one will be different, so that their advantage is precisely the opposite of that "no surprise" uniformity on which motel chains pride themselves. What you do get is the personal flavor of a family atmosphere in a private home. In popular tourist areas, state or local tourist information offices or chambers of commerce usually have lists of homes that rent spare rooms to paying guests, and such a listing usually means that the places on it have been inspected and meet some reliable standard of cleanliness, comfort and reasonable pricing. A nationwide *Guide to Guest Houses and Tourist Homes USA* is available from Tourist House Associates of America, Inc., P.O. Box 355-A, Greentown, PA 18426.

YOUTH HOSTELS. New Orleans has only two youth hostels, but both are conveniently close to the center of town. *Marquette House International Hostel* is a member of the International Youth Hostel Association. Rates are $18 a night for members and $22 for non-members. It has 60 beds, TV lounge, dining room, kitchen and patio. *Hostel on Burgundy* is a much smaller place, having only 3 rooms and 6 beds. The rate is $10 a night, and the hostel provides linens, kitchen and bath. Advance reservations are required.

For nationwide hostel listings check *The Official American Youth Hostels Handbook* by Michael Frome, which lists 240 or more U.S. hostels with maps; published in 1981, costs $6.95. Alternatively—and you need not be a member—write to American Youth Hostel Association, Inc., 1332 Eye St., N.W., 8th Fl., Washington, DC 20005. If you do join the association, a copy of the *Hostel Guide and Handbook* will be included in materials sent you.

New Orleans' YMCA International Center offers ideal budget accommodations for students, men, women and married couples from all over the world. It is conveniently situated in the Central Business District, 9 blocks from the French Quarter, 5 blocks from the Superdome and a short ride to the Garden District. It offers full athletic facilities (pool, gym, sauna), restaurant, TV lounge and a self-service laundry.

DINING OUT. For evening meals, the best advice is to make reservations in advance whenever possible.

Most of the better restaurants are fussy about customers' dress, particularly in the evening. For women, pants and pants suits are now almost universally acceptable. For men, tie and jacket remain the standard. Shorts are almost always frowned on for both men and women. Standards of dress are becoming more relaxed, so a neatly dressed customer will usually experience no problem. If in doubt about accepted dress at a particular establishment, call ahead.

If you're traveling with children, you may want to find out if a restaurant has a children's menu and commensurate prices (many do).

When figuring the tip on your check, base it on the total charges for the meal—not on the grand total, for that total includes a state or city sales tax. Don't tip on tax.

Restaurant Categories

Restaurants in the New Orleans area are categorized in this volume by type of cuisine: Creole, French, seafood, Chinese, etc. Within each type of cuisine, restaurants are further divided into price categories as follows: *deluxe, expensive, moderate* and *inexpensive.* As a general rule, expect restaurants in the French Quarter to be higher in price than in other sections of the city. Most neighborhood restaurants are surprisingly inexpensive. We should also point out that limitations of space make it impossible to include every establishment. We have, therefore, included those which we consider the best within each type of cuisine and price range.

Although the names of the various categories are standard throughout this series, the prices listed under each category may vary from area to area. In every case, however, the dollar ranges for each category have been clearly stated.

Deluxe: This indicates an outstanding restaurant of which New Orleans has many. The restaurant in this category usually has a superb wine list, excellent service, immaculate kitchens, and a well-trained staff. It will have its own well-deserved reputation for excellence, perhaps a house specialty or two for which it is famous and an atmosphere of elegance or unique decor. As in all other categories, this price does not include cocktails, wines, cover or table charges, tip or extravagant house specialties.

Expensive: In addition to the expected dishes, it generally offers one or two house specialties, wine list, cocktails, air conditioning, a reputation for very good food and an adequate staff, an elegant or unusual decor and appropriately dressed clientele.

Moderate: Cocktails and/or beer, air conditioning (when needed), clean kitchen, adequate staff, better-than-average service. General reputation for good, reasonably priced wholesome food.

Inexpensive: The bargain place in town, it is clean, even if plain. It will have air conditioning when necessary, tables (not counters), clean kitchen and will attempt to provide adequate service.

Chains: There are several restaurant chains, some of them nationwide, that offer reliable eating at excellent prices. Some of those operating in New Orleans are: *Denny's, Shakey's Pizza Parlor, Pizza Hut,* and *Sambo's. Holiday Inn* and *Ramada Inn* motels often offer all-you-can-eat, fixed-price buffets on certain days. New Orleans' *Popeye's Fried Chicken* chain cooks up delightfully spicy fried chicken and Cajun rice.

 TIPPING. Tipping is a personal expression of your appreciation to someone who has taken pleasure and pride in giving you attentive, efficient and personal service. Because standards of personal service are highly uneven, you should, when you get genuinely good service, feel secure in rewarding it, and when you feel that the service has been slovenly, indifferent or surly, don't hesitate to show this by the size, or the withholding, of your tip. Remember that in many places the help are paid very little and depend on tips for the better part of their income. This is supposed to give them incentive to serve you well. These days, the going rate on *restaurant* service is 15 to 20 percent on the amount *before* taxes. Tipping at counters is not universal, but many people leave 25¢ on anything up to $1, and 10 percent on anything over that. For *bellboys,* 50¢ per bag is usual. However, if you load him down with all manner of bags, hatboxes, cameras, coats, etc., you might consider giving an extra $1 or more. For one-night stays in most *hotels* and *motels* you leave nothing for the maids. If you stay longer, at the end of your stay leave the maid $1–$1.50 per day, or $5 per person per week for multiple occupancy. If you are staying at an *American Plan* hostelry (meals included), $1.50 per day per person for the waiter or waitress is considered sufficient and is left at the end of your stay. However, if you have been surrounded by an army of servants (one bringing relishes, another rolls, etc.), add a few extra dollars and give the lump sum to the captain or maître d'hotel when you leave, asking him to allocate it.

For the many other services you may encounter in a big hotel or resort, figure roughly as follows: doorman, 50¢–$1 for taxi handling, 50¢–$1 for help with baggage; bellhop, 50¢ per bag, more if you load him down with extras; parking attendant, 50¢–$1; bartender, 15 percent; room service, 10–15 percent of that bill; laundry or valet service, 15 percent; pool attendant, 50¢–$1 per day; snack-bar waiter at pool, beach, or golf club, 15 percent; locker attendant, 50¢ per person per day; golf caddies, $2 or $3 per bag, or 15 percent of greens fee for an 18-hole course; barbers, 15 percent; shoeshine attendants, 50¢; hairdressers, 15 percent; manicurists, 50¢–$1.

Transportation: Give 25¢ for any taxi fare under $1 (which you are not likely to find anywhere anymore) and 15–20 percent for any above. Limousine service, 20 percent. Car rental agencies, nothing. Bus porters are tipped 25¢ per bag, drivers nothing. On charters and package tours, conductors and drivers usually get $5 to $10 per day from the group as a whole, but be sure to ask whether this has already been figured in to the package cost. On short local sightseeing runs, the driver-guide may get 25¢ per person, more if you think he has been especially helpful or personable. Airport bus drivers, nothing. Redcaps, in resort areas, 50¢ per suitcase; elsewhere, about the same or a little less. Tipping at curbside check-in is unofficial, but the same as above. On the plane, no tipping.

Railroads suggest you leave 15–20 percent per meal for dining-car waiters, but the steward who seats you is not tipped. Sleeping-car porters get about $1 per person per night. The baggage porter at the railway station averages about 25¢ or 35¢ per bag.

SENIOR CITIZEN AND STUDENT DISCOUNTS. Some attractions in the New Orleans area offer discounts to senior citizens and students. Some may require special city-issued senior citizen identification, but in most cases showing a driver's license, passport or some other proof of age will suffice—"senior" generally being defined as 65 or over for men and 62 or over for women. Museums often post special senior citizen rates. Those places offering student discounts are generally somewhat more stringent in their proof requirements—a high school or college ID, international student traveler card, or evidence of age may be requested.

Many hotels and motels also offer special rates to senior citizens and students. It's best to call ahead to make sure these rates are available at the place of your choice.

Visiting senior citizens 65 or over can obtain, at no cost, the discount travel pass by appearing in person with proof of age, at the Regional Transit Office, 1001 Howard Ave. in New Orleans' Central Business District (for further information call 569–2620). This card enables senior citizen transit riders to pay only 20¢ fares between the hours of 9:00 A.M. and 3:00 P.M. and from 9:00 P.M. to 7:00 A.M. weekdays and all day Saturdays, Sundays and holidays. During peak weekday hours, (3:00 P.M. to 7:00 P.M.) Senior citizens must pay the full price of 60¢ (for further transit information, call 569–2700).

DRINKING LAWS. In Louisiana, the minimum age for the consumption and purchase of alcohol is 18—however some establishments won't serve patrons under 21. In New Orleans, alcoholic beverages—by the bottle or by the drink—may be purchased at any time of the day or night, 24 hours a day. Package sales are made in liquor stores, groceries and drugstores. Most restaurants, bars, nightclubs and pubs are licensed to serve a full line of beverages, while some have permits to serve beer and wine only. Proof of age is required.

BUSINESS HOURS, HOLIDAYS AND LOCAL TIME. New Orleans and its environs, like the rest of the United States, are on Standard Time from the last Sunday in October until the last Sunday in April. In April the clock is advanced one hour for Daylight Savings Time, and in October it is turned back an hour. The entire state lies within the Central Time Zone, which is an hour earlier than the Eastern Time Zone, 6 hours earlier than Greenwich Mean

Time, and more or less 16 hours earlier on the clock and the calendar than Sydney, Australia, depending on whether Sydney is on Daylight Savings Time.

Business hours for banks in New Orleans are pretty much like the rest of the country, by and large 9:00 A.M. to 3:00 P.M. in the Central Business District with some opening earlier or staying open later. Most banks also remain open from 4:00 P.M. to 6:00 P.M. Fridays. Shops open at 9:00 A.M. or 10:00 A.M., and most department stores open at 10:00 A.M. Offices operate from 8:30 A.M. to 4:30 P.M. or 9:00 A.M. to 5:00 P.M.

Most businesses and banks are closed the following holidays (the dates are for 1984): New Year's Day, January 2; Mardi Gras, March 6; Memorial Day, May 28; Independence Day, July 4; Labor Day, Sept. 3; Columbus Day, Oct. 8; Veterans Day, Nov. 11; Thanksgiving Day, November 22; Christmas Eve Dec. 24 and Christmas Day, Dec. 25.

In addition, banks, businesses and government offices also may be closed on Jan. 2; Lincoln's Birthday (federal agencies only—after all, this is a Southern city), Feb. 12; Good Friday, April 20; All Saints Day Nov. 1; and Nov. 12. Unlike most parts of the country, New Orleans and Louisiana have Sunday "blue laws" that require most retail businesses to close on Sundays. This does not affect restaurants, bars, hotels, drugstores, groceries, etc.

 CAMPING. There are many excellent campgrounds, some offering unique opportunities, such as floating down a National Scenic River in an inner tube, within an hour's drive of New Orleans. The sites are busiest during the summer months when reservations are recommended but not necessary. Most are north of New Orleans. A few are listed below.

Cherokee Beach and Campground. Four miles east of I–55 on State 442 near Tickfaw. 345–8485. 340 RV sites; unlimited camping. Inner-tube floats down Tangipahoa River, canoe and inner-tube rentals. Rates: $8 per couple, $1 each additional person; family rate, $8 per couple, $2 per child, ages 6–18.

Yogi Bear's Jellystone Park. North of Robert on State 445. 542–1507. 300 sites (water, electricity, sewer and concrete patios available). Man-made lake, 2 pools, gameroom, skating rink, water slide, paddle boats, canoes, bicycles, mini-golf, lounge, fishing. Rates: $16, $14, $13 per party of 5; $2.50 each additional person.

KOA Campgrounds of New Orleans. U.S. 51 exit off I–55 near Hammond. 345–9646. 110 sites (water, electricity, sewer). Stocked fishing pond, pool, planned activities. Rates: $12 full hook-up, $11 water and electricity per couple; $2 each additional person under 18.

Ponchatoula Beach. On State 22, east of Ponchatoula. 386–6844. 100 sites water and electricity, 60 primitive camping, 9 furnished cabins. On Tangipahoa River. Concession stand, gameroom, boat launch, canoeing, tubing. Rates: Cabins, $30–55 per night; $10 water and electricity per party of 4; $7 tenting per party of 3, $2 each additional adult, $1.50 child. Cabin reservations required.

Safari Indian Creek. State 40 exit off I–55 near Independence. 878–6567. 180 RV sites. On Natalbany River. 2 pools, gameroom, adult lounge, planned activities, movies, canoeing, fishing, stocked pond. Rates: $12 per party of 5; $2 each additional person.

Tchefuncte Family Campground. State 40, four miles west of Abita Springs. 796–3654. On Tchefuncte River. 150 full hookups (water, electricity, sewer). Picnic area, motor bike trail, hiking trail, pool. Rates: $10 full hookup, $8 primitive (without water and electricity) per party of 4, $1 each additional person.

KOA Campground, Slidell. State 433 exit off I–10. 643–3850. 74 sites with water and electricity, some sewer sites available. 2 pools, mini-golf, game room, store, planned activities. Rates: $10 tenting, $10.50 water and electricity, $12 full hook-up per couple, $2.50 each additional person. Mardi Gras rates: $17.50 per couple, $2.50 each additional person.

Lazy J Campgrounds. State 41 between Talisheek and Bush. 886–3701. 17-mile canal, skiing, fishing, boating, boat launch. Rates: $5.50 per trailer, tents usually not allowed.

New Orleans Travel Park. 7323 Chef Menteur Hwy. 242–7795. 95 sites (23 water and electricity only). Pool, laundry, bus tours into New Orleans. Rates: $15 per couple, $1 each additional person.

Other useful addresses are the *National Campers and Hikers Association,* 7172 Transit Rd., Buffalo, NY 14221; and *Kampgrounds of America, Inc. (KOA),* P.O. Box 30558, Billings, MT 59114—a very helpful commercial camping organization. *Adventure Guides, Inc.,* 36 East 57th St., New York, NY 10022, publishes a book, *Adventure Travel (Source Book for North America),* which gives details on guided wilderness trips, backpacking, canoeing, rock climbing, covered-wagon treks, scuba diving and more. Also the New Orleans Sierra Club recently published a book, *Trail Guide to the Delta Country* ($7.50 plus 75¢ mailing) on camping, canoeing, hiking, tubing and birding in the area. For a copy send check, cash or money order to *Sierra Club Trail Guide,* 111 S. Hennessey St., New Orleans, LA 70119.

RECREATIONAL VEHICLE PARKS. *New Orleans Travel Park* (eastern New Orleans), 7323 Chef Menteur Highway (U.S. 90). Full services, bus to and from French Quarter.

Riverboat Travel Park (eastern New Orleans), 6232 Chef Menteur Highway (U.S. 90). Full services, bus service to and from French Quarter.

Pets are allowed at both of the above RV parks.

FARM VACATIONS, GUEST RANCHES, HEALTH SPAS AND RESORTS. None of these facilities exist in southeastern Louisiana. However, a number of magnificent pre-Civil War plantation houses offer overnight accommodations, and several of them also have very fine restaurants. Weekly rates at these homes are also available. For a fuller description of these plantations, see the Excursions Outside New Orleans chapter in this volume and write to the Louisiana Office of Tourism, P.O. Box 44291, Baton Rouge, LA 70804, for additional information and brochures. Some of these places were and are the finest examples of plantation architecture in the Lower Mississippi River Valley.

 FISHING. Louisiana has gained a worldwide reputation for its excellent year-round fishing, both saltwater and freshwater. And the miles of rivers, lakes, bayous and marshes around New Orleans, plus the Gulf of Mexico, offer an excellent opportunity for this fishing action. Popular freshwater fish are largemouth bass, bream, crappie, catfish and spotted bass. Saltwater fishing offers, among others, speckled trout (spotted weakfish), redfish, flounder, sheepshead, drum, pompano, tarpon, croaker, king mackerel, red snapper, grouper and dolphin.

Nonresident licenses are $6 per year or $3 for seven days for residents of states other than Arkansas, Mississippi, Alabama, Florida and Texas. Licenses for those states are: Arkansas ($15.50 per year, $7.50 for seven days), Mississippi ($20 and $7), Alabama ($10.25 and $4.25), Florida ($10.50 and $5.50), and Texas ($15 and $4.50). Licenses can be obtained in advance from *Louisiana Department of Wildlife and Fisheries,* Licenses Section, 400 Royal, New Orleans, La. 70130 (tel. 504–568–5635).

Freshwater Fishing: Freshwater fishing is at its peak during spring, fall and early summer months.

In most cases, at least a small boat and motor is necessary for optimum results. Noted freshwater fishing spots in the immediate New Orleans area are:

The bayou, stream and river systems that feed into Lakes Pontchartrain and Maurepas from the north. They include the Tangipahoa, Tchefuncte, Tickfaw, Amite and Blind Rivers.

The Pearl and Bogue Chitto River systems. The Pearl River forms the Southeastern Louisiana boundary with Mississippi.

The canals adjacent to Interstate 55 from Ponchatoula to Laplace.

The canals and bayous around Lac Des Allemands, southwest of New Orleans

The shoreline brackish waters of Lakes Pontchartrain and Maurepas.

Fishing conditions in the above areas vary greatly with water and weather conditions. Local newspapers weekly list the current hot spots and best bait to use. The New Orleans Newspaper, *The Times-Picayune/The States-Item* carries its report on Wednesdays.

Saltwater Fishing: New Orleans is surrounded on the south, north and east by excellent waters for "inshore" saltwater fishing. In addition, the hundreds of offshore oil drilling platforms in the Gulf of Mexico provide hot spots of "offshore" saltwater fishing. Fishing party boats are available for day-long excursions to the offshore rigs where the catch varies from redfish to king mackerel. "Inshore" fishing areas include Lake Pontchartrain, the Rigolets, Hopedale, Shell Beach, Delacroix Isle, Violet, Point a la Hache, Lake Borgne and Lafitte. Gilbert Cousin (643–5432) on US 11 south of Slidell offers boat and motor rentals for fishing the "Trestles," a railroad bridge spanning eastern Lake Pontchartrain and a good area for speckled trout fishing.

"Offshore" fishing is usually good to excellent year-round, but can be exceptional during the winter months. Large fishing party boat excursions are available for $25 to $50 per day per person and include everything necessary for a successful outing to offshore hot spots. Smaller charter boats for parties of 6 to 12 range from $350 to $450 per day.

Some charter firms in the immediate New Orleans area include:

Bluewater Charter Fishing, 3220 25th Street, Metairie (837–2314); *Fishing Boat Information Service,* 941 Mouton, Metairie (282–8111); *Gulf-Delta Fishing and Charter,* 616 Codifer Blvd., Metairie (831–3026); *Captain Gil Fallon Dolphin Sports Fishing;* 1809 Madison, Metairie (834–8696); *Charter Boat Captain Don,* 164 Blanche Drive, Avondale (436–4420).

Numerous other charters are available out of Empire, Grand Isle and the Mississippi Gulf Coast.

HUNTING Louisiana, including the immediate area around New Orleans, offers excellent hunting for fowl (ducks, geese, quail, wild turkey, dove, snipe), and game (deer, rabbit, squirrel and other small game).

Seasons vary by the area of the state and year. Information can be obtained from *Louisiana Department of Wildlife and Fisheries,* P.O. Box 15570, Baton Rouge, LA, 70895 (tel. 504–925–1095, 925–1096). To give you an idea of seasons, usual periods are deer (November–January), dove (split seasons from September–December), quail (November–February), rabbit (October–November), squirrel (October–January), ducks (split seasons November–January), geese (split seasons from November–January), turkey (March–April), snipe (November–February).

While resident licenses are sold at most sporting goods stores, nonresident licenses may be harder to obtain. Information and order forms for getting licenses in advance can be obtained from Louisiana Department of Wildlife and Fisheries, License Section, 400 Royal, New Orleans, LA 70130 (tel. 504–568–5612). Licenses can be bought at this office.

Nonresident fees for residents of states other than Arkansas, Mississippi, and Texas are $25 annual, $10 for three days, $20 for big game (including deer). Licenses for Arkansas residents are $36.50 (annual), $15.50 (3 days) and $77 (big game). Mississippi residents pay $30 (annual), $20 (3 days) and $30 (big game). Fees for Texas residents are $42.75 (annual), $15.25 (3 days) and $58 (big game).

Charter duck hunting trips are available from six commercial operations in South Louisiana. Rates range from $125 to $150 per day per person which usually includes prior night's lodging, food, and a guide—everything but gun and shells. The two closest to New Orleans are *Honey Island Swamp Tours* (106 Holly Ridge Road, Slidell, LA 70458, tel 504–641–1769) and *Reach Out Landing* (Box 400, Four Point Road, Dulac, LA 70353, tel. 504–563–2590). The others, in Southwest Louisiana near Lake Charles, are *Cajun Hunting Club* (Sweet Lake, Route 2, Box 366, Lake Charles, LA 70605, tel. 318–598–2209), the *Catch and Kill Club* (Hackberry, LA 70645, tel. 318–762–3391), *Spring*

Hunting Club (Pecan Island Route, Box 95, Kaplin, LA 70548, tel. 318–737–2215) and *T and S Wildlife* (710 West Prien Lake Road, Suite 201, Lake Charles, LA 70601, tel. 318–478–3662).

 STATE AND NATIONAL PARKS. Three state parks, a state commemorative park, a national historical park plus national and state wildlife preserves are all within an hour's drive of New Orleans.

State parks charge $1 per car up to four persons and 25¢ for each additional person. Tent and trailer camping fees are $3 per day for unimproved sites (without electricity) and $5 per day for improved sites. Reservations for these campsites are not accepted.

Fairview Riverside State Park. Ninety-eight acres of picturesque moss-draped oaks off State 22, two miles east of Madisonville. Close to Lake Pontchartrain Causeway. Near the banks of the Tchefuncte River, about 2 miles before it empties into Lake Pontchartrain. Tent and trailer camping. Freshwater fishing. Saltwater fishing (by boat). Free 30-acre picnic area. Waterskiing on wide river.

Fountainebleau State Park. Over 2,700 acres on the north shore of Lake Pontchartrain, east of Mandeville on US 190. Nature trails, large picnic area, beach, swimming pool, tent and trailer camping, group campsites, playground. Close to Lake Pontchartrain Causeway.

St. Bernard State Park. About 18 miles southeast of New Orleans on State 39. About 350 acres on the Mississippi River with viewing points of the river. A network of man-made lagoons offers canoeing and fishing. Tent and trailer camping, fishing, boating, nature trail, swimming, picnic areas.

Fort Pike State Commemorative Area. About 23 miles east of downtown New Orleans on U.S. 190. Overlooks the Rigolets, a waterway passage into Lake Pontchartrain. The Fort, set on a 125-acre site, was constructed shortly after the War of 1812 to defend navigational channels leading into New Orleans. Fort Pike is a museum in itself. Picnicking area. Public boat launch into prime saltwater and freshwater fishing areas.

Bogue Chitto National Wildlife Refuge. 17,000-acre refuge in the Pearl and Bogue Chitto River swamps in northeastern St. Tammany Parish. Scenic preserve with meandering network of bayous, rivers and streams. Scenic boating, canoeing, fishing and hunting area. Accessible by boat only through three public boat launches off State 41, north of Hickory; off State 21, north of Bush; and off Mississippi 43 at Walkiah Bluff Water Park. Special hunting laws apply to refuge. Temporary primitive camping permitted in certain areas. For information call or write Bogue Chitto National Wildlife Refuge, 1010 Gause Blvd., Bldg. 936, Slidell, LA 70458, tel. (504) 643–5817.

Pearl River Game Management Area. State site of almost 27,000 acres in eastern St. Tammany Parish. Includes Honey Island Swamp and nature trail. Prime fishing, hunting, boating and canoeing area.

Chalmette National Historical Park. 141 acre park commemorating the Battle of New Orleans, a decisive battle during the War of 1812. Off St. Bernard Highway between New Orleans and Chalmette.

HINTS TO HANDICAPPED TRAVELERS. Presently, many New Orleans public buildings and hotels provide specially marked parked places for handicapped people. Handicapped drivers in Louisiana are issued special license plates.

For travel tips for the handicapped, write: *Consumer Information Center,* Pueblo, CO 81109. Hints include always requesting specially equipped hotel and motel accommodations and making reservations. Allow plenty of time if meeting bus, train or plane schedules. Be sure your wheelchair is clearly identified if it is carried with other luggage. Check out restroom facilities and, if driving, allow frequent, refreshing breaks. Travel lightly and informally.

Additional information can be obtained by writing to the *Society for the Advancement of Travel for the Handicapped,* 26 Court St., Brooklyn, NY 11242. This organization has presented awards to both Ramada and Holiday Inns for their programs to provide wheelchair ramps and room modifications for handicapped guests.

Access to the National Parks, a handbook for the physically disabled, describes facilities and services at all U.S. National Parks and costs $3.50. *Access Travel,* a brochure, provides information on 220 worldwide airport facilities. These publications are available from U.S. Government Printing Office, Washington, DC 20402. A booklet especially for people with lung problems is available for $1.25 from George Washington University, Rehabilitation Research and Training Center, Ross Hall, Suite 714, 2300 Eye St., N.W., Washington DC 20037.

For a free copy of Amtrak's *Access Amtrak,* a guide to their services for elderly and handicapped travelers, write: Amtrak, National Railroad Passenger Corporation, 400 North Capitol St. N.W., Washington, DC 20001. Handicapped travelers and senior citizens are entitled to 25 percent off regular coach fare, when the one-way coach fare is at least $40. A special children's handicapped fare is also available, offering qualifying children aged 2 to under 12 years a special savings—37.5 percent of the applicable one-way regular adult coach fare.

In New Orleans, the Regional Transit Authority has a number of buses in the city public transit system that are equipped with hydraulic lifts to assist handicapped riders. In addition handicapped persons may obtain, at no cost, a discount travel pass for use when riding New Orleans public transit by appearing in person at the Regional Transit Office, 1001 Howard Ave., in the Central Business District. This card enables transit riders to pay only 20¢ fares between the hours of 9:00 A.M.–3:00 P.M. and 9:00 P.M.–7:00 A.M. on weekdays and all day Saturdays, Sundays, and holidays.

Many of the hotels and motels listed in this volume will make special efforts to comply with needs of handicapped guests. Phone or write in advance for reservations and mention any special needs or requests. Hotels and motels offering handicapped facilities have been noted in the *Practical Information* section.

POSTAGE. At press time, rates for international mail from the United States are as follows: *Surface* letters to Canada and Mexico are at the U.S. domestic rate: 20¢ for 1 ounce or under, 37¢ for 2 ounces or under, but these rates actually get airmail carriage to those countries. Surface letters to other foreign destinations are 30¢ for the first ounce and 47¢ for up to 2 ounces. Airmail letters to foreign destinations other than to Canada, Mexico and some Caribbean and South American countries are 40¢ ½ ounce, 80¢ 1 ounce, $1.20 for 1½ ounces, $1.60 for 2 ounces. Postcards (except for Canada and Mexico, which go airmail for 13¢) are 19¢ for surface mail and 28¢ for airmail to any foreign destination. Standard international aerogram letters, good for any foreign destination, are 30¢, but of course nothing may be enclosed in them. Postal rates are no exception in this period of inflation, so check before you mail.

SECURITY. New Orleans is a wonderful place to have a good time, but an enjoyable visit to the "Big Easy," as New Orleans is called, can be easily spoiled by violence and theft. There are certain sections of the city that should be avoided altogether by visitors. Other sections should be avoided at certain times of the day and night. Perhaps the best way to see the city is to sign up for a guided bus or walking tour—there's safety in numbers.

The French Quarter is a great place during the day and it is generally safe for those who simply enjoy strolling about. When visiting the Quarter at night, stick to Royal, Bourbon and Chartres streets. There are usually a number of people just like yourself milling around enjoying the sights. Avoid the dark side streets and alleys. Many a vacation and holiday has been spoiled by a holdup and mugging.

To visit the old colonial St. Louis cemeteries behind the French Quarter, take a guided tour during the day and never go alone—especially at night. They are adjacent to crime-ridden, low-income federal housing projects.

Also avoid walking at night in the Central Business District, particularly in the area near the Superdome, Union Passenger Terminal, and Hyatt Regency Hotel. If you are traveling in and out of these areas at night, take a cab. Seamy slums are located nearby and criminals venture out to prey on unsuspecting visitors.

If you are planning a visit to the Irish Channel or Garden District, plan to go there by car or guided tour bus. Once there, walking along Magazine Street, with its hundreds of antique shops, is generally safe.

A good general rule of thumb is to avoid walking anywhere at night except in the heart of the French Quarter.

As in most other places in the world these days, don't leave money or valuables in your hotel room. Hotels themselves are magnets for professional thieves. Always be sure to lock your doors—even when you are inside. For valuables, use the safe-deposit boxes offered by hotels; they are usually free.

Carry most of your funds in traveler's checks, and be sure to record the numbers in a separate, secure place. Watch your purse or wallet, especially in

CONVERTING METRIC TO U.S. MEASUREMENTS

Multiply:	by:	to find:
Length		
millimeters (mm)	.039	inches (in)
meters (m)	3.28	feet (ft)
meters	1.09	yards (yd)
kilometers (km)	.62	miles (mi)
Area		
hectare (ha)	2.47	acres
Capacity		
liters (L)	1.06	quarts (qt)
liters	.26	gallons (gal)
liters	2.11	pints (pt)
Weight		
gram (g)	.04	ounce (oz)
kilogram (kg)	2.20	pounds (lb)
metric ton (MT)	.98	tons (t)
Power		
kilowatt (kw)	1.34	horsepower (hp)
Temperature		
degrees Celsius	9/5 (then add 32)	degrees Fahrenheit

CONVERTING U.S. TO METRIC MEASUREMENTS

Multiply:	by:	to find:
Length		
inches (in)	25.40	millimeters (mm)
feet (ft)	.30	meters (m)
yards (yd)	.91	meters
miles (mi)	1.61	kilometers (km)
Area		
acres	.40	hectares (ha)
Capacity		
pints (pt)	.47	liters (L)
quarts (qt)	.95	liters
gallons (gal)	3.79	liters
Weight		
ounces (oz)	28.35	grams (g)
pounds (lb)	.45	kilograms (kg)
tons (t)	1.11	metric tons (MT)
Power		
horsepower (hp)	.75	kilowatts
Temperature		
degrees Fahrenheit	5/9 (after subtracting 32)	degrees Celsius

large crowds and on public buses—a popular scene for pickpockets, who are highly skilled and usually don't look like sinister criminals. If planning to attend crowded events such as Mardi Gras, men should consider putting their wallets in some other pocket than the usual breast pocket or back pocket. Women should not hang their handbags on the backs of their chairs in restaurants. Enjoy casual acquaintances—but at a distance. Never leave your car unlocked, or valuable articles in plain sight in the car even if it is locked. Terminal counters and hotel check-in desks are also favored spots for lurking opportunists. Remember, security will enhance your visit to this great city.

 EMERGENCY TELEPHONE NUMBERS. In New Orleans proper, the emergency numbers used most often are: *police* 821–2222, *fire* 581–3473, *ambulance* 821–3232. In nearby Jefferson Parish, the numbers are: *police* 368–9911, *fire* 368–9911, *ambulance* 368–9911. By the World's Fair in May 1984, New Orleans hopes to have an enhanced 911 emergency number for police, fire, ambulance and paramedics. Jefferson Parish will not have the 911 call number until January 1985.

INTRODUCTION

New Orleans: "The Big Easy"

by
JOHN R. KEMP

John R. Kemp has written and edited four books relevant to the cultural, socio-economic and political histories of New Orleans and Louisiana including his most recent book, New Orleans: An Illustrated History. *A native New Orleanian, he is former Chief Curator of the Louisiana State Museum's Historical Center. Currently Mr. Kemp is a general assignment reporter and feature writer for* The Times-Picayune/The States-Item *in New Orleans.*

New Orleans, known to generations as the Crescent City and more recently as the "Big Easy," is a city whose magical names conjure up

23

images of a Gallic-Hispanic and Caribbean heritage in a predominantly Anglo-Saxon nation. It is an amalgamation of cultures from many parts of the world blended in such a way as to form a unique city and people. It was founded by the French on the banks of the Mississippi River in 1718, taken over by the Spanish in 1762, regained by Napoleon in 1800, and sold to the United States in 1803.

During its more than 250 years of history, New Orleans has survived yellow fever and cholera epidemics, Indian wars, slave uprisings, economic depressions, revolts, conspiracies, hurricanes, floods, the American and French Revolutions, the Civil War and Reconstruction, racial riots and political corruption. Today, its jazz, *Vieux Carré* (the French Quarter), cuisine, Mardi Gras and port are known worldwide.

It is a city whose mystique has captured the imagination of generations of writers and motion picture and television producers. New Orleans is a city of tourists, *beignets* (New Orleans French doughnuts), Creoles, aboveground cemetery tombs, William Faulkner's French Quarter, Tennessee Williams' *Streetcar Named Desire,* Walker Percy's *Moviegoer,* and John Kennedy Toole's *Confederacy of Dunces.*

As San Francisco is often called the most Asian of Occidental cities, New Orleans could be considered the most northern Caribbean city. Perhaps journalist A. J. Liebling best characterized the city when he described New Orleans as a cross between Port-au-Prince and Paterson, New Jersey, with a culture not unlike that of Genoa, Marseilles, Beirut, or Egyptian Alexandria: "Like Havana and Port-au-Prince, New Orleans is within the orbit of a Hellenistic world that never touched the North Atlantic. The Mediterranean, Caribbean and Gulf of Mexico form a homogenous, though interrupted sea."

Colonial New Orleans was very much a part of the economic, political, and social milieu of the French and Spanish Caribbean. The city's earliest population consisted of lesser French and Spanish gentry, tradesmen, merchants, prostitutes, criminals, church clergy, farmers from the fields of France and Germany, Acadians, Canary Islanders, Indians, Africans, Englishmen, Irishmen, English-Americans. Later came Italians, Greeks, Cubans, Vietnamese, and people from the earth's four corners.

A visitor to the city may be shocked to hear a New Jersey-styled accent spoken in one section of the city, while in another part of town, hearing an interesting blend of New England and Southern. Tune your ear for the familiar "choich" for church and "zink" for sink, and particularly for the "downtown" greeting, "Where y'at!" New Orleans' Southern accent has a lot less magnolia and mint julep than, say, a Mississippi or South Carolina accent.

New Orleans is a city of both the Old and New South with characteristics common to most American port cities. Present are the beautiful tree-shaded, azalea-lined streets and avenues, charming gingerbread-draped Victorian cottages as well as drab ghettoes, sprawling suburbs and skyscrapers. There is prosperity and poverty, gracefulness and garishness, altruism and callousness. Above all, it is a place where the pursuit of pleasure is a full-time business. New Orleans perhaps has more churches and barrooms per capita than any other American city, and its citizens enjoy a political scandal almost as much as a Mardi Gras parade, professional football game, or a sack of salty, raw oysters.

Contrary to the once popular saying, New Orleans is not the city that care forgot. It cares, but is is not quite sure what to care about sometimes. Despite high crime and unemployment rates, life still comes easy.

Perhaps much of New Orleans' special flavor has been preserved by its relative isolation from the rest of the nation. It stands like a curious island of Roman Catholicism of the Mediterranean variety in a Southern sea of hardshell Protestantism that looks upon New Orleans as "Sin City." To reach New Orleans, wrote novelist Walker Percy, who now lives in Covington, Louisiana, across Lake Pontchartrain from the city, the traveler must penetrate "the depths of the Bible Belt, running the gauntlet of Klan territory, the pine barrens of south Mississippi, Bogalusa and the Florida Parishes of Louisiana. Out over a watery waste and there it is, a proper enough American city, and yet within the next few hours, the tourist is apt to see more nuns and naked women than he ever saw before."

The demography of New Orleans has changed since the close of World War II. Although the city prospered during the war years, its population continued to fall behind that of other American cities. By 1950 it was no longer the South's largest city; it fell into second place behind Houston. By 1970 the Crescent City dropped to fifth place in the South, and the 1980 census showed it slipping even further behind. Census returns that year also showed the decline of population while surrounding suburbs grew dramatically. To no one's surprise, the 1980 census also revealed that blacks outnumbered whites.

Since racial integration in the early 1960s, tens of thousands of white families have moved to the sprawling suburban communities surrounding the city. Thousands of acres of soupy marshlands have given way to tract houses and shopping centers. The new brick houses with green lawns and central air conditioning were a lot more attractive to working-class whites and blacks than those century-old, drafty and cramped "shotgun" cottages in the city. Unfortunately, the flight to suburbia destroyed most of New Orleans' old neighborhoods.

Many whites, especially young and affluent couples, refused to abandon the city. They, along with white elite families, remained behind to buy up and renovate declining Victorian neighborhoods. Their work, courage and good taste have revitalized entire neighborhoods. The restoration craze in New Orleans has had an enormous influence on real estate values in older sections of the city and also has spread to the Central Business District, which is experiencing its biggest economic and construction boom since the 1850s. During the 1960s and 1970s, developers thought everything old had to be destroyed to make way for the new. Scores of building dating from the 1850s and earlier gave way to the wrecker's ball. In more recent years, however, developers have found it profitable and desirable to adapt pre-Civil War buildings to modern use. The results have been magnificent.

One glance at the city's skyline quickly reveals that the Central Business District is taking on all the trappings of a Sun Belt city. During the last decade, the CBD has experienced phenomenal growth, with more than a dozen new skyscrapers rising above New Orleans's 18th-century suburb. Major oil companies have built regional corporate offices here, and big-name hotel chains, including Hyatt-Regency, Hilton, Marriott, and Sheraton, have constructed luxurious highrise hotels in the district. The energy is dynamic, and the CBD is experiencing an explosion in construction and development it has not seen in over a century. For many years the CBD was stagnant. There was little growth. But in the mid-1960s with the widening of Poydras Street and later in the early 1970s with the construction of the $160 million-plus Louisiana Superdome—despite the controversy surrounding its construction, things began to change. Business and community leaders, fearing the CBD would dry up with the growth of suburbia, began making a conscious and concerted effort to revitalize the old commercial district. Their success has been staggering.

Across Canal Street from the CBD is the heart of Old New Orleans, the French Quarter. The *Vieux Carré,* laid out in 1718 by French engineer Adrien de Pauger, has all of the charm and mystique of a historical community. But most visitors, and some local real estate promoters, forget that the French Quarter is a living city where people live, work and play. Its architecture, history, hotels, restaurants and, of course, Bourbon Street are world famous. The Quarter is a fascinating place. Natives look upon it with reverence and disgust, but despite it all, they make regular pilgrimages to the Quarter to keep in touch with their past. They may curse and vilify it, but they love it like an errant child.

The contrasts in the Quarter can be mind-boggling. It possesses grace, beauty and elegance as well as vices that would have made Sodom and Gomorrah minor league.

New Orleans is a city where one never runs out of things to see and do. There are nightclubs, restaurants, museums, historic houses, jazz, blues, opera, symphony, amateur and professional sports, and theater.

There are walking tours, riverboat tours, bus tours, and tours by limousine and airplane. Or there is just sitting on the levee and watching the ships go by.

New Orleans' cultural activities may not have the same glitter as other major cities, but they are well established. Opera has been in the city since the late 18th century. The New Orleans Philharmonic Symphony now has a permanent home in the recently restored Beaux Arts Orpheum Theater in the Central Business District. The Audubon Park Zoo, once a disgrace, is now one of the best in the country. The city also offers a number of first-rate museums and historic houses. The Louisiana State Museum in the French Quarter is among the largest and best historical museums in the nation, and the New Orleans Museum of Art in City Park has gained an impressive international reputation. The Saenger Performing Arts Center on Canal Street is another recently restored vaudeville theater that now books big-name entertainers and Broadway road shows. There also are several other theaters in the New Orleans area that offer good entertainment.

New Orleans and jazz are synonymous. This is the city where it all began. Once confined to back streets, alleys and saloons, New Orleans jazz has made its way to all parts of the world. There are several places in the city where jazz is performed regularly, but the best place of all to hear it is at Preservation Hall in the French Quarter. As one New Orleans jazz musician put it: "It's a feeling. Just like when you get the spirit on you in church." New Orleans clubs also have other types of music ranging from "rock" and blues to blue grass. To hear it all, try to attend the New Orleans Jazz and Heritage Festival in late April.

New Orleans' night life comes in two forms—music and food. There are scores of clubs all over the city, ranging from pricey nightclubs to inexpensive neighborhood bars, where one can hear middling to excellent jazz, blue grass, rock, country-western and just about any other sound invented by man.

Dining out is a hallowed New Orleans tradition. Dining out to a New Orleanian is a full evening experience that can last several hours. New Orleans restaurants are justly famous, and the city's rich, spicey Creole food is known the world over for its unique flavor and origins. Antoine's, Galatoire's, Brennans, Broussard's, Commander's Palace have their deserved reputations. In addition there's K-Paul's Louisiana Kitchen which serves up Cajun food—the countrified version of Creole cooking. There are also scores of lesser-known restaurants all over the city that prepare relatively inexpensive New Orleans dishes, especially seafood dishes. New Orleans is an epicurean's fantasyland.

New Orleans architecture, like its food, is a *patois* of many cultures tempered by a semitropical climate. The architecture of the French Quarter, despite the area's name, is not really French. It is a combination of French colonial, Spanish, Greek Revival and Victorian. Most of the Quarter was rebuilt beginning in the late 1790s, after the devastating fires of 1788, 1792 and 1794. Although there are a few French colonial and a number of Spanish buildings remaining, most of the structures in the Quarter were erected after the 1803 Louisiana Purchase.

Uptown New Orleans is known for the Garden District, Greek Revival mansions and gingerbread-draped Victorian cottages. The uniquely New Orleans Creole cottage, dating from the early 19th century, is a common site in Faubourgs Trémé and Marigny adjacent to the French Quarter. Esplanade Avenue, which is the lower boundary line of the *Vieux Carré,* has a number of mid-19th-century, English-style townhouses and high Victorian architecture. Early examples of the Caribbean influence in early New Orleans architecture can be found in the colonial plantation houses along Bayou St. John near City Park. Several preservationist and historical groups in the city offer fascinating architectural walking tours of New Orleans neighborhoods.

Mardi Gras is the time of year dedicated to fun. Despite the millions of people milling about the streets, it is, perhaps, the safest time of year to visit the city. Everyone has a good time regardless of social status. Parades begin about two weeks before Mardi Gras Day, or Shrove Tuesday (40 days before Easter). It is a wonderfully silly time of year devoted to the old silk-stocking carnival balls (by invitation only), the newer and more egalitarian carnival organizations, street bands, marching groups, masquers, parties, balls and over sixty parades. When the parades pass, highbrow and lowbrow alike shout the familiar call, "Throw me somethin', Mister!" and scramble on the ground, fighting over trinkets and doubloons thrown from the floats. St. Charles Avenue, Canal Street and Bourbon Street form a single river of glowing humanity on Mardi Gras Day with the number of people in the streets reaching over a million. But midnight Tuesday, it all comes to an abrupt end, and the Lenten season begins the next morning on Ash Wednesday. Sparser lines queue up at local churches for the traditional ashes on the forehead.

Keep in mind that prices are a little higher in New Orleans during Mardi Gras, so bring along a few extra dollars. If driving, don't park your car illegally on or near a parade route; police will tow it away and it will cost you over $100 to get it back. Also, try to get a copy of Arthur Hardy's annual *New Orleans Mardi Gras Guide.* It costs $2.95 on local newsstands, and it contains detailed descriptions of all parades, schedules and routes.

Hotels in New Orleans run the full range from deluxe to inexpensive. With the exception of the Pontchartrain Hotel on fashionable St. Charles Avenue, all of the best hotels are located in the French Quarter and Central Business District. Generally, these also are the most expensive. In addition to the highrise deluxe hotels, there are a number of smaller and more intimate hotels and guest houses in the Quarter and Uptown that are quite comfortable and reasonable priced. During the last decade, there has been a building boom in the New Orleans hotel world with all of the major hotel chains trying to outdo each other in building higher and more luxurious accommodations, offering nightclubs with big-name entertainers, tours and attractive package deals.

And then there is always New Orleans' unpredictable weather to contend with. The summers are long and hot, and winters alternate between cold and damp, to sunny, cool, springtime-like balmy weather. So if you're coming in the winter, bring along jackets and coats to be on the safe side—an umbrella also would be a good idea.

New Orleans and New Orleanians are anxiously looking forward to the 1984 Louisiana World Exposition, appropriately dubbed "The World of Rivers: Fresh Water as a Source of Life." The site of the fair is an 82-acre stretch along the city's old riverfront warehouse district in the CBD. City officials are expecting up to 15 million people, or 10,000 a day, to visit the fair that will run from May 12 through November 11, 1984. The city also is expecting horrendous traffic, parking and other problems in the CBD once the fair gets under way. "Every day will be like Mardi Gras," one official said. One of the designers of the fair said, "I want people to feel the way you would feel if you saw Paris for the first time." In all, 13 architectural firms and over 100 architects and engineers were involved in putting together the fair's "eclectic" design. It will include pavilions and exhibits from all over the world, including the Vatican, outdoor theaters, Mardi Gras-style parades, and a 2,300-foot-long Wonderwall midway. Once again New Orleans has the opportunity to do what it does best—throw a big party.

A LEXICON FOR THE NEW ORLEANS VISITOR

New Orleans has several distinct accents. Uptown New Orleans (Garden District, St. Charles Avenue, the University Section) has a soft almost cultured Southern accent (picture Rhett Butler in *Gone with the Wind*) but not as pronounced as a South Carolina or Georgia accent— and certainly not as strong as in neighboring Mississippi. Early 19th-century New Orleans had strong commercial and familial ties with New York and New England, which may account for this softer sound.

And then there is "downtownese"—a broad, swaggering play on the English language closely akin to parts of Brooklyn and New Jersey.

The following translations of commonly used "downtownese" and other commonplace New Orleans words will be of immense help to visitors.

Nu Orlins, New Orl-yins—New Orleans.

banquette—sidewalk.

bayou—stream or creek.

batture—unsettled land between the river and levee.

beignets (bin yeas)—A New Orleans-style French doughnut.

cafe au lait (cafay o lay)—New Orleans coffee served with warm milk.

Cajun—Acadian. Descendants of those French Canadians of Acadia who settled in Louisiana in the late 18th century.

Cajun cooking—the more rough-and-ready version of Creole cooking developed in the country.

Camelback house—house with one story in front rising to two stories in the rear.

cayoudel—mutt or cur dog.

choich—church.

crawfish—crayfish. A local delicacy.

Creole cooking—a distinctly New Orleans, Louisiana style of cooking mingling food know-how from French, Spanish, Caribbean and other cultures.

ersters—oysters.

gallerie—front or rear porch.

geezum—golly, or By George!

gris gris (gree gree)—Voodoo hex or curse.

"Hey man, what's happenin'?"—Hello! How are you?

hun or *dawlin* (honey or darling)—A favorite greeting by older shopwomen.

Krewe (crew)—Mardi Gras social club.

lagniappe (lanyap)—something extra given, such as in a baker's dozen.

levee—dike built along river's edge to keep contiguous land from flooding.

mah nez—mayonnaise.

Make groceries—Going to the market, or shopping.

Muffuletta—Local Italian sandwich made with large oval Italian bun with olive salad, imported cold cuts and cheese.

neutral ground—divider down the middle of a street or avenue, usually called medians in other American cities. In 19th-century New Orleans, the median down the middle of Canal Street was the "neutral ground" between the French Quarter and the American Sector, now the Central Business District.

parish—in addition to ecclesiastical parishes, Louisiana's counties are called parishes.

Pass by—"I'm gonna pass by my mama's house," meaning "I plan to visit my mother." Pass by usually means to visit.

Po' boy—famous New Orleans sandwich made with French bread and a variety of stuffings, ranging from roast beef to oysters.

Shotgun house—narrow house with rooms in a straight line from the front to the rear.

stoop—front steps.

streetcar—trolley.

"Where y'at!"—a familiar downtownese greeting, meaning "Hello! How are you?"

zink—sink, or washbasin.

New Orleanians seem to have the most fun with their street names. The following are names of streets and their New Orleans-style pronunciations:

Burgundy—Bur-gun-dy with emphasis on *gun*.

Calliope—Cal-lee-ope.

Chartres—named for the city in France, but pronounced charters.

Clio—Ca-lie-o, or the letters and number C.L. 10.

Conti—Con-tie.

Erato—E-rat-toe.

Melpomene—Mel-po-mean.

Milan—My-lan.

Tchoupatoulas—Chop-a-tool-us.

Terpsichore—Terp-see-core.

THE STORY OF A UNIQUE
AMERICAN CITY

New Orleans History

by
JOHN R. KEMP

John R. Kemp has written and edited four books relevant to the cultural, socio-economic and political histories of New Orleans and Louisiana. His most recent books is New Orleans: An Illustrated History. *A native New Orleanian, he is former Chief Curator of the Louisiana State Museum's Historical Center.*

New Orleans is the child of many parents. French-bred for the first half-century of its existence, it passed several succeeding decades as a charge of mother Spain, before its adoption by the United States at the turn of the 19th century. In its time it has seen the arrival of British, Irish, German, West Indian and African immigrants (to name a few) who, like near-and-dear aunts and uncles, have all had something to say about the city's behavior and appearance.

What this has produced is a city of unique character, whose atmosphere and ambience seem to combine elements from a half-dozen nations or more. Its history is in large part a story of assimilation, of the confluence of peoples and cultures that has given New Orleans its very special flavor.

It is also, however, the story of a river city, and because the river did, in truth, play a major role in bringing many people to the region, a bit must be said about it before anything can be said about the city.

The Mississippi River

Called "The Father of the Waters" by the Indians, "Rio del Espiritu Santo" by early Spanish explorers, "Fleuve Colbert" and "Fleuve St. Louis" by the French, and today sometimes simply referred to as "The Big Ditch," the Mississippi is one of the world's great rivers. From Lake Itasca (in Northern Minnesota) south to the Gulf of Mexico, it runs 2,300 miles, joining three other major American rivers along the way: the Missouri, the Ohio and the Arkansas. So wide is its reach that it drains, together with its tributaries, all or part of thirty one states.

The value of the Mississippi to early settlers of the New World, and the role it played in New Orleans' development, are clear with a glance at any map of the United States. There were great natural riches hidden in the mid-American continent. The problem was how to get them to a port for shipment to places where markets waited. The Mississippi provided a solution: by sending goods down its serpentine length, traders could avoid the many problems involved in lugging them over a thousand miles of what was then quite difficult territory.

But sending goods down the Mississippi meant there had to be a port at its mouth to receive them, where European ships could dock and unload the finished work that was to be traded for the rougher material from upriver.

The Spanish were the first to explore the Mississippi, in the early 16th century, but it was the French who made the first efforts to settle there. Exploring the area in 1682, Robert Cavelier, Sieur de la Salle, claimed the land around the river in the name of King Louis XIV, and then returned to France. There he raised a colonizing expedition with promises of vast riches hidden in the unexplored New World, and easy exploitation of Spanish trade routes. La Salle sailed in 1684, but settled for some reason not at the mouth of the Mississippi, but on what is now the Texas coast. The small colony failed, and la Salle was assassinated by his own men as they tried to walk back to Canada.

Urged on by one of his ministers, Louis Phelypeaux, Comte de Ponchartrain (in whose honor Lake Ponchartrain, above New Orleans, is named), sent a second expedition in 1698. Led by a Canadian, Pierre le Moyne, Sieur d'Iberville, and his brother, Jean Baptiste le Moyne, Sieur d'Bienville, it reached the Mississippi on March 3, 1699; auspiciously, Mardi Gras day. Soon the brothers and their settlers were at work on the first of a series of posts and settlements set up along the river. The first was on Dauphin Island, at the mouth of Mobile Bay; a half-dozen more followed in the next twenty years.

Work, however, wasn't without its interruptions. In September, 1699, Bienville encountered a British warship anchored on the river, apparently searching out a suitable site for a British colony. Bienville paddled a canoe up to the ship and ordered the British to leave, or face destruction at the hands of an entirely fictitious French fleet waiting just up the river. The British captain hoisted anchor and sailed away, waving his fist and vowing to return. The site of the encounter, about 12 miles downriver from New Orleans, is still know as English Turn (*Detour des Anglais*).

In France, meanwhile, Louis XIV was growing weary of his still-young colony. Beset by continental wars and domestic troubles, in 1712 he turned over the worry (and expense) of colonial rule to a man named Antoine Crozat, granting him a 15-year exclusive charter that included all commercial rights. Crozat struggled in vain for five years before his charter was secured by another interested entrepreneur, John Law. Law, a Scotsman, had convinced Philippe, Duc d'Orleans, that the colony could be profitable if properly administered. With the colonial charter in their possession, the two began to send thousands of French settlers and African slaves, as well as hundreds of German and Swiss farmers. They settled upriver from New Orleans in an area called *Côte des Allemands* where their descendants still live.

The First French Settlements

New and willing settlers made a new settlement necessary; and when, in 1718, Bienville established one, it must have seemed only natural to name it after one of the colony's new charter-holders—the Duc d' Orleans.

Bienville chose a site about thirty leagues upriver. It had been an Indian portage with good elevation and had easy access to Lake Pontchartrain through Bayou St. John where a few Frenchmen had settled ten years earlier. The company wanted the town built further upriver; but Bienville claimed that his site was high and dry and safe from floods and hurricanes. Progress was not rapid. By the end of 1718, just a few palmetto huts stood in the dense forest. In 1719 a hurricane and flood stopped work, and two years later, after efforts had resumed, another hurricane blew everything down.

(In fact, subsequent history has cast a bit of doubt on the wisdom of Bienville's choice of location. Truth is, being so near to sea level causes not a few problems for New Orleans. Larger buildings often must be constructed on concrete or wooden pilings for stability, and underground cellars are about as common as blinding snowstorms in the city. Many parts of the city were built on reclaimed swamp and marshland. As a result, it is common to see old houses and buildings with cracked and sagging walls whose foundations never fully settle. Moreover, the city keeps a score of pumping stations working around the clock, draining water off through a network of canals that run above and below ground.)

In the spring of 1721, Adrien Pauger was sent to oversee the settlement's construction. Pauger enjoyed a good deal more success than Bienville had. In less than a month, despite the hostile terrain he and ten soldiers had laid out three streets facing the river. By the end of the year, the small settlement had almost 470 inhabitants. And in 1722, the capital of Louisiana was moved from Biloxi to New Orleans, a status the city held for over a century. That same year another hurricane struck, and destroyed almost everything that stood.

Despite the calamities, a visiting French priest was impressed with what he saw and predicted great things for the area: "I have the best grounded hopes for saying that this wild and deserted place, at present almost entirely covered with canes and trees shall one day . . . become the capital of a large and rich colony. . . . "

A young Ursuline nun, arriving from her native France seven years later, apparently was relieved when she arrived in the colonial capital and found that New Orleans was taking on the trappings of a permanent settlement. She noted in a letter to her father home in France:

Our city is very pretty, well constructed and regularly built. The people have worked and still work to perfect it. The streets are very wide and are laid out in straight lines. The main street is nearly a league in length. The houses are very well built of "collombage et mortier." They are white washed, paneled and filled with sunlight. The roofs of the houses are covered with tiles which are pieces of wood in the shape of slate . . . it suffices to say that there is a song sung openly here in which the words proclaim that this city is as beautiful as Paris.

Growing trade and commerce were behind much of New Orleans' expansion; it was rapidly becoming a major American port. Despite the first explorers' fantasies, gold and silver did not come pouring out of the New World's wilderness; what did come, however, though considerably less dazzling, was only somewhat less profitable. Vast quantities of tobacco, lumber, indigo, animal hides, naval stores and other local products floated down the river to the new city where ships from France, Spanish Florida, the West Indies and the British Colonies waited with stores of spices, cloth, cutlery, utensils, wines, foods, and other such to trade for them. New Orleans became a commercial center, connecting Europe and the West Indies with the back country and upper regions of the Mississippi.

Not that trade was without its difficulties. Storms, poorly built ships, privateers, colonial wars and financially shaky entrepreneurs all added to the risks of colonial commerce. There were other troubles as well.

Early Troubles

The Chickasaw Indians (nudged on by westward-moving British on the Atlantic seaboard) fought the French in battle for very near the length of their colonial rule. And when the young colony was not at war, it was more than likely embroiled in one or more of the many political and religious intrigues that spot its history. Bienville and his successors were often at odds with the church, company, royal and military officials.

By the mid-18th century, however, even more serious trouble was brewing.

In 1754 the long-running dispute between France and England over who-owned-what in America erupted into war. Dubbed the "Seven Years War" in Europe and the "French and Indian War" by British colonists, it ultimately eliminated France as a colonial power in America—for a while, at least. Despite an alliance with Spain (organized in the war's last years), France was defeated, and, in 1763, ceded to England all French territory east of the Mississippi, keeping for itself just two small islands in the St. Lawrence seaway.

Not included in the package, however, was New Orleans, which, along with all the Lousiana territory west of the Mississippi, had been signed over to Louis XV's cousin, King Carlos III of Spain, in the secret Treaty of Fontainebleau, in 1762.

Louis gladly turned Louisiana over to his cousin. The colony was costing him his royal shirt, and the merchant class in France wanted nothing more to do with it. Carlos III, on his part, accepted the unprofitable holding as a buffer to keep the British away from nearby Mexico.

Spanish Colonial Rule

Louisiana Frenchmen generally opposed the change to Spanish rule. When the first Spanish governor, Don Antonio de Ulloa, arrived, he did little to court their favor. In addition to committing several breaches of local etiquette, he enacted a series of commercial decrees that severely restricted the colony's trade, and had a devastating impact on its already-sagging economy. By October 1768, the colonists had had enough. Led by a former colonial attorney general, Nicolas Chauvin de Lafreniere, the settlers drove Ulloa out of Louisiana in a bloodless coup.

Retaliation from the mother country was quick. In July 1769, the Spanish fleet dropped anchor at the mouth of the Mississippi. On board its ships were General Alexander O'Reilly, an Irishman in Spanish service, and 2,600 Spanish soldiers. O'Reilly ordered the arrest and trial of the rebellion's leaders and in October Lafreniere and five others were sentenced to death. Six other rebels were sentenced to prison; the rest were granted a general amnesty. Before the firing squad, according to one account, Lafreniere sounded a call for liberty: "I do not fear death . . . the cry of liberty has been heard, it will conquer later."

The rebellion squashed, O'Reilly settled down to the business of governing Spain's new territory, the first of a series of successful Spanish administrators.

The American Revolution overlapped with the administrations of two of O'Reilly's successors, Don Luis de Unzaga y Amezaga, and Bernardo de Galvez, affording both the opportunity for an attack on their British colonial rival. The Spanish, through the Louisiana colony, sent supplies and munitions to the American rebels, and allowed American raiding parties to launch forays into British West Florida out of New Orleans. Galvez even went so far as to disrupt British shipping along the Mississippi.

Galvez, however, achieved considerably more than simple harassment of the British. He and his successor, Esteban Miro, opened New Orleans' gates to a great variety of peoples by establishing an open-minded immigration policy that welcomed British-Americans fleeing the Revolution, as well as Acadians (whose descendants are Lousiana's famous Cajuns) fleeing Canada, who settled largely outside the city. Natives of the Canary Islands came and settled just below New Orleans (in what is today St. Bernard Parish), and almost 500 Malagans set themselves down along Bayou Teche (near today's city of New Iberia). By 1785 the city's population had reached 5,000.

New Orleans' growth, however, did not rid Governor Miro of difficulties. Fights with the westward-moving Americans plagued him constantly; and in 1788, the city suffered an enormous fire that almost destroyed it entirely,

The Fire of 1788

It began on Good Friday, in the early afternoon. According to local legend, a candle ignited the curtains in a private chapel, but the priests would not allow alarm bells to be rung on the solemn Christian holy day. In less than six hours nearly four fifths of the city was destroyed. Among the buildings razed were the Church of St. Louis, the Presbytere, O'Reilly's Cabildo, the corps de garde building, and the jail. Spanish officials, through the generosity of Don Andreas Almonester y Roxas, rebuilt many government buildings and the church.

The city did enjoy two gains as a result of the fire: the establishment of its first fire department, and the creation of its first suburb, Fauborg St. Mary (today's Central Business District, above Canal Street) on the plantation of Madame and Don Bertrand Gravier.

Miro was followed by Don Francisco Luis Hector, Baron de Carondelet, a native of Flanders in Spanish service. He must have been a busy man. During his tenure as governor, he opened the colony's first theater in 1792, on St. Peter Street; created the city's first police department; ordered streetlights throughout the city; founded the colony's first newspaper, *Moniteur de la Louisiane,* in 1792; and rewrote the city's building codes after the devastating fires of 1792 and 1794. (Buildings more than one-story high had to be constructed of brick and located near the sidewalk, or *banquette.* Roofs had to be red or green tile; wooden tile was forbidden.)

Carondelet's exceptionally capable governorship, was somewhat rudely interrupted by the French Revolution. When Louis XVI was beheaded in 1793, Spain and France declared war, and New Orleans' predominantly French population rallied to their (somewhat distant) countrymen's cause. Mobs roamed the streets calling Carondelet a *cochon de lait* (suckling pig) and shouting "Liberty, Equality and Fraternity." Revolutionary pamphlets poured into the city from France, urging New Orleanians to revolt against Spain.

Carondelet brought in troops and outlawed publications concerning the Revolution. Diplomatically, he also gave refuge to French aristocrats fleeing the revolution, which won him back some favor with the Louisianians.

Still more problems were waiting for Carondelet upriver, where westward-minded Americans (usually Kentuckians, whom the New Orleanians called "Kaintocks") were raising an old issue: commercial travel along the Mississippi.

During the American Revolution, the colonists had assured the Spanish that they had no designs on Louisiana. But by the 1790s their assurances began to carry less weight. American use of the river had grown; so too had American desire for free navigation along its length.

As time passed, the situation worsened. Spanish officials in New Orleans occasionally seized American flatboats; the Americans responded with rattling sabres, urged on by the "Kaintocks," who called for an invasion of the Louisiana Territory.

An almost certain war was averted in 1795 by the treaty of San Lorenzo (also known as the Pinckney Treaty, after one of its chief negotiators). Spain gave the Americans free navigation of the lower Mississippi and the right to deposit commercial goods in New Orleans warehouses for three years. Spain also recognized U.S. claims concerning the border of Spanish West Florida.

Carondelet's administration ended soon after the treaty's signing, in the summer of 1797, but not before one last significant event. In 1796, Etienne Boré, at his plantation upriver from the city (on a site now largely occupied by Audubon Park), revolutionized the production of sugar by granulating it. Although natives had planted sugar cane for decades, Boré made sugar production a profitable industry.

By the time of Boré's discovery, and Carondelet's resignation, New Orleans was a very different place from the tiny frontier outpost settled 30 leagues north of the Mississippi's mouth 80 years before. It had become a major North American city, with a population close to 10,000 whose port handled cargo from all over the world, and whose well-earned reputation as a gay and colorful city was already well-established. Mardi Gras was being celebrated regularly (though it wasn't yet the extravagant carnival of parades seen today), and Creole food, that combination of French, Spanish, West Indian and African cuisines for which New Orleans is so justly famous, had already found its place on the local palates.

The 19th Century

But for all the change of the 18th century, the opening of the 19th was to bring even more. In France, Napoleon had taken power, and re-established the country as a formidable military force on the continent. In 1800 he forced Spain to retrocede Louisiana to the French. New Orleans was back in the hands of its first colonial parents, though Spanish officials continued to run the colony.

This news sat poorly with U.S. President Thomas Jefferson, who feared war with France had become inevitable. The issue that concerned him, naturally enough, was free navigation along the Mississippi:

There is on the globe one single spot, the possessor of which is our natural and habitual enemy. It is New Orleans, through which the produce of three-eighths of our territory must pass to market . . . The day France takes possession of New Orleans . . . from that moment we must marry ourselves to the British fleet and nation.

Interesting words from the man who penned the Declaration of Independence. To solve the problem, Jefferson resolved to buy New Orleans and a portion of West Florida bordering the Mississippi, including the Baton Rouge area. But Napoleon, anxious for money to fund his imminent war against England (and reasonably sure that he would lose the land to either England or America when war came anyway) went Jefferson one better; he offered to sell the entire Louisiana Territory.

The Louisiana Purchase

On April 29, 1803, the American emissaries, Robert Livingston and James Monroe, agreed to pay $11.25 million for Louisiana and, at the same time, to write off $3.75 million in French debts, setting the territory at a total cost of $15 million. After the sale, Napoleon commented: "This accession of territory affirms forever the power of the United States, and I have just given England a maritime rival that sooner or later will lay low her pride." A little short on cash, the U.S. borrowed heavily from banking houses in London and Amsterdam to complete the deal.

The "Americanization" of New Orleans officially began with the appointment of its first U.S. governor, William Charles Cole Claiborne (actually Jefferson's third choice; James Monroe and the Marquis de Lafayette had already turned down the job). It was furthered by a sudden influx of young businessmen from the Atlantic seaboard who came down to set up branch offices of Eastern commercial houses around the port. Most settled in the bustling Faubourg St. Mary—the "American sector," as it came to be called.

Of course, it may not have been business opportunities alone that lured people down. New Orleans had gained a reputation for West Indian atmosphere, European elegance, and vice. Perhaps the most infamous section of town in those days was "The Swamp," a district filled with bordellos and saloons located behind the American sector, in the vicinity of today's Super Dome. It was a wild place, where a life was not worth a picayune (a coin worth about 6 cents).

Frequent visitors to the district were the Mississippi flatboatmen (personified by the legendary Mike Fink), who made their way downriver from Kentucky and the Ohio and Missouri river valleys to sell their goods in the city. After celebrating in town, they either walked back up to the Ohio along the Natchez Trace, or literally pulled their boats back up the river.

By 1810, New Orleans was the fifth largest city in the United States. One historian has described the era as one of "excitement, uproar, flux, boom and bust, disasters, disappointments, and achievements." The city's population had soared to 24,000 residents, and they now enjoyed an opera house and theaters, fine homes and new suburbs. But there were problems, too, that came with the city's growth—perhaps most serious was the filth, decay and generally unhealthy conditions that spread throughout it. Recurring yellow fever epidemics took thousands of lives in 1804, 1808, 1811, and 1813.

Statehood and Steamboats

1812 saw a brief respite from the disease, and, almost as if in celebration, brought with it three momentous events for the region. On April 30, Louisiana was made a state—the nation's eighteenth. At about the same time, New Orleans watched a new type of transportation come down the river and tie up in front of the Place d'Armes (Jackson Square). It was the steamboat *New Orleans,* captained by Nicholas I. Roosevelt, the product of a joint effort by Robert Livingston (one of the two Americans who arranged the Louisiana Purchase) and the engineer and inventor of the steamboat, Robert Fulton. In the (quite correct) belief that steamboats would carry the region's economic future, the two somehow convinced the territorial legislature to grant them a monopoly for all commerce on western territorial waters. To the everlasting good fortune of every other person who hoped to work the river trade, a New Orleans court broke the monopoly in 1817.

Steamboats opened a new era; they soon became the river's most popular means of transporting goods and passengers in either direction. The river became a highway, and remained so for several decades.

1812 also brought war against the British. Though its first effect on New Orleans was slight, it eventually came hard to the city. In 1815, Andrew Jackson, with a ragtag army of Louisianians, and helped by Jean Lafitte, his Barbarian pirates, and Tennessee and Kentucky volunteers, fought the British and stopped them in a bloody battle at Chalmette Plantation a few miles downriver from the city. Although casualty estimates for the Battle of New Orleans conflict, reports placed American losses at 13 killed and 39 wounded; British losses at 858 killed and 2,468 wounded. It is one of history's more brutal ironies that the battle took place two weeks after the U.S. and Britain signed a treaty ending the war.

Antebellum

The years between the Battle of New Orleans and the Civil War have been described as the city's golden era. By 1820 the population had reached 25,000, and during the next ten years it doubled. By 1840, a census counted 102,000 people within New Orleans.

The port was choked with seagoing ships and riverboats laden with sugar, molasses, cotton, raw materials from upriver, and refined goods from the continent and the Northeast. A traveler to New Orleans in the 1830s was impressed with the vitality of the city's port:

> With what astonishment did I, for the first time, view the magnificent levee, from one point or horn of the beauteous crescent to the other, covered with active human beings of all nations and colors, and boxes, bales, bags, hogsheads, pipes, barrels, kegs of goods, wares, and merchandise from all ends of the earth! Thousands of bales of cotton, tierces of sugar, molasses; quantities of flour, pork, lard, grain and other provisions; leads, furs, and from the rich and extensive rivers above; and the wharves lined for miles with ships, steamers, flatboats, arks, and four deep! The business appearance of this city is not surpassed by any other in the wide world, it might be likened to a huge bee-hive, where no drones could find a resting place. I stepped on shore, and my first exclamation was, "This is the place for a business man!"

With burgeoning commerce came prosperity, new construction, canals and railroads. The Carrollton Railroad (today's St. Charles streetcar) began operations in 1835 and contributed to the development of new suburbs and "Uptown" New Orleans. The American Sector above Canal Street adapted the neo-classical "Yankee-style" red-brick row building prevalent in the East. Affluent Americans and Creoles moved upriver to fashionable Coliseum Square or to the "Garden District" in the town of Lafayette (annexed to the city in 1852). Others built opulent homes along Esplanade Avenue on the downriver edge of the *Vieux Carré.* By the early 1830s the city had three distinct sections: the American Sector, the *Vieux Carré,* and the Faubourg Marigny below Esplanade Avenue. Faubourg Marigny was the creation of New Orleans' most colorful 19th-century bon vivant, Bernard Marigny, who, as legend has it, introduced New Orleanians to the game of craps.

Moreover, the city's landscape changed dramatically during this era. Above Canal Street rose the splendid St. Charles Hotel and Gallier Hall (City Hall) on Lafayette Square; while the new Custom House took its place at its foot. The French Quarter boasted the new U.S. Mint on

Esplanade Avenue, the new St. Louis Cathedral and the classical Pontalba buildings facing Jackson Square (built by the Baroness Pontalba, who fled to New Orleans after the 1848 revolution in France). There were several theaters, including the St. Charles Theater in the American Sector and the Theatre d'Orleans and French Opera House in the French Quarter.

Gentlemen had their private clubs, such as the Boston Club and Odd Fellows Hall. Much has been written about the early New Orleans custom that allowed affluent white men to keep mulatto and quadroon concubines, sometimes openly. An entire subculture in the city resulted from and revolved around this practice.

Mulattoes, quadroons and octoroons were people of mixed African and Caucasian ancestry. Mulattoes were the children of one black and one white parent. Quadroons had one-fourth black ancestry—one grandparent of African descent and three caucasian grandparents. Octoroons were of one-eighth African ancestry. During the Spanish Colonial and antebellum periods, most of these people were "free people of color"—not slaves. They also had separate societies from each other and generally one group did not associate with another. Many in each category were wealthy, but most were artisans, artists, musicians, domestics, and so on.

In addition to the pleasures of the parlor, one could enjoy one of the several art galleries, sailing, horseracing, and practically every known form of gambling. Also, a fine meal could be had at any one of the city's noted restaurants, including Antoine's which continues to delight diners.

There was intrigue in antebellum New Orleans as well; many plots were hatched for excursions into Latin America. Bank's Arcade, on Magazine Street between Gravier and Natchez was a favorite meeting place for the plotters of some of the 19th century's most noted escapades: the Texas Revolution (1835); General Narcisco Lopez's invasion of Cuba (1851); and William Walker's expedition in Nicaragua (1855).

The golden age also gave birth to one of New Orleans' most famous pasttimes: The Mardi Gras parade. Mardi Gras had been celebrated on the European continent, in one way or another, for centuries. The parades, however, were a New Orleans invention, begun in the 1820s when bands of masquers marched through the streets throwing confetti and flour (and sometimes lye) into the faces of onlookers. Vehicles were first used in 1839, and the first carnival organization, the Mistick Krewe of Comus, formed in 1857.

But through the years of prosperity and celebration, disease continued to stalk the city. The almost yearly visits of yellow fever, cholera and typhus, encouraged by widespread poverty, took thousands of lives; 8,000 fell to yellow fever in 1853, and another 2,700 in 1856. In that same year cholera claimed the lives of over a thousand people and tuberculosis killed 650. In addition to its other qualities, New Orleans was known as one of the unhealthiest cities in the hemisphere.

And still the population grew. Like other port cities, New Orleans received thousands of European immigrants during those years. Irish and Germans came in the greatest numbers; by the late 1850s nearly 25,000 Irish lived in the city. Many settled below Esplanade Avenue, or above the city in Lafayette or Carrollton. But the majority huddled together in tenements in the "Irish Channel" above Howard Avenue between Magazine Street and the river. The new arrivals had a strong impact on local politics, particularly on the emerging parties. Feelings ran high, and elections were often marred by riots and violent clashes between parties.

If the 18th century can be seen as New Orleans' childhood, then the antebellum period was its adolescence and young adulthood; by its end, the city had reached full maturity. Prosperous and growing, it possessed an international personality that distinguished it from every other city on the American continent.

But the Civil War was to change much.

Civil War New Orleans

On January 26, 1861, Louisiana seceded from the Union. It must have been especially difficult for New Orleanians, many of whom had strong commercial and family ties with the northeast and midwest. Less than three months after secession, the war began when Southern troops, under the command of New Orleans' own General Pierre Gustave Toutant Beauregard, opened fire on Fort Sumter in Charleston harbor. A month later a Union fleet blockaded the mouth of the Mississippi River, causing severe economic hardships in the city.

The Confederate flag waved barely a year over New Orleans before it fell to Union forces. In February 1862, the U.S. fleet, commanded by "Damn the torpedoes" David Glasgow Farragut, gathered near Ship Island off the Mississippi coast. Its objective—New Orleans. For over a month gunboats from the massive fleet bombarded forts Jackson and St. Philip protecting the lower Mississippi and New Orleans. In the early morning of April 24, the fleet attacked. A Union army officer later wrote: "Combine all that you have heard of thunder, add to it all that you have seen of lightning, and you have, perhaps a conception of the scene."

New Orleanians panicked when word reached the city that the Union fleet and army were on their way. There was no Andrew Jackson to stop the invaders this time. City wharves piled high with cotton bales, sugar, lumber, and other goods were put to torch to prevent them from falling into enemy hands. Ships and boats moored in the river were sunk. Mobs rioted in the streets while Confederate troops in the city withdrew hastily to Confederate territory north of Lake Pontchartrain.

When the Union fleet arrived and trained its guns on a panicked city, Mayor John Monroe refused to surrender. Farragut threatened to bombard the city, but backed down. After a brief standoff, a naval squad went ashore and lowered the Confederate flag. New Orleans, the Confederacy's largest city, had fallen.

Occupation and Reconstruction

On May 1, 1862, Major General Benjamin Butler, a Massachusetts politician before the war, entered the city with an occupying army. Although Butler accomplished considerable good for the city, succeeding generations of New Orleanians have vilified him for the rampant corruption he supposedly oversaw (and which earned him his nickname: "Silver Spoons" Butler). Many of his subordinate officers and civilian officials allegedly made fortunes buying and selling property confiscated from New Orleanians loyal to the Confederacy.

Perhaps Butler's most notorious act was General Order 28, which proclaimed that any woman caught insulting a Yankee soldier would be "regarded and held liable to be treated as a woman of the town plying her avocation." The order was condemned in the South, and denounced by Northern and European leaders.

At war's end, with the Union army in control and "Reconstruction" under way, an uneasy semblance of normalcy returned to the city. The port was reopened, and trade with Europe and northeastern ports recommenced. Theaters and operas played to packed houses; baseball and boxing arrived in the city (in 1869); and horse and steamboat racing resumed as popular pastimes. Who has not heard of the great steamboat race of July 1870 when the *Robert E. Lee* beat the *Natchez* from New Orleans to St. Louis in 3 days, 18 hours and 14 minutes?

But Reconstruction brought radical changes to New Orleans. Northerners, or "carpetbaggers," as they were known locally, came to the city seeking their fortunes in the confusion brought on by war and occupation. Local opportunists, called "Scalawags" by die-hard Southerners, worked within the U.S. Army-backed Reconstruction government, In fact, they were simply realists adapting to the existing order and a new South.

Thousands of newly freed slaves flocked to New Orleans from the plantations, looking for a new life. But once in the city, they glutted the job market, making it impossible for many to find work. New

Orleans' public schools were integrated, and the "Radical Reconstruction" state constitution of 1868 enabled blacks to vote. Also, blacks, for the first time, held political office, including the governor's office. P. B. S. Pinchback became Louisiana's first and only black governor when the state's white governor, Henry Clay Warmoth, was impeached by the state General Assembly in 1872. The state House of Representatives named the president of the state senate (Pinchbeck) to serve out the remainder of Warmoth's term (one month).

The social and political upheaval brought on by Reconstruction was often violent and bloody with street battles fought between native white New Orleanians and factions of the military-backed Reconstruction government. The bloodiest of these confrontations in New Orleans took place at the Mechanics Institute on Canal Street in 1866; at the "Battle of the Cabildo" in Jackson Square in 1873; and, in the "Battle of September 14, 1874," at the foot of Canal Street.

Withdrawal of federal troops in April 1877 brought an end to almost fifteen years of Reconstruction. It also ended a flicker of hope that black New Orleanians would enjoy the same constitutional rights and protections as whites. With the end of Reconstruction came home rule and New Orleans' Gilded Age.

The last two decades of the century was an era of conscious boosterism, booms and busts, corruption and reform, labor unrest and racial retrenchment. With a population of more than 216,000, New Orleans was still the largest city in the South. Large and boxlike Victorian homes, decorated with mass-produced gingerbread frills, sprang up along major avenues and thoroughfares.

And then there was the Fair.

The Late 19th Century

Designed to show the world that New Orleans was part of the economically healthy and industrially progressive South, the World's Industrial and Cotton Centennial of 1884–85 was a multimillion dollar effort. To finance it, city boosters sold shares to private investors, raised $1.3 million from Congress, and even squeezed $100,000 out of the city itself. Set on 249 acres of Upper City Park (now Audubon Park) the Fair opened on December 17, when President Chester A. Arthur pressed a button at the White House to signal the start of festivities.

There were problems. Financial and organizational difficulties plagued the Fair from the beginning. Moreover, exhibits were, for the most part, scanty and lackluster. One historian described the 31-acre Main Building as an example of "typical nineteenth-century eclecticism." A less-kind contemporary called it an eyesore.

Only one million of the expected four million visitors appeared, though there are several explanations for this. The Fair was held during the winter, which made travel from northern and midwestern cities difficult. And, possibly, the city's reputation for frequent yellow fever epidemics also kept visitors away.

Whatever the reasons, the Fair closed its doors just six months after opening, up to its Southern honor in debt. Attempts to revive it a year later failed. But though a financial disaster, it wasn't a complete failure. It *had* given New Orleans a progressive sheen in the public eye. And it did much to encourage the development of Uptown New Orleans into fashionable neighborhoods.

But despite the boom-town atmosphere of the 1880s and 90s, mass violence was still a frighteningly common occurrence. Labor and racial issues provoked riots in 1892, 1894, 1895, and 1900. But undoubtedly the most infamous instance of a mob at work during those days was the assassination of Police Chief David Hennessy, and the lynchings that followed.

In October 1890, in the midst of an investigation of warring Sicilian gangs in the city, Hennessy was shot down while walking home. It was reported that before he died, he whispered to a friend that the "dagoes" shot him. In a citywide roundup, 19 Italians were arrested; 10 were charged with the killing.

After a long and emotional trial, the jury acquitted seven of the accused, and declared a mistrial for the remaining three. The city exploded. Local newspapers and community leaders urged the population to avenge Hennessy's death. A lynch mob marched to the parish prison on Trémé Street (behind today's Municipal Auditorium), forced their way in, and shot or hung every Italian prisoner they could find.

Later, the U.S. paid the Italian government a conciliatory $24,000. Local newspapers, however, generally praised the mob's actions; and several months later, a grand jury concluded that the Mafia did exist in New Orleans, it had killed Hennessy, and that the lynchings were justified, because the courts had failed justice.

Storyville

There were political and municipal reforms through the last decades of the 19th century as well. A civil service system replaced patronage in city government, and municipal services and utilities were modernized. But perhaps the most notable "reform" of the day was the creation of Storyville—the infamous red light district that gave New Orleans such names and places as Basin Street, Josie Arlington, Countess Willie Piazza, Lulu White, and Mahogany Hall.

The district was named after Sidney Story, a reform-minded council-man who wrote the bill creating it. Located behind the French Quarter above Basin Street, it was an attempt to control prostitution by confining it to a designated section of the city.

Storyville has often been called the birthplace of New Orleans jazz. But according to jazz historian Al Rose, though Storyville may have been "a forge in which some of the pure gold jazz was smelted," it was not the music's original home. Jazz, says Rose, was born in the dance halls and saloons of New Orleans' lakefront resorts in Milneburg and Bucktown, and along South Rampart and Bourbon streets.

The infamous tenderloin, created by a reform movement, was officially shut down during World War I at the insistence of Secretary of Navy Josephus Daniels. Federal authorities were afraid young soldiers stationed in New Orleans (a long way from home) might be corrupted by the district's alluring bawdy houses and *demi monde*. Prostitution continued in the city on a grand scale nevertheless. The city's mayor remarked at the time, "You can make prostitution illegal, but you can't make it unpopular." Closing Storyville pushed jazz upriver to Memphis, St. Louis, Kansas City, Chicago and the world. Today, a federal housing project stands in place of the old district.

20th Century New Orleans

New Orleanians entered the 20th century with an air of optimism. North and South put aside their differences to defeat the Spanish in the Spanish-American War, in 1898. Uptown continued to grow with new mansions along St. Charles Avenue and higher skyscrapers in the Central Business District hovered over the early 19th-century buildings of the old American Sector. During the first decade of the new century, three presidents—William McKinley, Theodore Roosevelt and William Howard Taft—visited the city.

Many of the city's cultural and educational institutions had their beginnings at the turn of the century as well. The New Orleans Symphony Society and the Louisiana State Museum (Cabildo and Presbytere) were founded in 1906; Loyola University and Isaac Delgado Museum of Art (now the New Orleans Museum of Art) opened in 1911. Four years later Xavier University was established. At about the same time, *La Petit Theatre du Vieux Carré* also began its long and still-continuing career across the street from the Cabildo. And, the French Quarter became a popular haven for young artists and writers as then little known William Faulkner.

The year 1900 also was an important date in the city's political history. It was the year the Tammany Hall-like Regular Democratic Organization, usually referred to as the Choctaws or Old Regulars, began its three-decade-long control of city government. Any mention of New Orleans politics during those years should include Old Regular, Mayor Martin Behrman, who headed the machine for seventeen years; Governor and, later, Senator Huey Long, demagogue or hero (depending on one's point of view) who broke the machine's back; Mayor Robert Maestri (1936–1946), who once asked President Franklin Roosevelt, "How ya like dem ersters (oysters)"; and, reform Mayor DeLesseps S. "Chep" Morrison (1946–1961).

But, problems remained. Despite sporadic economic growth, New Orleans began to fall behind other American cities. According to census figures, the Crescent City dropped from the nation's ninth largest city to twelfth by 1900 and then to sixteenth by 1918. While Memphis, Atlanta and Baltimore doubled their populations, New Orleans increased by only 25 percent.

Still New Orleans like other American cities prospered during World War II; and after the war, the city became a leader in the petrochemical industry thanks to its close proximity to the offshore oil and gas fields. During the 1960s and 1970s, New Orleans also played a major role in the nation's space program. The Michoud Space Center, located on the old Michoud Plantation in eastern New Orleans, built the Saturn S-1 booster rockets for the Apollo Program.

In spite of it all, New Orleans continued to slip behind other major Southern cities. Although the city's population increased from 494,573 to 570,445 between 1940 and 1950, it was no longer the South's largest city, but had dropped to second, behind Houston. By 1970 the Crescent City had fallen to fifth largest city in the South and the 1980 census saw the city slipping even further behind other Southern cities. During the ten-year period studied, the city's population actually decreased from 593,471 in 1970 to 557,515 in 1980. At the same time, surrounding suburbs grew dramatically. A number of factors, including white hostility to integration of the city's public schools, and fear sparked by the city's rising rate of crime, have sent many people into the surrounding communities. Because of this, many of the city's old ethnic neighborhoods are no more.

But while some people are fleeing, many are staying in the city. A recent trend is the purchase and renovation of dilapidated Victorian homes in old blue-collar neighborhoods. In fact, the restoration craze has spread to the Central Business District, which has an abundance of 19th-century architecture. In addition, construction of the Superdome in the early 1970s (despite the political controversy that marred its early years) and the subsequent building boom in the CBD has given the city an economic vitality it has not seen since the 1850s.

Today, most New Orleanians are anxiously looking forward to the 1984 World's Fair: "The World of Rivers: Fresh Water as a Source of

Life." Although the fair will tax the city's already strained resources and services, New Orleans officials and business leaders—like their predecessors in 1884—are hoping the fair will advertise the Crescent City to the world. "The World of Rivers," located on an 82-acre stretch of riverfront in the old American Sector's warehouse district, is expected to draw eleven million visitors and $2 billion.

Over 260 years have passed since Bienville's engineers and work crews built the first palmetto huts at the crescent in the river. Today, New Orleans, the Crescent City, the Big Easy, is scarred, decayed and often brutal. But its people, cuisine, its alluring 19th-century mystique and Caribbean-like culture make it like no other city in the nation.

NEW ORLEANS WAY OF LIFE

Heritage, Festivity, and Charm

by
D. CLIVE HARDY

D. Clive Hardy is the Archivist at the University of New Orleans. Among the many publications specializing in New Orleans history and culture to which he has contributed are 250 Years of Life in New Orleans, *published by the Louisiana State Museum, and* Arts Quarterly, *published by the New Orleans Museum of Art.*

First impressions of New Orleans are sometimes deceptive. Freeways approaching the city pass through endless suburban sprawl where the view shifts between flimsy residential tracts and discordant commercialism. In the city's core the view will change abruptly but not for the better. New Orleans has a reputation for romance, but vistas of tarmac parking and massive corporate towers are not romantic. Take heart; with a minimum of observation you will soon discover that your initial impressions were deceptive and your misgivings unwarranted.

You will also discover that New Orleans is different from any city you may have visited, and indeed, it is unlike any city in North America. Behind its 20th-century facade there exists an exotic 19th-century city that even then was foreign to Americans. If you have traveled widely you will probably recognize something in the life of the city that is reminiscent of Europe and in particular its Mediterranean regions. Generations of visitors have experienced the similarities and, with very few exceptions, they have written appreciatively of the city and its unique public culture.

New Orleans exudes an intangible charm that even the most passive observer finds hard to resist. However, to fully appreciate this fabled city, you should know something of its history, geography, and the various peoples who have settled in it and come to regard it as home.

Site and History

To understand why New Orleans is so different from other American cities, you should first think of it as an island, which of course it was considered during much of its early history. New Orleans rests on some of the finest high ground of the Mississippi's delta. Fronting on the great river, it was immediately surrounded on its other sides by vast swamps that were themselves bordered by lakes and rivers. In its early history virtually all traffic had to enter and leave by boat. In fact, early settlers frequently referred to the narrow strip of land as the Isle of Orleans.

Thinking about New Orleans as an island at the mouth of the vast Mississippi basin helps to explain its uniqueness. As the only major port for the whole of the Mississippi Valley, the city was able to maintain an assured economic base without being bypassed or overwhelmed by the more aggressive, business-dominated Anglo-America. Rich cargoes from the American interior gave New Orleans many years of easy prosperity without great exertion which might have transformed its culture. The enriched merchants could thus afford to build and sustain opulent hotels, great restaurants, posh gaming rooms, and flourishing theaters. Flushed with wealth, this urban leadership turned New Orleans into an urbane metropolis on the rude frontier of a largely rural continent.

Monetary profits, however, are not the only forms of wealth. While the city's commission merchants were extracting fortunes from outbound cargoes, inward bound cargoes from Europe and Africa enriched its basic culture. Beginning in the 18th century and rapidly accelerating in the 19th century, a flow of immigrants passed through the city in search of a better life. For most, the city would be only a way station to frontier communities and farms of the upper valley. Many, however, remained in New Orleans. Here, immigrants from France, Spain, Ireland, Germany, and Italy and unwilling Black slaves from Africa and the Caribbean blended their Old World cultures. Tightly packed and confined in growth to a small area of high ground bordering the Mississippi River, the polyglot population was forced into close contact which fostered a civic tolerance of ethnic differences, first as a necessity and eventually as a matter of course. This tolerance of ethnic variety was in turn passively nurtured by the French and later Spanish rulers who differed from Anglo-American authorities in their benign attitude toward cultural differences. Even free and enslaved Africans were allowed to maintain Old World practices as they were nowhere else in North America. And the retained cultures were not isolated but absorbed and influenced by the prevailing French culture. Unintimidated by Anglo-American social pressures to conform, the new arrivals seasoned the city's Gallic culture to produce a hybrid way of life. Food, music, architecture, and festival, in addition to other social mores, became an amalgam of the tastes of those who lived in colonial New Orleans. The resulting culture created a city unlike any other on the North American continent. Thus, the Isle of Orleans became a cultural melting pot before the fabled Ellis Island of schoolbooks.

New Orleans is insular for reasons other than geography. South Louisiana and New Orleans share a common French heritage but are distinctly different in several important ways. For example, outside of New Orleans, Acadians (or Cajuns as they are more commonly called today) constitute the great bulk of south Louisiana's population. Originally French-Canadians from New Brunswick and Nova Scotia, the Acadians were uprooted and transported by the British following the late 18th-century French and Indian War. Thousands found their way to Louisiana where they settled along the numerous bayous that lace through the southern portion of the state. As fishermen and small farmers, they remained essentially an isolated and rustic folk well into the 20th century. By contrast, the Creoles of New Orleans (roughly any native born, non-Indian New Orleanian) were an urban and, at least in their own minds, urbane people. Creoles and Acadians shared a common Gallic heritage and Catholic religion, but the similarity stopped there. To the New Orleans Creole the Acadian was and remains at best a quaint country fellow whose main recommendation is a robust sense of humor.

New Orleans Creoles may note the subtle differences between themselves and others in south Louisiana, but they look upon Louisianans north of Baton Rouge almost as members of a foreign country. Traveling north from New Orleans one quickly senses a change in both landscape and people. Flat vistas abruptly change to rolling hills, and forlorn cypress swamps are replaced by endless pine forests. The change in the people is as notable. If they are white, their origins will go back to the British Isles, and if black to Africa; but almost certainly the religion of all will be Protestant, though just as certainly not Lutheran. The tone of their speech will vary from soft to hard but the accent nevertheless will be distinct and their diet as dramatically different from New Orleans as the cuisine of Dover, England, from that of Calais, France.

To the north of New Orleans the state becomes part of the greater South. Culturally, little distinguishes such north Louisiana cities as Monroe or Shreveport from other cities across the region. Pan-fried steak or chicken is much the same in Monroe as in Selma, Alabama. And if per chance the coffee proves better in Monroe, the odds are good that the chef is newly arrived from New Orleans.

The point, of course, is that the culture of New Orleans is unlike the culture of north Louisiana, or by extension, the South. Indeed, while it may surprise many readers and even shock some New Orleanians, the truth is, except for its location, New Orleans is no more a Southern city than San Francisco, Milwaukee, or Philadelphia.

New Orleans, in fact, shares more similarities with many northern cities than with any of the cities of the South. For example, Milwaukee, Cincinnati, and New Orleans, unlike southern cities, all have a significant number of citizens of German origin. And unlike southern cities, each of the three supported numerous breweries before the conglomerate and advertising wars of recent years destroyed all but a handful of giants. Today, of all southern cities only New Orleans can lay claim to a locally owned brewing company, Dixie Beer.

Other similarities between New Orleans and northern cities abound. The local telephone directory will reveal the same repetition of Irish and Italian names as directories in Boston and New Jersey, and by comparision far more than the directories of Atlanta, Memphis, or Houston. If the O'Briens of New Orleans are today more concerned with Mardi Gras than events in Belfast, and if New Orleans citizens of Sicilian origin are less concerned with Columbus Day than with the freshness of their French bread, it only speaks for the assertion of New Orleans as a melting pot.

Much of the city's way of life, to be sure, would be familiar to a visiting American: automobiles are pervasive, national advertising beckons and franchized fast-food chains are growing. But Creole cottages, bowls of gumbo, marching jazz bands, and sequined black "Indians" remind you that this is a different and unusual place. It is not different because French is still spoken occasionally, or because you can also find Italians or pizza, Jews or synagogues, Irish or green beer, blacks or spirituals, Latinos or flamenco. You can find any of those ethnic characteristics elsewhere in America. Nor is it because *all* those characteristics can be found here. Chicago, Los Angeles, New York, Boston, or Baltimore would have similarly commingled populations and cultures. Its difference is due instead to historical circumstance, geography, and just plain luck. A new, open, unique culture and sense of identity deveolped in New Orleans—a rich common lifestyle.

Creole Culture

For most Americans the word Creole is synonymous with the distinctive features of New Orleans, and in general the association is historically accurate. In the era of European expansion the term was originally used to distinguish the children of colonial settlers from native peoples. In Louisiana it took on cultural and political implications as hordes of Anglo-Americans swarmed into the territory following the annexation. It designated and united the native-born, mainly French-speaking population in its efforts to resist cultural and political subjugation by the newcomers. While a majority of the early European settlers were French or Spanish by heritage, the term Creole included anyone, save Indian, born in Louisiana—even the child of an American. In essence, the term Creole and native were interchangeable. More important, in its modern usage the term reveals and has much to do with what is essential in the city's culture. To understand the meanings of the word is to look into the city's soul.

When a knowledgeable New Orleanian refers to someone as a Creole, he usually means that the individual is a member of the city's old French-speaking community. If he feels the need to be more specific, he may refer to the individual as a black Creole or a white Creole. In either case he has just revealed one of the city's more interesting aspects: the existence of two Creole communities, one white and one black. Both groups share many attributes and a common cultural heritage, but racism and historical circumstances have steadily driven them apart into separate communities with little contact between the two.

For most Creoles, black or white, the subject is a delicate one. In colonial times, the line between these communities was not so sharply drawn. But time and events have altered attitudes, and today the matter is best avoided in the company of either group.

New Orleans is especially rich in folklore and much of it concerns the Creole and his world. Indeed, in the pantheon of New Orleans mythology the Creole is supreme. There are other heroes in the Elysian temple—for example, General Beauregard, Bernard de Marigny, Jelly Roll Morton, Saint Expedite—but even these are mostly Creoles or, like Saint Expedite, personages with proper Creole connections. Perhaps because the Creoles are today no longer such a distinct and visible part of the community, New Orleanians feel a special nostalgia for them. Certainly few subjects are so close to their heart, and if they sense a receptive audience, they will happily share their abundant knowledge of the subject.

From such earnest informants you would probably learn, for instance, that the Creoles are the descendents of aristocratic French and perhaps Spanish colonials. Your informants will tell you how Creole children supposedly received a mandatory French education. The boys often went to Paris and the girls to one of the local convents administered by French nuns. In addition to their studies in French literature, poetry, and music, the girls in these convents were tutored in the various arts of homemaking and the social graces. With this training the Creole girl would return to New Orleans society, there to enjoy an endless round of balls until, very shortly, a proper marriage could be arranged. In such a marriage the Creole girl would finally assume her ordained role in Creole society as a homemaker, gracious hostess, doting mother, and loving wife. For Creole boys the Paris schooling would include not only the *belle-lettres,* music, philosophy, and perhaps mathematics, but especially the rounded sophistication so necessary for an aristocratic gentleman. This last would be acquired by attendance at the opera, the races, and, of course, those Parisian gatherings where, as men of the better class said with an amused wink of the eye, a boy can learn about the world. Along the way he would, of course, acquire an appreciation of good wines, proper tailoring, impeccable manners, and such similar attributes as might be expected in an urbane French gentlemen.

The next chapter in this romantic tale brings the elegant young man home from Paris. Increasingly the city to which these young Creoles returned was changing, however, and not for the better. In the Creole's view the trouble all started when the colony was transferred to the United States in 1803. With American control life had taken a turn for the worse, with no relief in sight. The Americans, led by an officious new governor named Claiborne, were turning the world of the Creole upside down.

The myth about the early American newcomers is well fixed in the local lore. Before the annexation there had been only a few of them— mostly rough, unkempt, and uncouth riverboat men, often drunk and swaggering on the levee or in the marketplace. After 1803, however, their coarse numbers seemed to increase by the week. And even among those few who were not ruffians off the river, all they talked about was business—never opera or the theater or any of the proper pursuits of a gentleman. But what can one expect? the Creoles must have asked among themselves, when even the American leader, Mr. Claiborne, speaks *Francais enfantin.* For the Creoles one word summarized it all: *barbare!*

But the Creoles survived. According to the legend they drew into themselves and avoided contact with the Americans. The Creoles, to their everlasting glory, preserved the highborn culture and manners of their fathers in a world gone mad with Anglo-American interlopers. True to their aristocratic code, the Creoles refused to engage in unseemly business dealings or associate with the uncouth Americans. Instead, they retreated into the old section of the city and there established their own closed society.

New Orleans, as a result, became a divided city, with Canal Street as a partition, or neutral ground, between the two worlds. Above Canal (Uptown) a new American city arose, while below Canal (Downtown) the *Vieux Carré* and the *Faubourgs Trémé* and *Marigny* became bastions of the old Creole world. Although the retreat cost the Creoles dearly in power and money, their stand continued an aristocratic code that even the Americans came finally to accept.

This legend, your local informant would assure you, is the true story of the Creole. You may also hear at some point in this account, that whatever you may have heard or read, there is no truth to the popular Yankee notion that Creoles are of mixed race. With assertive finality he will insist that there are no Creoles with any trace of African ancestry.

It is a good story, but like many good stories it is a mixture of some fact and much fiction. Most New Orleanians love it and will accept no other. The myth eases the burden of today's threadbare gentility or even blue-collar condition. To know that one is descended from aristocrats is self-gratifying in the extreme. For the more fervent it offers hope of betterment where fate has been unkind.

Historians, however, have presented a somewhat more mundane view of the Creole. They have questioned two tenets that are especially important in the Creole myth. These are the fanciful notion of the Creole as an urbane, polished aristocrat, and the even more fervent conviction that all Creoles are white. In the first instance they have demonstrated that the city's Creole society included a broad spectrum of economic and social classes, wherein not surprisingly, humble, uneducated Creoles vastly outnumbered elite Creoles. What is surprising in the historians' account, however, is the dearth among even the Creole gentry of high culture and other attributes usually associated with an elite class. Most evidence, including the testimony of many well-educated and reliable visitors, speaks almost as a single voice on the general lack of education and high cultural attainment among the city's Creole elite. Indeed, visitors seldom noted elegant manners among the Creole gentry. Some reliable observers on the other hand have even reported that the "Creole of Creoles," Bernard de Marigny, preferred using his fingers to the more usual knife and fork when dining.

That the Creoles in general lost out to the Anglo-Americans in the city's 19th-century economy is well documented. Recent historians, however, cannot attribute the defeat to any disdain of money or rough business practices. What Creoles lacked was training and experience.

Historians have also questioned that the Creoles reacted to their defeat by withdrawing into their own world where outsiders and in particular Anglo-Americans were rigidly excluded. In actuality, Creole society by its very openness to ethnic variety and cultural difference made possible the unique culture of New Orleans.

There was, of course, ethnic conflict between the Creoles and the Americans. Like any people, the Creoles resented the brash questioning of their values by newly arrived Anglos who often voiced disdain for cultural differences. Many Anglos, for example, were openly shocked by the Creoles' great enjoyment of worldly pleasures on Sunday. That the Creoles were frightened by the sudden Anglo horde after the annexation is not surprising. Any people confronted by a massive influx of aliens speaking a foreign tongue would have been. It was not, however, Anglos *per se* that the Creoles united against, but rather Anglos *en masse* that they perceived as a threat.

But what were the Creoles' qualities, and more important, what is the heritage of the Creoles that yet endures in the life of the city? The Creoles' qualities, simply put, were a friendly openness and sensate nature that expressed itself in a *joie de vivre*. These simple but fundamental qualities nurtured the culture in which native and visitor alike can partake and enjoy even today. Where the basic Puritanism of Anglo-America sought to deny or at least severely inhibit worldly delights, the Creole's open, sensate nature encouraged and celebrated worldly delights. The city's festivals, cuisine, and music derived from many sources, but all were nurtured by these basic Creole qualities.

The city's carnival with its bacchanalian Mardi Gras is a notable example of the Creole's Latin delight in worldly pleasures. Similar examples are the frequent neighborhood parades and, of course, jazz funerals. These last, with their unique music, are in part African in origin. However, it was the Creole's love of festival and tolerance of ethnic variety which permitted their transition from Africa and nurtured their evolution in New Orleans. Like jazz, the celebrated Creole cuisine of New Orleans is in part derived from Africa, but again it was the Creole's sensual delight and tolerance of cultural variety which initially allowed and then encouraged the African contribution which was so essential to its unique and full development.

But what of the Creoles today? Or more to the point for a curious visitor: what and where are the Creoles today, or indeed, how can one even recognize a Creole when one sees one? In today's usage a Creole is usually understood to be a member of the city's old French-speaking community. Unfortunately, members of this group are today not as easily distinguished from other citizenry. Public use of the French language which once identified them is now rare; the few who can still speak the language confine its use largely to the home or private gatherings. Some of the remaining French speakers may still be found in the homes and neighborhoods of their fathers and grandfathers, but most have scattered throughout the city.

Downtown New Orleans

The city's old French Quarter is illustrative. From its establishment until the late 19th century, it was the center and principal abode of the Creole. In the first years of this century, however, the Creole started an abandonment of the area that by the 1920s left only a handful of his compatriots. Indeed, even the French Market, which had sustained the Creole as much in soul as in body, remained French in name only. With his departure the French Quarter became successively a Sicilian enclave, a preservationist cause, a speculator's delight, and a gay paradise.

Racial bias has also complicated the matter. The city's Creole community is really two communities, one black and one white, each residing in separate and reasonably distinct geographic areas with boundaries that occasionally overlap and blur. Most black Creoles today reside in the city's sixth and seventh wards in an area roughly bounded on the east and west by Elsyian Fields and Orleans avenues and on the north and south by Broad and Rampart streets. St. Bernard Avenue cuts through the center of the area and serves as its main boulevard. The importance of the street in the psyche of the community is emphasized by its imposing residences and the prestigious Autocrat Club, a black Creole equivalent of the city's elite white Boston Club.

Off of St. Bernard Avenue the architecture becomes less imposing but more typically New Orleans. Two clues, however, suggest that the neighborhood is not altogether typical. The small Protestant churches so prevalent in the city's other black neighborhoods are only infrequently found here. Most black Creoles are Catholic, and Protestantism has made little headway in the community. Small neighborhood restaurants, however, are not uncommon. Their menus offer a surprisingly large variety of Creole dishes most usually of excellent quality at reasonable prices.

A significant number of the black Creoles who live in the area are skilled tradesmen: bricklayers, plasterers, carpenters, and similar crafts which they and their forefathers have dominated for generations. A few, more entrepreneurial, have prospered in undertaking, insurance, catering, and similar enterprises. Still others have entered the professions, usually as schoolteachers, but occasionally as lawyers or doctors. Touched by the American notion of upward mobility and the promises of the 1960s and 1970s, many have moved on to the suburbs of eastern New Orleans or even to California and the never-never land of the American dream. Most, however, are deeply rooted in the community and will live out their lives in the neighborhood.

Unimpeded by the legal and social restrictions that until recently burdened black Creoles, the city's white Creoles have been more mobile. Many—in particular the more affluent and elite—have abandoned the old, traditional Creole neighborhoods for the more fashionable Anglo Uptown sections of the city or even suburbia. Except for their French names and Catholic religion most are hardly distinguishable today from their Anglo-Saxon friends and neighbors.

There are, however, two areas to the south and southeast of City Park where white middle-class Creoles reside in large numbers. One is roughly the triangular section enclosed by Carrollton Avenue, Canal Street and City Park Avenue. The other can be loosely thought of as the area on both sides of Esplanade Avenue between Broad Street and City Park. Both neighborhoods were built up in the late 19th and early 20th centuries by a white middle-class overflow that included a large percentage of Creoles. These were the areas into which a substantial number of Creoles moved as they abandoned the French Quarter and receded out along Esplanade Avenue toward City Park. Most knowledgeable observers believe that the Creoles residing in these areas are the last, fairly cohesive remnants of the city's white Creole community.

Both neighborhoods are mainly residential and reflect a general prosperity. Many of the larger, more pretentious residences in both areas are late Victorian or Edwardian, although occasionally you will see a Creole cottage dating from the mid-19th century or a bungalow from the 1920s. The overall effect is of an earlier time which comes not so much from the architecture but from a noticeable lack of attention to current fashion. It is also very distinctly New Orleans and charming.

There is one other area in New Orleans with a large—perhaps the largest—concentration of Creoles. It extends approximately from Esplanade Avenue to a little below the Industrial Canal, and from the river to about Claiborne Avenue. While the area includes portions of the city's seventh and eighth wards, the greater part of it falls within the ninth ward. Although it is only a fractional part of the ninth ward, most New Orleanians regard that as *the* ninth ward or, as they would say, the "great" ninth ward.

While the area has many black Creole residents, it is mainly noted for its white working-class population which includes a large percentage of Creoles. The city's other ethnic groups are all well represented in the population, although Germans appear to be the most numerous.

In general, the area's architecture reflects the working-class origins of its residents. Single and double shotgun residences dating from the late 19th and early 20th century abound, interspersed here and there with camelback residences of the same period, or occasionally a 1920s bungalow. Many homes lack front yards and are set right up to the property line with small stoops extending onto the public sidewalk. This and the gregarious nature of the citizenry no doubt led to the very old but still popular New Orleans custom of stoop sitting wherein residents pass the time of day by sitting on their stoops and chatting with neighbors and passers-by.

Lack of maintenance is more usual than unusual in the area, but a surprisingly large number of buildings are models of care. The unfortunate New Orleans penchant for tasteless remodeling is all too common, but probably no more prevalent than elsewhere in the city. A notable characteristic of the neighborhood is the mix of dwellings and small business establishments, the latter often catering to neighborhood needs. Thus, in any short stretch of perhaps a block or two, it would not be unusual to find a corner grocery, an auto repair shop, and, perhaps, a small seafood market randomly interspersed among family dwellings.

Bars and nightclubs are both common and very popular in the area, as are dance halls. These last are probably more plentiful in this area than in any other section of the city. New Orleans has a reputation as a dancing town and the people in the ninth ward are apparently determined to uphold it.

While the neighborhood's restaurants are not as ubiquitous as its bars, very few of the bars in this area serve liquor without any food. New Orleanians seldom separate eating and drinking in public. Small bars and restaurants are very common in these old Creole neighborhoods. They cater to a largely working-class crowd, and usually lack linen napkins and similar amenities. The food, however, is almost certain to be good, and is often vastly better than what is served in many of the city's better hotels. Some are spectacular, and their patrons naively believe everyone in America eats as well—until they leave New Orleans.

In general the vast majority of Creoles have been true to their basic nature. They have remained on the downtown side of Canal Street and reveled in their essential *joie de vivre*. They welcomed the various immigrant groups that entered their world in successive waves and in the end "Creolized" them. In consequence, the downtown section of the city remains today a reflection of what is most essential about New Orleans.

Uptown New Orleans

The Anglo-Americans were another matter. While some regarded the Creole's Catholicism with an open suspicion, others were publicly critical of his Sunday afternoon pleasures in a cafe, or worse yet, his dancing at a ball on Sunday evening. Some Anglo-Americans were impudent enough to suggest that he had better give up his French language and learn English—*this* in the land of his birth! Finally, when they failed to Americanize him they washed their hands of him and went above Canal Street shaking their heads and suggesting that he would be sorry.

Unable to control the Creole and dominate his culture, the Americans turned to building their own world upriver from Canal Street. To awe the Creole, and no doubt bolster their own self-confidence, the Americans hired renowned architects and set them to building their commercial halls and opulent homes. Because the best land was on the elevated natural levee that closely followed the river, American development moved upriver in a ribbon-like swath adjacent to the river. The swath itself was divided roughly into three parallel streams of population that set a pattern of residential development in the Uptown American sector.

Not all of the upriver side of Canal Street is occupied by Uptowners. The swath between Magazine Street and the river became a white working-class neighborhood while the area beyond Baronne Street to the swamps became, in the years following the Civil War, a black neighborhood. Though the pattern still exists today, it has eroded in the decades since World War II. This is especially evident in the corridor between Magazine Street and the river, an area that in many ways resembles the downtown side of Canal Street. The houses are perhaps a bit more appealing because of the greater abundance of ornate woodwork called German gingerbread. Front yards, though very small, are more numerous, but many houses are also set flush with the sidewalk and stoop sitting is as common here as in the area below Canal Street. The mix of small business establishments and dwellings exists but not so thoroughly as in the ninth ward. Bars and restaurants are common enough—though again not so plentiful as in Creole downtown—and are noted for their friendliness and reasonable prices.

The area, however, is changing. For a decade or more preservationists have been moving into the area and this pressure coupled with speculation is altering the population. Much of the restoration is excellent but some is not so good. More important, however, is the yet open question: Will gentrification disrupt the living patterns and change a style of life?

The center swath of American development, roughly the area from Magazine to Baronne streets, with Saint Charles as its major thoroughfare, developed into an elite residential core. Here Anglo bankers, merchants, cotton and sugar factors, and professional men built great manor homes that reflected their success and eminence in the city's American community. Today many of their descendants still live in this fashionable area where a residential address is an important social symbol.

The section's architecture reflects the attitudes of the Anglo-Americans who built it. Coming from a society where homes were thought of as individual residences with surrounding gardens, they had little understanding or appreciation of the Creole's French Quarter, which was derived from the Mediterranean idea of connected residences with interior courts. Not surprisingly, they chose the tradition they understood. It was also a tradition that gave the Americans greater opportunity to exhibit their success for all the world to see.

Uptown architecture reflects the fashion that was popular at the time of its construction. Thus, a drive along St. Charles Avenue or Prytania, two of the area's important traffic arteries, will reveal the shifting *haut monde* tastes of the 19th and 20th centuries. Residences closer to Canal Street, and thus among the earliest, reflect the classic esthetic of that earlier time while those in the far Uptown usually exhibit the greater flamboyance of later decades and Edwardian times. Over the years saplings have become ancient oaks, and gardens have luxuriated, and what was once an area of scruffy *nouveau riche* development is now a luxurious and mellow area of great charm.

Most of the area's residents are just as charming. Time and comfortable circumstance have had their effect and the people are now mellow and delightful like vintage port. They have also been "Creolized."

Because the Americans could not dominate the Creole, a curious thing occurred. The Creole's infectious culture enthralled the Americans with the delights of Creole lifestyle. In the matter of drinking, Americans of the 19th century needed little encouragement. But food was something else. Coming from an Anglo culture where food was simple and lightly seasoned, the Americans were at first repelled by the exotic strangeness of Creole food. Eating, however, was a necessity and the local restaurants only served Creole dishes. Even in their homes, the well-to-do could not escape Creole cooking as the cooks whom they hired were black Creoles who could not prepare a dish without garlic or at least green onions and thyme. Gradually, what Anglo-Americans at first rejected became acceptable and then actually enjoyable. Prominent European travelers whom they occasionally entertained in their homes, praised the cuisine and encouraged the culinary conversion. To have *Viscomte* d'Abzac remark on the pleasure of dining in one's home was heady indeed!

Of Krewes and Clubs

The American mania to control the Creole culture was successful in one important instance: Carnival. At first, of course, they disapproved. It interferred with business, disturbed public order, and had no practical purpose that *they* could see. Indeed, the public debauchery and rowdyism had initially bothered the Americans so much that they banned it for a long period. The ban, of course, like a ban on rain, did not work too well and eventually it was dropped. Finally in 1857 the Americans succeeded in capturing Carnival by staging a parade and ball that caught the public's imagination and gave Carnival its basic modern form. Within a few years a large part of Carnival became a very private affair with participation in balls serving as a symbol of social standing. The Uptown Americans would control such participation through private men's clubs.

Today, Carnival is at the core of Uptown social life. For the Uptown male, membership in one or more of the older Carnival krewes (the New Orleans name for such organizations) is a badge of ultimate distinction. The fact that such membership is not publicly known is of small concern to the true Uptowner who is little taken with mass fame; it is known to his intimates where it counts. Ladies, on the other hand, do not belong to elite Carnival krewes but gain their satisfaction from having a daughter chosen as a queen or maid in one or more of the numerous balls that are given by such organizations. For the debutantes such honors are the New Orleans equivalent of being presented at the Court of Saint James. Indeed, for an Uptown girl it is ultimately far more important than presentation at the British Court.

Uptowners have at least partially captured another Creole institution: Antoine's Restaurant. If you see someone slip past the line waiting at the entrance to this establishment you can be fairly sure that it is not a Creole but almost certainly a wealthy Uptowner. Inside, this same Uptowner will be served by his private waiter who has served him for years. If your own waiter takes a liking to you he may show you one or more of the private dining rooms named for illustrious Carnival krewes. In them you will see illuminated wall cases displaying crowns, sceptors, and other memorabilia from these organizations. The remarkable relationship of this old Creole restaurant with Carnival and Up-towners is further illustrated on each Monday before Mardi Gras when it closes to the public and privately serves Proteus, an elite Carnival krewe with largely Uptown membership. Thus, Antoine's on occasion is virtually a private club of Uptown New Orleans.

The city's elite private clubs are an important part of both the Uptown world and Carnival. While only some of the clubs are direct sponsors of individual Carnival krewes, the memberships of such clubs and krewes are very largely interchangeable. The location of these clubs in the city's commercial district mainly relates to the use of their dining rooms as a midday convenience to members, but their location specifi-cally on the parade route results from their close ties with Carnival. The latter permits members and their guests to observe and toast the parading krewes from reviewing stands which are erected each year over the public sidewalks adjacent to the clubs. On one or another of these stands, queens and maids of such elite parading krewes as Proteus and Comus, and the Monarch of Carnival, Rex, receive and give hom-age as the parade passes. Among the older and more illustrious of these clubs are the Boston, the Louisiana, and the Pickwick.

Possibly because the membership of such clubs is restricted to males, Uptown ladies have formed clubs of their own. The two most promi-nent of these are the elegant Orléans Club on Saint Charles Avenue and the smaller but equally exclusive Le Petit Salon on Saint Peter Street. Because the latter is below Canal Street in the French Quarter, it is something of an anomaly in the social dichotomy of Uptown and Downtown. Its membership, however, is largely Uptown.

The importance of clubs in the world of the Uptowners is such that several have even been formed for the children of Uptowners. Thus, from puberty through high school Uptown children are initiated into the basics of Uptown society by clubs like Ice Breakers, Eight O'clocks, and Valencia. On the other hand, for Uptowners the right school is as important as the right club. For Uptowners this means schools such as McGehee, Sacred Heart, Newman, and Country Day. The last named is not in the Uptown area but in the old section of Metairie; this section is really an Uptown suburb unlike the rest of Metairie.

Detecting Uptowners

The Creole habits of dining, drinking, dancing, and cavorting became part of the Uptown lifestyle. Indeed, their genteel form of *bonhomie* has made the Uptowner both a figure and conveyor of status. Though the Uptowner would blush at such a characterization, he is not naive about all of this. To maintain his status a great deal of attention is given to symbols. Clothing, for example, is one of the more obvious badges. Natural-cut, conservative suits with cordovan shoes, button-down collars and handsome foulard or rep ties are standard men's wear for most business occasions and informal cocktails. Leisure suits and clothing made of double-knit polyesters with a luminous shimmer are not part of the Uptowner's wardrobe. People who wear such apparel do live Uptown but they are not Uptowners.

Even the children of Uptown families wear the badge of "Uptown" with pride and aristocratic bearing. Despite some of the hazards of living in the older neighborhoods of a large city, Uptown teenagers would consider the thought of living outside the neighborhoods along upper Saint Charles Avenue almost as a sentence of exile. They are horrified by the suburbs, mock the *nouveau riche* of the lakefront and the middle class of Gentilly, and seldom venture on the downtown side of the French Quarter.

Paralleling the other side of the prosperous Uptown corridor of genteel wealth is a poor settlement that runs along Claiborne Avenue. In the 19th century this area was a vast back swamp. In the years following the Civil War, it was the area into which large numbers of ex-slaves from the plantation country moved. Lacking the skills of the black Creoles, these blacks became the city's main unskilled labor force, a condition which still exists for many of their descendents. Many older black Creoles still refer to the blacks who live in the area as "American Negroes." Today it remains a generally depressed section with few interesting sites. The appearance of the neighborhood is generally ramshackled with very few homes or commercial structures of merit. Small Protestant churches are a common sight but the small restaurants that were once common are now disappearing, victims of franchised fast food outlets.

The area's two most famous sons were both musicians. One, Buddy Bolden, is thought by some experts on jazz to have been the musician who first made the transition from ragtime to Dixieland. The other, Louis Armstrong, helped to make it popular around the world.

The Lakefront

In the years shortly after the turn of the century modern drainage methods and men with axes cleared the vast back swamp that gave the area its name. With that impediment gone the area from approximately Broad Street to the lake was opened for development.

A pamphlet advertising lakefront real estate at the time argued that the city's old Creole architecture was rapidly losing favor. It assured the reader that the planned community on the lakefront would be like the golden west of California; that restrictions would protect home-owners against any Chinese laundry springing up on the corner. In the seventy years since then the area has become settled and today it is very much as promised. The Creole's influence will not be found in the area. It is almost devoid of restaurants, bars, and public festival; indeed, it differs little from suburban America. It is not old New Orleans.

Epilogue

You may wonder on your return to the airport what it is about New Orleans that has given the city its reputation. You will see the ironwork and unusual buildings of the French Quarter and the stately antebellum homes in the Garden District, but somehow that would only scratch the surface of the city's charm. To avoid such disappointment, you should realize before you explore the city that New Orleans is notably lacking in things that are usually associated with a great, modern city. There are no monumental buildings or truly great museums or surging masses of humanity such as you will find in New York or Chicago. And there certainly are no city vistas as can be seen in San Francisco.

New Orleans essentially is a way of life which is difficult for a tourist to capture while riding in a tour bus. The closest you can come to capturing it on a weekend trip would be perhaps a dinner in a restaurant and a stroll through the French Quarter or an older neighborhood. Under those conditions the best restaurant would probably be a crowded, boisterous restaurant, preferably on a Friday night when natives seek out their favorite haunts. As for strolling in the French Quarter, do it without an itinerary or schedule. At lunchtime stop at the Central Grocery on Decatur Street and buy a Muffuletta and a Barq's root beer. Take the repast to the Moon Walk on the levee by Jackson Square, find a bench and relax. You won't be disappointed.—you'll have found what New Orleans' reputation is all about.

A CITY OF CELEBRATION

Mardi Gras and Other Festivals

by
ERROL LABORDE

Errol Laborde is author of Mardi Gras! A Celebration, *and is associate editor of* Gambit *newspaper. His articles have appeared in* New Orleans Magazine, Guide Newspapers, *and the* Vieux Carré Courier. *He has won several awards in annual competitions sponsored by the New Orleans Press Club, including on two occasions the Alix Waller Award, the Press Club's highest honor for writing achievement.*

It is Mardi Gras night and the last parade is preparing to move. A stern-looking man who is in charge of the flambeaux carriers walks down the street, simultaneously lighting fires on both sides as he makes his way. Soon the street is an elongated arc of golden, bouncing flames spouting from flambeaux, fuel-lit jets attached to poles carried by muscular black men dressed in flowing white smocks. For the next two hours or so the flambeaux carriers will dance down the streets of old New Orleans illuminating segments of the parade as though time, and technology, were suspended in the 19th century. With the fires lit, the flambeaux carrier boss orders his workers into line.

Sound penetrates the eeriness of the golden glow. Miscellaneous notes, drumming and tooting, gradually come together as though formed by the haze. The shriek of whistles pierces the air. Official-looking men with walkie-talkies in their hands bark commands. "Let's get going" reverberates through the confusion. Suddenly that confusion becomes a streamlined procession moving along Napoleon Avenue then turning right onto oak-lined St. Charles Avenue, the main artery of fashionable Uptown New Orleans. From within a car bearing the markings of a local radio station, the driver gives his first report over the air to those along the way, "the parade of the krewe of Comus is on the way."

Comus himself rides near the head of the parade, a masked god of Roman origin perched on a throne atop a float, like a monarch reviewing his passing kindom. Those in the crowd wave to him, to which Comus responds by lifting his golden goblet as a salute. The light of the flambeaux torches down below sparkles off of his rhinestone and sequin costume.

Mounted knights and dukes, Comus' entourage, steer their steeds through the crowds like lieutenants awaiting the call of their general. But in the power structure of Mardi Gras it is actually the captain, one of the mounted men with plumage flowing from his helmet, who is in charge, not the monarch. This power-behind-the-throne rides a horse several yards in front of Comus' float.

Spectators along the parade route, however, have little concern for organizational charts. They are at once dancing, gyrating or keeping time to the passing bands then reaching, yelling, extending their arms upwards to receive trinkets as the floats that follow the monarch pass in front of them. Each float tells a story of some long-ago legend, but on the streets it's the same old story, the folks are participating in the one particular custom that makes the New Orleans Mardi Gras unique to any carnival, indeed any parade, in the world. The spectators are not merely spectating, they are caught in the fervor of trying to catch "throws"—beads, toys, and most of all, doubloons.

From his position on the float the masked rider looks down at the waves of hands swaying like a sea as the tide rolls in. With each passing float the tide rises. From within that sea, girls flirt, men gesture for attention. They are caught in the fury of desperately trying to catch what will become the next day's junk. The thrill of the hunt comes not so much from the prize as from the capture.

Meanwhile, Comus' float progresses, leading the parade into the business district, onto Canal Street, where he toasts his queen in front of the Pickwick Club. The parade then twists toward Rampart Street, a strip immortalized in song by the blues but that suddenly, once more, hears march time reverberating off of its old buildings. The marches will soon be over, however. As Comus reaches the Municipal Auditorium his procession is ending and, with his passing, Carnival is coming to a close for another year.

For weeks prior to this last parade, there have been many parades rolling along the streets of the greater New Orleans area—some old, some new; some modern, some traditional; some with women riders, most with men, a few with both; some all white, some racially mixed, some all black. On Mardi Gras, while Comus prepares for his evening march, the streets of New Orleans are packed with revelers watching the antics of the black krewe of Zulu and the spectacle of the grand march of Rex himself, the King of the Carnival. In surrounding suburban parishes (counties), lesser parades also roll along the highways. But of all the parades, it has always been Comus who has the prerogative of being last—because it was Comus who, back in 1857, started it all.

History

Mardi Gras came to the area that became Louisiana literally as soon as Frenchmen arrived. It all began on March 3, 1699, the date that a party headed by Pierre le Moyne, Sieur d'Iberville, reached the mouth of the Mississippi River after having explored its route. History, of course, is vague in detailing the event, perhaps Iberville's men didn't know that the date happened to be Mardi Gras. It is tempting to want to believe that Iberville and his men *did* indeed know that their arrival day was Mardi Gras and that as they sat around the campfire that evening, they lifted a cup to the season. Centuries of toasts would follow. Back in France, however, as indeed through much of Europe, the Christian custom of celebrating on the day before the three-day Lenten period of fasting was well established. The English called the day Shrove Tuesday. The French referred to the day as Fat Tuesday—the day of feasting before fasting. Where the French kingdom spread, so did the French words for the day, "Mardi Gras," literally fat Tuesday.

Christianity had adapted a pagan celebration of the rites of spring and altered it significantly, giving it a religious significance. Early accounts of pagan celebrations consist of tales of purification rites at which sinners would run naked through the field past priests who would lash at them with whips made of goat skin. This was a method of repentence. The Roman upper class used the day as a special occasion for orgies, a practice which quickly spread throughout the apparently status-conscious lower classes.

Christianity lent the celebration a religious purpose, but not all of the bawdiness was lost. Early reports of the Parisian carnival tell of public lynchings followed by the bodies being carried through the streets. Other places celebrated the day in more conventional ways with masking, dancing, and celebrations.

At first the rugged frontier town of New Orleans didn't know what to do with Mardi Gras. The celebration consisted of drunken brawls along the dusty streets. It was an occasion to be dreaded by the respectable people of the day. At times various maskers would cavort in the city's streets in keeping with the customs back in the old country.

Not until the Marquis de Vaudreuil came to power in 1743 was a bit more dignity added to Carnival. Vaudreuil was the French governor of Louisiana who served during the reign of Louis XIV. He must have seen himself as an extension of his king in the new world, for he tried to duplicate the pageantry and pomp of his king. Vaudreuil imported fine materials with which to stage elegant parties and balls. Thus the city began to develop social grace. It is uncertain just how capable Vaudreuil was as an administrator but he brought lace to a burlap town.

Balls became a part of the social season in New Orleans—a season that stretched from the winter through early spring and that avoided the humid, mosquito-infested delta summers.

Beginning on Twelfth Night, January 6, the last day of the Christmas season and the first day of the Carnival season, the town's aristocrats would disguise themselves for the *bals masque*. Just as the customs of the Roman upper class were adapted by the lower classes so were the carnival balls in new New Orleans. Eventually the balls became plentiful and varied. Probably the most whispered about was the quadroon ball to which white creole gentlemen would steal away to win the favors of the light-skinned "colored" ladies on the dance floor. Come Twelfth Night each year, New Orleans was a city having not just a ball, but many all over town. The carnival parade still did not become an important part of Carnival for many years.

Not that people didn't try. There were many failed attempts in the early years to stage an annual parade. Beginning in 1852, one group known as the Bedouins, named after the tribesmen of the Middle East, put together a few serpentine processions, but ultimately, as with all other efforts, their parade came to an end. Outside the gracious social setting of the ballroom, Carnival was just rowdyism dominated by spirits rather than spirit.

That was why a group of young men from Mobile, Alabama, were so disappointed when they moved to New Orleans. In Mobile, which like New Orleans had a French heritage, there had been a custom of an annual organized parade to celebrate the carnival season. The men set out to fill the void by staging a parade in New Orleans. They began planning in late 1856 so that by Mardi Gras evening 1857 word spread around town that a spectacular parade was about to take to the streets.

From along Magazine Street the glare of torchlights could be seen that night accompanying a rolling tableau headed by a comical-looking monarch identified to onlookers as Comus, the god of mirth. Following Comus were more glittering mule-drawn floats carrying masked riders. Marching bands and beaming papier mâché heads were dispersed throughout the procession of floats.

Perhaps only a god in his mirthfulness could immediately appreciate the fact that Mardi Gras, this French holiday, was being rescued for the predominantly French New Orleanians by men from Mobile of English ancestry. It might have been Comus' prank on the French that the parading group called itself the Mystick Krewe of Comus, adopting the Anglican spelling. And it would be Comus' spell on parades to come that all Carnival organizations would henceforth refer to themselves as "krewes."

With Comus came continuity. Each year from then on The Mystick Krewe held its parade, giving Carnival its one real public attraction. The krewe also set the guidelines for the customs of Carnival. The word "mystick" was taken seriously. To this day, Comus' identity is never revealed. The person chosen to be the god is hidden behind a mask. The position of the captain, the krewe boss, evolved; his identity, too, remains a secret. Comus was the organization adopted by New Orleans aristocracy and thus came the marriage between high society and Carnival.

But for all his contributions to the New Orleans Carnival, Comus merely set the stage. In 1872 the main act began.

It all started innocently enough: The Russians were coming, and New Orleanians were excited. Word reached New Orleans in 1872 that His Imperial Highness Alexis Alexandrovich Romanov, the brother of the heir apparent to the Russian crown, planned to visit the city as part of the western swing of his trip to the United States. The duke, whose itinerary included buffalo hunting with General Custer, was, coincidentally, to be in town for Mardi Gras.

To honor the visiting royalty the local citizenry thought it might be appropriate, and fun, to conjure up its own royalty. A parade during the day was organized for the duke's entertainment, headed by a make-shift monarch dubbed Rex, Latin for "king." Dutifully the duke sat at a reviewing stand and watched the procession which no doubt entertained the common folks on the streets more than it did the duke. History does not record if the duke was amused by the musical selections of the passing band. Since local gossip had it that Alexis had his royal eye on Lydia Thompson, a musical-comedy performer whose show "Bluebeard" was currently in New Orleans, many of the bands played one particular song from the show. Over and over Alexis listened to the melody of "If Ever I Cease to Love," a somewhat forgettable song that was immortalized that day. Rex was such a hit with the spectators that his parade became an annual event. His is now *the* major parade on Mardi Gras, and Rex himself is recognized as the King of Carnival. "If Ever I Cease to Love" has survived as the official song of Carnival.

Alexis returned to Russia perhaps never realizing that he would be a much more important figure in the New Orleans history books than those of Moscow.

Like the Mystick Krewe, the Rex organization drew its membership from the local aristocracy and there were apparently plenty of aristocrats to spread around. A third organization, the Knights of Momus first paraded on New Year's Eve of 1872 then eventually moved its parade to a date in the week before Mardi Gras Day. Several years later the god of the sea was honored as the Krewe of Proteus took to the streets. Other organizations came and went, but Comus, Rex, Momus, and Proteus have survived, not only as founders but as symbols of the traditional, secretive, high society Mardi Gras. They have given Carnival its mystique, thus its continuity.

Nothing about Carnival ever remained exclusive to the upper class in New Orleans and parades were no exception. Over the years more and more krewes formed—not out of blue blood, but of mixed bloods. By the 1950s, the traditionally mule-drawn floats gave way to the more practical method of pulling them by tractor. Although the Knights of Babylon and the Krewe of Hermes predate World War II, they are relatively young by Mardi Gras standards. Other groups followed to the extent that the Carnival parade calendar is now filled with at least one parade per day every day beginning a week and a half before Mardi Gras. And that's just in the city. The suburban Mardi Gras has also grown into a pageant of less historic, but equally eager parade groups.

In the late 1960s two new krewes startled New Orleanians. The krewes of Bacchus and Endymion brought huge double-decker floats to Mardi Gras. The floats depicted popular themes—as opposed to the more esoteric titles of the traditional krewes—and carried celebrities, some of whom wore the spectacular costumes of the new organizations. Bacchus and Endymion were the new wave krewes—created to be spectacular enough to serve as tourist attractions. Their parades, on the Saturday and Sunday evening prior to Carnival day, draw crowds equal to that of Rex. Both Bacchus and Endymion represent modern Mardi Gras. While they have indeed boosted tourism, those who run the krewes are probably no more progressive in their thinking or more committed to the city than those men from Mobile who in 1857 decided that Carnival needed a parade.

The People

One hesitates to categorize people but it becomes necessary in explaining Mardi Gras. Through the years many exclusive Carnival clubs evolved. The exclusivity of the clubs sometimes makes Carnival seem discriminatory—except that any faction that wants to can, and generally does have its own club exclusive to itself. The first krewes consisted of white male aristocrats which, by New Orleans standards, meant only those of French or English heritage.

Eventually the white middle class got involved generating parades and balls. Meanwhile the Illinois Club, a high society black Carnival organization, began staging balls. Then there was a schism which lead to the formation of the Young Men's Illinois Club. Nowadays, both black organizations are part of the Carnival calendar.

On Mardi Gras morning the first parade to hit the streets of downtown New Orleans is that of Zulu, the African warrior king. Zulu, founded in 1909, is the largest predominately black organization, and Zulu's parade is one of the most popular in all of Carnival. The popularity doesn't stem so much from the parade design (the group uses second-hand floats) as from the organization's custom of handing out painted coconuts. The Zulu coconut has become such a coveted item that there was a bit of a scandal in 1981 when Zulu officers discovered that someone had been selling counterfeit Zulu coconuts. Consequently, the krewe now places small labels on the base of each coconut to prove it's the real thing.

NOMTOC, another black parading organization, marches on the "west bank," the section across the river from New Orleans. The group's name, incidentally is an acronym for "New Orleans' Most Talked of Club." There is good reason to dispute the claim made by that name but, after all, it's only a parade.

There are two methods of Carnival participation that are totally unique to the black community: the flambeaux carriers and the Mardi Gras Indians.

In recent years there has been the kind of social discussion one might expect about maintaining the tradition of black males carrying the torches. Critics have wondered if the practice wasn't an uncomfortable reminder of slave days. It's a debate that has not been resolved, yet the tradition continues. There is no law forbidding white men—or females of either race—from carrying flambeaux, and those who do carry the torches are compensated for it by the krewe and by spectators who toss spare change. While the debate continues, the fact remains that the site of flambeaux approaching and illuminating the oak-lined streets is one of the most impressive in all of Carnival.

A far more sophisticated form of involvement, however, is that of the Mardi Gras Indians. The Indians consist of neighborhood "tribes" of blacks dressed in elaborate American Indian costumes rich in feather and beadwork. On Mardi Gras morning the Indian tribes roam the streets that border downtown New Orleans, meeting each other and going through a series of tribal dances and chants. It's a custom that dates at least to the last century but that has only recently been discovered by documentarians. The Indians have not neecessarily wanted their new-found fame and some groups are not receptive to interviews and picture taking.

No one is sure of the exact origin of the Indian custom, although the suggestion has been made that it could trace back to early intermarriage between blacks and Choctaws. There also seems to be a bit of Caribbean influence in their chants.

Each tribe is headed by a chief whose authority is as unchallenged as that of a captain in a Carnival krewe. By tradition new costumes are made each year to be worn on Mardi Gras and then again on March 19th, St. Joseph's Day—a day which Catholic New Orleanians consider exempt from Lenten restrictions. Twice a year the Mardi Gras Indians perform their rituals which are indigenous, authentic and found only in New Orleans.

There are two women's parades in downtown New Orleans: these are the krewes of Iris and Venus. The parades roll on the Saturday and Sunday afternoon before Carnival. Neither parade ranks among the best, but both are noted for the elaborate costumes of their riders and captains. The parades are worth seeing for no other reason than the grand headdresses worn by some of the officers. Both organizations also stage Carnival balls at which the costumes are fully displayed. Several other women's groups either parade or stage balls throughout the rest of the farflung domain of the New Orleans Mardi Gras.

There is no group of people whose participation in Mardi Gras is as visually dazzling as New Orleans' sizeable gay community. *New Yorker* magazine once described Mardi Gras in New Orleans as being equivalent to the Harvard–Yale game for the nation's homosexual community. That was obviously written before the pro sports boom for today it would be much more accurate to equate it with the Super Bowl in terms of the extent of involvement by gays. There are no exclusively gay parade organizations but there are at least eight gay groups that stage their own Carnival balls. The scope of something can sometimes be measured by the amount of specialization within it. Within the gay Mardi Gras there are elitist organizations and those that are broad in appeal. There are groups that closely parody the "straight" balls and groups that make fun of them. For some groups the dress and costuming are quite conservative, others are known as "tits and ass" organizations. There is a lesbian krewe as well as a fledgling black gay organization. Although all of the gay groups operate out of New Orleans, most of their balls are held in the Civic Auditorium in neighboring St. Bernard Parish. The reason has to do more with circumstance than social policy. As most of the gay groups are relatively new, the aged New Orleans municipal auditorium's time slots are already filled with older organizations. The St. Bernard facility also has the type of stage setting appropriate for gay balls which tend to resemble Las Vegas reviews more than Southern debutante cotillions. Invitations to the gay balls are difficult to obtain and highly prized. Some of the costumes, however, can be spotted on Mardi Gras being paraded through the French Quarter heading to and from the various masquerade contests. Many of the gay maskers impersonate women; some do not. The costumes are inevitably among the best in all of Carnival.

Something unique to the gay Mardi Gras is an umbrella organization which serves to evaluate the various gay organizations' balls for the purpose of giving awards in such categories as best queen and king costumes. (There is no higher honor at a gay ball than to be selected as the queen.) The group is known as the AGGI—the Academy of the Golden Goddess Incorporated. An Aggi award is won in the face of tough competition. To win the trophy for this "Super Bowl" you have to compete with the best there is.

Social Significance

On one level Mardi Gras is engrained into the social structure of the city. Approximately 18 organizations—of which only four, Comus, Momus, Rex and Proteus, have parades—are considered to be high society. At the balls of these organizations the various debutantes for the year are escorted and presented to their monarchs. A debutante who is a maid of one society ball may be queen of another. Entry into the select circle of debutantes is determined by lineage more than wealth (although making the round of debuts is hardly a pastime for poor folk) with most notoriety going to the girls selected to reign as queens of Rex and Comus.

Most members of the society organizations belong to at least one of several exclusive men's clubs. The affiliation between the krewes and the clubs dates back as far as the early days of Comus. For example many members of the Rex organization (officially known as "The

School of Design") have lunch at the Boston Club on Canal Street. On Mardi Gras the Rex parade stops in front of the club's white mansion long enough to allow Rex himself to toast his queen who waits on the reviewing stand. The roster of the Pickwick Club contains many members of the Mystick Krewe of Comus while the Knights of Momus discuss their business at the Louisiana Club. The connection between the business elite and high society is so strong that there is an infamous story about a prestigious law firm that, upon noticing that some of its secretaries were from the ranks of debutantes, reclassified their job titles to "paralegals."

There is much tradition among the society organizations, with one of the most important being the meeting of Rex and Comus. Near midnight of Mardi Gras evening Rex leaves his ball and is escorted to the municipal auditorium's other ballroom where Comus is receiving his court. In the waning moments of the Carnival season, Rex and his queen greet Comus and his queen. Carnival custom recognizes Rex as the symbol of the people and Comus as the symbol of tradition and high society. It is more than symbolic that in this ceremonial conclusion of Carnival, Rex bows to Comus—in this act, the people bow to society.

What to Do

Carnival is a movable season. Since Mardi Gras is the day before Ash Wednesday, its date each year is affected by the date of Easter which follows forty Lenten days later. Thus the date of Mardi Gras can fall somewhere between early February and early March. Generally the later the Mardi Gras date the better. February is one of New Orleans' coldest periods, especially the first half of the month. There have been some Carnivals when participants had to fight freezes in order to salute the coming of spring.

A late Mardi Gras, however, is delightful as "Spring Fever" seems to add to the festivity.

Whatever the date of Carnival, the parading starts nearly two weeks earlier and continues daily until midnight of Mardi Gras. Most visitors, however, will likely see the last four days. Many hotels have four-day packages beginning on the Saturday afternoon before Mardi Gras and lasting Wednesday through the morning after Carnival. With the city's hotel boom and the increased availability of rooms, some hotels now allow rentals for less than four days. Nevertheless, the Saturday before Carnival is the time to be in New Orleans because it begins what amounts to a four-day weekend.

That Saturday afternoon the krewe of Iris, one of two all-female krewes, winds through Uptown New Orleans and through the business district. It's a good time to get acquainted with the Carnival turf. All of the parades move along Canal Street between the river and North Rampart Street as well as along the segment of St. Charles Avenue intersecting Canal Street between the 600 and 700 blocks.

At whatever parade you go to the main activity is catching "throws" tossed from floats. Throws originated with the first parade of the Twelfth Night Revelers in 1879. The parade had a holidays theme and one float depicted Christmas. Riders on that float threw small "gifts" to the parade watchers. The custom caught on although that krewe's practice of parading lasted only a few years.

Doubloons (aluminum "coins" stamped with the krewe's insignia) are generally the most popular throws though among the most difficult to catch. Glass beads from Czechoslovakia were once thrown from the floats but because of political tensions, the market shifted to the Orient, most notably to Hong Kong, where plastic beads were the specialty. The most coveted beads are the ones that bear a krewe medalion. Beads can more easily be snatched from the air than doubloons and you'll find that many people wear them as an adornment to their carnival dressing.

Saturday evening Endymion, one of the truly grand parades, marches. The krewe is known for its costuming, particularly the headpieces of the maids and dukes who ride mini-floats, and for the elaborateness of its double-decker floats. It is a visual, large-scale, not-to-be-missed parade and one of the major attractions of the entire Mardi Gras celebration.

Sunday is a day full of parades beginning with Thoth, then Venus, another women's parade, and followed later in the afternoon by the Krewe of Mid-City. Mid-City is not a large-scale parade like Endymion, it more closely resembles the traditional Carnival parade. But there are few parades that are prettier than that of the Mid-City Krewe. Nor are there many parades that sound better. The parade includes organized competition among some of the South's top high school bands contending for the "Greatest Band in Dixie" honors. Mid-City was the first krewe to use animation on its floats. The animation was originally powered by Boy Scouts concealed within the floats who turned cranks which moved papier Mâché heads, hands and other features that decorated the floats. It is the only parade whose floats are made from bright-colored foils. Mid-City's is a picturesque parade designed for daylight.

Mid-City clears the streets in time for the crowds to regroup in preparation for the arrival of Bacchus. Bacchus is one of the super parades akin to the likes of Endymion. It is also the parade that introduced celebrity watching to Mardi Gras. Bacchus broke the custom of honoring one of its own as king, opting instead to import celebrities to play the role of the god of wine. In 1969, Danny Kaye served as the first Bacchus, starting a line of succession that has included Bob Hope and Jackie Gleason. The Bacchus parade is one of the big events of Carnival.

On Monday during the day, New Orleans briefly slips back into its workday mode. There is only one parade that evening, the krewe of Proteus. Go to the Proteus parade for an idea of what the traditional 19th-century Carnival parade was like. Tractors have replaced mules at pulling the floats and some electric lights supplement the illumination. Still Proteus is a good old fashioned parade and is one of only a few that still uses flambeaux carriers. The Proteus king's float, with the sea god framed by a huge pink sea shell and seahorses, is one of the grandest of all. To many krewes the king's float is as personal as a signature and few have a signature as quaint and picturesque as Proteus.

Mardi Gras—Tuesday—is a day of almost continuous parading. Some costumed marching clubs begin their trek early, playing music all along the way. There are no floats in the marching clubs, just musicians having a good time. The scream of their motorcycle escorts and the fluttering of their banners usually announces their coming. Two groups to watch for are The Jefferson City Buzzards, the oldest of the marching clubs, and Pete Fountain's Half-Fast Marching Club. Fountain can usually be spotted playing his clarinet somewhere in the middle.

Zulu's parade is not far behind the marching clubs. This black organization is known for the colorful hand-painted coconuts that it gives away. But don't count on catching one. The Zulus are not allowed to actually throw the coconuts (they could make dangerous projectiles) so they must be passed out instead. Coconuts are hard to come by—they tend to be handed to friends along the way. Zulu beads, however, are also a favored item and they are literally up for grabs among the throws.

Around noon his majesty Rex, King of Carnival, approaches Canal Street. The Rex parade is a spectacular one with sharp bands and original and well-designed floats. Rex's float is a classic with a huge burgundy and gold crown serving as a canopy for the king. (Since the word "rex" is latin for "king" it is considered a redundancy to refer to the King of Carnival as "King Rex.")

Rex's parade captures the essence of Mardi Gras. It is a traditional parade full of customs and secrecy (the identity of the Rex captain is a must for locals who want to be in the know) yet it is as visually spectacular as the new wave krewes. From atop his majesty's royal bandwagon a jazz group plays occasional renditions of "If Ever I Cease to Love" and the Mardi Gras colors of purple, green and gold decorate the parade. If you can only see one parade make it Rex.

If by the time Rex and his 25 floats pass and you still haven't caught any throws, you still have plenty of chances. Rex is followed by two truck parades; Elks Krewe of Orleanians and the Krewe of Crescent City. Both parades consist of flatbed trucks, some as elaborately decorated as the finest floats. Approximately 250 trucks pass, each carrying nearly 40 riders, giving the determined parade goers at least 10,000 chances to make their catch.

Comus, the father of the New Orleans Mardi Gras, ends Carnival with his evening procession. His is the oldest and most traditional of the krewes and one of the smallest. By the time he rolls down the city's streets most of the carnival crowd has left for home leaving the parade to the Carnival aficionados and those who are in no condition to move even if they wanted to. The masked Comus, saluting the crowd with his goblet, is not looking for crowds anyway; his ride is for the sake of tradition.

Besides the parades, the people themselves are also worth watching on Mardi Gras. Masking is the order of the day, although it's an order not always followed. St. Charles Avenue between Canal Street and Lee Circle becomes a promenade for some of the better maskers. There's no point, after all, in having a great costume if you don't show it off. The most elaborate and outrageous costumes, however, will no doubt be found in the French Quarter. The streets of the Quarter are like a bazaar, but what a bizarre bazaar it is.

Parades once rolled though the Quarter but were banished in 1974 for fear that in the event of a fire in the historic Quarter, a parade would block access by the fire engines. The Mardi Gras ecology of the Quarter has changed. Where once people stared down from balconies at the riders on passing floats, the many wrought-iron balconies themselves have become the new attraction. From those balconies some people throw trinkets; others, at the crowd's urging, perform impromptu strip-teases. The legacy of the pagan rites of spring has not been totally lost in the French Quarter.

There are several costume contests in the Quarter at which gays are usually the stars. To find a contest, either follow the crowd or if you see a bigger than life, buxom "woman" escorted by a small entourage, follow her, she-he may be one of the contestants.

Carnival balls are the sort of thing that people hear about but usually don't get to see. Invitations (they're never referred to as "tickets") to the more socially prominent balls are difficult to obtain unless you happen to know someone who knows someone who . . . Even at that, the invitation lists are carefully screened. Despite their public reputation the balls, after all, are private parties and people tend to give priority to their friends when inviting guests to their parties. Because of Rex's status as King of Carnival, invitations to his ball are a bit easier to obtain, but it still takes connections. In fact, krewe members only invite whom they choose and the invitation list is frequently scrutinized by a screening committee. Tickets to dinner dances are generally handled through krewe members and are not for public sale.

Bacchus and Endymion, the two new wave krewes, do not have traditional balls. They stage supper dances instead. Bacchus' is in the Rivergate Convention Center and Endymion's is in the Super Dome. Both buildings were constructed with delivery doors tall and wide enough to allow huge floats through them, which is exactly what happens as the respective parades finish their route by encircling their supper dance. Admissions to the supper dances are by purchased ticket.

There is, of course, a lot to behold in Mardi Gras that is free. Promoters refer to the New Orleans Carnival as the "Greatest Free Show on Earth." That's an oversimplification of course—somebody has to pay—and that somebody is the people attending the balls and participating in the parades.

The Season: The Beginning and End

Mardi Gras begins on Twelfth Night, there's no mistake about it. That evening the Phunny Phorty Phellows, a krewe that has appeared and reappeared since the 19th century, boards a streetcar (New Orleanseze for "trolley") and rides along the route of St. Charles Avenue streetcar. While the streetcar rumbles down the track, a jazz band plays and the Phellows dance. It's their way of announcing to those along the route that Carnival has arrived.

Meanwhile at the muncipal auditorium the Twelfth Night Revelers stage the first society ball of the season. And all around the city bakeries and supermarkets stack "king" cakes on the shelves. Over the next few weeks parties and even office coffee breaks feature the cakes into which a tiny doll or a bean has been hid. By tradition the person whose slice contains the foreign object has to host the next king cake party. It is one tradition that is frequently violated—not with the Phorty Phunny Phellow, however. As their streetcar turns onto the Carrollton Avenue track, king cakes are served to determine that year's "Boss" and Queen. It doesn't take long for the traditions to start rolling. And they will continue to roll throughout the Carnival season.

Depending on the date of Mardi Gras, the length of the Carnival season fluctuates, but it always ends the same way. Police lines in the French Quarter begin to gently disperse the crowds as the final hour approaches. The clock hands at the St. Louis Cathedral begin to signal midnight. Rex bows to Comus; street cleaners pick up the litter. It's almost tomorrow when celebration and hedonism come to an end and the Lenten fasting season begins.

OTHER FESTIVALS

The Jazz and Heritage Festival

Perhaps because of Mardi Gras' influence, New Orleans is a town with a penchant for celebration—celebration that now continues year-round. The austere Lenten season is sandwiched by festivity: Carnival on one end and the New Orleans Jazz and Heritage Festival on the other taking place in April or May. Next to Mardi Gras, the "Jazz Fest" is the city's biggest celebration. It began in 1967 as a small one-weekend festival and has been growing ever since.

Most of the activity for the festival is centered at the Fair Grounds racetrack right in the infield area where booths and stages and perfor-mance tents are constructed for the two consecutive three-day (Friday, Saturday and Sunday) weekends of indigenous music, food and crafts. The Fair Grounds is located in the Gentilly area of the city, near the lakefront.

There is an admission charge for the Jazz Fest, but for the money participants can spend the entire days keeping time to musical groups of various types, ranging from a simple fiddler to large-scale bands. Name celebrities, such as Fats Domino, perform along with street musicians. One of the most popular attractions is always the gospel tent where foot-stomping choir-robed soul choruses would raise the roof if it weren't tied down. Spanning the two weekends of the festival, ap-proximately 300 musical groups perform with a total of about 3,000 musicians.

Between sets, festival goers can buy native foods (such as crayfish pie and alligator soup) from the forty or so food booths, or shop for native crafts. The less ambitious can merely lie on the grass and develop their first tan of the new spring while listening to the music and watching the people. In fact, people-watching at the Jazz Fest is as much fun as anything else.

During the weeks of the Jazz Fest there are also satellite concerts held in places around town such as the tourboat *S.S. President*. All of the concerts charge an admission.

There was a time when the city was losing touch with its musical heritage. The Jazz Fest is an attempt to correct that. Judging from its success, the attempt is successful. For information, see the Seasonal Events section of the *Practical Information* chapter for details.

Spring Fiesta

On the Friday after Easter the Spring Fiesta parade winds through the French Quarter. The parade, called "A Night in Old New Orleans," is a greatly scaled-down version of a Mardi Gras parade, but it inaugurates a 19-day period of home tours to some of the area's classic residences. Among the guided tours are those that go to homes in the French Quarter, the uptown Garden District, the historic mansions along St. Charles Avenue and the plantations in East and West Feliciana parishes as well as along Bayou Teche in Cajun country. The Spring Fiesta is a no-hassle, low-key event that offers a good opportunity to observe actual better homes and gardens as they once were and as they have been preserved. To visit the homes, you must obtain tickets at the Spring Fiesta office. (See Seasonal Events section of the *Practical Information* chapter for details.)

Lesser Celebrations

St. Joseph's Day (March 19) and St. Patrick's Day (March 17) are actively celebrated by the Italians and the Irish, respectively. Beginning two days before St. Joseph's Day, several homes and institutions in the New Orleans area open to the public to display their St. Joseph altars—altars made of food in honor of the patron saint of the Sicilians. On the Saturday after St. Joseph Day there is an Italian parade through the French Quarter, and on the same day, the Irish stage several parades throughout the area, including the Quarter. On that weekend there is also a St. Joseph's festival at the Italian Piazza on Poydras Avenue.

Halloween is one of New Orleans' secrets. Halloween is, of course, celebrated everywhere, but not the way it is in the French Quarter. Next to Mardi Gras, Halloween night in the French Quarter is one of the busiest nights for masquerading. It's a great night for merely walking around and looking. On the day after Halloween, All Saints Day, locals honor the dead by taking flowers to the cemeteries. The day offers an opportunity to visit some of the city's historic and picturesque graveyards, which include the remains of early governors, pirates, and voodoo queens. In New Orleans, even cemeteries are part of the ongoing celebration.

NEW ORLEANS FOOD AND DRINK

Creole and Cajun Cooking Plus Other Delights

by
TOM FITZMORRIS

*Tom Fitzmorris is the only regularly published restaurant critic in
New Orleans. He is currently editor and publisher of* The New Orleans
MENU *magazine of restaurant criticism, cooking and wine. His daily
reports on restaurants and cooking were featured on radio as was his
weekly three-hour talk show on food and wine. He is co-director of the
New Orleans Chapter of Les Amis du Vin and was previously editor-in-*

chief of the monthly New Orleans Magazine *and a weekly avant-garde newspaper,* Figaro.

Few American cities can be identified as world-class culinary capitals. New Orleans, which is universally recognized as one of them, has a further distinction. It's the only place in the United States with a fully developed, comprehensive regional cuisine on a scale with the regional cuisines of Europe. Creole and Cajun cooking (which are respectively the city and country versions of the south Louisiana cuisine) have approaches to every foodstuff available to them. And their influence is so widespread that it's difficult to find restaurants—even ethnic ones—that are free of Creole touches.

Creole or Cajun?

Defining Creole cooking is as difficult a task as describing what makes French food French or Chinese food Chinese. One can say that Creole cooks tend to use more salt, pepper (both red cayenne and black), oil (both as part of a dish and as a medium for deep-frying, especially of seafood) and garlic. However, there are distinctly Creole dishes with none of those things, and you can make a very non-Creole dish using all of them.

A common starting point in much old-style Creole cooking is the roux, made by combining flour and either butter or oil and cooking it to the degree of darkness desired for the dish. The roux acts as a medium for the other ingredients and as a thickener. However, the trend in recent years has been to a lesser reliance on roux, partly in response to public preferences for lighter dishes. If you want to experience the older style in its full, glorious heaviness, the place to go is Antoine's, the oldest restaurant in the United States and a solid traditionalist.

Cajun cooking is little-seen in New Orleans proper—Cajun being a country thing, centered in Lafayette. Cajun cooking is typically a much more rough-and-ready style than Creole, with heavy-handed use of both herbs and spices. Its practitioners, the descendents of the Acadians who were exiled from Nova Scotia 250 years ago, developed their cuisine in order to make the poor-quality foods at their disposal palatable. It also works well on good foodstuffs. The only place in New Orleans with authentic Cajun cooking is K-Paul's Louisiana Kitchen, where the robustness of the style is unfettered.

Both Creole and Cajun cooking benefit from a wealth of raw materials, especially seafood. Fresh seafood is available from the estuaries adjacent to the Gulf of Mexico and from Lake Pontchartrain all year-round. Most of the shrimp eaten in this country come from these waters; they are a very common ingredient in Creole cooking and much less expensive than elsewhere. Other local favorites are redfish (a sort of sea bass), speckled trout (not a trout at all, but a saltwater weakfish), crabs (both hard- and soft-shell), oysters, and crawfish.

A few words about those last two. The preferred service of oysters is at a marble-topped bar, where they are opened before the diner and eaten raw with a sauce of horseradish, catsup, lemon juice, and Tabasco. Orleanians eat raw oysters in quantities and at prices which are alarming to Europeans, simply because the supply is so bountiful. The ones that aren't eaten raw go into a large number of baked and stewed dishes; the most famous of them is oysters Rockefeller. The dish was created by Antoine's, and, because of its richness, was named for the richest man in the world at that time. The sauce, tinged with Pernod, involves pureed greens whose exact proportions vary from restaurant to restaurant.

Crawfish (the local spelling and pronunciation of "crayfish") are strictly a seasonal item and the staple of Cajun cooking. They resemble small lobsters and have a delicate, refined flavor all their own. From about December through May they are served in many restaurants (although sometimes you have to ask for them) in a panoply of forms. The most common are crawfish *etouffee* (a well-seasoned stew with rice) and crawfish bisque (a very thick, reddish soup, powerfully seasoned, with a scattering of stuffed crawfish heads in the bowl). However, once again, the preference among local diners is for something simpler: a large pile of hot boiled crawfish, still in their shells, salty and peppery, spread out in a big platter or on newspaper and eaten by the dozen. The procedure of "squeezing the tips and sucking the heads" ejects the tail meat and brings forth the delicious fat in the thorax of the animal (the second part of the procedure is optional).

The prelude to most seafood repasts is a bowl of gumbo, a thick, lusty soup made in as many different styles as there are cooks. Two general categories appear, however. The more common is seafood or okra gumbo, which contains a variety of fish and shellfish thickened with okra. The other is *filé* gumbo, which is usually made from a chicken stock and often contains chicken. It also can have almost anything else, but andouille (a heavy, spicy ham-and-garlic sausage) and oysters are common. Both are served with rice and are rather spicy. First cousin to gumbo is jambalaya, an oily yet somewhat dry rice stew with shrimp, chicken, sausage, and seasonings. Jambalaya is a well-Creolized descendant of Spain's paella.

You may have noticed by now that Orleanians eat an unusually large amount of rice. It is in fact an integral part of many Creole classics, and nowhere is this fact more celebrated than in the example of the universal New Orleans Monday dish, red beans and rice. These are kidney beans which simmer all day long with a host of seasonings, sausage, and pickled pork. They are hearty and somewhat creamy in texture, served over steamed rice, usually with a length of smoked sausage. Virtually every restaurant in town features it at least for lunch on Mondays; some of the better places are Marti's, Maylie's, the Camellia Grill, Arnaud's Grill Room, Eddie's, and Buster Holmes.

Sandwich and Steak Institutions

New Orleans has two distinctive sandwiches that have practically eliminated sliced bread from lunch. The first is the poor boy (or "po' boy") which resembles the grinder, hero, or submarine sandwich in appearance but is quite different. The bread is an elongated crisp, light form of French bread which evolved for the purpose of making poor boys. It's filled with a meat or seafood and usually "dressed" with mayonnaise, lettuce, tomatoes, and pickles. The king of the poor boys is the roast beef, in which the sought-after merit is "sloppiness." This is generated by the large amount of gravy spooned inside. On Fridays the volume leader is the oyster loaf (a form of poor boy), in which fried oysters are jammed onto buttered, toasted French bread. However, there is hardly an ingredient that has not been tried in a poor boy sandwich. The list of possibilities is long.

The best poor boys are to be found at Mother's, Parasol's, R&O's, and Uglesich's. Many other restaurants have them at lunchtime as well.

The second local sandwich specialty is the muffuletta. This is a giant affair, easily enough for two people, combining ham, salami, mozzarella, and provolone on a thick, round, seeded Italian loaf. The distinctive flavor of the sandwich is provided by the olive salad, consisting of olives, of course, and other vegetables marinated in an herbal, garlicky, oily dressing. The originator of the sandwich and still the best purveyor of it is the ancient Central Grocery across from the French Market.

Surprisingly, New Orleans is one of the greatest steak towns in America. The quality and availability of heavy aged prime beef are high, with prices to match. And, predictably, there is a New Orleans version of the great American dish. Steaks are served in a shallow lake of butter sauce which not only provides sizzle but also adds a certain mellowness and toastiness to the crusty beef. The best purveyors are Del Frisco's, Ruth's Chris, The Butcher Shop, The Crescent City, and Charlie's.

Ethnic Influences

The ethnicity most often associated with Creole cooking in New Orleans is French. However, there is what could be called a Creole

Italian cuisine here, as well. It's just as distinct, robust, and spicy as French Creole and has provided some of the greatest local culinary classics. The most convincing manifestation of Creole Italian cooking is a roadhouse called Mosca's just outside of town. Here unique, simple, and eminently memorable dishes are prepared with shrimp, oysters, and chicken; the restaurant's food is one of the greatest gastronomic pleasures imaginable. A second restaurant with a great Creole Italian creation is Pascal's Manale, which originated one of the two or three best dishes in town: barbecued shrimp. These are not barbecued in any generally accepted sense, but are huge shrimp baked with shells and heads intact in a sauce of butter and pepper. Very messy, but marvelous.

The Italian influence on New Orleans dining, especially in the past half-century, is so strong that many restaurants exhibit a hybrid: Italian-French Creole. And if that's not convoluted enough for you, consider this: the majority of the hands-on practitioners of all kinds of cooking in New Orleans are black, as they always have been. It's impossible to discuss New Orleans food without considering the black influence. It in turn has its roots in the Caribbean, where one finds foods very similar to those favored by Orleanians.

The Creole cuisine is so strong an influence that other ethnic cuisines —American among them—have never made much of an impact. There are many Chinese and Latin American restaurants, but few of any merit. The Middle East and Eastern Europe are only scantily represented. There are many Yugoslavians here, but they have for the most part become the steak and seafood experts rather than vendors of their national cuisine (the one exception is Drago's, which has a wonderful Yugoslavian menu). And even the quest for a "pure" French or Italian restaurant becomes difficult.

Topping off the Meal

Regardless of how one begins an evening of dining, it wouldn't be complete without an ending at one of the two French Market coffeehouses (one of which isn't in the Market at all anymore—it's in Metairie). The menu at both the Cafe du Monde (in the French Quarter) and the Morning Call (Metairie) consists of beignets-square—shaped fried doughnuts that are airy inside and served under a drift of powdered sugar—and cafe au lait. The coffee blend is very strong, dark-roasted, and mixed with chicory. Even if you usually drink your coffee black, you'd better take this with hot milk.

What Really Matters

Behavior in New Orleans restaurants is also a bit different. A careless sort of *joie de vivre* prevails, both for the customers and the personnel, even in the grander restaurants. It frequently overrules standards of decorum and, at times, good manners. For many Orleanians, dining out is not a prelude or ancillary activity, but the entire evening's agenda. In a favorite restaurant, the particular waiter a regular Orleanian customer always uses (and sometimes passes on to the next generation) becomes a good friend. The Orleanian will make himself very much at home and throw a small private party at table. Naturally, the waiter gets chummy. This familiarity and informality are often mistaken by the uninitiated as either incompetence or rudeness; Antoine's and Galatoire's are notorious for this.

Nor is elegance of surroundings very much stressed. Orleanians are a bit suspicious of fancy places, and unless the restaurant has atmosphere born of either its incredible patio or long history, chances are it will have little atmosphere. Indeed, the best food in town is found in the most ordinary dining rooms (Mosca's, Manale's, and Galatoire's come immediately to mind).

If you consider polish as a *sine qua non* for a great restaurant, you may conclude that New Orleans is a great food town but not a very good restaurant town. That fact notwithstanding, the high end of the local restaurant spectrum has prices that match all but the most astronomical elsewhere. And while some expensive restaurants have less expensive lunches, many of them keep the same menu and prices all the time. But the expenditure of larger sums probably will not make the peak New Orleans dining experience more likely. In fact, the opposite is probably true.

MUSIC IN NEW ORLEANS

And All that Jazz

by
VINCENT FUMAR

Vincent Fumar writes feature articles and reviews centering on the local and national music scene—particularly jazz, rhythm and blues and various popular music forms—for The Times-Picayune/The States-Item. *In addition, he is former music critic for* NOLA Express *and has contributed to the* Vieux Carré Courier, Figaro, Performance Magazine, Wavelength, *and the* New Orleans Jazz and Heritage Festival Book.

In a city where jazz bands are featured at Sunday brunches and in funeral processions, there are few who would dispute the significance of New Orleans' musical culture and its impact on the 20th century, and many who would claim it as the hothouse of America's sole indigenous art form.

Why is New Orleans cited as the birthplace of jazz? The answer is simple—no one has yet located its origin elsewhere, and the city was the first place that the music took root and was cultivated.

Like most aspects of New Orleans history, the story of jazz (and its sister form, rhythm and blues) is rife with legends and misconceptions. It did not, for instance, spring full blown from a Storyville bordello. Nor did it always enjoy wide public acceptance. An 1890 newspaper cartoon depicts a Basin Street combo performing on a balcony; below as men and women hold their ears and shout in protest, dogs roll over the howl, and one nearby resident screams, "For God's sake, stop!"

Historians generally agree that jazz resulted from the interplay between two disparate social elements in the community, that of the classically trained downtown Creoles and their largely unschooled (and equally uninhibited) Uptown counterparts. But that's only part of the story.

While armchair musicologists usually are content to describe jazz as a fusion of African and European elements—which it is—little has been noted of the pre-jazz era of New Orleans music. After all, the city was the first in America to establish a permanent opera company, which resided in the French Opera House on Bourbon Street and became so popular that it toured New York and Philadelphia by the 1820s; it proved that the South was not solely the domain of frontier hayseeds.

Also, the city produced America's first recognized classical virtuoso, Louis Moreau Gottschalk, a pianist and composer who won the admiration of Chopin. Surely such influences filtered down to the Creoles of color, whose musical preferences leaned toward the light classics, and to newly emancipated blacks who had no one to tell them about the so-called limitations of their battered, second-hand instruments. Given the city's interest in light classics and European martial music, it was only a matter of time before such elements, along with those of ragtime and Sousa marches, met the slave and minstrel song, and that most elusive of style, the blues, to form an awesome musical mosaic that eventually spread around the world.

Jazz, then, was influenced in structure and feeling as much by the French quadrille and the Cuban habanera as it was the African work song. It was a formal music with folk-idiom influences, and was performed most often in places where drinking and dancing could be found.

As anyone who lived in the city during the first years of the century will attest, music could be heard virtually anywhere and at all times of the day. Whether from mule-drawn advertising wagons or at the social gatherings of the wealthy, ragtime pianists, collective-improvisation groups and "sweet" bands filled the air every day of the year.

Perhaps the most frequently cited location of jazz activity was Storyville, the legalized prostitution district just outside the French Quarter. As noted by residents and visitors alike, New Orleans was by most ethical standards the wickedest city in America (some insist today that things haven't changed much).

It was in Storyville around the turn of the century that one of the most colorful, and sordid, chapters in the city's history was played out. Legalized bordellos such as the Mahogany Hall were operated by Lulu White. The celebrated Josie Arlington, Countess Willie Piazza and Gypsy Shafer operated similar establishments. While the burgeoning music form jazz was performed in the parlors of these licensed sin centers, an equal amount of ragtime piano, popular sentimental tunes and light classics was also heard. It was in the taverns and the dance halls on the fringes of the district, such as the Tuxedo, Anderson's Saloon, the Funky Butt, the 101 Ranch and the 28 Club that the bluesier and more improvised style of jazz was heard.

Whether formal or strictly improvised, the music soon developed masters, typically piano "professors" such as Tony Jackson (the author of the song "Pretty Baby") and Ferdinand "Jelly Roll" Morton (who sidelined as a procurer and insisted that jazz must have "Spanish tinges"). Both had reputations for playing in any given style and commanded high salaries.

The Storyville era ended in 1917, when the Secretary of the Navy ordered the closing of all red light districts located within five miles of navy bases. Despite serious lobbying efforts from a coalition of madams, saloon owners and even city officials, the order was obeyed. Although splintered the vice trade was hardly eradicated—activities simply moved into other neighborhoods.

While the musical exploits of Morton and Jackson were concentrated in the red light district, the area above Canal Street suffered no lack of pioneering masters, whose efforts were sparked mainly by cornetist Charles "Buddy" Bolden, who is regarded as the first jazzman for the simple reason that no one has ever been able to name anyone who played jazz before him.

Since Bolden never recorded, we are forced to rely on the accounts of those who claim that he had a tone as big as a house, played the blues unlike anyone before or since, and would routinely send dancers into a frenzy. Unfortunately, Bolden was no paragon of mental stability. He reportedly went berserk during a street parade in June 1907, and was subsequently committed to the East Louisiana State Mental Hospital, where he died in 1931.

A six-year-old child named Louis Armstrong heard Buddy Bolden outside the Funky Butt Hall, but he apparently wasn't so impressed by Bolden's cornet as he was with the sound of Joe "King" Oliver, who had informally assumed Bolden's cornet mantle. It was Oliver and clarinetist Sidney Bechet who transported the New Orleans style northward, several years before Armstrong who didn't leave town until Oliver summoned him to Chicago in 1922. It was there, after a stint with Oliver's Creole Jazz Band, that Armstrong inherited the crown from the declining Oliver.

Today, Armstrong is memorialized by Louis Armstrong Park on North Rampart Street. One of his early cornets is on display at the New Orleans Jazz Club Collection at the Louisiana State Museum (housed in the old U.S. Mint building on Esplananade Avenue). Bolden's Philip Street home was demolished long ago, as was Storyville, whose site is now occupied by a housing project and several undistinguished commercial buildings.

Where to Hear Jazz Played

It would be nice to report that traditional New Orleans jazz has been zealously guarded, but it isn't so. True, its memory is preserved, but its practice, at least in authentic styles, is limited to the work of a handful of scrupulous revivalists, such as the Louisiana Repertory Jazz Ensemble, which regularly performs in clubs and concert settings alike.

But that doesn't mean that the visitor to New Orleans will find little jazz. Those seeking the truer style will be heartened to discover that the likes of trumpeters such as Alvin Alcorn and Teddy Riley can still be heard around town, usually in hotel clubs such as in the Marriott and the Hyatt Regency.

In the French Quarter, much of the tourist traffic finds its way to Bourbon Street venues that often don't feature groups particularly satisfying to purists. The most common complaint is that such practitioners play too fast, too loud and too heavy-handedly "Dixieland" (a term not interchangeable with traditional New Orleans jazz, but rather a designation of its revival in the 1940s).

However, while an evening's sampling of Bourbon Street might reveal a cursorily packaged Dixieland diversion or two, a little planning will reward both the jazz buff and dilettante alike. Preservation Hall (726 St. Peter) has featured some of the city's long-time practicing jazzmen of the past two decades—or more. The residence of the Preservation Hall Jazz Band, naturally, is always crowded, and some complain that the line outside is too long even on week nights. Regular attendees rarely complain, though, since they know enough to show up 30 minutes before show time and avoid the long lines.

Elsewhere downtown, Duke's Place (atop the Monteleone Hotel, 214 Royal) is the home of the Dukes of Dixieland, of course, who have taken their sound somewhat beyond the limits of their name, but not outside those of jazz. The new Blue Angel (225 Bourbon) is one of the first jazz clubs one encounters on Bourbon (as approached from Canal). The alternating groups are two good ones, Connie Jones' Crescent City Jazz Band and George Finola and the Chosen Few. In the next block, the Famous Door (339 Bourbon) offers Roy Liberto's Bourbon Street Five and Leroy Jones and His Jazz Group. Stellar trumpeter Al Hirt, recently closed his club, Basin Street South, but you can still hear Pete Fountain at the Hilton which showcases the renowned clarinetist from Tuesday through Saturday.

But not all of the best traditionalists are found in the French Quarter, nor on a regular basis. Visitors checking *The Times-Picayune/The States-Item's* listings are likely to discover the whereabouts of guitarist-raconteur Danny Barker (an ex-Cab Calloway and Duke Ellington sideman), the New Leviathan Oriental Foxtrot Orchestra or the New Orleans Ragtime Orchestra (featuring the dean of American jazz critics, William Russell), any one of which is likely to open up a whole new world of music appreciation.

On the modern front, the New Orleans jazz community might seem like a divided camp. Bebop-style groups have existed in the city for years, as have free-form modernists and contemporary-commercial stylists.

Modernists enjoy a larger following than ever now. Clubs such as Tyler's (5234 Magazine) feature the best modernists nightly. Pianist Ellis Marsalis (father of the jazz dynasty that includes sons Wynton and Branford) can be heard there. Also, stalwarts like James Black, Red Tyler, John Vidacovich, George French and Ramsey McLean are regulars. The adventurous might also want to try Mo' Jazz (614 Bourbon), the Crescent City Cafe (601 Chartres), and the Maison Bourbon (641 Bourbon) for a variety of jazz styles.

The Jazz Funeral

A special note must be made of that rare event, the New Orleans jazz funeral. The custom has suffered something of a black eye in recent years, primarily due to the involvement of nonmourners. The ritual, accorded deceased jazzmen—or nonjazzmen who happen to belong to certain social clubs, is an ancient one wherein a brass band's burial dirges become joyous sendoffs once outside the cemetery gates. In recent years, exuberant mourner-celebrants and sightseers have combined to make such events too disorderly for public officials and members of the deceased's families. On several occasions, there have been more photographers at the grave site than actual mourners. The jazz funeral simply isn't quite what it used to be, and any visitor chancing upon one would do well to keep a respectful distance. It is, after all, a funeral.

Rhythm and Blues

For many New Orleanians, the sound of the city isn't represented so faithfully by an old-style jazz band as it is by the rhythm and blues style that brought the city national recognition in the 1950s. It is a music of shouts, shuffles and slow blues, which enjoys a larger audience than ever, thanks to the numerous revivals it has undergone long after its golden age waned.

The New Orleans rhythm and blues style is a direct outgrowth of jazz, of course, and the influence still holds strong. For all practical purposes, the style began in the late 1940s, when record producer Dave Bartholomew (a jazz trumpeter) began to record some of the city's better young blues talent, most notably a gifted pianist name Fats Domino. For several years afterward, it seemed that Bartholomew and Domino could make nothing but hits, and national record companies took notice. Soon, half of the small record labels in America wanted the New Orleans sound, which was characterized by driving saxophones, boogie-woogie-accented piano and Latin beats.

The formula worked beautifully not only for Domino, but also for Smiley Lewis, Shirley and Lee, the Spiders, James "Sugarboy" Crawford, Lloyd Price and countless others who enjoyed national fame through records made at the city's chief record studio, J&M at Rampart and Dumaine. Out-of-town producers couldn't ignore such success, so by 1955 Little Richard and Ray Charles were recording with New Orleans musicians on their regular stops in town.

By the late 1950s, with popular music tastes changing a bit, the young Allen Toussaint began to update the local sound with more of a punchier, ragtime-like flavor. Thus began the second era of New Orleans rhythm and blues, with artists such as Ernie K-Doe (who had the nation's No. 1 hit in 1960 with "Mother-In-Law"), Irma Thomas, Aaron Neville and Lee Dorsey enjoying the national spotlight. With the advent of modern recording techniques, a fickle public and bad business decisions, however, New Orleans began to wane as a recording center in the mid-60s.

Since then, through the sporadic revivals, the cream of the city's rhythm and blues community has experienced renewed popularity and even a certain respectability, owing to its overdue recognition as a classic pop style. Without looking too far or spending an exorbitant amount of money, certain of the performers can still be heard. Tipitina's (501 Napoleon Avenue) has been something of an informal home for the style, and any night of the week one can catch the Neville Brothers (the city's most popular group), Earl King or the Dirty Dozen entertaining a packed dance floor. Cover charges are usually low, except for nationally known acts, and the house tends to get crowded in a hurry.

Clubs that feature rhythm and blues along with other types of music are The Maple Leaf Bar (8316 Oak Street), where one might catch the piano virtuoso James Booker or the stylings of the Dirty Dozen Brass Band. A homey, neighborhood establishment, it also houses a laundromat. Jimmy's (8200 Willow) features both contemporary rock and rhythm and blues groups—and also gets crowded in a hurry. The Dream Palace (534 Frenchman Street, 943–7223) features a musical grab bag nightly. `

It should be noted that casual dress is tolerated at all of the above-mentioned clubs, as is drinking and dancing. Only the prices (both for drinks and cover charges) differ.

Cajun Music

Certainly one form indigenous to south Louisiana is Cajun music, a folk form heavily dependent on a fiddle-and-accordion sound, but with a rhythmic emphasis and style of vocal phrasing not ordinarily associated with American folk forms. Its most famed exponents are fiddler Doug Kershaw (the Ragin' Cajun who is also a country-and-western artist) and accordionist Clifton Chenier (who is known as the master of zydeco, a primarily black style of Cajun music).

Since the center of the Cajun music world is South-Central Louisiana, New Orleans is actually but a satellite of the Cajun music form. Kershaw and Chenier occasionally perform in the city, as do the likes of Dewey Balfa, the Mamou Hour Cajun Band, and Rocking Dopsie & the Cajun Twisters. But in general the music is under-represented in the city's clubs. A worthwhile side trip to Lafayette (154 miles west of the city) and its environs (Abbeville, New Iberia, Crowley and Opelousas) should satisfy the curious.

The New Orleans Jazz and Heritage Festival

Perhaps the crowning jewel of any musical excursion in the city is the annual New Orleans Jazz and Heritage Festival, which is held throughout the city, usually in the first week of May (though occasionally events will commence at the tail end of April). Considered by many seasoned festival goers to be the finest music festival of its kind in the world, the Jazz Fest, as it's locally known, features something for everyone. Not only jazz, but also rhythm and blues, Cajun, gospel, blues, country and western, bluegrass and rock 'n' roll are showcased in one vast panorama of musical wonderment.

The Jazzfest is divided into several sections. Two weekends are reserved for the Louisiana Heritage Fair, held on the infield on the Fair Grounds racetrack in the old Gentilly section. Here, from several different stages and gazebos, one can sample all forms of music indigenous to the region, along with various local foods and beer. The affair has grown rather large in recent years, but the rewards waiting at the end of the long lines will be remembered for a long time.

While hundreds of entertainers are featured at the Heritage Fair portion of the festival, the evening concerts dwell on name entertainment (usually a name local attraction such as Fats Domino or Allen Toussaint) with a renowned jazz star. Most of these evening concerts are held on board the riverboat *President,* which plies the Mississippi while the entertainers perform. A trip to New Orleans is one thing, but a trip to New Orleans during the Jazz and Heritage Festival is almost the equivalent of getting a double dose of the city. Information on the festival can be obtained from the Jazz and Heritage Festival office at 1205 N. Rampart Street, 522–4786.

Tennessee Williams

Lillian Hellman

Truman Capote

MOONLIGHT AND MALAISE

The Literary Tradition in New Orleans

by
THOMAS BONNER, Jr.

Thomas Bonner, Jr., is the author of William Faulkner: The William
B. Wisdom Collection. *His articles on Southern literature have appeared
in the* Southern Quarterly, *the* Mississippi Quarterly, *and in the* Xavier
Review, *which he presently edits. He reviews books regularly for the New
Orleans newspaper,* The Times-Picayune/The States-Item. *A graduate
of Tulane University, he is a professor of English at Xavier University of
Louisiana. In addition, he is a member of the executive council of the
Society for the Study of Southern Literature.*

Lafcadio Hearn once wrote of a graveyard in New Orleans: "Out of the haze into—such a light! An azure haze! . . . All the streets were filled with the blue mist . . . voiceless the city and white . . . crooked and weed grown its narrow ways . . . old streets of tombs these." Some ninety years later the moonlight haze was replaced by Walker Percy's malaise: "What is the malaise? you ask. The malaise is the pain of loss. The world is lost to you, the world and the people in it, and there remains only you and the world and you no more able to be in the world than Banquo's ghost." The literary perspectives in New Orleans have indeed shifted over the years. Albert Goldstein, who once was an editor for *The Double Dealer,* observed: "The long parade of New Orleans literary achievements is a robust spectacle of many phases and cycles."

In the aftermath of the Civil War, New Orleans, the only major city in Louisiana and at that time the queen city of the South, began to assimilate North American culture; its most notable mark of that process was the demise of French literature and the development of a literature in English. The French novels largely were imitative of Dumas; the poetry similar to French romantics like Lamartine. The drama, however, raised social issues like slavery. Two American literary movements effected this new culture for this European city: the local color interest that had intrigued editors of magazines such as *Harper's* and the social consciousness that had begun to emerge in writers like Stephen Crane. Lafcadio Hearn, George Washington Cable, Grace King, and Kate Chopin were the major writers in English during the 19th century in Louisiana.

Most writers here—even to the present—are immigrant Louisianans. They have come from afar and find their material in this strange place; some have gathered it and continued their journeys to write it all down later; others have started to write shortly after their immersion in this humid climate.

Nineteenth Century

Lafcadio Hearn, born off the coast of Greece and educated by Jesuits in Europe, came to New Orleans in 1877 after a stint in Cincinnati as a journalist. There he made his reputation on his reporting and investigating murders. For ten years he was charmed by the exotic environment of southern Louisiana. His *Creole Sketches* and *Chita: Memory of Last Island* contribute to the local color literature of the period; however, Hearn's works offer more of an impressionistic view—a considerable difference from the detailed realism of most local color writers. Color and shape dominate his descriptions with the result of creating a distinct atmosphere: "The wind has waned and veered; the flood sinks slowly back to its abysses—abandoning its plunder,—scattering its piteous waifs over bar and dune, over shoal and marsh among the silences of the mango-swamps, over the long low reaches of sand-grasses and drowned weeds, for more than a hundred miles." Hearn writes, "It is a spectral dawn: a wan light, like the light of a dying sun." But the pull of realism in the extreme which dominated Hearn's murder reporting also shows up in his descriptions of scavengers over the bodies of hurricane victims: "Her betrothal ring will not come off, Giusseppe; but the delicate bond snaps easily: your oyster knife can sever the tendon." Hearn left this port city for the Caribbean and then Japan, where he is considered a major American writer.

A native of New Orleans, born in 1844, but one forced by public opinion to flee the city for the Northeast later in his career, George Washington Cable not only recorded the Creole environment but also criticized its hierarchial and unchanging nature in *The Grandissimes* published in 1880. Set in 1803 and early 1804 during the process of the Louisiana Purchase, the narrative focuses on a people who in October had been residents of a Spanish colony, in November a French colony, and in December an American territory. While Cable takes obvious delight in describing the architectural environs of the *Vieux Carré* and the charms and manners of the Creole ladies and gentlemen—black and white—he suggests a covertly captive atmosphere in which people are in a sense owned by means of the statecraft of international cession. Furthermore, he explores a society which clings to an outmoded social structure in the face of such dramatic changes. What made the novel so very real to its local readers was that the Civil War and Reconstruction era was so fresh that they too could identify willingly or unwillingly with a "foreign occupation." The central story within the story, that of the Black Bras Coupe, reveals Cable's abilities to examine people outside the dominant society and to suggest differences among them, notably through his distinctions of African tribes at Congo Square. His lecture tours on the Southern question and his promulgation of school integration made it difficult "to go home again."

Grace Elizabeth King found Cable's depiction of Creoles in New Orleans in violation of her own perspective and experience. A resident of Louisiana and New Orleans, she was educated at the Institut St. Louis, a private Creole school. In 1885 she told Richard Watson Gilder that she thought Cable's fiction discredited Creoles and favored Negroes. Answering a challenge from Gilder, editor of the *Library of Southern Civilization,* she wrote "Monsieur Motte," in which she emphasizes the loyalty of a quadroon during Reconstruction toward the child of her former owners. After three collections of short stories, she wrote her best novel *The Pleasant Ways of St. Medard,* an account of a family's experience during Reconstruction. In that work one finds descriptions of downtown New Orleans near Jackson Barracks. In one of her works she comments on mothers not letting their daughters out on the streets in that neighborhood when the soldiers were out on pass. King's female characters, in the process of growing up, are vital, as they emerge victorious over many of the static and reactionary situations and customs of daily life.

After several youthful visits to New Orleans, Kate Chopin moved to the city shortly after her marriage in 1870. For ten years she experienced life in the American Quarter, the upriver side of Canal Street, and visited frequently in the French Quarter, the downriver side. In the early 1880s when the cotton market declined, her husband moved to Cloutierville, Louisiana, near Natchitoches and the legendary site of Harriet Beecher Stowe's *Uncle Tom's Cabin.* During these years she absorbed the environment, climate, people, and spirit of Louisiana. After her husband's death and two years of managing a plantation, she returned to her native St. Louis, where her writing career begins. Her first novel *At Fault,* set on a plantation in northwestern Louisiana, explores the dilemma of divorce in a traditional Catholic community. Much of her fiction seems at the very fringe of 19th-century life; she even controls her settings to complement that concern. It is on Grand Isle that Edna Pontellier of *The Awakening* begins to have impulses beyond her matrimonial bonds, the walks on the beaches along the Gulf of Mexico suggesting the coming of a decisive moment. In New Orleans she lives on Esplanade at the lower edge of the old quarter, and as she yields to the surges of passion and self-knowledge she moves from her husband's townhouse into the small pigeon house. While much of Chopin's fiction records life in the city and country areas, one can easily find thematic uses of the descriptions. In "A Matter of Prejudice," she offers an excellent psychological study of the reluctance of an elderly Creole woman to accept her son's marriage to an American. Here geographical considerations are one with psychological barriers. Throughout her works one finds women in decisive positions, asking questions, attempting, and acting to resolve them.

Twentieth Century

The French Quarter, once the social, cultural, and financial center, receded from the light of progress and accomplishment which shone across Canal Street in the early 20th century. By the early 1920s, writers and artists had begun to move into this old, decadent, and inexpensive quarter of New Orleans. Sherwood Anderson and William Faulkner were among the "emigre-writers."

Anderson lived with his wife Elizabeth in the Pontalba apartments (540B St. Peter) along Jackson Square. This midwesterner discovered for himself the exotic black culture of the old city, which gave his imagination a new horizon. *Dark Laughter* reveals his early and naive interest in black characters, whose laughter appears free and natural in their mockery of white society. The short story "A Meeting South" forms not only a glimpse of New Orleans as a New World left bank, but it offers in the character David the best glimpse of the young William Faulkner, who considered himself a poet but who also masqueraded as a wounded World War I flying hero. David had "a very gentlemanly little smile on his very sensitive, rather thin, lips . . . the slight limp, the look of pain . . . the little laugh . . . He got up from his chair and went limping, dragging one foot after the other, across the patio and lay on the bricks." Anderson would later figure in two Faulkner books set in New Orleans.

Faulkner came to the Crescent City in the mid-twenties. He stayed with the Andersons for a while and then moved into a spare room at 624 Orleans Alley (Pirates' Alley), where he worked on his first novel *Soldier's Pay.* Anderson agreed to help him publish it if he did not have to read it, but Faulkner repaid this gesture with a satiric portrait in his and Spratling's *Sherwood Anderson and Other Famous Creoles,* a collection of sketches and caricatures of French Quarter personages.

Faulkner, later to win a Nobel Prize for literature, captured life in the French Quarter in his novel *Mosquitoes* (1927) and in the sketches for the New Orleans *Times-Picayune* and *The Double Dealer* (collected in *New Orleans Sketches*). *Mosquitoes* reflects the literary and artistic coterie that swirled about writer Lyle Saxon's apartment (612 Royal St.) and Spratling's second apartment (632 St. Peter). He describes the character Dawson Fairchild, who closely resembles Anderson, as "a benevolent walrus too recently out of bed to have made a toilet." The conversations at the gatherings in the Quarter and on board a yacht in Lake Pontchartrain reveal an artistic self-consciousness, an awkward but reliable picture of the spirit of this fertile environment.

Complementing the lost generation-atmosphere of *Mosquitoes* is the romantic and decadent tone of *New Orleans Sketches.* Faulkner describes the city as "a courtesan, not old and yet no longer young, who shuns the sunlight that the illusion of her former glory be preserved." At dusk Jackson Square is "now a green and quiet lake in which abode lights round as jelly fish, feathering with silver mimosa and pomegranate and hibiscus beneath which lantana and cannas bled and bled." On the river, "Two ferry boats passed and repassed like a pair of golden swans . . . the river curved away in a dark embracing slumber to where a bank of tiny lights flickered and trembled, bodiless and far away."

The literary life spilled over into the Café du Monde and the bars where Faulkner conversed with such writers as Roark Bradford, who was on the staff of the *Picayune* and who wrote the stories that inspired Marc Connelly's *Green Pastures.* Scott Fitzgerald viewed the city across a Garden District cemetery for a few months. Oliver LaFarge wrote *Laughing Boy* while he was at Tulane composing reports on his expeditions to Central America. It was in this remarkable atmosphere that the short-lived *The Double Dealer* was born. Julius Friend, Albert Goldstein, and John McClure were the founding editors of this periodical which published Ernest Hemingway's first professional literary writing, a fable titled "A Divine Gesture." Newspapers in the city have been integral to the cultivation of the city's writing environment since the 19th century. McClure continued that spirit in his "Literature and Less" pages in *The Times-Picayune*. Albert Goldstein, who also wrote for the paper, published satirical sketches of the city's inhabitants in "Albert's Noo Awlins" through the 1970s.

In the 1930s and '40s, both visiting and local writers found New Orleans attractive and provocative. Hervey Allen used Vincent Nolte's (537 Royal St.) autobiography in writing *Anthony Adverse*. John Erskine wrote *The Start of the Road,* which explores Walt Whitman's brief residence here in 1848 when he wrote for the New Orleans *Crescent.* Hamilton Basso, then in New York, described his native New Orleans at Mardi Gras in *Days Before Lent* and portrayed the Huey Long era with *Sun in Capricorn* (Robert Penn Warren also covered Long in *All the King's Men*). John Peale Bishop conveyed his impressions of Decatur Street to *New Yorker* readers, and Stark Young reveals the city's influence in *Feliciana.*

Saxon, who wrote *Children of Strangers* about mulatto life near Natchitoches, was in charge of the W.P.A. writers' project in Louisiana. Robert Tallant, Edward Dreyer, and he produced *Gumbo Ya-Ya: A Collection of Louisiana Folk Tales,* a lively work which includes a list of superstitions, for example, "a collector or a salesman will never return if you sprinkle salt after him"; and a glossary of colloquialisms like this one— *la banquette,* a sidewalk in any other town. Tallant wrote the *Mrs. Candy* novels which lightly satirize local society. *Mrs. Candy's Saturday Night* seems to be the general favorite, although *Angel in the Wardrobe* has its champions. Another writer whose work extended beyond 1950 was Frances Parkinson Keyes, a popular romantic novelist, who lived in the old Beauregard house at 1113 Chartres. *Dinner at Antoine's,* set in that famous restaurant, is her best known work.

Major American writers continue to come and go. Natives Lillian Hellman, who drew on her early years in New Orleans for *Toys in the Attic* and other plays, and Truman Capote, who is often seen at the Royal Orleans Hotel, still manage to contribute to the local literary milieu. William March of *Company K* and *The Bad Seed* spent his last years in the city. Eudora Welty's visits are reflected in her novels and stories. And Tennessee Williams, whose *A Streetcar Named Desire* immortalized the Elysian Fields Avenue neighborhood near the river and the French Quarter, lived on and off through the years in an apartment across from Marti's restaurant on Dumaine until his death in 1983.

New Orleans has had two Pulitzer Prize-winning novelists, Shirley Ann Grau and John Kennedy Toole. Grau, married to writer and philosopher James K. Fiebleman, won the award for *Keepers of the House* (1964). However, *The House on Coliseum Street* offers a perceptive view of Uptown New Orleans, especially the Garden District: "There was no traffic, there never was. The houses always looked closed and deserted, their galleries dusty and empty. No one ever walked by. The sidewalks . . . had been cracked and broken by the roots of the oaks and camphors and magnolias." There is something decadent about the very air in this old city as Grau describes it: "The air was very still, and almost cool. The night jasmine and sweet olive had gotten all mixed up. They hung heavy and thick like streaks in the still air, or like incense at a funeral."

The late John Kennedy Toole won his award posthumously with *Confederacy of Dunces* (1981). Ignatius J. Reilly, an eccentric with a medieval world view, leads his readers in rollicking fashion through another side of the city—the Irish channel, which has much of the mood of Toole's own neighborhood, Elysian Fields Avenue near the river. The peculiar Brooklyn–New Orleans accent exists in a glorious state in the novel and in these areas: "I'm beat. I just finished opening four dozen ersters out in the backyard. . . . That's hard work, believe me, banging that erster knife on them bricks." The characters, like Santa Battaglia and Reilly's mother, can be found not only under the clock at D. H. Holmes on Canal Street but in the bars, restaurants and churches near the river.

A National Book Award winner in 1962, Walker Percy has written *The Moviegoer,* a novel which presents a compelling study of a man making his own way against the clutches of a traditional New Orleans family. Percy uses Binx Bolling's movie going as a means of "certification" of reality: "If he sees a movie which shows his very neighborhood, it becomes possible for him to live, for a time at least, as a person who is Somewhere and not Anywhere." Bolling's search includes leaving his old family in the dark, close, tree-covered Garden District and moving to the openness of Gentilly (out Elysian Fields toward the Lake): "There are not so many trees and the buildings are low and the world is all sky. The sky is a deep bright ocean full of light and life." Percy, who lives in nearby Covington and who has been known to spend an afternoon in the city at the Maple Street Book Shop, used the New Orleans setting again in the more recent *Lancelot.*

Valerie Martin, John William Corrington, Berthe Amoss, and Peter Cooley are also writing in and about this old city. *New Laurel Review, New Orleans Review,* and *Xavier Review* publish the work of local as well as national and foreign writers. Book reviews appear on Sundays and Thursdays in *The Times-Picayune/The States-Item,* and writers read and discuss their work at the New Orleans Poetry Forum, the Maple Leaf Bar, and Congo Square Writers Union. Alice Claudel suggests the ambivalence which has attracted and repelled writers from Cable to Percy in these lines from "Unreal City":

> A friend said, "I thought
> the streets of the Vieux Carré
> were paved with gold."
>
> Riches for me were on the cobblestones
> of my own street, luring the stuffed-crab man,
> voice and aroma rising as one; and
> the long flat truck loaded with cotton bales,
> bound for the Warrier Service, snowing
> lint in our eyes as it passed.

If there is a common thread which leads into the late 20th century in the literature of New Orleans, it could be in the continuing conflicts of present and past, romance and reality—belonging and not belonging.

ART IN NEW ORLEANS

Visual Pleasures for the Adventurous

by
ROGER GREEN

Roger Green is the art and architecture critic for The Times-Pi-
cayune/The States-Item *newspaper as well as the New Orleans corre-
spondent for* ARTnews *magazine. Among the other publications he has
contributed to are* Art Voices South *and the* Franklin Mint Almanac.
*His monograph on the French painter Max Papart was recently pub-
lished in Spain.*

Some remarkable experiences await lovers of art in New Orleans, if
they are willing to seek out esthetic pleasures in relatively hard-to-find

places, and if they can agree to mentally extend the bounds of what is ordinarily understood as art.

New Orleans is not a city with strong artistic traditions. Few internationally famous artists and no art schools or movements ever developed here. Nor did any important collectors ever acquire masterpieces, which might today be the stellar attractions at local museums.

Yet New Orleans has in recent years become the site of considerable art activity. A surprisingly large number of artists today live and exhibit in the city, where studio space can be rented cheaply, and where pressures are all but unknown. New Orleans' art institutions and galleries regularly mount sophisticated, stimulating exhibits, showcasing efforts by both local and international artists. Moreover, and most important for the visitor, New Orleans' matchless physical environment never ceases to yield artistic experiences—"artistic" in the sense that strong emotional responses can be, and are, triggered by visual stimuli.

Jackson Square Artists

New Orleans' outstanding environmental attraction is the French Quarter or *Vieux Carré*, the original, 18th-century core of the city, today a picturesque, people-scaled neighborhood, reminiscent of Europe. As might be expected, the French Quarter is a place to find artists and art.

The nucleus of the French Quarter is Jackson Square, surely one of the loveliest urban spaces in America, and a haven for artists who exhibit their work on the square's surrounding, iron-spoke fence. Artists working at Jackson Square all are licensed by the city and daily set up shop in the fence's 200 spaces.

Working artists contribute to the remarkable ambience of Jackson Square, whose regular population also includes street musicians, mimes, magicians, jugglers, and vendors of helium-filled balloons. (One almost gets the impression on Jackson Square of stepping into a production number in a vintage movie musical.) However, the art for sale ranges from passable to embarrassingly bad.

Much in evidence are paintings of steamboats, plantation houses, jazz musicians, and swamps—all strictly for the tourist trade. Moreover, many of the Jackson Square artists are portraitists, catering to the identical trade with quick, creditable likenesses, executed on the spot with charcoal or pastel. The best way to select an artist for such a souvenir portrait (in the event that commissioning one seems fitting or fun) is to circle the fence until discovering the most personally pleasing work on display.

French Quarter Galleries

More serious art is exhibited in a number of commercial galleries at locations all over the Quarter. However, a certain amount of care should be taken in visiting these establishments as many of the most conspicuous and inviting galleries are in reality slick, cynical tourist traps whose stock-in-trade is overpriced, artistically worthless junk.

Typically, these galleries carry examples of sports or clown art (often offensively off-color), together with Impressionist-style views of Paris and facile dream images in the manner of Surrealism. This class of "art," mass-produced for tourist markets all over the world, equates in cultural significance with the cuisine at fast-food restaurants.

On the other hand, a number of worthwhile galleries are located in the Quarter, generally on the less-trafficked side streets, which can be found easily with a map. See "Art Galleries" in the *Practical Information for New Orleans* chapter for a rundown of French Quarter galleries, including their addresses and specialties. A tour of the galleries will help interested visitors to discover serious art, including creations by many intriguing local artists. Equally important, the act of seeking out the various galleries will result in a tour of the French Quarter somewhat removed from the beaten path.

Mention should also be made of galleries dealing in posters, which are locally produced in many cases and which make interesting, relatively inexpensive souvenirs. The creation of souvenir posters is actually a New Orleans industry, involving many of the city's most talented graphic artists. Frequently, New Orleans posters commemorate specific events, like each year's edition of Mardi Gras and the annual Jazz and Heritage Festival. Other posters celebrate distinctive aspects of life in the city, for example jazz and the consumption of boiled crawfish.

Flea Markets and Other Art Attractions

Another of the French Quarter's art attractions—one that may at first appear strange but that continues an important tradition in the history of art—is the flea market held each weekend in the so-called Lower French Market, near Esplanade Avenue.

To the Surrealists, working half a century ago in Paris, and powerfully influenced by the teachings of Freud, flea markets with their jumbles of cast-off items seemed to be metaphors for the workings of the human mind. For the visitor to New Orleans, the local flea market (a hodgepodge of furniture, bric-a-brac, clothes, appliances and magazines) is an excellent place to learn about Louisiana's pop culture and to indulge in nostalgia for the past.

Art attractions in the Quarter are easy to get to by foot and require no ingenuity or courage to deal with New Orleans' public transportation system. Other art attractions, located elsewhere in town, require some traveling but are definitely worth making an effort to see. Of particular interest uptown in this regard are the Contemporary Arts Center, at 900 Camp Street, and the collection of outdoor sculpture surrounding the K&B Building on neighboring Lee Circle.

The Contemporary Arts Center (known locally as the CAC) is New Orleans "alternative" art institution, much like The Kitchen and P.S. 1 in New York City. Founded in 1977, and occupying a cavernous, former drugstore warehouse on the fringes of the Central Business District, the Contemporary Arts Center is regarded by many Orleanians as the most exciting cultural institution in town.

Local artists regularly exhibit at the center, in theme shows and invitational exhibits, which are held all year-round. In addition, important traveling exhibits often find a temporary home at the center. Moreover, the CAC's numerous programs extend beyond the visual arts to concerts, films, theatrical performances, and dance recitals, plus art-related workshops and seminars in a variety of fields.

Located in a grim (but safe) neighborhood, the center is more comfortably reached by taxicab or bus than by foot. The Magazine Street bus, whose uptown route includes a stop one block from the center, leaves from the corner of Canal and Camp streets, by the Waterbury drugstore, adjacent to the Sheraton Hotel.

A short walk from the center (following St. Joseph Street in the direction of Lake Pontchartrain) is the traffic hub Lee Circle, distinguished by its towering columnar monument to the Civil War general, Robert E. Lee. Abutting the uptown, lakeside arc of Lee Circle is the K&B Building, a sleek, international-style office block, designed by Skidmore, Owings and Merrill and surrounded by a raised plaza filled with many remarkable examples of three-dimensional art.

The sculpture plaza is easy to spot: From a distance, and by virtue of the many oddly shaped constructions rising from it, the plaza somewhat resembles a cosmic amusement park. Among the internationally known sculptors represented are Isamu Noguchi, Henry Moore, Barbara Hepworth, Kenneth Snelson and George Segal. Visitors should also note that the benches and signs at the streetcar stops directly in front of the K&B Building are actually environmental sculptures created by Houston artist Frank McGuire.

The sculpture collection is financed by the Virlane Foundation, a local, nonprofit organization dedicated to increasing the public's appreciation of contemporary art, particularly sculpture. Admission to the plaza is free, and since the sculptures are all out-of-doors, they can be viewed anytime, any day.

Uptown Galleries

Located uptown from Lee Circle are many of New Orleans' most important art galleries. Other galleries, located considerably farther uptown, may be difficult for the visitor to reach. Many of these uptown galleries are clustered on or near Magazine Street, a long and in many parts an interesting artery, running parallel to the Mississippi River. Explaining the galleries' presence on relatively inaccessible Magazine Street are the exorbitant rents charged for commercial properties in the French Quarter, whose most successful entrepreneurs cater unabashedly to popular taste. (This circumstance explains the similarity of much French Quarter "art" to the food served in franchise restaurants.)

Besides art galleries, Magazine Street contains many second-hand and antique stores, ethnic restaurants and restored Victorian houses. However, the street also includes many bleak and unattractive stretches, with tumbledown houses and mean-looking shops. The best way to navigate Magazine Street is by private car, bus or taxi, stopping and getting out wherever the neighborhood seems inviting.

New Orleans Museum of Art

One final major excursion, to the New Orleans Museum of Art, is necessary for an art tour of the city to be complete. The museum is located in City Park, New Orleans' largest, and can be reached by either cab or the Esplanade bus. (The bus, traveling in the direction of the French Quarter, leaves from the corner of Canal and North Ramparts streets; it stops directly at the museum.)

New Orleans Museum of Art is—like a number of American museums—housed in a sprawling composite structure, combining a columned, neoclassical core with later, scrupulously unadorned additions that strongly resemble cardboard boxes. In the case of New Orleans, the original core was constructed in 1910, and was financed by a wealthy sugar broker, Isaac Delgado, after whom the museum was originally named. The additions, completed during the 1960s, more than triple the original building's floor area.

The museum's major attraction is not its permanent collection, which is only strong in limited areas. What makes the museum important is its practice of hosting big, international traveling exhibits, which frequently attract legions of visitors from out-of-state.

The practice of mounting such exhibitions was initiated in 1977–1978, when the museum presented "The Treasures of Tutankhamun," an exhibit that generated over $89 million in local tourist revenues, according to a study by the University of New Orleans. Subsequent "blockbuster" exhibitions have included "Peru's Golden Treasures," "The Search for Alexander," and "Honore Daumier 1801–1879, from the Armand Hammer Collection."

Despite its emphasis on traveling exhibits, the museum provides a permanent home for many splendid and significant works of art. Two of the strongest collections are photography and primitive art. Only a fraction of the museum's holdings in these areas are regularly displayed.

The decision to collect photography—well timed on the museum's part—became an official policy about ten years ago, just before the prices for historical photographs began to skyrocket. Today, the museum has an extensive and first-rate collection of camera art, including prints by such artistically diverse masters as László Moholy-Nagy, Alfred Stieglitz, Walker Evans, and James Van Der Zee.

The collection of primitive art became significant in 1977, when the museum acquired from the estate of financier Victor J. Kiam more than 175 carved wooden sculptures, from Africa, Oceania, and the Pacific Northwest. The outstanding sculpture in the collection, a squat "temple figure" with a towering headdress, was discovered by Captain Cook on his third voyage to the Hawaiian Islands in 1789.

Visitors to the museum may want to explore City Park, which has since the 1950s become undeniably seedy, but which is being rescued by an energetic group of volunteers called The Friends of City Park. One of the Friends' major restoration projects, which will be in progress for the next several years and which should be of interest to lovers of art, is the 7-acre rose garden behind the museum. Constructed during the 1930s by the Works Progress Administration, the Beaux Arts-style garden features pools, arbors, terraces, and formal planting beds.

The garden also features masonry lampposts, benches, and animal sculptures by Enrique Alferez, a colorful Mexican artist (now in his eighties) who has been visiting and working in New Orleans since the Depression years. Alferez' cast stone contributions to the rose garden are streamlined modern in style—as are his sculptures at other locations in the city, including the main entrance to Charity Hospital and the fountain at the Lakefront Airport.

Mardi Gras Art

New Orleans' best-known and most important artistic tradition is the city-wide street party known as Mardi Gras. This annual celebration, far from being an isolated occurrence, crystallizes the very ethos of New Orleans, whose citizens adore fancy dress, drinking and—in point of fact—any device that will permit them to avoid life's unpleasant realities. Not surprisingly, Mardi Gras' escapism requires elaborate decor, whose more spectacular manifestations can only be called works of art.

Some remarkable old Mardi Gras costumes and favors, dating from the turn-of-the-century, are preserved at the Old U.S. Mint in the lower French Market area, fronting on Esplanade Avenue. This restored 19th-century building, painted dark red, is one of the eight historical French Quarter properties comprising the Louisiana State Museum complex.

Visitors to New Orleans at Mardi Gras time will discover another art form that is unique to the city, the design of elaborate floats used in Carnival parades. The parades are staged by Carnival clubs or "krewes" in the two weeks preceding Mardi Gras day. Typically, all the floats in a parade will interpret a particular, pre-chosen theme, for example "Greek Myths" or "Broadway Shows."

Viewing the parades can be an exciting experience, particularly at night when masked marchers carry lighted flambeaux. The floats themselves have in recent years become objects of considerable beauty, by reason of a return—on the part of certain professional float builders—to time-honored methods of fabrication and decoration.

The float builders in question, Barth Brothers, today design parades for many of the city's most prestigious krewes. In returning to the old float building traditions, the Barths are preserving an art form that is truly indigenous to New Orleans.

Carnival floats are actually wheeled wooden wagons, rectangular in shape and pulled by tractors during parades. Decorating the wooden frames are "props"—i.e., outsized figures and objects made of papier-mâché. As old pictures at the Presbytere show, props have traditionally had curved, flowing lines, and have been painted in soft pastel hues. These formal traditions are today being continued in New Orleans, in a reaction against the use of garish, glossy props imported from Europe, which were seen in parades here for too many years.

Another response to Mardi Gras is New Orleans' "alternative" Carnival club, the Krewe of Clones, which is sponsored by the Contemporary Arts Center. Each year, the Krewe of Clones mounts a remarkable spoof-of-Mardi Gras parade about two weeks before Mardi Gras, with clever, topical floats and tongue-in-cheek pageantry. The spoof-parade —lest anybody doubt its validity as a form of art—has been funded since its inception in 1978 by grants from the National Endowment for the Arts.

The Clones parade is a timely event, and to be in New Orleans and miss it would indeed be a shame. This prospect raises the question, "How can the visitor know what's happening artistically in the city?" Happily, a number of readily available sources of information exist.

One is New Orleans' daily newspaper, *The Times-Picayune/The States-Item,* whose Wednesday art column lists upcoming art events for the week, and whose Friday entertainment supplement (called "Lagniappe") includes a comprehensive guide to cultural events of all kinds. The identical information can be found in the weekly, underground newspaper *Gambit,* which is available in vending machines all over the city. Both these listings also include restored mansions, specialized historical museums and other attractions.

Visitors can also obtain information about cultural events from The Arts Council of New Orleans. The so-called "arts hotline," 522–ARTS, plays a daily, taped message about special events. By calling the Arts Council at 523–1465, visitors can receive personal, detailed information about art happenings all over the city.

Finally, it should be noted that the people at most of the galleries and institutions listed in the *Practical Information* chapter are both knowledgeable about the local art scene and eager to be helpful to visitors. The very best of Southern hospitality, visitors will discover, works appropriately in the service of art.

CYPRESS AND BRICKS

Creole, Classic and Eclectic Architecture in New Orleans

by
ROULHAC TOLEDANO

Roulhac Toledano is the co-author of five books and author of numerous articles on New Orleans architecture and has inventoried some 8,000 New Orleans buildings in eight historic neighborhoods. Having taught New Orleans architecture at the University of New Orleans, she has also lectured on the subject widely throughout the South. For five years she wrote a column for a local newspaper in an effort to popularize restoration and the reuse of New Orleans' outstanding architectural inventory.

ARCHITECTURE **115**

Much that is said and believed about New Orleans "architecture" is largely myth. The French Quarter *(Vieux Carré)* is more Spanish than French and more American than either. The Garden District, famed for its antebellum mansions, boasts just a handful which pre-date the War Between the States. And the "gardens" would not be regarded as such by any proper Boston or Philadelphia lady who has done service in the Public Garden or Rittenhouse Square. And Union General Ben Butler, Reconstruction's version of the Ayatollah Khomeini, actually saved the city from plague and the New Orleans architecture from destruction when he was in charge of the occupation of the city after its fall in the Civil War. Finally, most of the cast iron gracing *Vieux Carré* galleries and in the Garden District was steamed in from Philadelphia and other points north.

New Orleans has more Greek Revival houses than Athens claims originals. But these classical flourishes are magnificent farces, merely additions forming pretentious posturings that resemble the fantasies of a wedding cake. New Orleans architecture, from the downriver Creole cottage; to the Uptown neo-classical mansion; to the Algiers Victorian gee-gaw; to the Irish Channel and back-a-town shotguns is just a series of big and little rectangular shapes, like shoeboxes, to which trim and decoration have been added according to the taste of the period and the pocketbook of the owner. This is known as "facade" architecture, its total emphasis being on the front elevation. Most of these facade grace notes and decorative touches found their inspiration in the *Modern Builder's Guide,* published by architect Minard Lafever in New York in 1833, and later from the sash and door catalogues of the time, where architectural details and elements could be ordered by number. From 1830 to 1900 the general maxim and final form of flattery appears to have been to love thy neighbor's Corinthian column or Morris wrought-iron or Greek-style entrance and emulate them.

But strangely (although little seems odd in this *Brigadoon en Bayou* where time often seems suspended) the city's vast amalgam of copy-cat eclecticism results in a magical cornucopia of architectural splendor in the swamp. While the purist in the temple of architectonics may sneer, any pilgrim with a touch of adventure and curiosity will discover unalloyed delights as a building watcher among the neighborhoods of New Orleans. It is difficult to scratch the surface, for there is enough here to fill eternity. But a note of warning! As you walk or ride, look up, because the misdirection of progress has seldom reached the upper levels of buildings where the proportion of cornices (those moldings that run along the tops of buildings), the shapes and workmanship of windows and other decorative detail bespeak an earlier era of good taste and refinement.

New Orleans, perhaps more than any other American city, is a living outdoor museum. Each of its historic neighborhoods comprises its own exhibition within the larger cityscape. Each neighborhood has building types and styles which, by their regional interpretation and their repetition along the streetscape, create for each suburb or faubourg (as the neighborhoods are called) a characteristic and individual ambience.

Downtown (downriver, really, because the Mississippi continues to dominate and delineate the living arrangements of the city) are the Vieux Carré, the old section of the city also called the French Quarter; Bayou St. John, site of the early Canadian rural settlement predating the Vieux Carré; the Esplanade, first of the grand avenues of what was to be America; and the first Creole suburbs or faubourgs of Marigny and Trémé. Only a short ferry ride across the river is the small Delta village of Algiers, a hodgepodge of Victoriana, although more antebellum houses may survive there than exist in the Garden District.

Upriver across Canal Street, which originally formed a great social divide between Creoles and Americans, is the Faubourg St. Mary, now known as the Central Business District. It is a collection of 19th-century wharves, warehouses, commercial buildings, rowhouses and storehouses, interspersed with skyscrapers, the first of which sprang up in the 1920s near and on Canal Street and since the 1970s have cropped up along Poydras Street. Uptown also boasts the Lower Garden District, a once collapsed version of the Garden District now rapidly being re-gentrified; the Garden District, the preferred historic area for New Orleanians; and St. Charles Avenue, one of the most spectacular streets in the country. Jefferson City, the University section, and Carrollton City, were all added on as the American city grew.

There are any number of ways to get a good look at the city's architecture. Sherwood Anderson preferred the Algiers ferry boat, while Walker Percy favored the St. Charles Avenue streetcar. Perhaps the most popular (and certainly the simplest) is to take a walk around.

A city's architecture can be enjoyed at almost any level of expertise from gawking to grave analysis. Gawking, however, is almost always more enjoyable when a bit of background is known. There are a number of books that describe New Orleans architecture in detail. Among them: *Lost New Orleans,* by Mary Cable (Houghton Mifflin, Boston); *New Orleans Architecture* (Pelican Publishers, Gretna, Louisiana), a several volume set supervised by an organization called Friends of the Cabildo; and *New Orleans: A Pictorial History, From Earliest Times to the Present Day,* by Leonard Huber (Crown Publishers, New York). If you'd like a more complete listing of what to see in New Orleans' neighborhoods than this essay provides, pick up a copy of the *Guide to New Orleans Architecture,* put together by the New Orleans chapter of the American Institute of Architects (AIA).

To aid the gawkers and their ilk, here is a brief glossary of some of the most common terms used to describe New Orleans' architecture:

portico—a porch or covered walk with cover provided by a column-supported roof.

segmental arch—an arch whose curve is not perfectly rounded.

pitched roof—a roof with two slopes that meet at a common ridge.

hip roof—one with four slopes, which rise from each of a building's sides.

mansard roof—one whose slopes rise at two angles, the lower half steeper than the upper.

dormer—a small, windowed structure that juts out from a sloping roof.

box columns—columns in the shape of a square.

rustication—masonry whose surface has been textured.

What follows is a series of very brief descriptions of some architectural sights in each of New Orleans' neighborhoods. Bear in mind that most of the houses are private homes that you may enjoy from the outside—do not expect to go in for a look around.

Vieux Carré—The French Quarter

Although actually predated by the settlements along Bayou St. John, the world renowned French Quarter or Vieux Carré (Old Square) will always be the heart and hub of New Orleans. Orleanians sojourning elsewhere invariably yearn for the French Quarter, even though they may not frequent it when they are in town.

The French established this colonial town in 1718. The Spanish took over the town of 3,000 French-speaking inhabitants in 1762 (although so few Spaniards came that no one seemed to notice it until 1768). They left a small city of 10,000 (still) French-speaking inhabitants. Spanish government prevailed, but so did the French language. The Louisiana Purchase of 1803 brought Americans flocking to the port to make a fortune, which many did; the Irish and Germans followed in the 1830s and 40s; then in the 1890s came large numbers of Sicilians, who so influenced life in the French Quarter that the back half from St. Ann Street to Esplanade Avenue became known as the Italian Quarter until shortly after World War II. All these groups left their mark on French Quarter architecture. Today it is a city within a city—an historic collection of architecture the like of which is not to be found anywhere. In 1939 most of the 100 square blocks bounded by Esplanade Avenue, the Mississippi River, Rampart and Canal streets became the first American neighborhood to be given legislative protection against alteration and demolition.

Military engineers and surveyors to the Crown of France should be given initial credit for this environment, now a continuous outdoor

New Orleans Architectural Sights (Select Areas)

Points of Interest

1) Algiers Court House (225 Morgan)
2) Beauregard House (1113 Chartres)*
3) Board of Trade Plaza (316 Magazine)
4) Cabildo*
5) Cornstalk-Iron Fence (915 Royal)*
6) Ewing House (605-07 De la Ronde, Algiers)
7) Gallier Hall (545 St. Charles)
8) Gallier House (1132 Royal)*

9) Hermann Grima House (820 St. Louis)*
10) Lafayette Square
11) Lafitte's Blacksmith Shop (941 Bourbon)*
12) Madame John's Legacy (632 Dumaine)*
13) Merieult House (525-33 Royal St.)
14) Napoleon House (500 Chartres)*
15) Payne-Strachan House (1134 First)
16) Piazza d'Italia (Poydras & Magazine)
17) Pontalba Buildings*
18) Presbytere
19) Rivergate (4 Canal)

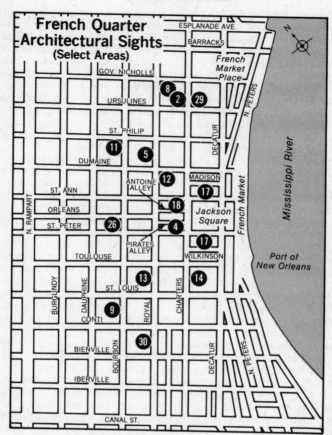

French Quarter Architectural Sights (Select Areas)

Points marked with an asterisk (*) are on the FRENCH QUARTER ARCHITECTURAL SIGHTS map.

museum and visible reflection of the culture, economics and lifestyle of almost three centuries. They laid out the grid pattern and the Place d'Armes (Jackson Square) in the 1720s. Pierre Le Blond de la Tour and Adrien de Pauger at that time originated the traditional lot sizes which marked the "look" of the city which continues today. Engineer in Chief Bernard de Verges was responsible from 1751 to 1768 for many structures of *bricque entre poteaux* (brick between posts) and *bousillage* (mud and moss between posts), with both utilizing the *colombage* system of timber framing with cypress. Lafitte's Blacksmith Shop (941 Bourbon), built late in the Spanish era, ironically reveals the French colonial structural method. The method employed handhewn cypress posts placed upright with diagonal posts set at intervals between with soft river sand brick filling the area between the framing members. Although the bricks and posts are now visible, they were originally covered with plaster or weatherboard. No self-respecting Frenchman or Spaniard would leave brick exposed, not only because they are soft and do not weather well, but because of esthetic preference.

Ignace Francois Broutin, Engineer to the King, designed the Ursuline Convent (1114 Chartres Street) in 1745. Completed about 1750, it was erected behind a convent which had housed the nuns since 1734. Although only eleven years old, the first convent was on the verge of collapse, and was demolished upon completion of the Broutin structure. The second Ursuline Convent is the only remaining French building standing in its entirety in New Orleans, and the only major French building remaining in the Mississippi Valley. The steep hip roof, small dormers, quoins and string courses dividing the structure's two and one half stories all bespeak its French origins.

Curiously, while Spanish authorities dictated building methods by law, few Spanish architects designed buildings. The Cabildo (then City Hall and the Calabozo or jail) was designed in 1795 by Gilbert Guillemard, a French architect in the service of Spain. Marcelino Menendez, an artisan from the Canary Islands, was responsible for the Cabildo's outstanding wrought-iron work. Its near twin, the Presbytere (separated from the Cabildo by the St. Louis Cathedral), was commissioned at the same time. Both buildings, appropriate to their Spanish colonial origins, resemble the neo-classic *Casa Real* of Antequera, Mexico. The slate mansard roofs added in 1847 by Louis Surgi project a French ambience to the pair.

Madame John's Legacy (632 Dumaine), a Spanish colonial residence, now an adjunct of the Louisiana State Museum, was designed by an American builder in 1788 in the French style for Don Manuel Lanzas, a Spaniard. This rare example of the raised basement, hall-less building surrounded by wide galleries is given an urban air because of its proximity to the sidewalk (banquette). Otherwise, with its casement openings (full length French doors), double pitch hip-roof, detached kitchen and outbuildings, it could be mistaken for a French colonial country house. Its builder, Robert Jones, was called Roberto Honess, disguising his American origins. Another important Spanish colonial contribution to the French Quarter is the Jean Francois Merieult House (533 Royal) now the Historic New Orleans Collection. It dates from 1792, but underwent extensive interior Greek Revival alteration in the 1830s; the mantels, woodwork and decorative plaster of that period distinguish the interior today.

A major Spanish colonial building, now Waldhorn's Antiques (339 Royal), was built in 1800 by Frenchman Barthelemy Lafon for a French Creole, Vincent Rillieux. The owner was the grandfather of French painter, Edgar Degas. Also dating from the late Spanish period is Brennan's Restaurant at 417 Royal built about 1802 for merchant Joseph Faurie. Both of these gems reflect Spanish influence with wide stucco bands around the windows and Spanish wrought-iron balconies supported by consoles or S curve wrought iron.

Restraint, conservatism, anonymity, simplicity of surface, delicacy of proportion, and sophistication in relationship of form might be considered passwords of continuing French traditions in Spanish colonial architecture. Spanish colonial urban buildings, whether one-and-one-half-story cottages, storehouses, commercial buildings or town residences, have relatively flat fronts, with a simple projecting masonry band outlining the building or delineating windows or segments of the facade, as seen at 731 Royal Street, the Montegut House (1799). A wrought-iron balcony, of restrained design, is traditionally supported by wrought iron S curve brackets. Many more intricate examples of wrought-iron design, however, like the balcony at 343 Royal, Waldhorn's Antique Shop (1800), are to be found on any French Quarter walk. Look for the *guard de frise* on many iron balconies. This iron guard with pointed elements was placed at dwelling boundaries to keep balcony hoppers at bay. A Spanish colonial facade often exhibits a wide *porte cochere* entrance. These wide arched openings were designed for carriages and have large double doors, usually with a smaller inset door for pedestrian traffic allowing passage to the rear patio. A good example is 532–34 Madison Street, a Spanish colonial structure where author Lyle Saxon lived before his death in 1946. *Porte cochere* entrances were often closed off with a handsome double gate of wrought iron.

What is visible from the street in the French Quarter is seldom a hint of the possible elegance and beauty within. Neither Spanish nor French dwellings utilized interior hallways, and a narrow flagstone or brick alley to the courtyard is seen in many French Quarter complexes. These guttered walkways may be seen through narrow wrought grills or lattice work, so popular here, but stemming from a Southern Spanish tradition. Other patios are accessible only through the residence parlors or the *porte-cochere,* like the handsome one at 619 Chartres, the Spanish colonial home (1795) of Suzette Bosque, Governor W. C. C. Claiborne's third wife.

Arches as enframements for doorways and windows are also characteristic of Spanish as well as French building. Pat O'Brien's courtyard at 718 St. Peter illustrates courtyard arches, built by Etienne de Flechier in 1792.

Stairways are accessible from both the patio and the main house in most Spanish colonial buildings. Although covered, they are not enclosed within the house. The Girod House stairway at 500 Chartres illustrates the custom. Service buildings or slave quarters of Spanish buildings exhibit interesting stairways, like the pair at Madame John's Legacy (Louisiana State Museum) at 628 Dumaine Street.

Spanish colonial patios are paved with 6 inch tiles, brick, or flagstone, carefully guttered for drainage as seen at the Merieult House, 529 Royal (Historic New Orleans Collection). Enclosing the patio are usually galleries of the main house, balconies and galleries of service buildings, and stables with brick walls between. The small, decorated-wood columns (called colonettes) used for gallery supports are notable features of Spanish buildings; they are delicately turned as seen at Madame John's Legacy.

Many features of Spanish-colonial design retained their popularity despite the end of Spanish colonial rule in 1803. The same builders continued their customs and the flow of French and West Indies French-speaking emigres and builders and architects continued. Thus the patio of the Salomon Prevost house at 830 Royal Street, built in 1808, looks Spanish colonial as does that of 625 Toulouse street, erected by Jean Antoine Demarchy in 1807, or the court at 520 Royal Street, dating from 1816, built for Francois Seignoret of Bordeaux, France. This early 19th-century amalgam of styles became known as Creole architecture, and predominated from about 1803 until the 1840s, when Greek Revival architecture, then by far the most popular style of design in the country, began to influence New Orleans design. Nonetheless, Creole architecture persevered, with little taint of American design, in the French Quarter and the Creole suburbs of Marigny and Trémé, well into the 1850s.

James Gallier, Sr., one of the best known 19th-century New Orleans architects, arrived in the city in 1835 after working on Mountjoy Square in Dublin and the Grosvenor estate in London. Henry Howard, another prolific New Orleans architect, came from Cork, Ireland, by mid-century. Both these men were involved with the handsome Pontalba buildings, which face Jackson Square on two sides. This complex was a project of Micaela Almonester, Baroness Pontalba, begun in 1849. She commissioned Gallier and Howard to design thirty-two, four-story rowhouses for commercial use at street level with luxurious rental townhouses on the upper levels. Each unit was provided with a three-story service wing and paved patio. The architects used exposed hard brick brought in from Philadelphia for the facades, an innovation for the Vieux Carré, where exposed brick was "de trop" since the early French period. Cast iron was used on the front galleries, one of the first uses of decorative cast iron in the city.

Visually the Pontalba buildings compliment the Cabildo, Presbytere and the St. Louis Cathedral which they flank. This is appropriate since the Baroness' father, Spaniard Andres Almonester y Rojas, put up most of the money for these three edifices.

The English and American traditions of the Pontalba buildings began to intrude elsewhere in the Vieux Carré as evidenced by James Gallier, Jr.'s granite front, side hall house at 1132 Royal, built in 1857 and the Hermann-Grima House (823 St. Louis), a center hall mansion designed by William Brand in 1837. Exposed brick, painted and penciled, wide center halls with interior stairways, and the inevitable embellishments emphasizing the entrance are distinguishing elements of the British or Anglo-American influence on New Orleans architecture. Both the side hall floor plan exhibited at Gallier House and the center hall floor plan evident at the Hermann-Grima house illustrate a turning away from the French and Spanish hall-less traditions. These are both museums, open to the public.

Creole design endured, despite the invasion of other types and styles; thus Louis J. Dufilho's pharmacy (514 Chartres), an 1837 three-and-one-half-story storehouse designed by J. N. B. de Pouilly, is an old-school design, with an arched *porte cochere* and an emphasis on the rear elevation and patio area. My own favorite, if one can have a favorite in this vast outdoor display, is the Tricou House (711 Bourbon) designed by the French architectural firm of Gurlie and Guillot. It is an exemplary 1834 masonry surface of two-and-one-half-stories with a garlanded wood cornice contrasting with a delicate wrought-iron gallery. There is an arched *porte cochere* beside two full length arched openings at the first level. This, with the segmental arched dormers and the facade proportions, bespeaks the building's Creole provenance.

French Quarter architecture, whether French, Spanish or Anglo-American leaves visitors with strong impressions. The memorable characteristics include dormers with arched heads, casement openings or French doors, projecting overhangs protecting the front elevations, galleries or balconies, gable ends, rythmical repetitions of architectural elements, like windows, columns, pilasters, brackets and arches, and finally, enclosed courtyards with charming multilevel service buildings.

But it is likely to be the ironwork that is perceived as the most visible and typical aspect of French Quarter architecture.

Wrought iron is fashioned by hammering or hand-working slag-bearing malleable iron. Light gray in color, it can be twisted, turned or stretched when hot or cold. The blacksmiths used up to thirty tools, most frequently hammers, tongs, chisels and anvils to produce simple designs or complex motifs, like monograms, flame shapes, volutes, and petals. The delicacy and refinement of wrought-iron design, its conservative scale and the repetition of a few simple and graceful patterns served the populace well until the mid-19th century. Then an explosion of cast-iron galleries occurred. They appeared as prominent features of new buildings and replaced discarded wrought-iron balconies on older buildings—and even sometimes the two were combined together. Decorative cast iron is made by pouring molten iron into molds. The molds could accommodate more complicated patterns, heavier designs and stronger support than the earlier wrought iron. The availability of the highly decorative cast iron coincided with the extravagant taste of the successful merchants, brokers and factors of New Orleans' Golden Age. Cast-iron galleries multiplied in ever more complex and opulent patterns. Proud new owners also wanted their decorative cast iron to be noticed so they painted it bronze, Chinese red, yellow ochre and Paris green—not the dull black presently associated with cast iron. The best known and most opulent example of cast iron in the French Quarter is the corn stalk fence at 915 Royal. Each gate post rests on an iron pumpkin and the corn stalks are entwined with morning glories.

Faubourg St. Mary—The Central Business District

Taking Thomas Jefferson's advice that New Orleans was the place to make more money than anywhere else in the Western World, 19th-century Americans flocked there by the boatload. They settled in Faubourg St. Mary—also called the American section and later known as the Central Business District—across Canal Street from the *Vieux Carré*. The area from Canal Street to Howard Avenue and the Mississippi River to Loyola Avenue is a reflection of New Orleans' Golden Age when cotton was king, sugar was queen, and quick fortunes could be made. Benjamin Latrobe, the eminent architect, remarked in 1819 that "in the Faubourg St. Mary and wherever Americans build, they exhibit their flat brick fronts with sufficient number of holes for light and entrance. . . . The old English side hall passage house with the stairs at the end is also gaining ground."

The point is well illustrated by the thirteen row houses in the 600 block of Julia Street, built in 1832 and designed by A. T. Wood for the New Orleans Building Company. The Preservation Resource Center, headquartered at 603 Julia, and the Historic Faubourg St. Mary Corporation are spearheading the restoration of this lovely row (as well as scores of others) to attract residents and restore the neighborhood ambience of the 19th century to the CBD.

Mixed among the row and storehouses are blocks of granite and brick front commercial buildings (even some of marble) built in the 1830s and 1840s by Irish, Scottish and Anglo-American immigrants to Louisiana. These remain as testimony to the South's great days when commerce was god among the new arrivals. W. H. Sparks put it aptly when in 1859 he noted that "the Anglo-American commences to succeed and will not scruple at the means, and this is called enterprise, combined with energy. (To the American Protestant) it is honorable and respectable to succeed, dishonest and disreputable to fail." Magazine Street in its heyday was proof of this dictum. The 300 block of Magazine exhibits a fine row of four-story commercial buildings designed by Lewis Reynolds in 1854. Across the street at the 400 block are five four-level stores in the Classic style dating between 1830 and 1850. Such commercial buildings have three openings across a width of twenty to twenty-five feet with granite or cast-iron pillars at the first levels, rising to support two or three stories of brick or granite. Each level has three double-hung windows having granite lintels and often, molded cornices. Also characteristic is a decorative brick architrave, sometimes with a parapet. The 300 block of Magazine also features the Board of Trade Plaza, an adaptation by Richard Koch and Samuel Wilson, restoration architects, of the 1850s commercial complex.

The heart of Faubourg St. Mary was Lafayette Square and Gallier Hall, built in 1845–50 to serve as City Hall. This imposing example of Greek Revival architecture designed by James Gallier, St., cost $342,-000 to build and was restored by the city in 1970 to be used for official city functions and cultural events. Vying with Gallier Hall as a major Greek Revival monument is the United States Custom House, 423 Canal Street. Construction was begun in 1848 and continued until 1881. A. T. Wood, J. H. Dakin, P. G. T. Beauregard, and finally T. K. Wharton assisted in the design and supervision. The "Marble Hall" in the Custom House is regarded as one of the finest Greek Revival interiors in America.

Canal Street is a major thoroughfare with a rich presentation of 19th-century commercial types and styles. The 600 block starts with a simple, distinguished 1833 commercial building, one remnant of five originals designed by architect William Brand. Adjacent to it is a late Victorian commercial building beside an 1870 example of Italian Renaissance Revival. The visual contrast in decoration among the buildings is interesting. The tallest building of the quartet possesses an elaborate cast-iron front, cast by a local foundry in 1850 for New

Orleans architect W. A. Freret, Jr. Another example of cast-iron fronts is the Krower Building just off Canal at 111 Exchange Street where the elaborate sculptural effect of cast-iron work may be appreciated. It was constructed in 1866 by James Gallier, Jr., and Richard Esterbrook. Fronts made entirely of cast iron were attached to the brick sides. Reportedly fireproof, they were later discovered to melt in fires.

Aside from commercial space, Canal Street had its share of townhouses and residences as well. The lone reminder stands at 824 Canal, erected in 1844 for Dr. W. N. Mercer who commissioned James Gallier, Sr., to design the house, which cost $18,700. Since 1884 the Mercer house has been occupied by the Boston Club.

Churches, too, were included in the development of the self-sufficient American section. In 1838 Irish Catholics hired James Dakin to design and erect St. Patrick's Church at 724 Camp Street for $115,000. After a dispute with the church managers over the stability of the partly finished church, Dakin's contract was cancelled. The Gothic style building, was completed in 1839 with designs of James Gallier, Sr. The church and Italianate rectory face and are flanked by major mid-19th century townhouses, storehouses, and commercial buildings in varying stages of restoration or decay.

The most exciting trend today in the Central Business District/ Faubourg St. Mary is an impetus toward preserving the historic warehouse district fronting the river. Block-long rows of mid-19th century sugar and cotton warehouses, wharves and industrial buildings provide memorable silhouettes and marvelous interior spaces of exposed brick and cypress. They are being renovated for modern use. Fulton and Front streets are also receiving notice today due to the nearby site of the Louisiana Exhibition Hall for the 1984 Louisiana World Exposition.

With completion of the Louisiana Exhibition Hall, the city and state will have anchored the financial and cultural life of the Central Business District with a series of bold strokes. These begin with the Rivergate Exhibition Hall at the foot of Canal, designed by the local architectural firm of Curtis and Davis in 1967; the Superdome, another Curtis and Davis project in 1971 placed in the midst of the city's financial, hotel, and retail trade center; followed by the Piazza d'Italia at Poydras and Magazine. The Piazza, a controversial public venture into post-modernism, was designed by Charles Moore in association with the local firm of August Perez and Associates in 1976.

The finest view of all that is and was the Faubourg St. Mary can be had from the top deck of the Canal Street free ferry. It leaves from the foot of Canal Street every thirty minutes, crossing the Mississippi to the village of old Algiers and back. From the ferry one sees the slick curtain wall of skyscrapers foisted upon the city since 1950, largely by out-of-state entrepreneurs and architects. They form a horizontal ribbon of glass and shiney surfaces along Poydras from the River to the Super Dome—a sharp contrast to the city's early 19th-century styles. It is generally agreed among New Orleanians that there is no such thing as good modern architecture.

Algiers

This area is an oddment—an exotic. Old Algiers (now called Algiers Point, after the river pilots' lexicon) remains a small, sleepy Delta village, existing in peaceful co-existence with the metropolis across the Mississippi. Although it was annexed by New Orleans in 1870 (still considered by some Algerines as an act of folly), Algiers remains as stubborn an entity as Quebec or the Basque country. No one is quite sure how it got its name. First a colonial abatoir (slaughterhouse) then a slave depot, the settlement became known as Duverjeville soon after 1805 when Barthelemy Duverje acquired the plantation eventually absorbed by the village of Algiers. Ship-building, farming, then railroading offered livelihoods to a population as mixed as the city across the river.

Although there are still more antebellum buildings here than in the Garden District, Algiers' original character changed radically shortly after annexation. The old French and Spanish colonial town (including the Duverje Plantation House turned courthouse) burned in 1897, and the lower coast plantations became ghosts along the Mississippi, lost to industry and oil storage tanks. Algiers was largely rebuilt as the sparkling late Victorian settlement that has remained virtually unchanged almost a century later. It is a short, delightful (and free) ferryboat ride from the foot of Canal Street. And it can be traversed leisurely and on foot in a relatively short time.

Directly across from the ferry landing squats the Algiers Court House, a splendid and forbidding architectural ogre dominating the levees which form the bend in the river. It is an 1896 Romanesque Revival counterpart of the original 1849 Gothic state capitol in Baton Rouge, holding sway over the river upstream. A few blocks downriver, 2009 Patterson at Valette, is the old Emporium, a two-story brick storehouse built about 1870 in the still popular late Classic style. Handsome cast-iron galleries with anthemion cresting cover a colonnaded walkway below featuring narrow iron colonettes. A period Tiffany glass panel recalls the building's days as the Renecky Shoe Store. It now houses an interior decorator's shop as well as the Algiers' office of Congressman Robert Livingston, named for his Hudson Valley patroon ancestor who was lured down to New Orleans by his friend, Thomas Jefferson.

One of the oldest antebellum houses to survive the 1897 fire is the Ewing House at 405–07 De la Ronde Street. It dates from 1849 and is often cited as one of Algiers' finest double houses. Rather than a great manor house, it is simply a large, well-built, two-story box, faced with grandiose wood pillars extending two levels to an imposing Classic-style cornice and edged below by a fine iron balcony. All this for a two-family rent house! Such pretentious examples of "facade" architecture, are referred to locally as having "Queen Anne front, Mary Ann sides," which is to say that the facades are sparklingly painted, while the sides, generally concealed by close alleyways, are left in weathered condition.

A neat center hall villa set low to the ground may be seen with its Classic-style gallery and architectural details embellishing the facade at 232 Valette Street. Standard to its type and style, popular in Algiers until 1870, are the gable sides, dormers and front gallery with wood pillars. Here a handsome cast-iron railing is complemented by a cast-iron balcony at the corner gable. A charming example of the Queen Anne cottage in its Delta interpretation remains at 1000 Brooklyn Avenue characterized by massing of a variety of forms, one pediment projecting beyond another, asymmetrical galleries, bays, contrasting textures and shapes, rustication, quoins, segmental arched openings, and decorative wooden elements used with abandon. Such Queen Anne cottages usually date from the 1890s.

No trip to Algiers is complete without a walk along Olivier Street from Opelousas Street to the levee where a variety of small-scale residences and storehouses reflecting the taste of Algiers is displayed crisply with the Delta sky as backdrop and the Mississippi River as foreground.

Lower Garden District

A steady stream of Americans, as well as Irish and German immigrants in the 1830s and 1840s, is responsible for the development upriver from Faubourg St. Mary. Known today as the Lower Garden District, it was planned by surveyor Barthelemy Lafon, who subdivided a number of small plantations within the bounds of Howard and Jackson avenues, the river and St. Charles Avenue as early as 1805. It became the first American suburb (predating the Garden District), having a more open landscaped setting than the urban Faubourg St. Mary which it abuts.

A park called Coliseum Place (where a planned coliseum was never built) was laid out in 1805, and streets were named after the muses— Calliope, Clio, Erato, Thalia, Melpomene. In this classic and sophisticated setting, the beautiful Greek Revival homes were appropriate.

Set back on their lots with a front garden, they formed the first semi-urban subdivision. Most were designed and built by immigrant architects from England, Ireland, and Scotland, like James Gallier, Sr., and Jr., Henry Howard and James McVittie or Anglo-Americans from New York such as Lewis Reynolds.

The Anglo-American inhabitants were well-to-do cotton factors, brokers and bankers who had come to New Orleans after the Louisiana Purchase. Judge Thomas Slidell, authors George Washington Cable and Grace King, architects James Gallier, Sr., and Thomas Kelah Wharton were among the notable English-speaking residents.

Yet the neighborhood began to wither as many of the homes were confiscated to house Union troops during the Civil War and the Occupation. Subsequently, all attempts at dignity and style were lost to continuing intrusions, demolitions, and abandonments, as residents fled to the newer and more affluent Garden District.

However, after more than a century, the 1972 distribution of Volume I of *New Orleans Architecture,* published by the Friends of the Cabildo, spurred the restoration of this neglected historic treasure trove. Now the houses on and around Coliseum Place remain as testament to the elegance and grandeur of this neighborhood.

St. Mary's Assumption Church (2030 Constance) built in 1860 by and for German Catholic immigrants became the center of the most extensive and outstanding nucleus of brick architecture in the city. Built for the Redemptorist order, the church is a beautiful exhibit of corbeling and molding in brick with arches, crosses, and niches projecting and receding to create a patterned surface.

St. Anna's Asylum at 1823 Prytania, built in 1853 by Robert Little and Peter Middlemiss, occupies a site donated by Dr. William Mercer, who asked that it be named after his daughter Anna. St. Anna's is one of the finest Classic-style structures in the city as a home for elderly ladies of the Episcopal diocese. A Doric portico is raised on scored piers. Sophistication is evident in the window design: those at the first level are post and lintel design, with full arched openings at the second level and segmental arched windows above.

Only in the Lower Garden District would something as unusual as the removal and restoration of the boyhood home of author and explorer Henry Morton Stanley occur. It was moved in 1980 from badly rundown Orange Street and relocated on Coliseum Place at 1721 Coliseum Street. There this charming, early Classic-style, frame center hall villa, built in 1837 by Stanley's adoptive father, further adds to the luster of the park. The one-and-a-half story residence has a lovely entrance with side lights and transom, flanked by two full length, double-hung windows on each side. A wide overhang extends from well-proportioned gable sides to cover a gallery with wood box columns and a diamond motif railing.

Garden District and Irish Channel

During the Civil War and Reconstruction, architects, builders, entrepreneurs, European immigrants and enterprising Americans (as well as carpetbaggers, scalawags and lottery kings) continued to swarm upriver to create what is now one of the city's finest neighborhoods and tourist attractions—the Garden District (Jackson Avenue to Louisiana Avenue, Magazine Street past St. Charles Avenue). Simultaneously, these same people arranged for the building of a working-class neighborhood south of the district along the adjacent river levees. This was soon dubbed the Irish Channel, for the vast numbers of Irish immigrants who found housing there.

The Garden District was an American spectacular, and unlike other neighborhoods, has remained a jewel throughout the 19th and 20th centuries. This beautiful array of galleried side hall houses, villas and gracious center hall mansions proclaimed an affluence, optimism and determination not implied in the careful, chaste, anonymous facades of the French, Spanish, and Creole sections. The Garden District was and is very American, and amazingly most of the houses were built during the Civil War and Reconstruction.

In 1832 Mme. Jacques Esnould de Livaudais, nee Celeste Marigny, sold the upriver plantation she had received in a divorce settlement. It was laid out in 1833 as a subdivision from Jackson Avenue (then Rue Panis) to Louisiana Avenue (then the Gran Course Wiltz) and from the river to just beyond St. Charles Avenue. By the late 1850s, American merchants and businessmen were reflecting their newly found wealth with their homes in the new faubourg. Their preference for Italianate design is most obvious at the Louise S. McGehee School, 2343 Prytania, built by architect James Freret for Bradish Johnson in 1870. A more restrained but equally handsome Italianate interpretation of the galleried center hall house is located at 1315 First Street. It was built by Samuel Jamison for J. W. Carrol towards the end of the Civil War. The Italianate taste is reflected in the segmental arch window design with the highly decorative molded cornices. Huge brackets, the parapet, the front gallery with central projection in cast iron, the side bay, and the side gallery reiterate the Italianate influence.

Prytania Street, not St. Charles Avenue, is the principal thoroughfare of the Garden District. A short walk along Prytania from Philip Street to Washington Avenue will reveal a typical segment of gracious living in this beautiful and romantic area. The Toby Westfeldt house at 2340 Prytania, dating from the 1830s, is a raised villa in the Greek

Revival style, one of the earliest buildings in the area. Surrounded with wide galleries and set deep on a large lot, it reflects the more rural feeling of the early days of the Garden District. It is said to be the model for the Cutrer's residence in Walker Percy's *The Moviegoer*. The original owner, Thomas Toby, was an early Texas speculator who lent money to Sam Houston to finance the Texas Revolution. As a result, Toby lost his house at a sheriff's sale for just $5,000. At this writing the house is on the market at the bargain price of just over a million.

Many other frame one-and-one-half-story villas in the Italianate style suggest the continuing evolution and American interpretation of the French raised basement tradition. One of many fine examples is located at 1327 Seventh Street. Inviting columned galleries lead to pilastered recessed entrances. Within are spacious center halls, flanked by pairs of high ceilinged rooms on each side. Wide pine floors, beautiful woodwork, plaster medallions and molding and marble mantels create an aura of gracious living.

The handsome masonry Payne-Strachan house at 1134 First is another of the earliest residences (1849) in the Garden District. It is an exquisite example of the two-story Classic center hall house with double level galleries. In a fitting historical footnote, Jefferson Davis died in this house in 1889.

Across Magazine Street and heading toward the river is the Irish District. Certainly less elegant than the Garden District, it is perhaps a more creative product of the energy and vitality of mid-19th century. There shacks, shanties, and wood boxes for single families or double occupancy, mostly one story, were thrown up with cypress frame or flatboat board construction. Irish and German immigrants pouring off the ships at the river's edge built these rent houses, working as hod carriers and laborers for contractors who could not obtain sufficient slave labor. Little did these men know that the results of their cheap labor and cheaper buildings—$500 to $5,000—would be, by the 1970s, one of New Orleans' most popular historic districts.

Demand for housing was such that use was made of the wood from flatboats that had floated downriver from Ohio, Kentucky, and Missouri bringing products to the port of New Orleans. The boats were dismantled and the lumber was re-used in house construction. These flatboat boards were set upright in the ground or placed vertically on sills. Sometimes they extended to provide two stories, being sawed off to make a gable roof line. Weather boards were nailed to the flatboat boards, and wallpaper with a cloth backing was applied on the inside. The front elevation of the resultant boxlike dwelling was decorated with woodwork ordered from the sash and door catalogs of the day. Box columns and simple cornices date the 1850s Classic-style examples. Paired brackets, segmental arch windows and cornices with parapets denote Italianate decoration of the 1860s and 1870s. Late Victorian scrolled brackets supporting overhangs for front porches or colonettes turned on a lathe represent the late 1870s and 80s. The result is surprisingly dynamic, esthetic, and lots of fun, especially to the large numbers of young people who have renovated their own Irish Channel treasures.

St. Charles Avenue

While Esplanade Avenue, bordering the French Quarter, once held sway as first among equals of America's avenues, its heyday is long gone. Nonetheless, New Orleans still possesses a grand boulevard, and anyone who has ever walked or driven along St. Charles Avenue with its tremendous live oaks and quaint streetcar will be hard pressed to find any street in America so magnificent. There remains some good-humored self-mockery among "Esplanade" families and "St. Charles" families. The latter claim that the Esplanade was for rich, money-grubbing Creole antebellum merchants, while the former maintain that St. Charles is for rich, money-grabbing American (post 1870) merchants. The two groupings now rub shoulders (and even mix genes) with alarming regularity.

From Louisiana Avenue uptown, the St. Charles Avenue homes and buildings are more opulent. Sacred Heart Academy (4521 St. Charles) was designed by Allison Owen in 1905 in the Classic Revival style with authentic New Orleans touches, such as colonnaded galleries and a cadence of arched openings, surrounded on three sides by a fenced courtyard. The 5800 block of St. Charles (between State and Eleanore) provides a beautiful sylvan setting for two elegant frame villa-style residences, surrounded by extensive gardens. The frame Italianate villa at 5800 St. Charles, at the uptown corner of Nashville Avenue, dates from 1870. Its raised basement and center hall plan with galleries and dormers is repeated in the adjacent Palacios House at 5824 St. Charles which was built in 1867 in a late Classic style. Nearby, at 5005 St. Charles, is the Clarke House, an Italianate mansion built in 1868 and now housing the Orleans Club. The epitome of the esthetic period is seen at the corner of St. Charles and Nashville Avenues at the downtown, river corner. Two large two-story frame houses (5724 and 5726 St. Charles) combine elements of the Eastlake, Queen Anne and other late 19th-century fads. Turrets, gables, multiple pediments, wood jigsaw work, turned colonettes are just a few of the profusions of forms frivolously combined for an eclectic effect in the two fantasies.

Audubon Park, and Tulane and Loyola Universities, were made possible by improvements brought to the area by the World's Industrial and Cotton Centennial Exposition of 1884–1885, which was located where the park now stands. To prepare for the exposition, streets in the area were improved and wharves were constructed along the river nearby to bring up building materials for the fair construction. After the exposition, these same wharves continued to receive building materials for the construction of Jefferson City and the University section. And, of course, for the universities themselves. Loyola was begun in 1904 and the Gothic Revival buildings there date from 1911. A feature of the Gothic Revival complex is Holy Name of Jesus Church designed in 1914 by the firm of DeBuys, Churchill and Labouisse. The Tulane campus, next to Loyola, is mainly Richardson Romanesque Revival, an 1894 homage to the famous Louisiana-born architect, Henry Hobson Richardson (1838–1886). The administration buildings of St. Mary's Dominican College, at St. Charles and Broadway, present in type and style a high contrast to their neighbors. The frame construction, with its wide galleries and ogee arches, is a reproduction of late Victorian, Indian, and Steamboat Gothic motifs combined by architect William Fitzner in 1882.

Audubon Place, a private street sold by Tulane University, was developed in 1894 and represents the local interpretation of the City Beautiful movement, as do the stone balustrades and gate posts leading to Audubon Park. The local interpretation and mixing of the Beaux Arts Classicism, the Neo-Classical Revival and the Georgian Period beginning in the early 1900s has been dubbed City Beautiful since the period coincided with the beginning of a conscious effort towards urban planning and coordination of the appearance of public amenities with the neo-Classic-electic taste in residential and commercial architecture.

Jefferson City, the University Section and Carrollton

The City of Jefferson, incorporated in the 1850s, linked together several small American upriver faubourgs from Louisiana Avenue to Octavia Street, and from the river to St. Charles Avenue. It remained rural, with a smattering of pretentious estates, until the World's Industrial and Cotton Centennial Exhibition in 1883. Similarly, five small villages upriver between Octavia and Carrollton City, now known as the University Section, also owe their appearance to the Fair. Within an amazingly short time the area abounded with examples of late Victorian (5349 Camp Street), Eastlake (4032 Prytania Street), Queen Anne (5433 Coliseum Street), and Edwardian (7030 St. Charles Avenue) styles of architecture—eclectic taste for an eclectic turn-of-the-century population.

The shotgun, however, became the hallmark of the area. This one-story frame house fits cozily on a standard 30' by 120' lot. Each dwelling is one room wide, with three to five equal-sized rooms extending to the rear. Invariably there is a front porch with wide overhang or a full, colonette supported gallery. The name derives from the fact the building is long and narrow like a shotgun barrel. Chimneys march one behind the other on a low hip roof while doors and mantels within progress front to the rear in a great commonality of space and form. It is as though the unheralded developers of the shotgun type had taken seriously Andrew Jackson Downing's admonition in his 1849 builders bible: "In every human habitation chimney tops ought to be conspicuous—they distinguish apartments destined for human beings from those designed for lodging cattle." A shotgun's kitchen is situated to the rear, with the bathroom, whether original or added, often a shedlike appendage.

The origins of the shotgun are conjectural, as are those of its close relative, the camelback. This is a shotgun with a second story over the back part, indicating the need for more space on one lot. The shotgun is ubiquitous throughout Uptown New Orleans, with rich variations of decoration. It is the epitome of "facade" architecture, front decoration tacked onto shoeboxlike buildings. Shotguns have been repeated all over town in a panoply of styles, appearing as early as 1850 in the Classic style in the Lower Garden District. Italianate examples are frequent in the Garden District, but the vast majority exhibit the deep overhang with scroll bracket supports, the wood fronts with quoins, dubbed late Victorian, dating from the 1880s. Not architect designed, most shotguns were built as rent houses for working-class people by wealthy developers who often constructed an entire block of identical shotguns. When prefabricated woodwork became available in catalogues, the combination of decorative detail created a lavish exhibition of design combinations along the streets. Turned columns, spindles and brackets (fretted, pierced and reticulated) abound and recall Oriental, Middle Eastern and Steamboat prototypes, all turning the Uptown streets of New Orleans into a giant puzzle of woodwork.

The City of Carrollton, at the Uptown river bend, represents still an earlier period of architectural development. It was founded in 1833 by railroad developers Laurent Millaudon, John Slidell, and Samuel Kohn. German surveyor Charles Zimpel laid it out and in 1852 it became the seat of Jefferson parish government. Henry Howard's courthouse at 719 Carrollton Avenue was designed in 1854 in Greek Revival style. It has been used as a school since 1874 when Carrollton, as well as the University Section, were annexed to New Orleans.

A contrast in style, but built in 1849, is one of the city's few Gothic-style residences at 1015 South Carrollton. Although popular elsewhere in America, the Gothic Revival style with deep gables and pointed arched windows was largely rejected by New Orleanians. The classical inspiration in architectural taste, as in literary preference, continued here through the 1870s. Here, however, is a gem, a brick English-inspired, Gothic-style house with an X-shape plan. Its picket fence and large verdant grounds provide an appropriate setting for this extraordinary brick country house.

The Esplanade

Begun on the downriver border of the French Quarter in 1805, the Esplanade is reputed to be the first "grand avenue" of America. Like its spiritual heirs, Mobile's Government Street and the Bronx' Grand Concourse, the Esplanade was allowed to deteriorate terribly. But, unlike its successors, the Esplanade is coming back.

The Esplanade extends from the Mississippi River to Bayou St. John, a distance of about three and a half miles. Forty years in developing, it reached the Bayou by 1850. It is an absolute storehouse of 19th-century architectural types and styles. Every decade of the 1800s is represented here in a rhythmical procession of columns, cornices, and rooflines, mile after mile. Types range from small square Creole cottages built before 1820 like 640 Esplanade to the large American brick townhouses with their pretentious entrances and monumental scaling like 741 Esplanade (1850). Contrasting are the Creole versions of the urban multilevel residence with its more delicate storehouse of 19th Esplanade (1847). Also seen here is a style called Second Empire, exemplified by 632 and 634 Esplanade, built in 1885–86 along with Queen Anne (2809 Esplanade, built in 1902), Edwardian (2127 Esplanade), and City Beautiful (2326 Esplanade) structures, and Mission Revival (2927), an early 20th-century style.

At the southern terminus of the Esplanade, just above the Mississippi, sits the old United States Mint, designed in 1836 by William Strickland on the site of the original French and Spanish fortifications which bordered the French Quarter down river. Related to Strickland's work in Nashville, Charleston, and Washington, the Mint's simplicity and restraint reflect the architect's clear, structural interpretation of the Greek Revival style. He selected an Ionic portico for the three-story building. Granite pilasters delineate the corners, and the scored plaster exterior surface was painted and penciled to resemble rustication. The building, 282 feet by 80 feet, with paving, fences, and necessary machinery cost $300,000, the building alone just $118,000.

Bayouward, large, opulent, multistory, side hall, galleried mansions sit all in a row of cynosures along this avenue. These come in assorted styles and colors of the mid-19th century: Classic, Italianate, and High Victorian. They are so prevalent along this stretch that they gave rise to the term "Esplanade Ridge Style."

Among the great mansions of the city is the Florence Luling House, once facing Esplanade, set deep in an entire square. Now it is tucked just off the avenue at 1438 Leda Street. Subdivision of the grounds in the 1920s with infill of incompatible and badly scaled bungalows completed the mutilation of James Gallier, Jr.'s magnificent 1865 effort. The city's most unusual and lavish example of the Italianate style, the house reflects the universal attributes of the style rather than the more regional and particular characteristics seen elsewhere in the city. The wide overhang projecting from the elevations, heavy balustrades encircling the house, a raised basement with rusticated surfaces, arched openings with keystones, and the projecting bays at the side of the structure denote a sophisticated interpretation of the Italianate style in the international vernacular. This entire monumental complex, including main building, wings, granite steps, the since disappeared iron fence, banquettes, terraces and outbuildings cost $24,000. In typical Creole fashion, Mr. Luling was outraged at the price and bitterly complained to the architect.

The Queen Anne-style center hall house at 2809 Esplanade is one of the more decorative late Victorian homes. The Dunbar House at 2453 somehow has survived alterations, which did not totally obscure the imposing slate mansard roof that reflects the Second Empire (1870) style. Nearby at 2306 Esplanade are the remaining sections of the Classic-style Musson-Degas House. It was once the home of a brother of the famous French artist, Edgar Degas. Degas lived here in 1873 when he painted in New Orleans. New Orleans architect Henry Howard is represented at his best in the 1859 Dufour-Baldwin House at 1707 Esplanade. This is an imposing Italianate side hall mansion with double galleries and featuring paired fluted columns.

Branching off the Esplanade to 2200 Bayou Road sits the late Spanish colonial plantation home of the Fleitas family. Built in the 1790s, it was moved to its present location about 1835 when a classic remodeling within included Greek Revival moldings and marble mantels. Spanish colonial characteristics are apparent in the hip roof, small dormers, turned wood columns, wide galleries, and full length casement openings (French doors). Adjacent to this, the only other house on the square, the Benachi-Torre House, is a *maison de maitre* or semirural, two-story manor house built in 1859. Beautifully situated on its spacious grounds, retaining some outbuildings, the double-galleried Classic residence has paired boxed columns between three openings, an unusual arrangement.

Faubourgs Marigny, Trémé, and Bywater

The Creole faubourgs were New Orleans' answer to the urban suburb. Faubourg Marigny came naturally into being as the French Quarter outgrew itself. Laid out in 1805 from the plantation of Bernard de Marigny, its original inhabitants were European immigrants, the expanding Creole population and emigres from Haiti and Ste Domingue, many of whom were free-persons-of-color. Faubourg Trémé is similar in origin and architecture with an accent on the large and prosperous French-speaking, free black population of the early 19th century. Life here is charmingly captured in the novel *Toucoutou,* written by Edward S. Tinker, of all things, a New York lawyer.

Marigny lies just across the Esplanade, downriver, and Trémé just across the Vieux Carré ramparts (Rampart Street). Creole cottages, built to the owner's taste, predominate. These hall-less, four-room, almost square, one-and-one-half-story cottages are represented in every form. They come with or without dormers, with galleries or with charming *abat vents* (overhangs). Most were placed at the *banquette* (sidewalk) or some were set back on larger lots. Some had side gables, others canted hip roofs. Some are built of brick and have common walls. Others are detached or semidetached with narrow flagged passageways to the all important patio with *par-terre* garden, the rear cabinet gallery, and the brick service buildings beyond.

The patio, situated behind the rear gallery of the main house and facing the front gallery or balcony of the service building, provided an outdoor, walled living area for the inhabitants of a Creole complex. Based on designs popularized in France at Versailles by André LeNotre, the patio was paved with a central axis out from which formal *par-terres* or beds were laid out symetrically. The beds were planted with orange, lemon or sweet olive trees, and edged with boxwood. The rear galleries had small rooms or *cabinets* at each end. The *cabinets* might contain a stairway, nurseries or dressing rooms. Facing the *cabinet* galleries across the patio were usually a two-story brick building with a gallery or balcony. These service buildings contained a kitchen, summer dining room, laundry, servants' rooms, or sometimes bedrooms for male family members.

The Dolliole-Clapp cottage at 1436 Pauger and its neighbor across the street at 1445 Pauger, the Boutin-Flettrich house, epitomize much that is Creole in New Orleans architecture. Built in 1820 by Jean L. Dolliole, an eminent French-speaking, free-person-of-color and builder, the Dolliole house has a picturesque flat-tile hip roof. The overhang with its characteristic cant adds charm as do the batten shutters, wrought-iron strap hinges, and narrow delicate window and door surrounds. Typically urban, the house is built low to the ground. The brick is, of course, plastered in the typical French and Spanish New Orleans style.

The Boutin-Flettrich house, built in 1825, is of brick-between-post construction and plastered. The sophisticated structure was built by an unknown builder for Antoine Boutin, a commission merchant. The arched-light dormers with pilasters and pediments are examples of the fine decorative detail found in the Creole areas. A high pitch roof has gable sides with edges projected upwards. The recessed doorway has fluted surrounds and a petaled fanlight bespeaking the Creole style. Notice also Federal elements, such as the Ionic pilasters. The narrow entrance is Creole as are the overhang, batten shutters, and rear cabinet gallery.

The church spires that punctuate the skyline throughout Marigny form a contrast to the small and intimate scale of the surrounding frame construction. In the 2300 block of Burgundy, St. Peter and Paul Church, designed in 1860 by Henry Howard, was built for an Irish Catholic congregation. Holy Trinity for the growing German Catholic population was designed by T. E. Giraud in 1853. Its neo-Romanesque style with onion-shaped domes dominates the area. Another spire at 3000 Daupine Street marks St. Vincent de Paul Catholic Church, a Lewis Reynolds' work, built in 1866 for yet another group of Germans. The applied and recessed brickwork of German and Irish artisans illustrates the fine masonry work by immigrants of the period.

A radically different type of architecture can be found downriver at Egania and Douglas streets in the Bywater section. There sit Captain Paul Doullut's two almost identical Steamboat Gothic houses that were built in 1905. Doullut's profession, steamboat captain, is reflected in the design and decoration of his houses. Encircling decks are festooned with wood garlands draped as balustrades. Ingenious and creative use of cypress ornamentation adds distinction to this pair of landmarks. Further along the levee at Delery Street is the New Orleans Barracks (now Jackson Barracks) designed in 1825 by Lt. Frederick Wilkinson. Remaining today is a handsome brick complex of parallelogram design with one picturesque sally gate, two towers, the officers' quarters and, nearby, the post magazine where the arms and ammunition were stored. Officers who were to become famous generals of the Confederate and Union armies saw duty at the barracks.

Marigny and Bywater (the neighborhood beside the river extending to St. Bernard Parish), presently undergoing revitalization, are emerging as a major art colony, spiritually akin to New York's Soho district. Trémé is also showing signs of improvement. A principal landmark of Trémé, America's first city-sponsored subdivision (1812), is Louis Armstrong Park, an urban renewal project beginning in the late 1950s.

Within Armstrong Park which fronts on Rampart Street are three important buildings that represent the history of the Creole suburbs and the birthplace of New Orleans jazz. French-speaking emigres from the West Indies came to New Orleans in 1808, re-establishing their Masonic Lodge in temporary quarters. In 1820 Bernard Thibaud designed Perseverance Lodge #4 for these Masons. Ten years later, Francois Correjolles and Jean Chaigneau built beside it a beautiful *maison a etage* (two-story building) for the Lodge. Creole and black jazz bands performed there for social and cultural occasions of all types. It was here that many musicians developed their distinctive rhythms and style. Similarly, the Rabassa–de Pouilly house, dating from the early 19th century, is the only remaining residential building on the nine squares comprising the park. The house not only has architectural distinction, but it was the home of French architect J. N. B. de Pouilly who was responsible for much of the French Quarter and Creole suburb building inventory. The raised Creole cottage is built of brick-between-post construction, covered with weatherboard. It has the traditional hall-less Creole plan of four rooms, two across the front and two deep.

Bayou St. John and City Park

French Canadians settled between Lake Pontchartrain and Bayou Road before the founding of the city, beginning in 1704. While the original plantations of Canadians Juchereau St. Denis and Rivard Lavigne have disappeared, the ambience here continues to reflect the early French colonial period, where landholders presided over working indigo, rice, tobacco, and wax myrtle plantations.

The house which stands at 1300 Moss Street on the shore of Bayou St. John may incorporate the original Lavigne house, where this family resided for generations, industriously turning to farm staples and cattle after indigo had its day. They also provided tar, turpentine and lime for an active ship repair business.

At 1440 Moss Street stands the Pitot house, home to an illustrious array of residents. Spanish colonial planter-merchant Don Bartolomeo Bosque built the house about 1799. A major resident was James Pitot, French Creole Mayor of New Orleans. It is now a National Historic Landmark, open to the public by the Louisiana Landmark Society. The Pitot House boasts a steep hip roof covering deep galleries on four sides, leading to French casement doors with transoms. These lead into each room of the hall-less house, the wide galleries of which recall French colonial prototypes. The raised basement, with its heavy brick columns, supports the main level galleries. The columns and weatherboard exterior are characteristic of French building in New Orleans. Cypress vertical board fencing set into the ground adds to the French colonial aura.

Also on Moss Street along Bayou St. John (numbers 1454, 924 and 1342) are early 19th-century *maisons de maitre* (or country houses). These weekend getaway spots face the Bayou on properties which originally extended three acres deep. These were once extensive rural estates with *par-terred* gardens and orangeries, owned by city speculators, merchants, and developers, Creole and American.

The New Orleans City Park site was a working plantation from 1708 until 1850 when owner John McDonogh left the land to the cities of New Orleans and Baltimore. In 1891, Victor Anseman formed the City Park Improvement Association which developed the park and has managed it since 1896. Architectural embellishments are primarily Neo-Classic and Beaux Arts in the spirit of the early 20th century. There are bandstands, fountains, pavillions, arcades and most important, the New Orleans Museum of Art. The museum, built in 1910 by James Koch of New Orleans after designs of the Chicago firm of Ledenbaum and Marx, was a gift to the city by Isaac Delgado, a prominent Jewish philanthropist. He donated $150,000 for construction of the museum. According to the designers, the building, Neo-Classical Revival in style, was "sufficiently modified to give a subtropical appearance."

The Cemeteries

New Orleans' cemeteries merit special attention. Microcosms of 19th-century architectural styles, they have been celebrated as far back as 1834 when visiting architect Benjamin Latrobe described and illustrated them for publication. The fiction of George Washington Cable in the late 19th century and the film *Easy Rider* in 1969 featured them. These cemeteries with their aboveground burials, tropical planting, wide avenues of walkways, interesting alleyways and resultant visual appeal offer dimensions not available in other American cities. Here they are also esthetically appealing parks that have served through the centuries as promenades, concert sites, and meeting places.

The possibility of multiple use for cemeteries became a reality in 1788 when Spanish colonial officials established St. Louis Cemetery No. 1. It occupies the site between streets known today as Basin, Conti, Trémé and St. Louis near the French Quarter and the Central Business District. The Spaniards, in the Roman tradition long since established in southern Spain in the time of emporers Trajan and Hadrian, enclosed the site with high brick walls containing tiers of tombs for aboveground burials. Within the resulting square were avenues and paths with spaces for architecturally conceived multiple-burial family tombs. Soon, various benevolent societies provided multitiered tombs for members and their families, as well as handsome memorials. These and wall vaults soon became the established norm for New Orleans' cemeteries.

Varieties of scale, materials, and tomb designs based on Classic, Oriental, Gothic, and Egyptian motifs provide a rich diversity here. Sculptural ornamentation and its symbolism provides displays of both iconographical and purely ornamental designs. The small scale, and resulting cost savings, made possible exquisite examples of wrought- and cast-iron enclosures, seating and decoration. Picket tops and finials exhibit crosses, projectile points, urns, and *fleur de lys* in marvelous combinations. Wrought-iron swirls, lyres, scrolls, and arrow patterns, as well as the architect-designed ornate tombs of marble, granite, and masonry reveal great sophistication of conception.

St. Louis No. 2, built near its predecessor in Faubourg Trémé in 1823, occupies the square bound by Claiborne Avenue, N. Robertson, St. Louis, and Conti streets. Here the tradition of aboveground burials was solidified. Lafayette Cemetery No. 1, at Washington Avenue and Prytania Street in the heart of the Garden District, was established in the 1850s for the fast growing Lafayette City, formerly Faubourg Livaudais, and it belongs to the City of New Orleans, whereas the St. Louis cemeteries belong to the Archdiocese. Continuing the old Spanish layout and aboveground burial system, Lafayette provided burial sites for many of the German and Irish immigrants who succumbed to the devastating yellow fever epidemics of the 1850s and 60s.

The two cemeteries founded for and by fire fighting organizations provide special interest. Cypress Grove, also known as the fireman's cemetery, was founded in 1840 at the end of Canal Street on what was then the banks of Bayou Metairie (120 City Park Avenue). This was followed by Greenwood Cemetery, established for firemen in 1852 nearby (5242 Canal Boulevard). It appears to be the most crowded of the New Orleans' cemeteries with lots just 6 feet by 9 feet, some 20,500 of which are dotted with architectural entombments of great variety of style and type. There the Ladies Benevolent Association of Louisiana erected a Confederate Monument marking the mass grave of 600 Confederate soldiers.

The well-known Metairie Cemetery was situated in 1872 on top of the old Metairie Race Course, now bound by the Pontchartrain Expressway and Metairie Road, then Bayou Metairie (5100 Pontchartrain Boulevard). It was promoted as a cemetery without wall vaults, with a park-like appearance to contain elegant and grandiose tombs and monuments. Architect Benjamin F. Harrod utilized the 1 1/16 mile track racetrack as the cemetery's principal avenue. Memorials like St. Roch Chapel in the cemetery in the Marigny area (1725 St. Roch Avenue near Elysian Fields Avenue) was built for the German community. It well represents the working-class Catholics. The charming chapel, designed to resemble the chancel of a Gothic church, has great popularity which stems from the association of St. Roch with the alleviation of the suffering of crippled and infirm persons.

EXPLORING NEW ORLEANS

Touring the Big Easy

by
JOHN R. KEMP

New Orleans is a great city and a fun place to visit. Like any other city, it is divided into a number of sections and neighborhoods. However, very few of them are conducive to walking tours because of their size, general interest, and sometimes dangers to visitors. Since the early 1970s, New Orleans has been considered in terms of metropolitan New Orleans with all of its suburban communities included. Each has a flavor of its own. Metro-New Orleans includes the French Quarter (the original city also called the *Vieux Carré*), the Central Business District, Faubourgs Marigny and Trémé, Garden District, Irish Channel, Uni-

143

versity Section (Uptown), Carrollton, Lakefront, Gentilly, Bywater, and the parishes (counties) of Jefferson, St. Tammany and St. Bernard.

Finding one's way around any large city can present problems. New Orleans has its peculiarities as all cities do. Sometimes they can be confusing.

Most of New Orleans is divided into uptown and downtown with the streets running north and south from Canal Street—and that's where the confusion begins. Uptown usually refers to a section of the city that includes the Garden District, Irish Channel, University Section and Carrollton. Downtown can mean the Central Business District or most of New Orleans downriver (the Mississippi River, that is) from Canal Street. Canal Street is the dividing line between Uptown and Downtown. The closer you get to Canal Street driving on streets designated with north and south, the lower the block number. Downtown includes the French Quarter, Faubourg Marigny, Fauberg Trémé, and Tidewater areas. Uptown and downtown are also directions of travel.

If someone says they are going uptown or downtown, and are not referring to a special section of the city, he simply means he is traveling in an upriver or downriver direction. When New Orleanians give directions, they use the river, Lake Pontchartrain, and the directions uptown (upriver) and downtown (downriver) as points of reference. If you, the visitor, ask a New Orleanian for the location of a particular building, he or she will use the river and lake rather than the points of the compass to guide you. If you are driving in an upriver direction (uptown), everything on the left is riverside. Lakeside will be on the right. Facing downriver, everything on the left is lakeside and right, riverside. Try to keep that straight. For example, the Marriott Hotel is located at the corner of Canal and Chartres streets. By New Orleans direction, the hotel is on the downtown, river corner of Canal and Chartres because it is downriver (as the river current flows) of Canal Street and on the riverside of Chartres as opposed to the lakeside.

As to north and south streets, Canal Street is the dividing line. North streets head downtown (downriver) from Canal and south streets run uptown (upriver) from Canal. Remember upriver from Canal is south and downriver is north.

Hopefully, if you are not irrevocably confused, you are now anxious to see the Big Easy.

Bear in mind that like other large cities in the U.S., New Orleans has a very high crime rate, especially street crimes, and you should be careful where you walk day or night. Walking in the French Quarter and Central Business District during daytime hours is generally safe. The streets are filled with visitors and locals having a good time or going about their business, but remote and dimly lighted areas of both sections should be avoided at night. Also, be extremely careful at night around the Union Passenger Terminal and the Louisiana Superdome. If traveling to and from hotels and restaurants in that area, take a cab. The best ways to see other sections of the city and surrounding communities are by automobile or guided tour. These warnings are not intended to frighten you, but to help you enjoy New Orleans more.

French Quarter

Before beginning a formidable walking tour of the *Vieux Carré*, a visitor should know something about the Quarter's beginnings. The French Quarter was the original city of New Orleans. Although it has a definite Caribbean flavor and old world patina, New Orleans is an example of early city planning. It was laid out in a grid pattern with a large public square facing the Mississippi River.

The year 1718 is officially given for the founding of New Orleans, but the *Vieux Carré* did not begin to take on its current configuration until 1721.

The diplomacy and politics that went into naming the city's first streets were strokes of genius. As historian John Chase notes in his delightful book on the origins of New Orleans street names, *Frenchmen Desire Good Children,* Bourbon, Orleans, Burgundy, and Royal streets were so named in honor of the royal families of France. The Conti, Chartres, and Conde families were cousins to the Bourbons and Orleans. (Conde Street was once a section of Chartres Street from Jackson Square to Esplanade Avenue before the name was dropped in 1865. Chartres Street now extends from Canal Street to Esplanade Avenue.) St. Peter Street was named for Peter, an ancestor of the Bourbon family. Louis IX, the Saint-King, was honored with St. Louis Street and Louis XIII's widowed Queen Ann got St. Ann Street. Toulouse and Dumaine streets were named for Louis XIV's politically powerful royal bastard children. Chartres and Conde also were Louis XIV's sons-in-law and Louis XV's House of Burgundy also was remembered. Dauphine Street probably got its name from the financially powerful Parish brothers of Dauphine, France. They invested heavily in France's Louisiana venture. Of course, New Orleans itself was named for Philippe, Duc d'Orleans, who was looking after the French throne for the young Louis XV.

The French Quarter, unlike historical districts in other cities, is a living city. The buildings are not props in some historical re-enactment. People reside, work, and play here as they have done for over two and a half centuries. The aromas of age, garlic, and roasted coffee hang heavy in the damp air. The streets and alleys are often dirty and broken sidewalks make walking difficult at times. And yet this shabbiness adds

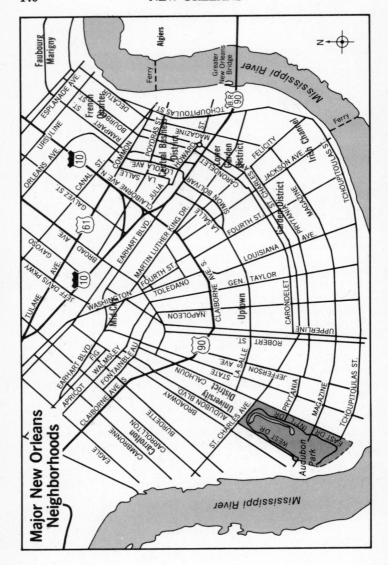

Major New Orleans Neighborhoods

French Quarter. The Vieux Carre, the Old Quarter, is where the city began in 1718. With its 18th- and early 19th-century buildings, it is the center of the city's cultural history. It is filled with many fine hotels, restaurants serving Creole food, historical architecture, museums, jazz and other night clubs, and an atmosphere foreign to most Americans. This is by far the liveliest area in New Orleans by day and by night.

Uptown. Uptown New Orleans generally includes several neighborhoods: the Central Business District, the Lower Garden District, the Garden District, the Irish Channel, the University Area, and Carrollton.

Central Business District. The CBD, lying adjacent and upriver to the French Quarter, is the heart of New Orleans' business community. It is the site of the 1984 Louisiana World Exposition, the Superdome, and many fine hotels. It was also the city's first suburb in the late 18th century where English-speaking Americans settled. Alive on weekdays with business people, this area quiets down during the evenings and particularly on weekends when workers are elsewhere.

Lower Garden District. Many fine houses dating from the 1830s to the 1850s are located in this area. Surrounded by a blighted area, the Lower Garden District is being revitalized by young affluent New Orleans couples. It was one of the finest residential areas of New Orleans before the Civil War. Use caution when walking in this area—and avoid walking here after dark.

Garden District. Adjacent to the Lower Garden District, this area is one of the finest residential neighborhoods in the country. Its magnificent High Victorian mansions date from the 1840s to the 1870s when Southern cotton was King and Louisiana sugar was Queen. This area is home to New Orleans' gentry.

University Area and Carrollton. The city's silk stocking district that surrounds Tulane and Loyola universities, Dominican College, and Audubon Park and Zoo. There are a number of fine restaurants, shops, and bars that cater to college students and Uptown residents.

Irish Channel. Rich in architectural styles, this has always been a working-class neighborhood. It has long been a depressed area but is now being slowly revitalized—however, try to avoid walking in this area. Also known for its hundreds of antique stores along Magazine St.

Mid-City. City Park, one of the largest urban parks in the country, is located on scenic Bayou St. John with its many fine examples of 18th-century West Indies plantation houses. Area residents are mostly descendants of Italian and French settlers. Also Metairie Cemetery, with its magnificently ornate above-ground tombs, is located in this area.

Lakefront. Scenic drive along Lake Pontchartrain shoreline. Great picnic area and very popular among New Orleanians. The University of New Orleans is located here.

Algiers. Easily reached by ferry from Canal Street, Algiers Point is a good example of a late 19th-century neighborhood on its way back. However, it is not the best place to walk at night. The area is populated mostly by old New Orleans families.

to the area's charm. Overhanging galleries and balconies block both sun and rain.

A visit to the French Quarter should begin in the very early morning before the midday sun burns off the morning river fog. The air is fragrant and the aged colors of the centuries-old buildings are so much more vivid in the soft golden sunlight. You can see the Quarter come alive with people bustling off to work, sidewalk artists pulling their carts off to Jackson Square and Pirates Alley, and folks bringing their produce to the Farmer's Market in the French Market. Also, you will probably discover a few people on the street—derelicts or revelers— who didn't make it home the night before. The streets, shops and cafes in the *Vieux Carré* are crowded with people seven days a week. At night, however, most of the action is located on Bourbon and Royal streets.

Jackson Square

The best place to start a walking tour is in Jackson Square, once called the Place d'Armes by the French and the Plaza de Armas by the Spanish. During the colonial era, the Place d'Armes was the town square where the militia drilled and town folk met. It also was the place where public hangings, beheadings, breakings at the wheel, and brandings were carried out. There are countless stories about public executions and floggings, but perhaps one of the most bizarre cases was in 1754. Several soldiers stationed on Cat Island just off today's Mississippi Gulf Coast mutinied and killed their oppressive and sadistic commander. The soldiers were later captured and executed in the Place d'Armes. Two were broken at the wheel with sledge hammers and a third, a Swiss soldier, was nailed alive in a coffin and then sawed in half.

The Place d'Armes was renamed Jackson Square in the 1850s in honor of Andrew Jackson, the hero of the Battle of New Orleans at the time of the War of 1812, who later became president of the United States. In the center of the square is an equestrian statue of Jackson executed by Clark Mills in 1856. It is actually only one of three cast: one is located in the center of Lafayette Park in front of the White House in Washington, D.C. and the third in Nashville, Tennessee, Jackson's home. On the base is carved "The Union Must and Shall Be Preserved." The words were placed there by General Benjamin Butler during the Civil War occupation of New Orleans by U.S. troops.

Today Jackson Square springs to life each day with tourists, artists, street musicians, jugglers, and a host of wandering minstrels that follow the sun and tourist trade.

Facing the square is St. Louis Cathedral with the Spanish Cabildo on the left and the Presbytere on the right. The first Church of St. Louis was built on the site in 1727 and destroyed by fire in 1788. The present church dates in part from 1794 with extensive remodeling in 1849. The stained-glass windows in the front of the Cathedral were donated by the Spanish government. Several colonial officials are buried beneath the floor. The Cathedral was renovated in the 1970s and it is the seat of the Archdiocese of New Orleans.

The Presbytere is the headquarters of the Louisiana State Museum complex. Under construction from 1795 until 1847, the building's original purpose was to house the priests who administer St. Louis Cathedral. It never served that purpose. After the Presbytere was completed, it was taken over by the government and served as a court-house until the early 20th century when it became part of the Louisiana State Museum. Facing the building you will notice to the right of the colonnade a strange oblong form made of iron. It's the *Pioneer*—the Confederate Navy's first submarine which they sank in Lake Pontchar-train in order to keep it out of Union hands. Inside, the Presbytere contains six exhibit galleries that feature important changing exhibits that pertain to the history of New Orleans and Louisiana. You will also find exhibits of antique toys, fashions, and fire fighting equipment.

The Cabildo (1795–1799) to the left of the Cathedral is also part of the Louisiana State Museum system and it too contains important historical exhibitions. There are eight exhibit galleries and you will find Napoleon Bonaparte's death mask which was made on the Island of St. Helena. The 1803 Louisiana Purchase transfer ceremonies took place in the Sala Capitular, located on the second floor of the Cabildo. The building got its name from the Spanish Cabildo—or council—that met there during the Spanish colonial period (1762–1803). After the Louisi-ana Purchase, the Cabildo became the city hall and later the home of the state supreme court. Located on the third floor is an excellent exhibition on the history of the steamboat and the Mississippi River. From April 29 through November 18, 1984, a special exhibit, "Louis XIV, the Sun King," will be shown.

Novelist William Faulkner, who once resided in a small apartment behind the Cabildo (at 624 Pirate's Alley), described this ancient seat of government as a "squat Don who wears his hat in the king's pres-ence, not for the sake on his own integer vitae, but because some cannot, gloomed in sinister derision of an ancient hoke; within the portals Iowa wondered aloud first, why a building as old and ugly could have any value; and second, if it were valuable, why they let it become so shabby."

The Louisiana Purchase transfer ceremony took place in the Cabildo in 1803 and in 1825 the Marquis de Lafayette used the place as his private residence during his visit to New Orleans. The mansard roof was added in 1847. Lying between the Cabildo and the Cathedral is

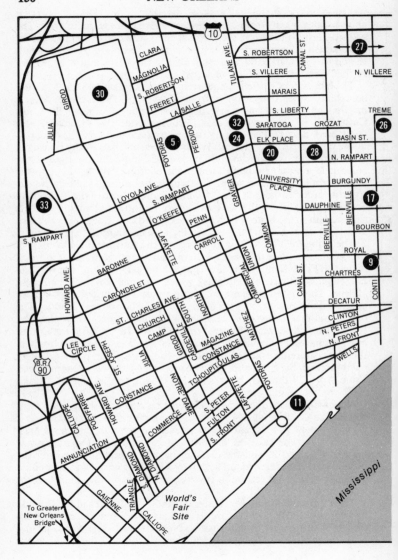

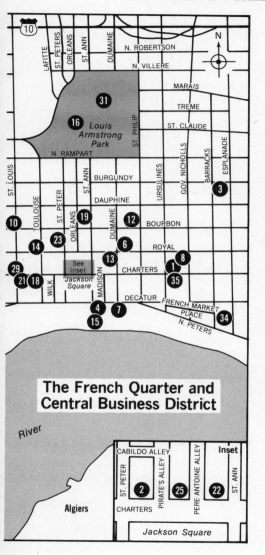

The French Quarter and Central Business District

Points of Interest

1) Beauregard House
2) Cabildo
3) Cabrini Doll Museum
4) Café du Monde
5) City Hall
6) Cornstalk-Iron Fence
7) French Market
8) Gallier House
9) Greater New Orleans Convention and Visitors Bureau
10) Hermann-Grima House
11) International Trade Mart
12) Lafitte's Blacksmith Shop
13) Madame John's Legacy
14) Merieult House
15) Moon Walk
16) Municipal Auditorium
17) Musée Conti Wax Museum
18) Napoleon House
19) New Orleans Spring Fiesta Mid-19th Century Town House
20) Orpheum Theater
21) Pharmacy Museum
22) Presbytere
23) Preservation Hall
24) Public Library
25) St. Louis Cathedral
26) St. Louis Cemetery 1
27) St. Louis Cemetery 2
28) Saenger Performing Arts Center
29) State Wildlife and Fisheries Building
30) Superdome
31) Theatre for the Performing Arts
32) Trailways Station
33) Union Station (Amtrak and Greyhound Depots)
34) U.S. Mint
35) Ursuline Convent

Pirate's Alley. Legend says that pirates once dueled there, but some observers say the alley's original name, Orleans Alley, was changed several decades ago for the tourist trade. Today, it is a popular place for sidewalk artists to display their work which varies in quality.

Jackson Square is bordered on the upper and lower sides by the Pontalba Apartments. They were built in 1851 by native New Orleanian Micaela Almonester, the Baroness Pontalba, who returned to New Orleans to escape the 1848 revolution in France. The story of the Baroness Pontalba is one of those interesting dramas history provides. Micaela was the daughter of Don Andres Almonester, a wealthy New Orleans merchant who financed construction of the Cabildo, Cathedral, Presbytere, and many other public buildings in the city after the great fire of 1788. Micaela married a distant cousin, Celestin Pontalba, and moved to France. Over the years, Micaela and her father-in-law, the baron, became deadly enemies. One day the aging baron decided to kill her. He quietly entered her boudoir, locked the door behind him, and shot her several times. Thinking she was dead, he turned the gun to his head and fired. The baron died, but miraculously she survived. Micaela then became baroness, divorced her husband, and returned to New Orleans with a substantial divorce settlement. With the settlement money she built both Pontalba buildings, often wearing pants and climbing ladders to inspect the work herself. When the buildings were completed, she and her children moved into apartment 508 and rented out the other apartments and ground level commercial spaces. The Baroness then went to work refurbishing and landscaping Jackson Square.

The upper Pontalba building (the one on the left facing the Cathedral) is owned by the city, while the lower building is owned and maintained by the Louisiana State Museum. The ground floors of both buildings house shops and cafés and the upper stories are private residences. A visit to the state museum's 1850 House in the lower Pontalba is well worth the effort. It is furnished in the style of an upper-middle-class New Orleans family residence of the 1850s. Also, notice the initials "AP"—Almonester Pontalba—in the grill work.

Perhaps the best view of the square at any time of the day is from the public viewing platform on the riverside of Decatur Street. Built by the city in the mid-1970s, it offers the full grandeur of the square and surrounding buildings. During the day the area is alive with fountains, street bands, jugglers and other sidewalk entertainers. It bustles with life and is a favorite spot for visitors.

Behind the viewing platform, the city also built the "Moon Walk" (named for former Mayor "Moon" Landrieu). It is one of the few spots in the city where the visitor can get a good front seat view of the river and ships. Actually, it is quite an exciting feeling to watch the steamer

The 1984 Louisiana World Exposition

May 12 - November 11, 1984

"The World's in New Orleans and they came to see the show at the World's Fair in Mardi Gras City." That's the message that has been sung across the country by the Fair's Musical Ambassadors since May of 1983, heralding the 1984 Louisiana World Exposition (LWE). The official mascot of the Fair, a Pelican named Seymore D. Fair, has also been ever-present. The Fair promises the best sights and sounds, and a wealth of experiences from around the world—not to mention the U.S. and the state of Louisiana—ranging from special exhibitions, food, music, performers, events, fine arts, and technology.

The United Nations designated the 1980s as "The Decade of International Drinking Water Supply and Sanitation." In keeping with that, the LWE's theme is "The World of Rivers: Fresh Water as a Source of Life." The aim of the Exposition is to create an environment where ideas, accomplishments, cultural traditions, and technology may be exchanged, and solutions explored, for maintaining the fresh water supply. This will be accomplished through thematic exhibitions, demonstrations, fountains, sculptures, and aquatic performances.

The Fair is a virtual celebration of the role of rivers in national and international life. The Fair spotlights the crucial link between fresh water and life-demands for it, and calls attention to the need to conserve and protect our freshwater resources from pollution and ecological disruption.

The $350 million World's Fair is hosted by the governments of the U.S.A., the State of Louisiana, and the City of New Orleans in conjunction with the Louisiana World Exposition, Inc. The choice of New Orleans is particularly appropriate as it is the nation's busiest port in foreign and domestic tonnage. Breezes from the Mississippi River offset New Orleans' notorious summer temperatures and all exhibits are air conditioned. In fact, roughly 55% of all exhibit and concession space is indoors. A feeling of coolness also pervades because of the network of fountains, water sculpture, waterfalls, lagoons, aqueducts, and the 1.5-acre Watergarden that adorns the site. The 82-acre LWE site stretches along the Mississippi River in New Orleans' historic warehouse district. It is adjacent to the Central Business District and just a short walk from the French Quarter. Some 11 million visitors are expected during the 6 months the Fair is open, with an estimated daily peak of about 71,000 people.

DATES AND TIMES

The Fair officially opens on Saturday, May 12, and closes on Sunday, November 11, 1984.

The Fair gates open daily at 10:00 A.M. The Pavilions close at 10:00 P.M. but the Fulton St. entertainment area doesn't close until 3:00 A.M.

THE FAIR SITE

The 82-acre site is bounded in the east by the Mississippi River; west, by South Peters St; south by Erato St.; and north by Canal St.

The main entrances are the Canal Gate at Girod and South Front Sts. and the Bridge Gate at Erato and South Front Sts. Both entrances are provided with ticketing facilities. The Canal Gate is accessible to pedestrians and cabs and the Bridge Gate is near the parking lot. From the Canal Gate, pathways lead to the main body of the site, marked by an open rotunda and vista opening to lagoons and lush tropical foliage. More pedestrian walkways lead to other areas of the site. A winding stream and shady walk lead you to the Great Hall Exhibition Center. It dominates the central area of the site and houses the Central Theme Pavilion, the Louisiana State Exhibit, and special exhibits. Opening off a pathway within the building are the state and corporate exhibits, plus performers on floating stages amid a cool leafy setting along the stream. Corporate and other temporary exhibits are located in the northern adjoining parcel of land and the Vatican Pavilion is nearby on South Front St. next to the Fulton St. Mall. At the river's edge, a riverfront promenade leads past the International Pavilion, the U.S. Pavilion, theme structures, and a riverfront park. The NASA exhibit is also here and features the U.S. Space Shuttle. Historic ships and naval vessels may be seen docked along the riverfront. This whole riverside development is tied by bridges to other areas of the site and to the main Exhibition Hall. The southern parcel contains the main performance area with the International Amphitheater and other performance tents.

ADMISSION/TICKETS

Admission prices for one day are: $15 for adults (ages 12–54); $14 for children (ages 4–11) and senior citizens (aged 55 and over). If tickets are bought for two consecutive days, the rate is $28 for adults and $26 for children and senior citizens. Children under 3 are allowed in free of charge. Special group rates are available. Season passes are also available for special group prices that will enable guests to visit the Fair on an unlimited basis.

A ticket to the Fair entitles you to unlimited rides on the automatic air conditioned monorail that loops around the site and through several pavilions, plus entry into all pavilions, exhibits and regularly scheduled entertainment at the 12 performance areas. The special star attractions at the International Amphitheater and the Vatican Pavilion require an extra ticket and are *not* covered by your general admission.

FACILITIES FOR HANDICAPPED TRAVELERS

The Louisiana World Exposition site has been developed barrier-free for total access to the handicapped. Wheelchairs, as well as motorized carts for the aged or infirmed, are available for rent on the Exposition grounds. Special tours are also offered for the blind and for the deaf (contact the hospitality office at 566–1984 to make arrangements).

In addition, the Louisiana World Exposition Committee for the Developmentally Disabled has provided a communications system for the speech and hearing impaired. The system, using special T.V. monitor and keyboard combinations, is located at the Fair Information Center. Six smaller devices are located in information booths at emergency services throughout the site. Transmission of the signal is through a standard telephone. (From now until the Fair opens on May 12, 1984, the central device at the Exposition Information Center has a special telephone number to call regarding general information for the Fair: (504) 566–2070. After the Exposition begins, the central device will be tied to the six smaller units on the site, giving on-site information to the disabled, as well as providing a link to off-site communications by telephone.)

TRANSPORTATION

To the Fair. New Orleans is accessible by air, water, rail, bus, and automobile.

By car: The main interstates into New Orleans are I-10, I-55, and I-59.

By bus: Trailways is offering special tour packages during the LWE that will include hotel arrangements and sightseeing tours in and around New Orleans.

By train: Amtrak is offering a variety of special tours ranging from 3- to 6-day stays and one tour offered especially for students.

By air: Delta, the official airline of the LWE, has developed a number of vacation packages linked to the Fair that are offered out of key foreign and domestic cities.

By boat: The official steamboat company of the LWE is the Delta Queen Steamboat Company which will offer 17 World's Fair cruises during the Fair and 16 World's Fair Holiday Cruises aboard the *Delta Queen* and the *Mississippi Queen* overnight paddlewheel boats.

Fair Site Terminals and Entries. There are 2 bus terminals at the Fair site: one for tour buses and the other for shuttle bus service. Both are located in the main parking area near the Bridge Gate. Shuttle buses depart on set schedules to satellite parking lots and selected destinations around New Orleans.

Taxi stands, pick-ups and drop-offs, are located at the Canal Main Entrance Gate and along South Peters at Girod Street.

Recreational vehicles, private cars, and tour and charter buses are being diverted to the Greater New Orleans Bridge at the end of the Fair site and passengers will enter the area by the Bridge Entrance gate.

Parking. 47 acres of land adjacent to the Fair site were leased from the Mississippi Pacific Railroad (MOPAC) for parking. The parking area is roughly bounded by Annunciation, Race, and Erato streets and the Mississippi flood wall. It accommodates approximately 5,400 automobiles and serves as the principal terminal for charter buses and shuttle buses. Security guards patrol the area and shuttle tram cars provide transportation from the lot to the Bridge Gate.

Two other parking areas accommodate about another 2,900 automobiles: one in Algiers at Teche and Lamarque streets (New Orleans' west bank) and the other at a location near Broad and Poydras streets.

Around the Fair. A 1.4 mile air-conditioned monorail ride will whisk you around the Fair site and through some pavilions. An estimated 3,500 visitors per hour will ride it. Your admission ticket entitles you to unlimited rides on the monorail.

The $12 million Aerial Gondola ride links New Orleans's west bank (at Teche and Lamarque streets in Algiers) to the east bank terminal located next to the New Orleans Convention and Exhibition Center (Great Hall) at the the Fair Site. The 3½ minute ride gives you a sweeping view of New Orleans and the Mississippi River. The cost is $3.50 round trip. Each car can carry up to 6 passengers and roughly 3,600 passengers will be transported every hour. Once the Fair closes, the aerial gondola will remain as a permanent commuter service.

INFORMATION SERVICES

The Louisiana World Exposition Center will answer any questions you have on how to get tickets, what's happening on the Fair site, how to get literature on the Fair, on-site entertainment schedules, emergency services, etc. Call (504) 525-FAIR (504-525-3247). In addition to the Fair information, the center can also provide information on events around the state of Louisiana. You can also write to the Tour and Convention Department, 1984 Louisiana World Exposition, P.O. Box 1984, New Orleans, LA 70158-1984. The main on-site information center is located at the Canal Gate entrance. Six other information booths are located throughout the Fair site.

PAVILIONS

Pavilions are being sponsored by countries and corporations, all keeping to the theme of Rivers and Freshwater as a source of life. The major exhibits can be found in the following pavilions.

The Great Hall (Convention and Exhibition Center). This is the largest structure on the site and features a water course that winds through the exhibits of the state of Louisiana and other state and industrial participants. The 140,000-sq.-ft. Louisiana State Exhibit features a narrated multi-media boat ride through a simulation of Louisiana's many facets—including swamps and the eye of a hurricane. Also housed here is the 28,000-sq.-ft. International Business

Center. Its purpose is to encourage U.S. and foreign businessmen to explore new trading opportunities and to provide them with the latest international marketing information and services. After the Fair closes, the Great Hall will become a permanent Convention and Exhibition Center for New Orleans.

The Central Theme (Cousteau) Pavilion was designed by the Cousteau Society, and, of course, is a freshwater exhibit. In addition to the Pavilion, the society's film of the Mississippi River expedition from New Orleans will be available at the fair after its initial showing on national television in the spring of 1984. The pavilion is located in the Great Hall, near the Louisiana Pavilion.

The Vatican Pavilion. Located on South Front St. next to the Fulton Street Mall. The pavilion was built in conjunction with the Archdiocese of New Orleans and designed to show off a wealth of art from the Vatican museums. A separate ticket is required for entry into this pavilion.

The U.S. Pavilion. The 87,000-sq.-ft. exhibit on the riverfront is a $10 million project sponsored by the Federal Government. It showcases American industry and the 50 states, while expressing the Fair's theme through audience-participation exhibits that tell the fresh water story from the science of a water molecule to the influence of rivers on American music, literature and art. Information is displayed from laser discs. Computer graphics and film sequences tell the story on T.V. monitors. The pavilion also features 2 theaters showing some 48,000 daily visitors an American fresh water resource adventure film featuring a 20-minute, 3-dimensional film by Guggenheim Productions, Inc.

International Pavilion. This 2-level, 370,000-sq.-ft. structure is situated directly on the riverfront promenade. You can enter the exhibit areas directly from the promenade or via escalators to the 2nd level entrance. The area is served by aqueduct systems pumping fresh water for exhibits. Covered pedestrian walkways connect the International Pavilion to the Exhibition Center. Among the many exhibiting countries are the lovely 21,000-sq.-ft. Japanese Pavilion, featuring Japanese gardens, a tea room, and an indoor river that operates a waterwheel leading to an indoor lake; the French Pavilion, showcasing advanced technology as related to water; the South Korean Pavilion; the Chinese Pavilion; and the Canadian Pavilion, illustrating the extent of Canadian concern about the effects of acid rain on fresh water.

Other Exhibits. Among the many other exhibitions that may be found at the LWE site are: the Petroleum Industries Pavilion, featuring an offshore oil rig and a 50,000-gallon aquarium complete with aquatic life and deep sea divers; the Women's Pavilion, sponsored by Women in the Mainstream, a local nonprofit organization; the Afro-American Pavilion, sponsored by I've Known Rivers, Inc., to present a record of Black progress in the U.S. and world community; the Energy Saving House, a 6,000-sq.-ft. exhibit on the south plaza of the exhibition site, consisting of a 2-level house designed to answer homeowners' questions about making their homes more energy efficient; the Travel Pavilion in the Exhibition and Convention Hall, featuring entertainment and information from a variety of travel-related companies; the AEEE Exhibit, representing the electric industry and presenting live entertainment plus an award-winning presentation entitled "Electricity;" an Aviation and Aerospace Pavilion featuring the space shuttle *Enterprise;* and a Transportation, Water, and Aquatic Life Exhibit.

ENTERTAINMENT

Throughout the Fair site, visitors will be amused and entertained by marching bands, jazz ensembles, international choral groups, the New Orleans Philharmonic Symphony, gospel singers, aquatic extravaganzas, and a host of other forms and styles of entertainment. Roughly 20,000 hours are scheduled with live music, dance, drama, and street performances during the run of the Fair. There are four floating stages that drift through the Fair's watercourse, as well as six mobile stages. Amusement and thrill rides are located at different areas around the site—including a chair lift offering a 1,500-ft. ride along the riverfront, a flume that will feature 16-passenger boats plunging down a 60 ft. waterfall, the Magic Room illusion ride, an antique carousel, and an 18-story Ferris wheel—the biggest in the United States.

Mardi Gras parades will wind through the Fair site twice daily, featuring real Mardi Gras Floats, a 26-member marching band, and guest bands from around the world. Spectacle in the Skies is a nightly fireworks and laser show. Other featured entertainment are water-ski shows on the river and daily air shows over the Mississippi with biplanes and skydivers.

American Showcase Theater. Part of the U.S. Pavilion, this theater seats 1,500. It is adjacent to an on-site T.V. studio operated by New Orleans' NBC affiliate WDSU. It sets the stage for U.S. ceremonies, college and high school marching bands, and live national T.V. broadcasts.

Aquacade. This very special arena seats 3,500. It features great entertainment in eight daily shows. The synchronized swimming revue is reminiscent of the one staged by Billy Rose in the 1939–40 New York World's Fair.

Centennial Gazebo. Seats 300. This stage features turn-of-the-century entertainment such as barbershop quartets and choral recitals.

Circus Internationale. With a seating capacity of 2,700 and 5 shows presented daily, it features the best acts from an international array of performers in a European-style one-ring circus.

International Amphitheater. This covered outdoor theater seats 5,600. It features popular national and international entertainers and musical and performing groups such as Julio Iglesias, Anne Murray, the Oak Ridge Boys, and the Stuttgart Ballet. *Note:* Separate tickets are required for shows here and prices vary according to the acts scheduled.

Jazz and Gospel Tent. Seats 1,500. There are over 10 hours of programmed music daily featuring New Orleans, regional, and international jazz and dixieland musicians, as well as vocalists.

World Theatre. This is the only indoor theater for live entertainment on the grounds and seats 1,200. Five shows daily feature a variety of entertainment such as Mummenschanz, the Swiss mime show, Lanterna Magika, Chinese acrobatic troupes, and so on. During the month of June, there is World Theatre for Children and Young Audiences, presenting twelve international theater troupes in daily performances geared to youngsters.

Wonderwall. This is a half-mile of performance areas, food, beverage, and merchandise concessions, amusements, viewing platforms, aviaries (stocked by the Audubon Zoo), sculpture, water, music, and much more. It stretches along five blocks of South Front St. and ends at the Ferris Wheel, serving as a divider between the Louisiana Pavilion and a cluster of renovated warehouses that now house shops and restaurants. The 2,300-foot panorama of architectural styles, shapes, and colors rises up to 3 stories high and is designed in 12-foot-long sections. An aqueduct channels water through a series of colonnades overhead and a ground-level watercourse meanders below. Its three performance areas feature mimes, puppet shows, and magic acts.

Artworks '84. Located at 1101 South Front St., near the Bridge Gate, this is a collection of exhibits of photography, contemporary crafts, films and videos, fine arts, and other art forms. This is an opportunity to watch artists from all over as they work. Visitors will be able to witness the creative process from the concept of a piece of work to its final product.

Operation Ship '84. This sailing regatta is scheduled for a number of times throughout the Fair's 6-month schedule. The first regatta takes place Memorial Day weekend. A parade of ships will pass the Expo site for several hours on Sunday, May 27, including sailing ships, luxury liners, container carriers, and paddlewheel riverboats. Nationally and internationally famous personalities will be on board, music will resound, and the day will culminate in a fireworks display. On Memorial Day, Monday, May 28, the "Yacht Parade of All Nations" takes place on Lake Pontchartrain with an expected 25,000 pleasure boats cruising the waters. Foreign boats will be decorated with flags while American boats will fly U.S. flags and those of their ancestral homelands.

"Operation Ship" also moves into play on Independence Day (Wednesday, July 4) when tall ships assemble in a salute to the armed forces, and on Labor Day (Monday, September 3), when the working ships of the world will be honored.

The final nautical tribute takes place on Columbus Day (Monday, October 8) in an homage to research vessels.

The Louisiana Folklife Festival. This is a program of Louisiana and Gulf Coast folklife featuring Cajun music, rhythm and blues, Creole cooking, folk architecture, boat building, and other crafts. The focal point is the craftsmakers areas—particularly the pirogue, lugger, canoe, and skiff builders. Demonstrations of boat building skills take place throughout the 6-month Fair. Finished boats will be displayed permanently at sites such as Planquemine Locks State Commemorative Area and Jean Lafitte National Historic Park in Louisiana. The center of the Folklife Festival is located in a historic warehouse building in the middle of Fulton St. pedestrian mall. The first floor of the warehouse is occupied by the crafts and demonstration areas, complete with boatmakers, a film and video room, a kitchen/demonstration area, a storyteller and workshop corner, an art and photo gallery, and a crafts shop where traditional craftsmakers display and sell their wares. The second floor of the 2-story warehouse is a performance stage seating 250–300 people. It features 14 live music performances daily and has an adjacent dance floor for performing groups and social dancing. The music and dance hall is open until 3:00 A.M.

9

FAIR SITE NEIGHBORHOODS ORIENTATION/LOCATOR

Centennial Plaza—embarkation/debarkation for the aerial gondola ride; Petroleum Industries Pavilion; America's Electric Energy Exhibit; 100-year-old carousel ride.

Great Hall—Louisiana and other state exhibits; central theme pavilion.

International Riverfront—International Pavilion, U.S. Pavilion; Space Shuttle *Enterprise* on loan from NASA, International Amphitheater.

Fulton Mall—food and merchandise; late-night spots; Reunion Hall; Vatican Pavilion.

Bayou Plaza—Wonderwall; Aquacade; Conergy Exhibit; Watergarden; Chrysler Transportation Pavilion; Union Pacific Pavilion.

Festival Park—Cajun and Louisiana related food, arts, crafts, and entertainment; Jazz and Gospel Tent; German beer garden; Artworks '84; Rooftop Bar and observation deck; Italian Village.

SPECIAL EXHIBITS

The Waters of America: 19th Century American Paintings of Rivers, Streams, Lakes, and Waterfalls. A joint project sponsored by the Historic New Orleans Collection (HNOC) and New Orleans Museum of Art (NOMA). Located in HNOC's new CBD building at Poydras and Tchoupitoulas streets, close to the Canal Entrance Gate. The exhibit runs from May 1–November 18, 1984. Approximately 75 paintings by the nation's great 19th-century artists depicting inland waterways of the continental U.S. The exhibit features artists such as Thomas Cole, Albert Bierstadt, Frederick Church, Winslow Homer, and Thomas Eakins. Separate entrance fee is required.

The Sun King: Louis XIV and the New World. The exhibit was conceived and developed by the Louisiana State Museum in cooperation with the Reunion des Musées Nationaux de France, the Association Francaise d'Action Artistique, and public and private collectors in France. The show runs from April 29–November 19, 1984 at the Cabildo fronting Jackson Square. The exhibit displays approximately 190 objects, including articles from Versailles, the Louvre, and the National Archives of France, plus paintings, tapestries, furniture, sculpture, manuscripts, original maps, printed works, and precious pieces—many of which have never traveled outside

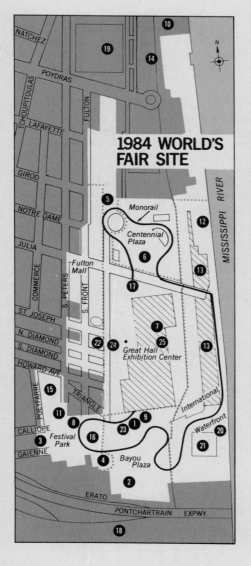

Points of Interest

1) Amusements and Concessions
2) Aquacade
3) Artworks '84
4) Bridge Gate
5) Canal Gate and Main Information Booth
6) Centennial Gazebo
7) Central Theme Pavilion
8) Circus Internationale
9) Ferris Wheel
10) Ferry Terminal
11) Food Festival
12) International Amphitheater
13) International Pavilions
14) International Trade Mart
15) Italian Village
16) Jazz and Gospel Tent
17) Louisiana Pavilion
18) Parking and Bus Drop-off
19) Rivergate Convention Center
20) Space Shuttle *Enterprise*
21) United States Pavilion
22) Vatican Pavilion
23) Watergarden
24) Wonderwall
25) World Theater

of France before. Louis XIV became king of France at age 5 and reigned until his death in 1715. The exhibit focuses on Louis' contributions to the development of Western civilization and to the exploration and settlement of the New World. Separate entrance fee is required.

FOOD AND BEVERAGES

Native Louisiana cuisine as well as national and international fare are featured at the nearly 75 restaurant concessions and theme bars scattered around the site. The 11,500-sq.-ft. Miller Beer Garden, an indoor restaurant, bar and lounge with an outside patio seating 750 is sponsored by Miller High Life—the official beer of the World's Fair. Pete Fountain's Reunion Hall is a 17,000-sq.-ft. restaurant space with an additional 3,000 sq. ft. of dance floor and live entertainment: daylong dixieland Jazz bands and Big Bands in the evening.

Natchez plying the river side by side with gigantic oil tankers and modern cargo ships.

Decatur Street to Esplanade Avenue

Certainly a good cup of coffee would be appropriate at this point. Facing the Decatur Street viewing platform is the Café Du Monde. The Café Du Monde is world famous for its rich tasting *café au lait* (coffee and chicory with warm milk) and warm *beignets* (French doughnuts) that you sprinkle with confectioners sugar.

Proceeding downriver on Decatur from the Café Du Monde, a walk through the French Market is particularly rewarding. The colonnaded marketplace behind the Café Du Monde dates from the second decade of the 19th century. Until the mid-1970s, it was still a viable market providing seafood, vegetables and fruit for French Quarter residents. During the French Market renovations of the 1970s, produce stalls gave way to gift shops, restaurants and other tourist attractions. The face lift caused a great loss to the aged patinated ambience of the old French Market. However, there are several good restaurants here and the visitor should sample a New Orleans praline (a hard sugary candy with pecans) at Aunt Sally's Praline Shop or at a dozen or so other places in the Quarter that sell the local delicacy.

The second colonnaded section of the French Market, dating from the 1820s, continues down Decatur across the street from where the first section of the market ends. Both markets, sagging with age and neglect, were renovated in the 1930s by the federal Works Progress Administration. Without question one of the most interesting establishments in that section of Decatur Street—although not located in the French Market—is Central Grocery (923 Decatur). Dating back to the turn of the century, it is one of the few Italian grocery stores left in the city. The population of the Quarter in the early 20th century was mostly Italian. Walking through Central's front door one is greeted by a marvelous aroma of olive salads, imported herbs, spices, and cheese stacked on barrel heads and shelves that extend to the ceiling. Central Grocery also prepares what has become one of New Orleans' most popular sandwiches, the muffuletta—a delectable treat on a large Italian roll stuffed with a variety of Italian cold cuts and cheese bathed in a green and black olive salad. A half sandwich is enough for the normal appetite and an entire muffuletta can adequately feed two or three people. With a comfortably full belly, one is now fortified to continue a tour of the Quarter. The Marketplace in the next block (1015 Decatur), which is separate from the French Market, is an excellent example of how entrepreneurs have adapted many old French Quarter buildings to modern use. The interior was gutted and replaced with two levels of attractive shopping stalls, arts and crafts, gifts, antiques, etc., and a mini New York-style deli.

Beyond the St. Philip and Decatur Street market is the old Farmer's Market, a long steel shed build by the Works Progress Administration during the Great Depression of the 1930s. It is open twenty-four hours a day, seven days a week. To one side of the Farmer's Market, the side opposite the river, is old Galatin Street, once notorious for its bordellos and saloons where visitors of yesteryear were stiffed and shanghaied. Today, Galatin Street's *demimonde* has been replaced by vegetable warehouses and run-ins with the law seldom amount to anything more than a double-parked truck. The lower end of the market near the old U.S. Mint has a thriving flea market on weekends from early morning until dark where one can secure anything from old phonograph records and coins to hand plows. The flea market is especially popular among Quarterites.

Behind the market at the corner of Esplanade Avenue and Decatur Street in the old U.S. Mint building. Its massive scale overwhelms the surrounding area.

It was built in 1835 during the administration of President Andrew Jackson as the first major branch of the U.S. Mint and is now the oldest remaining Mint building in the U.S. During the early days of the Civil War, the Mint served as the Confederacy's only mint. It never really got into full operation under the stars and bars, turning out fewer than ten prototype coins. They are extremely valuable today. After the fall of New Orleans in 1862 the Union army housed Confederate prisoners there. After the war, the Mint resumed its minting operations until 1909 when a change in government minting operations forced its closure. Between 1909 and the late 1970s, the magnificent Greek Revival building served, among other things, as a federal jail and Coast Guard office. For about the last twenty years it sat mostly dormant, used as a storage warehouse for the Louisiana State Museum and city Civil Defense. It is the oldest existing mint building in the United States. The Louisiana State Museum restored the building in the late 1970s and it now houses several historical exhibitions on New Orleans jazz and Mardi Gras and two important research libraries and archives—the Louisiana Historical Center and the Amistad Research Center. Two major collections in the Louisiana Historical Center are the French and Spanish Louisiana colonial archives and the New Orleans Jazz Collection, one of the world's most extensive collections of New Orleans jazz sheet music, recordings, photographs, books, memorabilia, and musical instruments—including Louis Armstrong's first trumpet. Also located in the Mint is the Louisiana Visitor Information Center which provides information on the culture and history of New Orleans and Louisiana. The Amistad Research Center is one of the country's most important historical research centers with extensive collections of documents, books, photographs, and recordings pertaining to the history of black Americans. The two research centers are open to researchers only.

During the restoration of the building, architects discovered that it originally had been painted reddish brown to simulate brownstone buildings in the Northeast. The museum, for the sake of restorative integrity, painted the building.

Across Esplanade from the Mint is Ruby Red's. Although the place is dimly lighted and the floor ankle deep in peanut shells, Ruby's makes the best hamburger in town.

This side of Esplanade is the beginning of a section of town called Faubourg (suburb) Marigny. It was founded in the early 1820s by New Orleans' most colorful *bon vivant* Bernard de Marigny de Mandeville, or simply Bernard Marigny. He gave the streets of his faubourg such names as Good Children, Craps, Frenchmen, Love, and Desire (setting for Tennessee Williams' *A Streetcar Named Desire*). Desire Street crosses St. Claude about a mile from where Esplanade and St. Claude intersect. (In 1850 Good Children was changed to St. Claude Avenue, Craps to Burgundy Street, and Love to Rampart Street.) Strolling through these areas can be dangerous because of their high crime rate and visitors are advised to see the faubourg's unique early 19th-century cottage architecture by automobile or guided tour.

Chartres to Conti Streets

Resuming our walking tour of the Quarter, continue up Esplanade away from the river to Chartres Street (runs one block parallel to Decatur). This section of Chartres Street is a quiet residential area of the Quarter that reflects the true nature of the Vieux Carré. It has not become an outdoor sideshow like some areas of the Quarter.

The first cross street on Chartres is Gov. Nicholls Street. There are several buildings in the 1100 block of Gov. Nicholls worth a brief detour. The Clay House (618–620 Gov. Nicholls) was built *circa* 1828 for John Clay, brother of statesman Henry Clay (not open to the public). During the 1890s, Frances Xavier Cabrini used it as a school. Cabrini later became St. Frances Cabrini.

At the corner of Gov. Nicholls and Royal (1140 Royal Street) is the LaLaurie House, or the "haunted house" (not open to the public). Stories about this house have fascinated generations of New Orleanians and visitors alike. In 1831 Madame Delphine LaLaurie acquired the house from her father. It became one of the social spots in the city. But rumors persisted that something was amiss in the LaLaurie household. In 1833 a neighborhood woman told police she saw Madame LaLaurie beating a small slave girl who subsequently fell to her death in the courtyard below. Madame LaLaurie was simply fined in court for the offense. A year later a fire broke out in the house and neighbors broke in to save what they could. But when they got inside they found a half dozen or more starved and emaciated slaves chained to a wall. A newspaper story the next day suggested that Madame LaLaurie may have started the fire. Shortly after an angry mob gathered in front of the LaLaurie house, a carriage carrying the LaLaurie family raced from the house and through the mob to a ship waiting at Bayou St. John. The LaLauries fled to Europe never to return again in their lifetime. After the Delphine's death, her body was secreted back to New Orleans where it was buried. Local legend says that when the moon and wind are right, the mournful cries of the tortured slaves can be heard coming from the LaLaurie garret.

Returning to Chartres Street, the 1100 block has several excellent examples of early 19th-century New Orleans architecture. The Soniat House (1133 Chartres) was built in 1829 for New Orleans aristocrat and planter Joseph Soniat du Fossat (not open to the public). The wrought-iron work was replaced in the 1860s with the cast-iron lace work that now graces the building's facade. A couple of doors down (1113 Chartres) is the 1827 LeCarpentier House. It is an unusual style of architecture for the French Quarter with its raised portico on the sidewalk and formal English garden sideyard. It is also called the Beauregard House as Civil War General P.G.T. Beauregard, a New Orleans native, rented a few rooms here shortly after the War Between the States. In more recent years, the house was the home of Frances Parkinson Keyes, who wrote popular novels about the area and the general. The house, furnished in the New Orleans Victorian style, is open to the public.

Across from the LeCarpentier House is the old Ursuline Convent (1114 Chartres). It is oldest French colonial building in New Orleans—designed in 1745 and completed in 1750. During the colonial and antebellum eras, Ursuline nuns taught local Indian, black, and white girls. The nuns moved to a different location in 1824. During the 1830s, the state legislature met here and later it served as headquarters for the archdiocese of New Orleans. The archdiocese has restored the old convent and guided tours (only) are available Fridays at 1, 2, and 3 P.M. Group tours are also available (call 561–0008).

Moving up Chartres toward Jackson Square, special note should be taken in the 900 block. At 910 and 921 Chartres are two excellent examples of New Orleans French Quarter courtyards, or patios. The one in the interior of 921 Chartres is especially nice because of the long carriageway leading from the street to the damp, serene, and lushly green patio. These are private residences and not open to the public.

You will have to enjoy the view from the sidewalk. But take heart; there are several large and lovely patios in other sections of the quarter that are open and to be enjoyed by the public. We will get to those later in our walking tour.

Before returning to Jackson Square on Chartres, another brief detour is in order. At Dumaine Street, turn right and walk a half-block to 632 Dumaine. This is the Jean Pascal House, also known locally as "Madame John's Legacy." The name is purely fictitious so don't bother your head about who Madame John might have been. The house was built in 1788 and rebuilt in 1789 after the great fire of 1788. It was constructed in the French Louisiana colonial style to resemble the original house destroyed by the fire. But this time it was built closer to the banquette (sidewalk) to conform to post-fire Spanish building codes. The house got the name Madame John's Legacy because it was the setting of George Washington Cable's late 19th-century short story, "Tite Poulette." Madame John's is part of the Louisiana State Museum system and it contains an excellent exhibition on Louisiana colonial furniture. The state restored the house in the early 1970s—an obviously busy decade for the Quarter.

Back to Chartres Street. Another point of local trivia is the building housing the Chart House Restaurant on the corner of Chartres and St. Ann streets across from the Presbytere and Jackson Square. Earlier this century the building housed a spaghetti factory. Actually, the building is several buildings joined together by a mid-19th century facade. The interior has been tastefully restored and what was once the center courtyard is now a glass-covered atrium leading to the restaurant above.

Continuing past the Presbytere and Cathedral to the 600 block of Chartres, the weary walker might be ready for a cup of tea or coffee and a piece of pastry. Le Marquise (625 Chartres) is a delightful French pastry cafe owned and operated by a native Parisian. His croissant are excellent. There is a rear patio with a few tables and chairs where one can enjoy the pastry and ambience of the old Quarter.

If something more substantial than pastry is desired, the Napoleon House and Masperos' Exchange are both a couple blocks farther up on Chartres at St. Louis Street. They serve substantial sandwiches and both are French Quarter landmarks. Maspero's was a slave exchange in the early 19th century and the Napoleon House is one of the most interesting places in the Quarter day or night. Part of the building was constructed in 1814 as the home of New Orleans Mayor Nicholas Girod. Local legend has it that Girod offered his home to Napoleon during his exile on St. Helena. In 1821 Girod and others collected money to buy the schooner *Seraphin* to rescue Napoleon, but before the expedition could get under way, word reached New Orleans of the emperor's death. For the last fifty or sixty years, the Napoleon House, with its weathered exterior, airy, high-ceilinged interior, tiled floors, flaking sepia walls and everpresent classical music in the background, has been a favorite watering hole of local artists and writers. Around the corner from the Napoleon House in St. Louis Street is another New Orleans culinary landmark. No history, no architectural splendors, but one of the best Po-boy restaurants in town—Johnny's. Po-boys are New Orleans' equivalent to submarine or hero sandwiches—only with sometimes more creative fillings such as fried oysters. There are also a number of antique and specialty shops in this area of Chartres. Generally, they are not as expensive as the pricy antique parlors on neighboring Royal Street.

Turning the corner at Chartres on to Conti Street (one block up from St. Louis) and walking away from the river, you'll see Exchange Alley cutting in from the left. During the early 19th century, fencing masters had schools there to teach New Orleanians the art of the rapier. Now you will find gift and specialty shops there as well as restaurants and offices.

Royal Street to Esplanade

The corner of Royal and Conti streets was the city's banking center during the first half of the 19th century. The columned building on the uptown-river corner (334 Royal) was built in 1826 to house the Bank of Louisiana. Today, it is headquarters of the Greater New Orleans Tourist and Convention Commission, open daily from 9 A.M. to 5 P.M. Not only does it provide a free cup of coffee to visitors, but also has a wealth of tourist information about the city and surrounding environs. Directly across Royal Street (343 Royal) stands the Bank of the United States building, built in 1800. It is the oldest bank building in the city and now houses Waldhorn Antiques—the Saks of antique devotees. Across from Waldhorn's and facing Royal Street was another bank, the Louisiana State Bank—note the "LB" in the grill work. The Louisiana State Bank opened its doors in 1821 in this building designed by architect Benjamin Latrobe, one of the architects of the U.S. Capitol in Washington, D.C. Manheim Galleries (403 Royal), another chic antique gallery, is now located here.

Occupying the fourth corner of Royal and Conti streets is the state Wildlife and Fisheries Building. Since its construction in 1908–1909, it has served as a state court building, federal appeals courts, and state office building. The state has recently decided to renovate it for use as courtrooms. A few years ago there had been some talk about converting it into a concert hall or opera house, others suggested the city courts, and a local television personality suggested the building be razed and a park be built on the grounds with an underground parking lot. Meanwhile, most of the building remains empty.

Royal Street with its fine restaurants, hotel and antique galleries is unquestionably the most interesting street in the Quarter. Across from the Wildlife and Fisheries Building is Brennan's Restaurant (417 Royal), one of the city's notable eating establishments. Brunch at Brennan's is a memorable experience and every visitor to the city should try it. The building itself was erected about 1801 as a residence for the maternal grandfather of French Impressionist painter Edgar Degas, who visited and worked in the city for a short time. In 1805 the Banque de la Louisiane bought the property—note "BL" in the iron work. Fourteen years later, the bank folded and the building once again became a private residence. Andrew Jackson was wined and dined here during his 1828 visit to the city. It later became the home of 19th-century world chess champion, Paul Morphy.

At the corner of Royal and St. Louis is the Royal Orleans Hotel, one of the best in the city. It was built only a few decades ago with the same outward appearance as the once popular 19th-century St. Louis Hotel that occupied the same spot.

Turning the corner into the 700 block of St. Louis is another New Orleans dining institution, Antoine's Restaurant (713 Royal). It is known worldwide for such French and Creole dishes as Oysters Rockefeller and Pampano en Popilotte. Next door to Antoine's is the Epitome Tobacco Shop. According to its proprietors, they decided to open the shop after dining at Antoine's one night because they couldn't find a decent after-dinner cigar anywhere in town.

Resuming our tour of Royal Street, there are several points of interest in the 500 block. The Merieult House (533 Royal) was one of the few houses in the Quarter to escape the fire of 1794. It was the home of Jean Francois Merieult and his wife, Catherine McNamara Merieult. According to a popular story surrounding the early years of this house, the Merieults were visiting Paris when a representative of the Emperor Napoleon asked Madame Merieult for some of her red hair. Apparently the emperor wanted it as a gift for some Turkish sultan. But Madame refused. The house is now owned by the Kemper and Leila Williams Foundation and houses the Historic New Orleans Collection—a superb research library and archives, and an extensive collection of historical documents and objects (see Museums).

Across the street at 536 Royal is the Casa de Comercio, built after the 1794 fire. It is a classic example of Spanish colonial architecture in New Orleans. The upstairs apartments are not open to the public but you are obviously welcome in the ground-level shops (open Monday through Friday from 8:30 A.M. until 4:00 P.M.). Next door (520 Royal) is Maison Seignouret, built in 1816 by the city's most famous furniture maker, Francois Seignouret, a native of Bordeaux, France. Seignouret and other New Orleans furniture makers of the time, such as Prudent Mallard, who came to the city in the late 1830s, were famous for their massive and ornately carved furniture. Such opulently styled furniture was appropriate for the high ceilings and airy rooms of that time. (Incidentally, the high ceilings and large windows enabled local residents to endure the long, sweltering summers.) Seignouret and Mallard's style of furniture can be found today in many of the city's private homes and museums, and in the plantation houses in the lower Mississippi River Valley. In trying to identify Seignouret's furniture, look for an "S" carved subtly into the ornate embellishments. The building is now occupied by a local television station and the interior courtyard, which is open to strollers, is well worth seeing.

The Court of Two Sisters (615 Royal), built in 1832, has a magnificent courtyard where one can dine and enjoy the establishment's ample bar. The "two sisters" were Emma and Bertha Camors. They operated a "fancy and variety store" at this location for over twenty years during the late 19th century.

The double-galleried buildings (621–639 St. Peter Street) at the corner of Royal and St. Peter streets, built in 1840 by Jean Baptiste Labranche, is one of the most popular street scenes in New Orleans. Its intricately ornate iron galleries are the best examples of cast iron work in the city. Private apartments occupy the upper levels and typical French Quarter retail shops are located on the ground floor.

Also at the corner of Royal and St. Peter is the city's "first skyscraper" (640 Royal). This three-and-a-half-story building was constructed in 1795–1811 as the residence of Dr. Yves Le Monnier. Notice the initials "YLM" in the iron grillwork. The upper floors are private residences and shops occupy the street level. It just goes to show that everything is relevant when one can easily see the modern skyscrapers towering in the background.

The Cathedral garden in the next block of Royal Street offers a peaceful setting, with a good rear view of St. Louis Cathedral. Writer William Faulkner resided in the small ground-floor apartment in the building on the right, 624 Pirate's Alley, during his stay in New Orleans in the 1920s. It was here in 1925 that Faulkner wrote his first novel, *Soldier's Pay.* The marble monument in the middle of the garden was presented by Napoleon III's minister of navy in memory of the French sailors who died in New Orleans while serving as volunteer nurses during one of the city's many deadly yellow fever epidemics. The garden was once called St. Anthony's Garden in honor of Père Antoine (Antonio de Sedella), a popular Spanish priest who served in New Orleans from 1770 until his death in the 1820s.

Crossing Royal to the left and entering the 700 block of Orleans Street, you will have the opportunity to visit the embodiment of one of the city's historical ironies. Located at 717 Orleans Street is the Orleans Ballroom (Salle d'Orleans), housed in what is currently the Bourbon Orleans Hotel. Built in 1817, the magnificent ballroom on the second floor was once the scene of the city's famous early 19th-century balls where quadroon mothers would introduce their *café au lait*-skinned, racially mixed daughters to young white aristocrats during the ball. After hard negotiations between the shrewd mothers and the young men, the daughters would become mistresses and reside in the small cottages near Rampart Street. In the early 1870s, Thomy Lafon, a black philanthropist and born a free man of color in 1810, bought the old ballroom and gave it to the Sisters of the Holy Family, a black order of nuns. The nuns converted the building to an orphanage for black children and the upstairs ballroom held celebrations of a much different sort: it became a chapel. The nuns sold the building to the hotel in 1964 and the ballroom has been restored.

Walk back to Royal Street and continue to the 900 block. The Miltenberger House (908–912 Royal) was the 1858 birthplace of Alice Heine. Alice was a member of the Miltenberger family and related to German poet Heinrich Heine. At the age of 17, she married the Duc du Richelieu, and after his death five years later, Alice became the first American princess of Monaco in 1889 when she married Prince Albert of Monaco. The two-story ornate cast-iron lace-work galleries were added in about 1858. The three upper stories are private apartments. Shops and offices are on the street level.

A few doors down at 919 Royal, Andrew Jackson was fined $1,000 for contempt of court shortly after the Battle of New Orleans. Seems as though the local folk thought him a bit high-handed after turning away the British at the city gates. Today the building houses a hotel called, of course, the Andrew Jackson. In the same block (915 Royal) is the famous corn stalk cast-iron fence painted green and yellow to look like corn. The original house behind the fence burned years ago and the newer one has been converted into a popular French Quarter hotel. The fence was made in Philadelphia by Wood and Perot and shipped by sea to a Dr. Joseph Secondo Biamenti who had purchased the property in 1834.

Throughout the Quarter the visitor will notice the large number of Victorian and early 20th-century houses that have replaced older French Quarter buildings destroyed by fire or simply neglect. The 1000 and 1100 blocks of Royal provide good examples of this historical mixture.

Of particular note in the 1100 block is the Gallier House (1132 Royal). Built in the late 1850s, it was the residence of renowned New

Orleans architect James Gallier, Jr., son of architect James Gallier, Sr. (You will see many of his works during your stay in the Crescent City.) The house has been meticulously restored and furnished. Guided tours of the house show how the upper-crust lived just prior to the Civil War (see Museums).

Bourbon Street to Canal Street

Moving over to Bourbon St.—although originally named for the French royal family the appellation is now more fitting since more bourbon is probably consumed here in one night than any other place in the city. Before the Civil War, Bourbon Street was one of the most fashionable residential streets in the city. Although it still has several fine homes and several good restaurants and nightclubs, "The Street," as it is called in Quarter parlance, is known world over for its second-rate strip joints, bars, souvenir shops, jazz parlors, and male and female prostitutes. In spite of all of this, or perhaps because of it, Bourbon Street is immensely popular among tourists. Throngs of humanity move like a great river current up and down the street most weekend nights and particularly during Mardi Gras and other festive occasions. Although the street has a sleazy atmosphere, it is much safer today than it was in years past when a Mickey Finn slipped into the drink of an unwary visitor was not uncommon.

Lafitte's Blacksmith Shop (941 Bourbon), with its brick-between-post construction, is an excellent example of early French colonial architecture in New Orleans. Whether the pirate, Jean Lafitte, or any of his Barbarian cohorts ever operated a blacksmith shop here is more legend than fact.

The building that now houses the Embers Restaurant at Bourbon and St. Peter streets once was called the Bourbon House. During the 1940s and 1950s, it was a popular hangout for artists and writers, including Tennessee Williams. Today, it is a popular Quarter bar.

A half-block over to the right on St. Peter Street toward the river are two contemporary landmarks—Pat O'Brien's bar and magnificent patio (open day and night), and Preservation Hall (726 St. Peter), famous all over the world for its pure New Orleans jazz. Here you can hear jazz played by old New Orleans musicians who learned their art in the same saloons and dancehalls as Louis Armstrong and King Joe Oliver. Preservation Hall regular George "Kid Sheik" Collar, whose wailing trumpet has delighted audiences for decades, once gave his own definition of jazz in a *Time* magazine interview: "It's a feeling. Just like when you get the spirit on you in church. You can't play this music unless you got the feeling to play it—and love it. Then you puts the feeling in the other people." Preservation Hall has not changed its appearance one bit since its doors opened in 1961. It's the same aging, tattered building, with dirty windows and peeling paint, but the "feeling" is there almost every night and it is the best place for unabridged New Orleans jazz.

Where the motel now stands at the corner of Bourbon and Toulouse streets was once the site of the French Opera House. Built in 1859, it was the theatrical and cultural center of New Orleans before its destruction by fire in 1919. Most of the Mardi Gras balls were held here before the fire; they now take place at the Municipal Auditorium on North Rampart Street. The site stood vacant until the present motel was built in the early 1960s.

The Absinthe House (238 Bourbon) is another one of those New Orleans' institutions. The building dates from the first decade of the 19th century and there has been an absinthe bar here since 1861. The bar got its name from the once popular absinthe drink, which is a strong licorice-tasting liqueur made originally from wormwood and other herbs. The genuine absinthe was outlawed in 1905 because medical scientists said wormwood caused insanity and other maladies. Absinthe is made today but without the wormwood and many a New Orleanian and visitor have enjoyed the Old Absinthe House's Absinthe Suisesse (a frothy mixture of Pernod, white anisette, water, egg white, powdered sugar, and cracked ice) and Absinthe Frappe (white anisette, Pernod, and water, served on ice in a tall glass). This is also one of the several places in the city where Andrew Jackson supposedly planned his strategy for the Battle of New Orleans.

A classical illustration of the changed character of the Quarter, and especially Bourbon Street is 327 Bourbon. For many years this building has been a bar, and at times third-rate nightclubs have occupied its rooms. Before the Civil War it was the residence of lawyer Judah P. Benjamin, U.S. Senator from Louisiana and Secretary of State for the Confederacy. Often called the "brains of the Confederacy," Benjamin fled to England after the South's fall. In England he distinguished himself at the British bar. One recent nightclub owner tried to capitalize on the history of the building by calling his establishment "Judah P's." Added to the gaudy nightclub spectacle were a pair of women's legs that swing in and out of the front window. Fortunately, that nightclub and the "legs" are gone.

Dauphine, Burgundy and North Rampart Sts.

Dauphine and Burgundy streets, one and two blocks over and running parallel to Bourbon, are interesting mostly for the French Quarter's early 19th-century architectural styles. But extreme care should be taken. Walking in this area can be dangerous, especially at night.

North Rampart Street (where the city's rear rampart was in the 18th century) is the rear boundary of the French Quarter. Across Rampart is another of the city's early 19th-century suburbs, Faubourg Trémé, often called "back-a-town" (back-of-town).

One of the more interesting places on North Rampart Street is Our Lady of St. Guadeloupe Catholic Church at the corner of Conti Street. The church was built in 1826 on the edge of the city and next to the cemeteries as a "burying chapel." The little church saw considerable use during the many 19th-century yellow fever and cholera epidemics. Today it is the police and firemen's chapel. Notice the statue of St. Expedite inside. Locals say the statue of the unknown saint arrived in a crate many years ago with no identification other than the word "expedite" stamped on the box.

Almost directly behind the church, on Basin Street, is St. Louis Cemetery No. 1 that dates from the 1780s. This cemetery, as well as others in New Orleans, is famous for its ornate aboveground tombs. They have been called cities of the dead. The usual reason given for this form of burial is that because of the area's high water table, graves can't be dug without striking water. That may be true, but the city's Mediterranean and southern European heritage probably had something more to do with the custom. Whites and blacks, free and slave, all were buried in the three St. Louis cemeteries. Walking through St. Louis No. 1, you will see the names of people who had a profound impact on the city's history and lore: Etienne Boré (who revolutionized the sugar industry), world chess champion Paul Morphy, Voodoo Queen Marie Laveau (note the *gris gris* Xs on her supposed tomb), and Homer Plessy (who described himself as "seven-eighths caucasian and one-eighth African blood." Plessy's 1892 challenge of Louisiana's Jim Crow segregation laws resulted in the famous 1896 U.S. Supreme Court decision *Plessy vs. Ferguson* that set up over a half-century of "separate but equal" laws throughout the South). St. Louis cemeteries No. 2 and No. 3 are directly behind No. 1.

Unfortunately, vandals searching for jewelry and other valuables have desecrated many tombs in all three St. Louis cemeteries. Also, a vast number are crumbling from years of neglect. An organization called "Save Our Cemeteries" was formed a few years ago to restore and preserve these New Orleans landmarks.

Again caution! The best and safest way to visit the cemeteries is by guided tour and in large numbers. The cemeteries are located next to Iberville Housing Project, a federal housing project and a high crime area.

The Iberville Housing Project, built in the early 1930s, occupies most of the city's old tenderloin district, once called Storyville. The City Council created Storyville in 1897 as an attempt to control prostitution in the city. The ordinance stated: "It shall be unlawful for any public prostitute or woman notoriously abandoned to lewdness to occupy, inhabit, live or sleep in any house, room or closet situated without the following limits." It then went on to define the boundaries of the twelve-square block area: Iberville Street from Basin to North Robertson streets; North Robertson from Iberville to St. Louis streets; and St. Louis along the St. Louis cemeteries back to Basin Street. How's that for progress! Several European and Asian countries continue to have such arrangements. But what started as a reform movement in the late 19th century became a *cause célèbre* for early 20th-century reformers who wanted the district closed. The creation of Storyville was only one of the city's many attempts to control prostitution. In the 1850s, the city required harlots to buy a license from the city to ply their trade. Storyville was famous for its magnificent pleasure palaces along Basin Street and the dozens of lesser bordellos and cribs. Jazz and blues also owe much of their early beginnings to the saloons of Storyville. Under pressure form the U.S. Government during World War I, the city closed the district. The government wanted to protect the morals of young soldiers stationed near New Orleans. Not much is left but a few houses here and there. However, it has left the city a legacy rich with names of such madams as Lulu White, Countess Willie Piazza, Josie Arlington and the infamous Blue Book, a directory of Storyville prostitutes handed out to visitors arriving at the train station. The little one-story brick building at the corner of Basin and Bienville streets is all that's left of Lulu White's two-story Mahogany Hall Saloon, celebrated in the jazz tune, "Mahogany Hall Stomp." After Storyville officially closed in 1917, prostitutes continued to ply their trade in the area although illegally. Police, who were regularly bribed, looked the other way. Most of the buildings in the old district were bulldozed in the early 1930s to make way for the housing project.

Mention should be made that Basin Street, of "Basin Street Blues," got its name from a late 18th-century canal that terminated in a basin near today's Municipal Auditorium (North Rampart and Orleans streets). The canal and basin, no longer used in shipping commerce, were covered in the early 20th century.

The Municipal Auditorium, built in the 1930s, is now part of the city's entertainment complex that includes Louis Armstrong Park and the Theater for the Performing Arts. The oldest and most prestigious Mardi Gras balls are held here, as well as prize fights, circuses, concerts, etc. Like many other places in New Orleans, the auditorium has one of those amusing anecdotes surrounding its early history. When the city first came up with the idea of building a multipurpose auditorium, a group of civic-minded citizens approached a city official and reportedly suggested a Greek amphitheater style. As the story goes, the official said he didn't think there were enough Greeks in the city to warrant such a style.

Directly in front of the auditorium and facing Rampart Street is Congo Square, or Beauregard Square. Perhaps more than any other place in the city, Congo Square can be said to be the birthplace of jazz. In the late 18th and early 19th centuries, blacks, both free and slave, congregated in the square on Sundays to dance and play music of African origins tempered by European music heard in the city. Their music had a strong influence on early 19th-century New Orleans-born pianist and composer Louis Moreau Gottschalk. Their influence can be heard in many of his compositions, such as "Le Bamboula" and "Calinda." Gottschalk traveled throughout the western world playing his compositions to critical acclaim.

This concludes our walking tour of the French Quarter. Now the visitor will have the opportunity to go back and enjoy what the Quarter has to offer.

Central Business District

Directly upriver from the French Quarter and across Canal Street is the Central Business District—the hub of the city's business and commercial community. The CBD was also the city's first suburb— Faubourg (suburb) St. Marie (now anglicized to St. Mary). From 7 A.M. to 6 P.M. Monday through Friday, the CBD is a beehive of business men and women, secretaries, shopkeepers, shoppers, and sales clerks rushing around in the canyon-like streets that run between the highrise buildings. On Saturdays the workers are elsewhere and the streets are less crowded. The CBD streets are generally empty on Sundays except for tourists walking to and from the French Quarter to their hotels.

The Central Business District runs approximately from Canal Street, called the widest business street in the country, to Howard Avenue and from the Mississippi River to Loyola Avenue in the general vicinity of the Louisiana Super Dome. Prior to the Civil War, this area of the city was known as the American Section because this was where most Anglo-Americans settled after the 1803 Louisiana Purchase.

After the great fire of 1788 that destroyed almost four fifths of the city, Madame and Don Bertrand Gravier subdivided their plantation and sold lots to New Orleanians and newcomers who no longer wanted to reside in the fire-plagued French Quarter. The Gravier plantation once had been part of the vast Jesuit plantation, confiscated by the colonial government in 1763 after the religious order was expelled from the colony.

Royal Surveyor Carlos Trudeau drew up plans for dividing the plantation into squares separated by streets with such names as Magazine (warehouses), Camp (Gravier's slave camp), Poydras (an investor), Julia (explained later), Carondelet (for the Spanish colonial governor), St. Charles (king of Spain), and Gravier, in honor of the developers.

The area grew slowly during the first decade but after the Louisiana Purchase, English-speaking Americans and immigrants began pouring into the city. Most settled in Faubourg St. Mary. During the next thirty years the suburb experienced a building boom unlike any other time in the city's past or future to this date. By the 1830s the area rivaled the *Vieux Carré* in commerce and population. By the 1850s, the faubourg was unquestionably the dominant commercial and political section of the city.

The Central Business District, with its striking architectural contrasts, has remained the city's financial center ever since. The area is rich with early 19th-century architecture commingled with the glass and concrete 20th-century monoliths.

Canal Street

Perhaps a walking tour of the CBD should begin at the foot of Canal Street at the river. Canal is packed from sunup to sundown with tourists and locals shopping at one of the many department stores or dining at cafes and restaurants, as well as business men and women scurrying from office building to office building between appointments. By the way, there was never a canal on Canal Street. There was a shallow ditch or moat in the late 18th century when New Orleans was a walled city, but an early 19th-century project to build a canal along "Canal Street" to connect the river with Lake Pontchartrain via the Carondelet Canal behind the Quarter didn't materialize. Also, the wide, raised concrete median down the center of Canal Street is called "neutral ground" in New Orleans, so named because it separated the French Quarter Creoles and the American Section. As a result, medians throughout the city have been called neutral grounds ever since.

Back to our walking tour. Standing in the neutral ground and facing in the direction of the Mississippi, there are several points of interest. *Warning:* Be careful as you stand on the neutral ground and be aware of approaching buses as they drive down the center of it (cars are not allowed on the neutral ground, however). Straight ahead is the ferry landing that connects Canal Street with Algiers Point across the river. By all means, take the round-trip ride on the ferry; its the best and most scenic free ride in town.

Plopped right in the middle of the neutral ground is a granite monument. The center section of the neutral ground in front of the ferry landing was cut off from the rest of the neutral ground a few years ago.

This section, containing the monument, stands alone in the form of a drive-around circle. The monument was built toward the end of the 19th century to commemorate the Battle of September 14, 1874, also called the Battle of Liberty Place by its white victors. It was the last battle between local whites with old Confederate sympathies and the militia representing the military-backed Reconstruction government in New Orleans.

In June 1874 local white Democrats, frustrated politically by the Republican Reconstruction government, formed the White League as a quasi-military force to drive the Radical Republicans from office.

On the morning of September 14, word reached White Leaguers that the predominantly black Metropolitan police force planned to intercept an arms shipment to the Leaguers scheduled to arrive that day. The attack was prepared. After a brief but fierce battle, complete with Rebel yells, artillery, and rifle fire, the Leaguers' 8,000-man army routed the 3,000 black and white militiamen and 600 Metropolitans, who ironically were under the command of former Confederate General James Longstreet. The battle took place at the foot of Canal Street, the Quarter and CBD. The Leaguers replaced city and state officials with their own appointments, but the victory was short-lived. President Grant sent more federal troops to reinstate Republicans. Reconstruction ended three years later.

During the 1960s and 1970s, many of the city's black leaders wanted the monument removed, saying it was a long lingering insult to the black people of the city. Others argued that the monument should remain as a reminder of our history. A compromise was struck. The offensive words, "Dedicated to White Supremacy," inscribed at the base, were covered. (Apparently some city officials added those words in the 1930s resurgence of elitist racism.) Every once in a while protestors will demonstrate in front of the monument or deface it with paint.

The ritzy towering building on the left (on the Quarter side) is Canal Place. Canal Place's 260,000 square foot retail mall houses some of the best fashion shops in the country, including Saks Fifth Avenue. Canal Place opened in 1980, is the first of a five-phased construction plan for the development that includes hotels and office buildings. This is a great and exciting area that has come a long way in recent years. It has become *the* fashionable place to shop in New Orleans. The area is lively seven days and nights a week with shoppers, visitors, conventioneers, and business people.

At the very foot of Canal Street stands the 33-floor International Trade Mart World Trade Center. Completed in the 1960, the ITM Building houses 28 foreign consulates and trade offices; a number of state and federal agencies dealing with international trade; and, 150 shipping, import-export and other private international businesses. At the very top of the building is a revolving bar and below that is an observation platform open to the public. Both provide magnificent views of the city and river. The Louisiana Maritime Museum, with its extensive collections of Mississippi River and shipping memorabilia, also is located on the 31st floor of the ITM Building.

Directly in front of the ITM Building is the spectacular Plaza de Espana, with its magnificent fountain. It was Spain's Bicentennial gift (1976) to commemorate New Orleans' colonial ties to Spain.

Next to the ITM Building is the 580,000 square foot Rivergate Exhibition Center, completed in the late 1960s and designed by the architectural firms of Curtis and Davis and Edward B. Silverstein and Associates. It is one of the city's most important convention centers, accommodating more than 17,000 people. The Carnival Krewe of Bacchus holds its annual ball here—complete with floats—the Sunday night before Mardi Gras. Architecturally, the interior of the building is quite interesting. Its 130,000-square-foot Main Hall is an engineering marvel, especially the clear-span, column-free vaulted ceiling. The Rivergate Exhibition Center is located near numerous hotels, although it does not offer overnight guest accommodations itself.

Several first-rate hotels have sprung up in the area within the last decade, such as the Hilton (jazz clarinetist great Pete Fountain performs here regularly), Sheraton, Marriott, International, and several more are on the drawing board. Five blocks upriver from Canal Street and the ITM-Rivergate complex is the new Louisiana Convention and Exhibition Hall and the site of the 1984 Louisiana World Exposition, "The World of Rivers: Fresh Water as a Source of Life."

Walk to the corner of Canal and Magazine streets to continue our tour of the CBD. For decades the whole Canal Street area was the city's main retail shopping area, but twenty years ago creeping signs of decay began to show. The area became nothing more than a long-deteriorating riverfront warehouse district with a string of sleazy saloons and flop houses that catered to seamen. Suburban shopping centers, with ample parking, proved more convenient to new suburban lifestyles and lured shoppers away from the decaying CBD. City officials and developers have been doing an excellent job in trying to reverse the decay since the early 1970s, however. Today it is a vibrantly new commercial center with handsome landscaping, internationally known plush hotels, fine restaurants, chic retail stores and flashy nightclubs. Oddly enough, they are all mixed in with the old junk shops, wig parlors, and cheap discount stores that still remain from the by-gone days. If the current trend continues—as it appears it will—the lower end of Canal Street near the River will become a fashionable place to visit and shop. Even now, it is alive day and night with people—both visitors and natives alike. But bear in mind that this new oasis is also an island, surrounded by dimly lighted and tough riverfront areas where unwary visitors who stray away could fall victim to muggers. Stay with the crowds and bright lights and you'll have a fine time.

The massive gray block-long building facing Canal Street from the French Quarter side is the U.S. Custom House (Canal and Decatur streets). It is located on the site of the long ago demolished French colonial Fort St. Louis. Construction on the Custom House began in 1848 and was substantially completed by the onset of the Civil War. Statues were supposed to be placed in the concave niches in the exterior walls, but, for some unknown reason, they never were. The building was renovated in the 1970s and its stately Marble Hall—measuring 120 by 100 feet and described by the American Institute of Architects as one of the finest late Greek Revival rooms in America—is worth the visit. It rises three stories and its fourteen massive marble Corinthian columns support a huge ceiling and skylight.

Fortunately, a number of early 19th-century commercial buildings still remain on Canal Street. Some of them have been nicely restored while others are hidden behind tacky and garish facades. Still others remain in sort of a limbo with their original facades visible but scarred by modern additions. The 600 block of Canal Street on the CBD side contains classic examples of Canal Street commercial architecture dating from the 1830s to the 1870s. Of particular note is 622 Canal. Built in 1859 and designed by noted New Orleans architect W. A. Freret, this building's sumptuously colorful facade has been described as the city's finest surving example of a cast-iron facade. In recent years the building has housed a number of retail stores. The interior has been modernized, and its original interior architectural designs have long ago disappeared. Unquestionably the most elaborate pre-Civil War building on Canal Street is the Pickwick Club (115 St. Charles St.) at the corner of Canal and St. Charles streets. Parts of this building date back to the 1820s. In 1865 it became the Crescent Billiard Hall and in 1950 the Pickwick Club, an exclusive private men's club from old and well-to-do New Orleans families (not open to the public). Note the striking contrast between the elegant Italianate upper stories and the modern, visually unpleasant shop fronts on the ground level.

A bit of Bavaria has its presence on St. Charles Street directly behind the Pickwick Club in the form of Kolb's German Restaurant (125 St. Charles). It is the closest thing New Orleans has to a German restaurant and it is an especially popular lunch spot for local business people. Although the iron-work, galleried facade may seem out of place for a German restaurant, the scene is typically New Orleans. Stepping inside is like entering any Munich *gasthaus*. The *gasthaus* ambience is there and the menu features an interesting mixture of typical German food along with such local Creole favorites as gumbo. Also notice the ancient ceiling fan slicing the air overhead. Follow the turning shafts and belts with your eyes to the source of power and you will see a mechanical man dressed in lederhosen cranking away. The several ceiling fans reportedly came from the 1884 New Orleans Cotton Centennial Exposition in Audubon Park. In keeping with tradition, Kolb's also hosts an annual *Oktoberfest.* Next door to Kolb's is the Pearl Restaurant. It is primarily a sandwich shop, but it has an excellent raw oyster bar in addition to great hot pastrami but be careful—they may try to serve it to you on French bread with mayonnaise!

Returning to Canal Street, note the classical white, three-story stuccoed building in the middle of the 800 block. This is the Boston Club (824 Canal), an exclusive men's club. The club was formed in 1841 and named after a then popular card game, Boston. The building was constructed in 1844 and it is the only remaining single residence in this section of Canal Street. Club membership and entry is strictly by invitation only.

Perhaps the most unusual or unique bit of architecture in the CBD is the Church of Immaculate Conception, or the Jesuit Church, at 132 Baronne (around the corner from the Boston Club). Its Moorish facade, with twin onion-domed towers, is a striking contrast to the surrounding architecture. Erected in 1929–1930, it is a replica of a church built on this site in 1851–1857. The original church had fallen into such disrepair that even renovation was impossible and it had to be razed. Much of the interior furnishings and materials were saved for the reconstruction. The interior design also has a strong Moorish flavor. The horseshoe arches are supported by ornately twisted columns crowned with detailed cast-iron capitals. The intricate cast-iron pews and the gilt bronze altar all came from the original 1851 church. The altar was designed for the church by architect James Freret and cast in Lyons, France. It won first prize at the Paris Exposition of 1867–1868. Although the statue of the Virgin Mary originally was destined for the royal chapel in the Tuilleries, the royal family was driven out of France during the Revolution of 1848. The statue was later sold in France to the New Orleans congregation for $5,000.

The Orpheum Theater and Fairmont Hotel Area

Back to Canal Street and on to the next side street, University Place—so named because it was the original 1834 site of Tulane University before it moved uptown in 1894. The Orpheum Theatre (129 University Place) with its recently restored Beaux-Arts polychrome terra cotta facade and Beaux Arts interior is the new home of the New Orleans Philharmonic Symphony. Built in 1918 the theater was one of the major stops on the Orpheum's vaudeville circuit and featured such big time vaudeville acts as Houdini, Bob Hope, and George Burns and Gracie Allen. The Mystic Krewe of Comus also held its Mardi Gras balls here from 1924 to 1929. In more recent years, the Orpheum was a first-rate cinema before it began to slip and show third-rate films. The City Council and state Legislature saved the building from demolition in 1979 when developers wanted to replace it with a 480-room hotel. A hint—if you plan to attend the symphony, the seats in the first balcony are the best. According to a New York theater critic who reviewed the primere performance in the summer 1982, "in the Orpheum's first balcony, the aural picture was transformed. The lower strings bloomed, the woodwinds piped up clearly, and the percussion did not sound like so many nails being rattled in a stone jug." The symphony season begins in September and runs through May. Philippe Entremont is the orchestra's musical director as well as its conductor. Other musical events also are scheduled at the Orpheum when the symphony orchestra is not performing there.

Across the street from the Orpheum is the 750-room Fairmont Hotel, one of the city's best. Long-time New Orleans residents still refer to it as the Roosevelt Hotel, named in honor of Theodore Roosevelt's visit to the city much earlier in this century. The hotel, which became the Fairmont in 1965, contains several fine restaurants, bars and a supper club which have all been popular among generations of New Orleanians. Of particular note is the Sazerac Bar that serves two famous drinks invented in New Orleans—the Sazerac Cocktail (sugar cubes, Angosture bitters, bourbon Pernod, lemon peel and ice) which dates from the mid-1800s and the Ramos Gin Fizz (gin, egg white, powdered sugar, lemon juice, cream, lime juice, and orange flower water) which has been popular since the 1890s. The Sazerac Bar is also a favorite watering hole among many New Orleans business people. The Blue Room supper club features big-name national and international entertainers on a regular basis. Check entertainment tabloid, *Lagniappe,* in Friday's *Times-Picayune* newspaper, *Gambit* newspaper or any of the several publications found in local hotel lobbies for information on who will be appearing on stage. The hotel's restaurants and bars are extremely popular day and night among New Orleans residents. The Fairmont also has the other trappings of a first-rate hotel, including lavishly decorated interiors, meeting rooms and attentive service.

Return to Canal Street and walk up a block to the intersection of Canal and Elks Place (which becomes Basin Street on the other side of Canal Street). At Basin and Canal stands a monument to South American hero Simon Bolivar. It is one of several erected in the city during the late 1950s and early 1960s to symbolize the city's close ties with South and Central America.

No walking tour of a city would be complete without at least a passing reference to a governmental complex. The New Orleans Civic Center complex begins at the intersection of Tulane and Loyola avenues (Elks Place becomes Loyola one block from Canal Street at Tulane Avenue). The complex includes the public library, the state Supreme Court, state office buildings and City Hall. As the drab glass and concrete architecture plainly reveal, the complex was built during the 1950s. The library is the headquarters of the New Orleans library system. It has the usual general reading stacks found in most libraries as well as special divisions on art, music, business, science, foreign languages, and New Orleans and Louisiana history. Occasionally the library holds film and lecture series that are open to the public. The Civic Center complex is open from 9 A.M. to 5 P.M. weekdays when it bustles with government workers, businessmen and women, lawyers going to and from court, and everyday citizens visiting government offices. The area should be avoided at night as it becomes deserted and forbidding.

The Superdome Area

The Louisiana Superdome, that colossal structure that somewhat resembles a doorknob, lies directly behind City Hall on Poydras Street. The Superdome is a gargantuan building by any standard. For the trivia minded: it seats 77,000 people for football games and up to 100,000 for other types of events. The parking garage has space for 5,000 cars and 250 buses. The roof covers 9.7 acres and the dome is 27 stories (82.3 meters) high. The largest building of its type in the world, it houses four ballrooms, a stadium club, two restaurants, five cocktail lounges, eight bars and a 166,000 sq. ft. concrete floor covered with artificial turf appropriately called Mardi Grass. Completed in 1975, the Superdome is home to the New Orleans Saints and Tulane University football teams, the annual Sugar Bowl football classic, in addition to a number of other annual sporting events. The surrounding neighborhoods are packed when these events take place. Despite the controversy surrounding its construction and $180 million-plus price tag, the Superdome launched a building boom in the immediate area spawning the revitalization of Poydras Street. Tours of the Dome are given daily.

Directly in front of the Superdome is the Hyatt Regency Hotel, 500 Poydras Plaza, with its huge interior atrium that rises almost the entire height of the building. The revolving lounge at the top of the hotel provides a stunning view of the city.

The Hyatt is across Poydras from City Hall. During daylight hours, the streets and sidewalks are very busy with traffic and pedestrians.

Visitors to this section of the city should take special care at night as the streets are practically empty after evening rush hour ends. The Superdome area is located on the fringe of an impoverished area of town and walking at night is extremely dangerous. Take a cab!

Return to Poydras and walk toward the river. The city widened Poydras in the late 1960s as part of the renaissance of the business district. Like the rest of the Central Business District, Poydras Street sidewalks are busy from 7 A.M. to 7 P.M., Monday through Friday. But often with change, something is lost. Many mid-19th-century buildings were razed to make way for new and taller office buildings. Today the CBD is enjoying an economic vitality it has not seen since the 1850s.

Cross South Rampart Street on Poydras. There isn't much left of the old South Rampart of jazz fame when early 20th-century saloons and brothels lined the street. On the left, at 1009 Poydras, you'll find Maylies Restaurant, a century-old eating establishment that serves multi-course meals in old New Orleans style. It also has a good bar. Partly because of its interesting old 19th-century architecture and partly because of the meals served, Maylies has been a popular weekday lunch spot among local office workers and business people for generations.

After a brief but tasty repast at Maylie's or one of the other area restaurants, a brisk walk back toward Canal Street through the city's banking and financial center would certainly help digestion—depending on the current state of the economy, of course. Carondelet and St. Charles streets, between Poydras and Common streets, are synonymous with banking in New Orleans. The lobbies of the Whitney and Hibernia banks are worth the visits. Each lobby is characterized by its huge, towering marble and granite neo-Classic interior that rises several stories. As the designer of these lobbies originally intended, they exude a feeling of fiscal strength, stability and soundness. The Hibernia Bank Building (Carondelet and Gravier), completed in 1921, was the tallest building in the city for almost four decades. Its small white cupola capping the 23-story building could be seen for miles. Today, it is dwarfed by concrete and glass skyscrapers that seemingly are popping out of the ground faster than bamboo shoots in an Asian rain forest.

Place St. Charles, a 53-story office-retail complex on the corner of St. Charles and Common, stands at the site of the old St. Charles Hotel. Three St. Charles hotels have occupied this spot, dating back to the 1830s. The first two were destroyed by fire. The most recent one, one of the first examples of period architecture built in the late 1890s, was demolished in the 1970s to make way for a much-touted architectural marvel that never materialized. For several years thereafter the site was used as a parking lot. The barren square was a constant scar that was a constant reminder to New Orleanians of how fragile our architectural treasures are.

Although demolition of pre-Civil War buildings ran rampant in the 1960s and early 1970s, adapting old buildings to modern use has become fashionable among the business community. Notice the superb restorations and commercial adaptations in the 300 blocks of both St. Charles and Carondelet streets. It is happening throughout the CBD. For example, the South Savings and Loan Building, 300 St. Charles Avenue, is an excellent example of how pre-Civil War commercial buildings are being beautifully restored. Also noticed the First Homestead across the street. Another example of this urban revitalization was the renovation of the Board of Trade Building and the creation of the Board of Trade Plaza in the 300 block of Magazine Street (2 blocks parallel from St. Charles toward the river) in the late 1960s. The Board of Trade Plaza consists of a raised classical courtyard with a large center fountain. It is enclosed on one side by a colonnaded breezeway and on the street side by a large iron picket fence. Also visit the Piazza d'Italia on Poydras and Tchoupitoulas near the Hilton Hotel. Built in the 1970s on the site of old produce warehouses, the Piazza's polychromatic pseudo-Roman piazza—complete with chrome columns and neon lights—has evoked extreme emotions by those who praise its excess and those who condemn it as a garish insult. At night the surreal atmosphere created by the neon lights, chrome and fountains seems an appropriate high-tech interpretation of the ancient world.

If you are down in this area of the CBD during the daytime when it's alive and bustling, there are two other spots to catch: Mother's Restaurant at 401 Poydras and the old Bank's Arcade. Mother's (open for lunch) unquestionably has the best roast beef and baked ham Poboys (hero-type sandwiches) in the city. The long queue in front of the counter each day at lunchtime attests to that appraisal.

The old Bank's Arcade (336 Magazine adjacent to the Board of Trade Plaza) was erected in 1833 to serve as a meeting place for merchants. But as history records, Bank's Arcade was more than a meeting place where local business deals were transacted. It also was the scene of international intrigues. Plotted within these walls were the Texas Revolution (1835) when agents for the revolution often spoke there to recruit New Orleans men to fight against Mexico; General Narcisco Lopez's ill-fated invasion of Cuba (1851); and, William Walker's adventurous military expedition into Nicaragua (1855). The arcade once took in the entire block. Notice the architectural similarities between the arcade and the Pontalba Buildings in the French Quarter. The arcade predates the Pontalbas by almost twenty years. What has survived of Bank's Arcade is now the corporate home of J. Aron & Company (oil and gas investors).

Continuing our walking tour of the CBD, return to St. Charles and Poydras by walking two blocks from Magazine Street away from the river and one block to the left. The yellow-chrome bank building at the corner was constructed in the early 1970s. Facing the yellow-chrome building is the Federal Reserve Bank.

Lafayette Square

Across the street from the bank is Lafayette Square, which is one block square and was once the political center of the city. Lafayette is the city's second oldest public square. It was the American Section's answer to the Place d'Armes (Jackson Square). When plans were drawn for this "new" section of town in 1788, the public square was given the name Gravier, in honor of the developers. It was rechristened Lafayette Square in 1824 during the Marquis' visit to the city.

The square has seen its share of New Orleans history, especially the bloody, riot-filled political campaigns of the last century. Perhaps the most bizarre example of 19th-century New Orleans politics was the mayoral election of 1858 when Lafayette and Jackson squares became armed and opposing quasi-military camps complete with artillery. The mob antics of the Native American Party, a secretive national political party representing the interests of the American section and known as the Know Nothings, reached a pitch when its members stole voter registration rolls and purged names not sympathetic to its party. Police and city officials did nothing. Creoles and foreign-born residents, often victims of Know Nothing attacks, formed the Vigilance Committee to ensure fair elections. The committee invaded and occupied the Cabildo, the arsenal in the rear of the Cabildo, and Jackson Square and proclaimed itself the city's provisional government. At the time, the Cabildo was a police station and court as well as one of the most historical and symbolic buildings in the city. With authorization from city officials, Know Nothing mobs armed themselves with rifles and artillery and occupied Lafayette Square. The French Quarter and American Section were armed camps. When the Know Nothings tried to invade the Quarter, they were met by rifle and artillery fire. After retreating hastily to Lafayette Square, the Know Nothings became so nervous about a possible Vigilance Committee attack (which did not come) that sharpshooters shot and killed members of their own returning patrols. Election day passed quietly with the Know Nothings winning the mayoralty and most other city elections. The Vigilance Committee dispersed peacefully after the election. Although no one was prosecuted, many of the Vigilance members hid for a while in nearby swamps until hunger got the best of them.

In more recent years, the square and surrounding neighborhood became home for skidrow derelicts. But much of that is changing as public officials, developers, property owners and preservationists make a concerted effort to restore buildings in the area to its former luster. While the area is quite safe during weekdays when it is a center of the bustling commercial district, it is a foolish and dangerous place to be at night when muggers are on the prowl.

There are three notable statues in the square. In the center stands the Clay Monument, a bigger-than-life bronze statue of early 19th-century American statesman Henry Clay, "The Great Pacificator." Clay, who had family connections in Louisiana and was a frequent visitor to New Orleans, died in 1852 in Washington, D.C. Eight years later the statue was unveiled at the corner of Canal and Royal streets where it stood for almost a half century. The city moved the monument to Lafayette Square in 1901 because of increasingly heavy traffic on Canal Street.

The bronze statue facing St. Charles Street and Gallier Hall is of John McDonogh. McDonogh came to New Orleans from Baltimore at the age of 22. Before his death in 1850, he had acquired a fortune and vast land holdings in and around New Orleans, including several plantations. Somewhat of a recluse during his life, McDonogh was one of the founders and chief contributors to the American Colonization Society founded in 1817 to return freed slaves to Liberia in Africa. In his will he divided his fortune between New Orleans and his native Baltimore for the construction of free schools. New Orleans built 36 public schools with the legacy. The bust was designed in 1898 by New York sculptor Atallio Picoirilli and paid for by nickle-donations from the city's school children. McDonogh's only request was that "the children of the free schools be permitted to plant and water a few flowers around my grave." McDonogh first was buried across the river on his Algiers plantation, but his body was moved later to Baltimore. New Orleans public school children continue to the present day to lay flowers at the foot of McDonogh's bust on the first Friday of each May.

On the far side of the square, facing Camp Street, is a bronze statue of Benjamin Franklin. It was donated to the city in 1926 by Henry Wadsworth Gustine, a Chicago businessman who enjoyed spending his winters in New Orleans.

Notice the architectural contrasts around Lafayette Square. The massive columned building facing the Square on St. Charles Street (545 St. Charles) is Gallier Hall, an architectural landmark and one of the best examples of Greek revival architecture in this part of in the country. Built in the late 1840s by architect James Gallier, Sr., a native of Ravensdale, Ireland, the building served as the New Orleans City Hall from 1853 to 1957. Most oldtimers still refer to it as old City Hall.

Because of political, cultural and economic rivalries between the Americans and the Creoles, the city was divided into three municipalities in the 1830s: the American Section (Second Municipality) above Canal Street; the French Quarter (First Municipality); and, Faubourg Marigny (Third Municipality) below Esplanade Avenue. For a brief period during the early 1850s, Gallier Hall served as Municipal Hall for the Second Municipality, but after the consolidation in 1852, City Hall was moved from the Cabildo in the French Quarter to Gallier Hall. The move symbolized the American dominance over the waning Creole community.

Gallier Hall has witnessed many strange sights during its 130-plus years. At various times during the 1850s and 1860s several different mayors had to be dragged kicking and screaming out of the mayor's office after losing their re-election bids. Federal troops lowered the Confederate flag flying high over City Hall when the city fell to Union forces in 1862 during the Civil War. New Orleans had the dubious distinction of being under Reconstruction longer than any other Southern city.

In 1932 Governor Huey Long (despot or hero, depending upon one's point of view) sent state troops to occupy City Hall during a political struggle with the mayor and the city's Old Regular political organization. The Old Regulars was a ward-style political organization in the Tammany Hall tradition, lacking any real political ideology other than "Democrat." On a lighter side, the venerable old building also has watched 130 years of Mardi Gras parades pass before its viewing stands. The mayor toasts the reigning krewe monarchs of many of the parades from Gallier Hall.

The city restored the hall in the 1970s. The mayor's office and parlor are well worth seeing. They are quite different from the chairman-of-the-board look of the mayor's office in the new City Hall in the Civic Center. Located in the basement is the New Orleans Recreation Department Theater (NORD Theater). It produces several highly entertaining plays each year with local talent. Check the schedule.

Before moving on from Gallier Hall, notice the relief figures of Justice, Commerce, and Manufacture in the pediment over the columns.

The long squat eclectic Italian Renaissance-style building facing the Square on Camp Street was the old Post Office building until the 1950s. Erected in 1914 and renovated in the late 1960s and 1970s, it now houses part of the federal court system. Occupying part of this site in the last century was Odd Fellows Hall, one of the most popular meeting places in the city.

Heading a block up Camp Street away from Poydras is St. Patrick's Church (724 Camp). The church, patterned after York Minster in

England, was built in the late 1830s as a place of worship for the city's newly arriving Irish Catholics. It was designed by the architectural firm of Charles and James Dakin, and completed by James Gallier, Sr., two of antebellum New Orleans' best known architectural firms. The vaulted, ribbed ceilings in the nave and sanctuary, with its stained-glass windows and murals, are graceful and worth the visit. The three large murals above the main altar were painted in 1840 by Leon Pomarade. Also notice the *faux boix* and *faux marble* walls that reportedly date from the 1872 restoration. Architectural historians also surmise that the rough cement exterior originally was scored stucco and painted to resemble building stones.

Renovation and Revitalization

Located a half block up at the corner of Camp and Julia streets is one of the most ambitious residential renovation projects underway in the city—Julia Street Row, also known as the Thirteen Sisters. The row of thirteen brick townhouses dates from the 1830s, and they take up the entire block between Camp and St. Charles. The project has been spearheaded by the Historic Fauborg St. Mary and the Preservation Resource Center of New Orleans, which has a membership of over sixty preservation and neighborhood organizations. On the other side of the street are skidrow tenements and service shops as well as a recently restored building housing law and other offices.

American-style townhouses were popular in New Orleans during the early decades of the 19th century. They are found in the Creole Faubourg Marigny, the French Quarter and, of course, in the CBD. Like Julia Row they were built by speculative developers and sold almost as quickly as they could complete them.

Before the Civil War, Julia Row was one of the finest residential neighborhoods in the city. But by the turn-of-the-century, as the city spread out and waves of poor immigrants arrived, the Row had already started its slow and painful decline. New Orleans writer Eliza Ripley, who lived in Julia Row during her early childhood, noted the former glory of the Thirteen Sisters in her book, *Social Life in Old New Orleans* (1912):

I wonder if anyone under seventy-five years of age passes old "Julia row" today and knows that those "13 Buildings" between Camp and St. Charles Streets have an aristocratic past, and were once occupied by the leading social element of the American colony residing in the early forties above Canal Street? "13 Buildings" it was called . . . and a decade later every one of them was tenanted by prominent citizens of New Orleans. There they lived and entertained a host of delightful guests, whose names were a power then, but whose descendants are perhaps little known today.

One of those frequent guests was Henry Clay, a lifelong friend of Ripley's father. Unfortunately the area is still scarred by a seedy skidrow. If the restoration momentum continues, Julia Row might once again be a prestigious residential neighborhood.

Incidentally, legend has it that Julia Street was named for Julia, a free-woman-of-color once owned by Julian Poydras, a wealthy New Orleans merchant and landowner. Others speculate that the street was named for Poydras himself whose nickname was Julie.

A walk through this area—recommended during daylight hours only—will spark the imagination of what can be done with the many architectural survivors that remain there.

Two blocks up Camp Street is the Confederate Museum (929 Camp). The building, designed by noted New Orleans architect Thomas Sully, was built in 1891. The museum contains numerous historical artifacts pertaining to the Confederacy and Jefferson Davis. Paintings, prints, photographs, daguerreotypes, ambiotypes of Confederate generals and soldiers, uniforms, Robert E. Lee's campaign silver service, medical instruments, battle flags, and weapons—including those belonging to New Orleans General P. G. T. Beauregard—are among the museum's treasures.

Next to the museum is a low, massive Romanesque building. This rather somber-looking redstone fortress originally housed the city library, known formally as the Howard Memorial Library, until the 1950s. It was built in 1888 according to plans drawn by noted American architect and Louisiana native Henry Hobson Richardson. A law firm now occupies the building.

Lee Circle Area

Across the street, at the intersection of Howard Avenue and St. Charles, is Lee Circle and the Robert E. Lee monument. Lee, of course, held the distinction of commanding general of the Confederate troops. As you may recall from history lessons, Lee married Mary Custis, the great granddaughter of Martha Washington, and was superintendent of the U.S. Military Academy at West Point from 1852 to 1853. He was also commanding officer of the troops that stopped John Brown at Harper's Ferry in 1859. Although Abraham Lincoln offered Lee command of the Union ground forces at the outbreak of the Civil War, Lee declined and resigned his commission. Instead he tossed his fate with that of his native Virginia and the Confederacy.

The drive to build Lee's monument began in New Orleans in 1870, the year of his death. Because New Orleans was deeply embroiled in Reconstruction at that time, the monument committee had a difficult time raising money for this tribute to the Confederacy's commanding general. By 1876 the committee had raised enough money to commission New York sculptor Alexander Doyle to begin work. But money shortages and other delays caused the work to proceed slowly. Finally on Washington's birthday, 1884, the long-awaited tribute to Lee was unveiled. Present at the ceremonies were Jefferson Davis, P. G. T. Beauregard, and a host of other former Confederate dignitaries. For the trivia minded: The granite column is 60 feet tall.

At one time Lee Circle, or Tivoli Circle as it was known earlier, was lined with fashionable homes. Amid the gas stations and office buildings that crowd the area, only one of the old houses—albeit modified—remains today.

Uptown

Uptown New Orleans, upriver from Canal Street, also includes the Central Business District, and several sections of the city: the Garden District, Lower Garden District, the Irish Channel, University Section, Carrollton, and Broadmoor. Each section is connected to the other as the city follows its winding course upriver. The Lower Garden District and Irish Channel are more or less continuations of the CBD. The Garden District is contiguous to the Lower Garden District and Irish Channel and so on.

Prior to the Civil War, most of these sections were carved from sugar plantations that lined the Mississippi River. Today, they include some of the nations' most elegant 19th-century neighborhoods (Garden District and Audubon Place). But Uptown also contains impoverished areas that could cause problems for sightseers.

Uptown New Orleans simply follows St. Charles Avenue which parallels the Mississippi River. The best way to see this section of the city, especially the Garden District and University area, is to take one of the many commercial guided tours. The guides know where to go and the points of interest. Because these areas are so vast and spread out, walking tours would be difficult and in some cases inadvisable. Another way to visit Uptown is to catch the St. Charles streetcar and pay the 60-cent fare to ride the oldest continuing railroad in the country—founded in 1835. Take the five-mile ride up St. Charles to the end of the line in Carrollton. Along the way you can get off and walk through the Garden District, and then reboard (pay full fare again) and continue on to the University and Carrollton areas. The ride is quite pleasant. In addition, you can see the lovely and stately St. Charles Avenue homes from the streetcar windows.

Lower Garden District

The Coliseum Square area, now usually referred to as the Lower Garden District, encompasses the area from Howard Avenue to Felicity Street and Prytania Street to Magazine Street. Dating from the early 1800s, it was for many years an elegant antebellum neighborhood but deteriorated into a slum a century later. Its fine homes dating from the 1830s to 1850s became third-rate flophouses and tenements. The area has made, and is continuing to make, a remarkable comeback since the early 1970s. This is due largely to a book published by the Friends of the Cabildo titled, *The Lower Garden District,* which drew the attention of young professionals to the area. Today more and more young affluent families are buying and renovating the old homes.

This faubourg, or suburb, was laid out between 1806 and 1810 by surveyor Barthelemy Lafon on land previously occupied by four plantations. Lafon's suburb begins on Howard Avenue and ends at Felicity Street. The main streets in the development were the *Cours du Colisée* and *Rue du Colisée* with a large triangular park in the middle. The park was to house a large coliseum for gaming events but it was never built. Lafon's plan was obviously a child of the neo-Classical era. The *Rue du Colisée* was an extension of Camp Street from the Faubourg St. Mary. Both street names were changed in the mid-19th century to Camp Street and Coliseum Street. The main avenues heading uptown from Tivoli Circle (later Lee Circle) and Howard Avenue were named Prytania, Nayades, Apollo, Bacchus, Hercules, and Dryades. Prytania and Dryades have kept their names to the present day, but Nayades became St. Charles Avenue; Apollo, Carondelet; Bacchus, Baronne; and Hercules, South Rampart. They became continuations of the streets in the Central Business District. Lafon's plan also included construction of the *Prytanée,* a French-styled preparatory school slated for Prytania Street, but, like the coliseum never came about either. According to New Orleans historian John Chase, Lafon's grandiose plan for the suburb didn't materialize for two reasons: Louisiana statehood in 1812 and the War of 1812 both of which put the city into an economic crunch. The lower Garden District flourished a few decades later. Only the street names remain from Lafon's big plan. There are few people on the streets in this area so visitors should not walk around here. Nearby slums make this area rather dangerous at times and you would be well advised to stay in your car or visit the area on a bus tour. The main sites to see are the early 19th-century architecture and building restorations. Many bus tours hit the high spots along Coliseum Street.

Garden District

The Garden District, bounded by Jackson Avenue to Louisiana Avenue and St. Charles Avenue to Magazine, is one of the finest residential areas in the country. It was once part of the now defunct city of Lafayette. Lafayette was created from the Livaudais plantation and developed in 1835 by Americans who were fed up with the Creole-dominated politics in New Orleans. Wealthy American merchants built fine homes here and it eventually became such a prestigious city that even Creoles moved in, building equally sumptuous houses. Most of the grand homes in the district date from the 1840s to the 1870s. Lafayette was annexed to New Orleans in the early 1850s. The portion of Lafayette now called the Garden District includes the area from Jackson Avenue to Louisiana Avenue and St. Charles Avenue to Magazine Street.

One normally visits the Garden District to see the beautiful homes, architectural styles, lush green gardens, and tree-lined streets. But in addition, there are several other points of interest that should not be missed. Magazine Street has hundreds of antique and speciality shops and art galleries. Commander's Palace (Washington Avenue near Prytania) housed in a fine Victorian building has been a popular Uptown restaurant among locals and visitors since the 1880s. Nearby is Lafayette Cemetery (visit during daylight only) dating from the 1830s, and the Rink (2727 Prytania St.), a large building housing several fashionable speciality shops, moderately priced book and gift shops, and a restaurant.

There are a number of magnificent mid- to late-19th-century homes in the Garden District that should not be missed. Although most of them are private homes and closed to the public, visitors still may enjoy the ambience and grace of these architectural styles from the street and sidewalk. McGehee Garden District Tours offer tours of the area by appointment. Also The Preservation Resource Center, 604 Julia St., 581–7032, offers occasional tours of Garden District homes. Call for schedules and information.

Starting at Lafayette Cemetery at Washington and Prytania avenues, continue down Prytania a couple of blocks toward Canal Street until you reach Fourth Street. Turn right on Fourth and about a block down toward the river is the Short House (1448 Fourth). In addition to the 1859 house that was built for Colonel Robert Short of Kentucky, the most interesting point of interest here is the cast-iron cornstalk-and-morning-glory fence. It is an almost exact duplicate to the cornstalk fence at 915 Royal Street in the French Quarter. And also like the one in the French Quarter, this one was made in Philadelphia and shipped to New Orleans before the Civil War. Return to Prytania Street, go one block toward Canal Street and then turn right into Third Street. On your left is the Robinson House (1415 Third St.), one of the largest and grandest houses in the Garden District. It was constructed in 1865 for a Walter Robinson, and it is believed to be the first house in New Orleans with indoor plumbing. Continuing on Third Street another block and again on your left is the Musson House (1331 Third)—the street numbers get smaller as you approach the river. The Musson House, built in the 1850s for Michel Musson (related by marriage to French Impressionist painter Edgar Degas), has one of the most stunning examples of lacy cast-iron galleries outside the French Quarter. At the next corner (Coliseum) turn left and continue two blocks to First Street. Turn right into First Street and continue toward the river to the 1100 block. On your right at 1134 First Street is the Judge Jacob U. Payne House. This opulent Italianate-style mansion was constructed in 1849–1850 with the use of black slave labor. Jefferson Davis, President of the Confederate States of America, died here December 6, 1889, during a visit to New Orleans. Continue down First Street to Magazine Street (a busy, two-way thoroughfare). Turn left on Magazine and drive one block to Philip Street and turn left again. Continue on Philip Street four blocks to Prytania Street and make another left turn into Prytania. On your right is the Louise S. McGehee School for Girls (2343 Prytania), an expensive and exclusive private school. The massive and imposing Second Empire-style mansion was built in 1872 for a wealthy New Orleans sugar factor, Bradish Johnson. It was designed by New Orleans architect James Freret, who studied at the Ecole des Beaux Arts in Paris. Tours are available by appointment, 561-1224.

Another of New Orleans more interesting historical neighborhoods is the Irish Channel. It lies directly below the Garden District between Magazine Street and the river.

Irish Channel

The Irish Channel, like the Garden District, was also part of Lafayette. It got its name from the Irish immigrants who settled here from the 1840s onward. Its parameters lie roughly between Magazine Street and the river and Howard Avenue to approximately Louisiana Avenue. By the Civil War in 1861, almost 20 percent of the city's population was Irish. The Germans made up the next largest immigrant group. They too settled in the Channel (as it is simply called) and on upriver farms. The Channel has always been a working-class neighborhood, but very few people of Irish descent still reside here. The area has been on the skids for the past twenty-five years or so and today it remains a depressed area populated mostly by poor blacks and Cubans who fled Castro's revolution. However, during the last decade, the Channel has become increasingly popular among young, white, affluent upper-middle class families who are buying and renovating the Victorian-era cottages. These pockets of revitalization may be found scattered throughout Magazine, Annunciation, Tchoupitoulas, and Constance streets and concentrate mostly between Jackson and Lousiana avenues. Also located in the Channel is the St. Thomas Street federal housing project—a rough and unsafe place for visitors and natives alike.

Of particular interest in the Channel are the Roman Catholic Redemptorist churches administered by the Congregation of the Most Holy Redeemer order, located on Constance and Josephine streets. Constance runs parallel to Magazine Street one block over on the river side. Josephine Street crosses Magazine about three blocks from Jackson Avenue. In the 1850s, the Redemptorists built three churches here to serve the three major Catholic ethnic groups—French, Irish, and Germans. The French church is gone, but St. Alphonsus (2029 Constance), the Irish church, and St. Mary Assumption (Josephine and Constance), the German one, still remain even though their original congregations are gone. Both churches were constructed in a baroque style and both are worth seeing.

Also located in this area (1729 Coliseum St.) is the boyhood home of explorer Sir Henry Morton Stanley of "Dr. Livingstone, I presume" fame. Stanley was born John Rowlands but later took the name of the wealthy New Orleans merchant who gave him a home. The house was moved to this location about three years ago from the 900 block of Orange Street. The parish School Board owned the land on which the house was originally located and wanted to use it. So as not to destroy the house, the building was sold at a public auction. The mid-19th-century house is not open to the public but there are plans to have it renovated.

The Channel is also known for the hundreds of antique shops that line Magazine Street. Magazine Street is relatively safe to walk around and you'll enjoy browsing through the shops there. The best and safest way to see the rest of the Channel is by car or guided motor tour. Walking in this area can be dangerous.

University Area and Carrollton

After completing your tour of the Irish Channel, you should not miss the opportunity to see the rest of Uptown New Orleans. The best place to begin the tour, if you're coming from the Irish Channel or Garden District, is to return to St. Charles and Louisiana avenues and head up

St. Charles. Heading Uptown by car or streetcar, there are a few other sites—homes, clubs, restaurants, churches—along St. Charles that should be noted.

Before getting on with the historical spots and architectural splendors, one must be mindful of equally important attractions—bars and restaurants. Seven blocks up St. Charles on the right is the 4141 Club, which is one of the most popular Uptown night spots for young, affluent Uptown New Orleanians. Great bar, food, and atmosphere. On with the tour. Two blocks from the 4141 Club Touro Synagogue (4338 St. Charles) was constructed in 1909 and named for New Orleans philanthropist Judah Touro, who died in 1854. Touro, born in Newport, Rhode Island, left considerable sums of money in his will for the construction of the first Touro Synagogue in New Orleans (since demolished) and Touro Infirmary (on Prytania Street one block from the intersection of Louisiana and St. Charles avenues), one of the largest hospitals in the city. Two blocks up St. Charles on the right hand side at 4521 St. Charles is the Sacred Heart Academy, a fashionable Catholic private school for girls dating from 1899. It is owned and operated by the Sacred Heart nuns. Five blocks up St. Charles on the right is the Orleans Club (5005 St. Charles). Originally a private home dating from 1868, the building is now the home of an exclusive women's social club. In the next block of St. Charles on the left side is the Milton H. Latter Memorial Library (5120 St. Charles). The building housing the library was once the home of silent screen star Marguerite Clark. But it later was purchased by the Latter family of New Orleans and given to the city as a library in memory of their son who was killed during World War II.

Continue up St. Charles and notice the varying but rich architectural styles of the houses and mansions along the way. One of the most spectacular and classical examples of turn-of-the-century architecture is the "Wedding Cake House" (5809 St. Charles). Known for its lavishly decorated exterior, the house is an architectural landmark along the avenue. Built in 1896, it is a private residence not open to the public. Another architectural gem along this section of St. Charles is located another five blocks up the avenue. On the left at 6330 St. Charles is the Round Table Club, a private men's social club dating from the 1890s. Located on the downtown side of Audubon Park, this Beaux Arts-styled former residence has a great view of the park from its side windows. Many a festive party has been held in this club, especially its annual ball held the Friday night before Mardi Gras. The ball is strictly by invitation only. Notice the massive two-story Tiffany stained-glass window on the downtown side of the building. The clubhouse is open to members only and their guests. Across the street from the Round Table Club are Loyola and Tulane universities.

Loyola and Tulane

Loyola University (6363 St. Charles) is owned and operated by the Jesuits. It dates back to 1840 when the Jesuits established the College of the Immaculate Conception in downtown New Orleans. Suffering from growing pains, the campus moved to its present location in 1911. It has been co-educational since 1915, and it is the South's largest Roman Catholic university. During the 1982–1983 academic year, the university had 4,682 students: 3,385 undergraduates, 671 law students and 626 graduate students. Loyola's campus is housed on five city square blocks: one block facing St. Charles Avenue and five blocks deep to Freret Street. Loyola is particularly known for its Law School, which concentrates on Louisiana's unique Napoleonic Code (the other 49 states in the Union use English Common Law). The large red brick Tudor-Gothic style church facing St. Charles Avenue to the left of Loyola's main building is Holy Name Church, built in 1918. It is part of the Loyola campus and also the parish church for this section of the city.

Tulane University (6823 St. Charles) next door began in 1834 as the Medical College of Louisiana. The name was changed in 1847 to the University of Louisiana, but when Paul Tulane, a wealthy New Orleans merchant, made a sizable bequest to the university in 1883, the university adopted its benefactor's name. The original campus was located on University Place just off Canal Street on the general site of the Orpheum Theatre. The St. Charles Avenue campus dates from 1894. Tulane is known worldwide for its fine medical school, which is located downtown on Tulane Avenue; its Delta Primate Research Center; and, the Middle America Research Center. It also has a respected law school, teaching both the Napoleonic Code and English Common Law, and a business school. Tulane has the oldest college of commerce in the nation. The campus is located on twenty-five city square blocks beginning on St. Charles and stretching back to South Claiborne Avenue. Also located on the Tulane campus is Newcomb College for Women. Originally, Newcomb (founded in 1886) existed as a private college for women without any connection to Tulane. But in 1918 the two institutions merged. In the 1982–1983 year, Tulane had 10,489 students: 6,616 undergraduates, 735 graduate students, 867 in the Law School, 164 in the School of Social Welfare, 353 in public health, 601 in Medical School, 441 medical residents, 396 business graduate students, and 316 engineering graduate students.

Of particular architectural note is Tulane University's main building, Gibson Hall. It was constructed in 1894 in the Richardsonian Romanesque style and designed by New Orleans architects Harrod and Andry. The building is open to the public.

Both Loyola and Tulane universities have very fine historical research collections. Loyola has microfilmed huge quantities of Louisiana colonial documents found in various French and Spanish archives. Tulane's Howard Tilton Library building contains the Latin American Library, the New Orleans Jazz Archives, Special Collections Division, and the Middle American Research Institute with its extensive collections of pre-Colombian art.

Audubon Park and Zoo

Directly across St. Charles Avenue from Tulane University is the main entrance to Audubon Park and Zoological Garden. The 400-acre park, which stretches from St. Charles Avenue back to the Mississippi River, is one of the most beautiful urban parks in the nation and a pleasant place for *daytime* strolls. The land making up the park was originally part of the 18th-century Foucher and Boré plantations. Louisiana's sugar industry was born here on Etienne de Boré's plantation in the late 18th and early 19th centuries with the first successful granulation of sugar. The city bought the property from land speculators in 1871 and created the Upper City Park. The 1884–1885 World's Industrial and Cotton Centennial Exhibition—New Orlean's first world's fair—was held here. The fair, which was a financial bust, featured exhibits from all over the world and a 31-acre exhibition building made entirely of wood. The object remaining from the fair is a large chunk of iron ore sitting in the middle of the park's golf course. About the turn of the century the park was renamed Audubon Park, for naturalist John James Audubon who spent much time in Louisiana earlier in the century, and rebuilt based partially on a plan drawn up by famed landscape architect Frederick Law Olmsted, who designed New York City's Central Park.

Audubon Park also offers a public golf course and swimming pool, tennis courts, horseback riding, bicycle rentals, picnic grounds (located throughout the park), jogging paths, and a miniature train that travels through parts of the zoo. The park is closed to automobile traffic on weekends. During that time it is reserved for bicycles and joggers.

The 58-acre zoo, located toward the rear of the park between Magazine Street and the river, was once an embarrassment to the city. Now it is unquestionably the finest park in this part of the country. Visitors can stroll through the picturesque setting at their leisure to see over a thousand animals living in natural habitat settings. Or you can ride the Mombassa Railway for a guided tour of the zoo. The zoo is divided into five main sections and several subsections. Each of the main sections—

Asian Domain, World of Primates, African Savannah, North American Grasslands, and South American Pampas—features animals native to those sections of the world. In addition, the zoo also has a sea lion pool, bird house and sanctuary, reptiles, aquarium, elephant rides, a children's petting zoo, restaurants, and gift shops. Scheduled for completion by mid-decade are the Louisiana Swamp and Australian exhibits. The zoo's board of directors and its allied group, the Friends of the Zoo, have done a magnificent job over the last ten years. Be sure not to miss Monkey Hill as you are walking through the African Savannah. Monkey Hill was a popular playground for two generations of New Orleanians. Before the zoo was expanded in the 1970s to included this section of the park, children had a great time running up and down the hill. After all, this approximately 50 ft. mound of dirt is the only hill in all of New Orleans. It was built by the WPA in the 1930s.

The zoo is open from 9:30 A.M. to 4:30 P.M. Monday through Friday; 9:30 A.M. to 5:30 P.M. (during daylight savings time) or 9:30 A.M. to 4:30 P.M. Saturdays, Sundays, and holidays. Admission is charged. The Friends of the Zoo sponsor activities at the zoo throughout the year. Check the newspaper or call the zoo for current events.

Elsewhere in the University Section

Off St. Charles, on the uptown side of Tulane University, is Audubon Place, the ritziest and most exclusive street in town. The street is blocked by a large and ominous iron gate and the neighborhood within is walled off so that no one can get in unless expected by one of its exclusive residents. The mansions that line both sides of this private street were built starting in the 1890s. The large columned white mansion on the corner of St. Charles and Audubon Place—the one that would put Scarlet O'Hara's Tara to shame—was the home of the late Sam Zemurray, founder of Standard Fruit Company. Zemurray started his fortune with a small cart selling overripe bananas from door to door. He eventually built a financial empire with tentacles reaching into the political backrooms of several Central American countries. The house, now owned by Tulane University, is the residence of the university's president.

About three blocks up St. Charles from Audubon Place is Dominican College for women at the corner of St. Charles and Broadway. The college was founded in the 1860s by the Irish Dominican nuns. The large galleried wooden building facing St. Charles was built in the early 1870s.

The Carrollton Area

The Carrollton section begins a block up from Dominican College at Lowerline Street. Carrollton got its name from General William Carrollton who camped here in 1815 during the Battle of New Orleans. St. Charles Avenue, following the river, makes a ninety degree turn to the north and becomes Carrollton Avenue. The large, rising parklike green expanse off to the left is the levee. You might want to hop off the streetcar here, climb the levee and watch the ships cruising the Mississippi. Old Carrollton was a popular resort for 19th-century New Orleanians. Today, the Riverbend area—as this part of old Carrollton is called—is a quaint old residential area with a number of small shops and cafes. The Camelia Grill (626 S. Carrollton) in particular, has been popular with two generations of Uptown residents and college students. Harry, a waiter at Camelia Grill and die-hard Yankee baseball fan, is a local institution. Other good restaurants in the area include Riverbend Restaurant, located where the river makes its wide turn about five miles upriver from Canal Street and St. Charles becomes S. Carrollton, and Campagno's Restaurant (7839 St. Charles). The latter has great Italian food and its fried oysters are hard to beat.

The multistoried, white-columned building across from the Camelia Grill on Carrollton Avenue is Benjamin Franklin High School. It is a public school for exceptionally bright students who must pass an entrance exam to go there. Built in 1855, it served as the Carrollton Town Hall until the town was annexed to New Orleans in the 1870s. Nearby Maple and Oak streets, with their numerous specialty shops and cafes, are the main shopping locations in old Carrollton. They bustle with shoppers during the day. The bars and restaurants on Maple Street are especially popular with students and faculty members from Tulane and Loyola universities. Some of the more popular watering holes and cafes are Phillips Restaurant (Maple and Cherokee streets), Vera Cruz (7535 Maple Street) and Bruno's (7601 Maple).

Bayou St. John and City Park Area (Mid City)

The Bayou St. John and City Park area can easily be reached by driving up Carrollton Avenue and past Canal Street. North Carrollton, a continuation of South Carrollton at Canal Street, ends at Bayou St. John and City Park. If you are in the French Quarter and want to visit Bayou St. John and City Park without traveling through Uptown, you can get there via Esplanade Avenue at the lower boundary of the French Quarter. Esplanade begins at the river and ends about three miles later at Bayou St. John and the main entrance to City Park.

Frenchmen settled along Bayou St. John (Bayou Ste. Jean on early maps) as early as 1708, ten years before the founding of New Orleans. Until early in this century, the bayou (the term generally means small creeks or rivers) was a major water highway connecting the French Quarter via a late 18th-century canal to Lake Pontchartrain. The Carondelet Canal, which led from the Bayou to Basin Street behind the French Quarter, was filled in early this century. There are a number of raised Louisiana colonial houses dating from the late 18th and 19th centuries located facing the bayou. The old architecture is great and so are the Po-boy sandwiches at Parkway Bakery located at Hagan and Toulouse streets, a block from where the bayou was blocked up and dead ends. Parkway is a very unpretentious neighborhood sandwich shop that bakes its own French bread. People fish around this area of the bayou all the time but it's not particularly good fishing. Water skiing is permitted at the lower end of the bayou near Lake Pontchartrain; however, most waterskiers prefer to use the lake.

Facing the bayou is City Park, once the 18th-century sugar plantation of Louis Allard. The oak-tree-lined main entrance to this 1500-acre public park is magnificent. It is one of the largest urban parks in the nation. The park grounds with its majestic live oaks and network of man-made lagoons are well worth seeing. Located at the foot of the entrance boulevard is the New Orleans Museum of Art. The museum has come a long way in recent years. It has hosted several major international traveling exhibitions, including "The Treasures of Tutankhamun," "Peru's Golden Treasures," "The Search for Alexander," and "Honore Daumier, 1801–1879." It has a fair representative permanent collection of art ranging from pre-Colombian and Far Eastern work to European, American and African masters. However, its strongest collections are Louisiana art, primitive art and photography, featuring work by such notables as Laszlo Moholy-Nagy, Walker Evans, Alfred Stieglitz, and James Van Der Zee. As you enter the park, the large stand of oak trees off to the left are the "Dueling Oaks" where 18th- and 19th-century New Orleanians settled disputes with rapiers, broad swords, pistols, knives, and shotguns. Although dueling was always outlawed, it was a commonly accepted way to uphold one's honor.

Located behind the museum building on Roosevelt Avenue is a beautiful formal rose garden. The garden and much of the park was built or improved by the Works Progress Administration during the Great Depression of the 1930s. The work of the WPA is evident everywhere.

In addition to the art museum, City Park offers three 18-hole public golf courses, tennis courts, a canoe and paddle boat rentals, a small amusement park and petting zoo for children, picnic grounds through-

out the park, and a miniature train. Concession stands are located on
Dreyfus Drive that begins on the south side of the museum circle.

The museum is open 10 A.M. to 5 P.M. Tuesday through Sunday,
except Thursday when it is open 1 P.M. to 9 P.M. Closed Mondays. There
is an admission charged but entrance is free on Thursdays.

City Park is bounded on the north by Lake Pontchartrain, City Park
Avenue on the south, Bayou St. John to the east, and Orleans Avenue
to the west.

Lakefront Area

The Lakefront area is easily accesible from anywhere in the city. The
easiest way to reach the lake from the Bayou St. John/City Park area
is via Wisner Boulevard which is a continuation of Carrollton Avenue.
Wisner Boulevard parallels the bayou which feeds into Lake Pontchartrain about three miles from the City Park entrance. Once you arrive
at the lakefront, a drive along Lakeshore Drive provides a pleasant
springtime and summertime outing. The West End section, about a
half-mile long, has a number of popular old-time New Orleans seafood
restaurants such as Brunnings and Fitzgerald's, that extend out over
the lake on wooden stilts or pilings. Also located at West End are the
Bucktown fishmarkets and the Southern Yacht Club (established in
1849). A magnificent view of the lake can be had from the yacht club's
breakwater that is easily reached from West End Drive. You can drive
your car out onto the breakwater and park.

Lakeshore Drive extends about five miles for almost the entire length
of the developed Lakefront area. It is a delightful drive during daylight
hours. You can park your car anywhere along the way, sit on the lawn
or seawall and enjoy the beautiful view and cool lake breezes. In past
years, New Orleanians flocked to the Lakefront at night to escape the
sultry summer nights in the city. Law enforcement officials have closed
Lakeshore Drive at night when large and unruly crowds of teenagers
began taunting passing motorists and causing problems for area residents.

Also located along Lakefront Drive are the University of New Orleans campus and the impressive Mardi Gras Fountain. The University
of New Orleans is a relative newcomer to the New Orleans academic
scene. It has come a long way since its creation in 1958. With its
16,000-plus student body, UNO is the second largest university in the
state. Louisiana State University in Baton Rouge is the largest. For the
history-minded visitor, the UNO campus was built on an old World
War II U.S. Naval air station. As late as the mid-1950s, aircraft carrier
airplanes sat in formation on the runway with their chevroned wings
folded skyward like so many praying mantis. UNO has gained a solid

reputation over the last twenty years for its academic excellence, especially in the liberal arts, sciences, and business. The university's Gulf South Research Institute, International Marketing Institute, and Center for Economic Development are important sources of economic information for the New Orleans and state political and business communities. The campus contains twenty major buildings, the oldest dating to 1961, including the new 10,000-seat Lakefront Arena. This new assembly center was completed in October 1983, and it will serve as a combined athletic and cultural center. It also has an olympic-sized swimming pool.

Located about a mile to the west of the campus along Lakeshore Drive is the impressive Mardi Gras Fountain. Built in 1962 "For the enjoyment of the people of and visitors to New Orleans," the fountain sprays, on a continuous cycle, a 60-foot cascading tower of water into the air. Lights, shining the Mardi Gras colors of green, purple, and gold, dance through the rising water, creating a colorful and gripping performance. Encircling the outer edge of the fountain, which is about 120 feet in diameter, are 69 6-foot square concrete pillars supporting the coats of arms of all of the Mardi Gras krewes in New Orleans history.

The entire length of Lakeshore Drive is packed with people on summer weekends. Thousands of picnickers, teenagers, and families flock to the Lakefront to lounge about on the wide expanse of greenery and to enjoy the cooling lake breezes. Most of the time it is difficult to find a place to park unless you get there very early. Unfortunately, the lake water is somewhat polluted and swimming is discouraged. However, water problems haven't kept people from enjoying the parklike beauty of the Lakefront. Incidentally, if you can find a parking spot, you can picnic anywhere along Lakeshore Drive—but you won't find any tables. Scattered along Lakeshore Drive you will find several picnic shelter houses with grills.

Located at the eastern end of Lakeshore Drive is the New Orleans Lakefront Airport, which handles mostly small aircraft. It is one of the busiest airports of its type in the country.

Hayne Boulevard basically is the continuation of the Lakeshore Drive east of the airport. Boulevard is a misnomer as it is no more than a two-lane winding road that follows the shoreline. Little Woods, as this area is called, is not particularly attractive. A high levee blocks one's view of the lake. Despite all of this, there are several outstanding seafood restaurants along here—such as Lakeview Seafood Restaurant (7400 Hayne Boulevard)—that are immensely popular with locals—and that kind of endorsement is hard to beat. These places are packed on weekends, especially Friday nights, so its best to go on week nights or call for reservations.

Metairie Cemetery

Metairie Cemetery, like the St. Louis cemeteries, is among the nation's most fascinating burial grounds. Like the others, it is a city of the dead, where New Orleanians built princely monuments and memorials to their own immortality. The best way to reach Metairie Cemetery is to drive out Canal Street away from the river. Canal Street ends at City Park Avenue. Turn left and drive one block to where Interstate 10 overpass crosses City Park Avenue. Turn right onto the I-10 access road. Keep to the left and drive about 20 feet then make a sharp left on the street continuing under the overpass. This street (which has no name), makes a sharp right on the far side of the overpass and will take you to the cemetery's main entrance a few blocks ahead. Follow the signs from City Park Avenue that clearly mark the way. The cemetery is open seven days a week during daylight hours. Drive your car through for a visit to one of the most interesting burial grounds in America.

Metairie Cemetery originally was the Metairie Race Course. Opened in 1838, for many years it was the finest racetrack in the South. Needless to say the track and Metairie Jockey Club fell on hard financial times during the Civil War and Reconstruction. A faction of dissenters broke away, formed the Louisiana Jockey Club, and in 1872 opened the Fairgrounds Race Trace, which still ranks high among the nation's racetracks. The circumstances surrounding the demise of the track has added another colorful chapter to the city's history or book of legends. As the story goes, the old patrician New Orleanians who sat on the track's board of directors blackballed Charles T. Howard, a politically powerful and immensely wealthy director of the Louisiana Lottery Company who also had close ties to the detested Republican Reconstruction government. Angered by the snub, Howard bought the track the following year (1872) and converted it to a cemetery. The cemetery was designed around the racetrack's main concourse that is still clearly visible from the air.

Many of the massive tombs are architectural splendors. There are gleaming white pyramids, Roman temples, Greek and Egyptian mausoleums, Moresque spires, towering monuments to deceased loved ones, and old-shaped tombs that almost defy description. Also located there are memorials and the tombs of Confederate veterans of the armies of Tennessee and Northern Virginia and the Louisiana Washington Artillery, which was formed at the Battle of New Orleans in 1815. The cemetery later saw action during the Civil War at the Battle of Bull Run (Manassas) and other major battles, and in subsequent wars.

Algiers Point

Algiers Point is on the west bank of the river directly across from the French Quarter. It is part of the city (Ward 15) and a very old residential neighborhood. How Algiers got its name remains a puzzle to historians. During the French and Spanish colonial eras, the royal governments and private entrepreneurs kept slave pens there to house new slaves brought in from the West Indies and Africa. Perhaps it got its name by association to the North African slave markets. Another theory has it that Spanish governor Don Alexandre O'Reilly, an Irishman in Spanish service, gave the point its name. O'Reilly arrived in Louisiana in 1769 to suppress a revolt in the colony.

The old courthouse that can be seen so clearly from the French Quarter side was built in the late 1800s. The best way to see old Algiers is by automobile. Catch the free ferry at the foot of Canal Street. It is a short, scenic and delightful trip, and the best free ride in town. You will exit the ferry at Algiers Point—where the land seemingly juts out into a bend in the river. Of particular interest is a twenty-five block area on the point.

The renovation and restoration craze has hit Algiers Point. Many fine late 19th-century houses and neighborhoods are on their way back, thanks to the foresight, courage, and good taste of young, affluent middle-class married couples who have taken the area in hand. Walking at night is not recommended, however, because the area is close to a desperately poor and crime-ridden area.

Also located on the West Bank are the U.S. Naval Base, the U.S Naval Station at Belle Chasse, and miles of new residential subdivisions and shopping centers. You may take a tour of the Naval Base, although there isn't too much to be seen.

Fat City

Fat City is suburbia's answer to Bourbon Street and other saloon strips around the country. Located in Jefferson Parish, Fat City is a collection of garish discos, bars and other night spots that mainly attract local "swinging singles" looking for fast times. Fat City grew up around the Lakeside Shopping Center as a result of Jefferson Parish's population and commercial explosion during the sixties and seventies.

The best way to reach Fat City from anywhere in New Orleans—be it the French Quarter, CBD, Uptown or wherever—is to get on the I–10 expressway and drive about five miles. Once on I–10 take the North Causeway exit ramp. As you exit on the ramp, be sure to keep to your right and merge to the right with the Causeway traffic heading north. Still staying on the right, exit Causeway Boulevard at Veterans Highway which is about 100 feet from where the I–10 exit ramp merges with Causeway Boulevard. Turn left onto Veterans Boulevard. On the right side, you'll notice Lakeside Shopping Center. Drive one long block on Veterans then turn right on Severn Avenue. You are now on the eastern edge of Fat City. Turn left at any cross street and you'll be right in Fat City.

A number of recently formed suburban Mardi Gras krewes include Fat City in their parade routes. Nearby Veterans Boulevard, with its anywhere U.S.A. look, is the main shopping area in the Parish. Vets, as locals call it, has several miles of shops, stores, dealerships, car lots, department stores, shopping centers, restaurants, and about anything else one finds in such areas.

Fat City is bounded by Veterans Boulevard, West Esplanade, Severn Avenue and Division Street. The Fat City area also has a number of very good specialty shops that sell everything from camera and computer equipment to dresses, gifts, and flowers, and restaurants such as Augie's (3837 Veterans Highway), Peppermill (3524 Severn Street), Little Cajun Cuisine (3201 Houma Boulevard).

St. Bernard Parish and Chalmette Battlefield

St. Bernard Parish lies directly below New Orleans and can be reached easily by automobile on Louisiana 46. If you head out of New Orleans on North Rampart Street, it becomes St. Claude Avenue at Esplanade Avenue and then turns into Louisiana 46 a bit farther on.

The parish was named for Don Bernardo de Galvez, a popular Spanish governor who defeated the British in West Florida during the American Revolution. During the colonial era, this area was known as *Terre-aux-bouefs*. Throughout the 18th, 19th and early 20th centuries, *Terre-aux-boeufs,* and later St. Bernard Parish (also called this in early 19th century) was strictly agricultural. The numerous plantations that lined both sides of the river produced huge quantities of sugar cane and sugar. Today, most of the plantations are gone, except for a few plantation houses scattered here and there. Those remaining are private residences. The levees are lined with shipbuilder and barge companies, grain elevators, docks, and a host of other industries. Many of the old cane fields are now sprawling, middle-class, residential subdivisions. However, in some of the more distant reaches of the parish, there are a number of small fishing villages that supply New Orleans with much of its seafood. These villages have such interesting names as Delacroix Island and Yscloskey and they are accessible by car.

In was in St. Bernard Parish that General Andrew Jackson defeated the British in the Battle of New Orleans in January 1815 on the Chalmette Plantation. Actually, the battlefield and fishing villages are the only points of interest to visitors.

Driving down from New Orleans on Louisiana 46, the battlefield is located in the town of Chalmette. Watch for the highway signs giving the battlefield location—you can't miss it.

The Battle of New Orleans was one of the last dramatic performances in what most American historians call the second war of independence (the first being the American Revolution). When, in 1812, the U.S. Congress declared war against Great Britain, England had been at war with France since 1803 and the United States found itself in a difficult position. Although the young nation professed neutrality in the conflict, both the British and the French seized American ships on the high seas. The U.S. reacted by passing the 1807–1808 Embargo Acts to prohibit trade with both countries; but while legal trade slowed to a trickle, smuggling rocketed. The British continued to seize American ships and impress their seamen, blockaded American ports, and continued to maintain British forts on American territory near the Great Lakes even though they had promised to withdraw after the American Revolution. By 1812 the U.S. had had enough.

The Americans fared well during the early phases of the war, but suffered numerous defeats in later battles including the capture and burning of most of Washington, D.C. By the spring of 1814 word reached New Orleans that the British planned to attack New Orleans and the lower Mississippi Valley. In almost mass confusion, civil authorities went about the task of erecting defenses about the city.

The British set up their base of operations on a group of islands off the Mississippi and Louisiana Gulf Coast. In command of the British ground forces was Sir Edward Pakenham, brother-in-law of the Duke of Wellington.

Throughout December 1814, the British brought in more troops and supplies while American General Andrew Jackson built his main battleline behind cotton bales, earth, and cypress logs along the Rodriguez Canal above the Chalmette plantation. On December 28 the British attacked to test the American line and then retreated. An artillery battle on the morning of January 1, 1815, silenced most of the British cannon.

Meanwhile 2,000 Kentuckians and other units arrived to reinforce Jackson's ragtag army of regulars, New Orleans volunteers, free blacks and Choctaw Indians. This brought the American line to about 4,000 troops to meet Pakenham's 6,000 to 7,000.

Shortly after dawn on January 8 two signal rockets raced into the sky from behind the British lines. Americans, waiting behind their

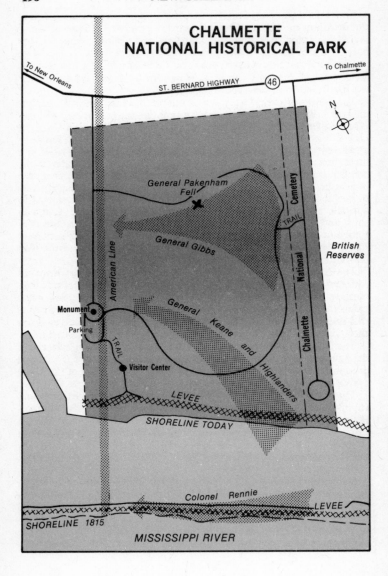

CHALMETTE NATIONAL HISTORICAL PARK

To New Orleans

To Chalmette

ST. BERNARD HIGHWAY (46)

N

General Pakenham Fell

General Gibbs

British Reserves

American Line

Monument

Parking

TRAIL

Visitor Center

General Keane and Highlanders

National

Chalmette

TRAIL

Cemetery

LEVEE

SHORELINE TODAY

Colonel Rennie

LEVEE

SHORELINE 1815

MISSISSIPPI RIVER

breastworks, could hear the drummers beating cadence and shrill cries of bagpipes wailing ancient regimental tunes. When the ground fog lifted, they could see three columns of British soldiers marching slowly toward them carrying fixed bayonets and scaling ladders. American cannon and sharpshooter fire decimated the British ranks yet on they came. Finally, the carnage became so great the British dropped their weapons and ran from the battlefield. Pakenham, trying to stop his fleeing army, rode up to his troops, shouting: "Shame! Shame! Remember you're British! Forward, Gentlemen, Forward!" A shot rang out from the American line and Pakenham fell mortally wounded. He later died and his body was shipped home to England in a keg of rum to preserve the body. Estimates place the American casualties at 13 dead, 39 wounded and 19 missing. The British reported 858 killed, 2,468 wounded, and many others missing. Ironically, in early February the British and Americans received word that the U.S. and Great Britain had signed a peace treaty at Ghent, Belgium on December 24, 1814—two weeks before the Battle of New Orleans took place.

Today, the battlefied is a National Historical Park administered by the National Park Service. The grounds are well kept and a walking tour is clearly marked for visitors. The Beauregard plantation house on the grounds, constructed in 1840 by James Gallier, Sr., for Judge Rene Beauregard, has been restored and now serves as a visitor's center. In addition to helpful information, it has historical exhibits including weapons and dioramas as well as a film presentation about the battle.

On the lower end of the battlefied, approximately in the vicinity of the British line, is the Chalmette National Cemetery, established in 1864. Buried there are Civil War casualties and veterans of the Spanish-American War, World War I, World War II, Korea, and Vietnam. Also interred there are three American casualties of the War of 1812 and, ironically, one British casualty of WWII.

Leaving the battlefield and turning south (right) on St. Bernard Highway, notice the brick ruins on the left and the avenue of oaks on the right. The ruins are the remains of Pierre Denis de la Ronde's 18th-century plantation house, *Versailles*. The oaks are called the Pakenham oaks for as legend has it, Pakenham died under these oaks from the wound he received during the battle. (Historians give no credence to the story.)

For those who would like to explore the area further, continue downriver to Plaquemines Parish, but there is little to see or do there except to enjoy a peaceful drive. Or, you could visit the Isleños fishing villages along La. 46 and Bayou Terre Aux Boeufs. These fishing villages are exactly that so don't expect to find the same picturesque version available in New England or Europe. Isleños culture, though changing, is still unique.

The "Isleños" of St. Bernard Parish

The largest of the Isleño villages is Delacroix Island. The population is growing but the culture is changing. "The Island" is not really an island, but a small strip of land along La. 300 and Bayou Terre Aux Boeufs in the lower end of the parish. There is no town hall, no mayor; the community is directly under the administration of the parish government. The Island was named in honor of the Countess Livaudais de Suan de la Croix, who built the Island's first church and school. Before that, the local residents simply referred to the area as St. Bernard Island or Isleños Island.

About 75 percent of the 500 or so residents of Delacroix Islands are Isleños, descendants of the Canary Islanders who came to Louisiana in 1779 during the colonial administration of Spanish Governor Bernardo de Galvez. A majority of the residents of other St. Bernard communities such as Reggio, Shell Beach, and Yscloskey are also Isleños.

The majority of the Isleños, those over 35 at least, still speak the 18th-century Spanish brought to Louisiana by their ancestors. Linguistic studies of the Isleño dialect have found the presence of Portugese, French and English words, but the language is basically 18th-century Spanish.

"Isleño Spanish is a dialect similar to Latin American Spanish," according to Samuel Armistead, professor of romance languages at the University of Pennsylvania. "It has a good number of words that are quite archaic with medieval origins which has lasted 200 years, but not in the written form."

The Isleños have been living in a predominantly French and then English culture for the last 200 years. French and English words were added to the language to describe things not included in the Isleño vocabulary.

Time is taking its toll on the community. As one old-timer said: "Delacroix Island is changing—there are too many strangers who don't speak Spanish but follow the English like American people." Older Isleños are uneasy about the changes and the failure of older generations to teach their ancient Spanish language to the young, for to them Isleño is not simply a name, it is a way of life, a tradition.

Preservation of the language and some of the old customs is under way. Spanish is taught in the schools and local historians are doing what they can to document and preserve Isleño history.

In addition to the language, there are two other cultural survivals: decimas and caldo. Caldo is a staple dish among the Isleños and consists of white beans and a variety of other vegetables cooked slowly with pickled pork. *Decimas* are folk songs sung in the ancient Spanish language that have passed Isleño history from one generation to another all the way back to the Canary Islands.

To get a flavor of the history of this area, visit the Ducros Museum and El Museo de Los Isleños. Both are located on La. 46 east of the village of St. Bernard (which is the same as St. Bernard Parish). Ducros Museum is open from 9 A.M. to 5 P.M. weekdays, admission free. El Museo de Los Isleños is managed by the National Park Service. It is open from 9 A.M. to 5 P.M. Saturday through Monday. The Museum displays the history of Isleños through photographs, exhibits, arts, crafts, tools, and other historical memorabilia. Admission is free.

St. Tammany Parish North of Lake Pontchartrain

If you are visiting New Orleans for any length of time and have an automobile at your disposal, a visit to the semirural pine forests north of Lake Pontchartrain would be a welcomed break from the bustle of the city. To get there drive west on Interstate 10 toward Baton Rouge. Upon reaching suburban Jefferson Parish, turn north and cross the 24-mile Causeway bridge—the longest in the world ($1 toll each way).

Prior to the American Revolution, St. Tammany Parish was part of British West Florida. Most of the older families residing in the parish are descendants of British settlers. The area forms a striking contrast to Gallic-Hispanic heritage of New Orleans.

St. Tammany is also called the Ozone Belt for its clean air and water. Bottled drinking water from St. Tammany wells has become a big industry in New Orleans—which gets its drinking water from the Mississippi River.

St. Tammany has been a haven for generations of New Orleanians looking for a cure to their ailments or simply escaping summer heat, pestilence or urban problems. But to those who simply are looking for a one-day or even a weekend outing close by, St. Tammany towns and countryside offer relatively inexpensive pleasures for the entire family.

In western St. Tammany, towns such as Mandeville and Covington, with their turn-of-the-century flavored commercial and residential districts, offer scores of interesting shops, galleries, eateries, and water holes. The area also has become a popular haven for artists and writers such as Walker Percy who resides in Covington.

Mandeville was founded in 1834 by Bernard Marigny, the Creole *bon vivant* who founded Faubourg Marigny below Esplanade Avenue in New Orleans.

A walk along Mandeville's parklike seawall is especially rewarding. One can sit under one of the many ancient live oaks and wax poetic, watch a breathtaking sunset on the lake or admire the many waterfront homes. Picnicking along the seawall is forbidden and the town gendarmes are quick to enforce the prohibition.

Mandeville also has more than its share of restaurants ranging from good to superb. The list includes Trey Yuen (Chinese food), Masthead, Rip's, Chaisson's, Terry's, Bossier's, and Bechac's with its Caribbeanlike atmosphere. The two most worthy of note are Trey Yuen and Bechac's. Trey Yuen, meaning crystal jade garden, is owned and operated by the Wong family. A visit to Trey Yuen is more like a visit to an oriental art gallery with its opulent decor reflecting thousands of years of Chinese history. Perhaps the most interesting work of art there is a 6-foot panel, gold-leaf woodcarving located over the wine rack. Made in Chachow, Kwangtung Province, it depicts in intricately carved images military battles, palace grounds and hunting scenes. The prices are reasonable and the food is superb.

Bechac's old world atmosphere is a welcomed change from the slick decor of most modern restaurants. Between 1860 and 1868, the building that houses the restaurant was the summer home of Bernard Marigny. By this time he had squandered most of his inherited fortune and lost his land holdings, including a sugar plantation in St. Tammany. Prices are moderate and the food is good, especially seafood dishes.

Unquestionably, the best Po-boys in town—New Orleans does not have a corner on this market—are served at Big Bear's, an unpretentious sandwich stand on U.S. 190.

Mandeville also has a number of antique and craft shops within walking distance of the lake.

If you can find nothing to satisfy your palate in Mandeville, there are two exceptionally outstanding restaurants in the small town of Lacombe a few miles east of Mandeville on U.S. 190. One is La Provence with French and Creole cuisine (expensive) and Sal and Judy's Italian cooking (moderately priced).

Perhaps the best way to see Covington to the north of Mandeville is to park your car somewhere in its downtown business district and walk. The old business district, with its curious New England street names, forms much of what was the original site of Covington when laid out by John Wharton Collins in 1813. Areas of town such as Lee Lane, North Columbia, and North Florida streets contain a number of antique and specialty shops housed in renovated cotages.

In recent years, the town has seen a considerable amount of private and commercial restoration of old buildings. Entire neighborhoods are on the rebound, as are parts of the business district. Perhaps the most notable example of the revitalization was the restoration of the old Southern Hotel building across from the courthouse on East Boston Street. It is now a courthouse annex.

The defunct old train station on North New Hampshire Street is now a restaurant—the Covington Depot (moderately priced and well-prepared food). Its well-stocked bar sidetracks many a weary businessman at the end of the workday.

For the sake of a historical footnote, the main dining room, furnished with a Victorian flavor, originally was the "White only" waiting room during the days of segregation. The "Colored only" waiting room is now in the kitchen. Coincidentally, the U.S. Supreme Court decision of Plessy vs. Ferguson in 1896, which set up the South's "separate but equal" Jim Crow laws, was the result of a racial incident aboard a train bound from New Orleans to Covington in 1892.

Many of the older residential areas with their abundance of oaks, pines, shrubs, and green lawns are especially eye-pleasing. Nearby Abita Springs and Madisonville, once bustling resorts and health spas, are now quaint but sleepy residential communities. They are worth the detour. The Long Branch Hotel, a turn-of-the-century favorite among visitors to Abita Springs, has been placed on the National Register for Historic Places and was recently renovated. The owners plan to make it a viable hotel again in time for the 1984 New Orleans World's Fair.

To those day-trippers enamored with the wonders of nature, picnics, sandy food, chiggers, and poison ivy, western St. Tammany has several large and beautiful state parks.

Fontainbleau and Fairview Riverside state parks are open seven days a week, twelve months a year for camping and picnicking. Both have electrical hookups for mobile campers for nominal overnight fees. There are no food and refreshment concessions, so bring your own supplies.

Fontainebleau was once Bernard Marigny's sugar plantation. Marigny seems to have had George Washington's same ubiquitous sleeping habits. Remnants of the old sugar mill can be seen on the grounds. The park (nominal admission charge) offers a nature trail through a magnificent pine and hardwood forest—a definite treat for the city dweller.

Fairview Riverside is northwest of Mandeville on the Tchefuncte (CHA-FUNK-TA) River and can be reached by La. 22. The 98-acre park and house were bequeathed to the state in 1962 by the estate of Frank Griffith Otis, a wealthy New Orleans mahogany importer.

For solitude and a closer communication with nature, visitors can rent canoes at Oceans 1 in Covington or take one of the guided canoe trips offered by the Canoe and Trail Shop in New Orleans.

No trip to St. Tammany would be complete without a drive through the rolling, emerald-green, thoroughbred and quarter horse farm country in the northwestern reaches of the parish.

To visit the horse country, drive north from Covington on the Folsom Road (La. 25) until you reach Bennett Bridge Road (La. 1078).

Clear Creek Stud Farm on Bennett Bridge Road is well worth the detour. Backtrack to La. 25 and continue north to Folsom. Drive west about 10 miles on the Bush-Folsom Road (La. 40), which winds, turns, and dips its way across the entire northern stretch of the parish.

Turn south on Old Military Road (La. 1082) and, after a few miles, you will reach Dorignac's thoroughbred horse farm—which is unquestionably St. Tammany's grandest.

Please note: these are private farms and not open to the public.

Continue on Old Military Road until you reach Military Road (La. 21). General Andy Jackson used this road on his way to the Battle of New Orleans—hence Military Road. Turn right on Military Road and be on the lookout for Sunny Brook plantation house on the left (not open to the public). Military Road, lined with ancient pines, oaks, and azaleas, is a pleasant drive back to Covington.

A special note: Try to remember the name of each road as well as its more impersonal highway number. If you lose your way, most old-timers in St. Tammany know the highways by their age-old traditional names. Their memories are hazy when it comes to recalling the numbers slapped on them by the Highway Department. However, highway maps use the numbers and not the local road names.

 SIGHTSEEING CHECKLIST. Visiting a city for the first time can be a harrowing experience if you don't know where to go or what to do—especially if your time is very limited. New Orleans, like all cities with a colorful past and present, has certain points of interest that should not be missed. The following is a quick reference of such places.

Audubon Park and Zoological Garden. A beautifully landscaped, 400-acre, century-old park in the center of the city's fashionable Uptown residential area. The 58-acre zoo is among the finest in the South. Audubon Park was the site of the 1884–1885 World's Industrial and Cotton Centennial Exposition, New Orleans' first world's fair. The zoo is open daily. Audubon Park can be reached by the St. Charles Ave. streetcar, automobile, or the *Cotton Blossom* sternwheeler that departs regularly from the foot of Canal Street. The main entrance to the park is in Uptown New Orleans at the 6800 block of St. Charles Avenue across from Tulane University. The zoo entrance, however, is off Magazine Street near the Mississippi River. It is about twelve blocks back from the park's main entrance heading toward the river.

Bourbon Street. This thirteen-block strip of nightclubs, striptease joints, garish T-shirt shops, restaurants, and hotels is perhaps one of the best known streets in the U.S. Bourbon Street was the city's most fashionable residential street in the early 19th century. Today it is best known for its jazz clubs and night life. It is particularly busy at night on weekends and during special events in the city, such as Mardi Gras, New Year's Eve, Sugar Bowl Football Classic, and when the Super Bowl is in town. During these times, a river of humanity flows slowly down this narrow street from late afternoon to the wee hours of the morning. Bourbon Street runs through the center of the French Quarter from Canal Street to Esplanade Avenue.

Central Business District. Prior to the Civil War, this area was called the Faubourg St. Mary or the American Section, where Anglo-Americans settled apart from the Creoles. Today the CBD is the city's financial and business district. It stretches from Canal Street above the French Quarter to Howard Avenue. The CBD contains a number of fine shops, restaurants, and galleries, and its modern monolithic skyscrapers form an interesting contrast to the district's antebellum commercial architecture. The CBD and the French Quarter below Canal Street is the architectural devotee's dream.

Chalmette Battlefield. Located below New Orleans in neighboring St. Bernard Parish (county). This is where General Andrew Jackson defeated the British in the Battle of New Orleans on January 8, 1815. The National Historical Park and Information Center is maintained by the National Park Service.

Contemporary Arts Center. Located at 900 Camp Street in the Central Business District, it is New Orleans' alternative art institution that features the work of local artists, traveling exhibitions, concerts, films, dance recitals, theatrical performances, and art-related workshops and seminars. Open from noon to 5 P.M., Tuesday through Sunday.

French Quarter (Vieux Carré). The *Vieux Carré* is one of the most famous historical districts in the Western Hemisphere. The French Quarter is bounded by the Mississippi River on the south, Esplanade Avenue to the east, Bienville Street to the west, and North Rampart Street on the north. It is a living museum displaying, free of charge, French and Spanish colonial and antebellum New Orleans architecture. The French Quarter is known worldwide for its Creole restaurants, shops, antique galleries, museums, Caribbean atmosphere, jazz, and Bourbon Street striptease parlors and bars.

Gallier House. Located at 1118–1132 Royal Street in the French Quarter, Gallier House was the residence of noted 19th-century New Orleans architect James Gallier, Jr. Restored and furnished, it is a superb example of how the upper half lived in mid-19th-century New Orleans. The Gallier House also has exhibition galleries on the history and culture of the city during those years.

Garden District. This area, which dates from the 1840s, is one of the finest residential neighborhoods in the country. Located in Uptown New Orleans between Jackson and Louisiana avenues, and St. Charles and Magazine Street, the streets and byways are filled with elegant and sumptuous classical antebellum homes and gardens. The area is easily reached by the St. Charles Avenue streetcar.

The Historic New Orleans Collection. 533 Royal Street in the French Quarter. Superb collection of colonial and 19th-century documents and artifacts. THNOC includes ten permanent galleries, featuring the colonial and antebellum history of New Orleans. In addition, the collection has two historic museum residences, a research center and gift shop. The buildings date from the late 18th century.

Jackson Square. Located in the heart of the French Quarter, Jackson Square was called the *Place d'armes* prior to the 1850s. Today the edge of the square is filled with sidewalk artists selling their wares and painting portraits for tourists. It is also a pleasant place to stroll and enjoy the ambience of the centuries old buildings that overlook the square.

Lakefront Drive and West End. Located along the Pontchartrain lakefront, this is a pleasant and scenic area that is beautifully landscaped. It is a favorite spot for New Orleanians during the hot summer months. Be sure to see the impressive Mardi Gras Fountain. West End is filled with seafood restaurants built out over the lake on stilts. It is a popular dining spot for locals, who know and appreciate good seafood. The University of New Orleans and Pontchartrain Beach Amusement Park are located along Lakefront Drive.

Louisiana Maritime Museum. 31st floor of the International Trade Mart Building at the foot of Canal Street. Offers a spectacular view of the Mississippi River and French Quarter. The museum features the maritime history of New Orleans.

Louisiana State Museum. 751 Chartres St. in the French Quarter. The LSM, with its eight historical buildings, is one of the largest historical museums in the country. The system includes the historic Cabildo and Presbytere, the Lower Pontalba Building, Madame John's Legacy (632 Dumaine Street), the old U.S. Mint Building (oldest in U.S. at the foot of Esplanade Avenue and Decatur Street in the Quarter), the Creole and Jackson houses, and the Arsenal (all three behind the Cabildo on St. Peter Street). The museum contains extensive exhibition and research collections pertaining to the history of New Orleans and the Lower Mississippi River Valley.

Mardi Gras. New Orleans biggest, noisiest celebration takes place this year on March 6 but festivities begin about two weeks prior to that.

Mississippi River Cruises. Seeing New Orleans from the river is an unforgettable experience. Several riverboats, including the *Steamer Natchez,* make regular two- to five-hour trips up and down the river night and day. The *Natchez* moors at the foot of St. Peter Street and the Mississippi River; others are moored at the foot of Canal Street and the river.

New Orleans Museum of Art. Located in City Park about five miles from the French Quarter along Bayou St. John and City Park Avenue. It is easily reached using Esplanade Avenue. NOMA has representative collections dealing with pre-Colombian, Medieval, European, American, African, and Oceanic art. It has strong primitive art and photographic collections. In recent years, NOMA has presented several major international traveling exhibitions, such as "The Treasures of Tutankhamun," "Peru's Golden Treasures," and "The Search for Alexander."

Canal Place. At the foot of Canal Street. This is one of the city's most impressive multi-use skyscrapers. It features top-drawer shops, such as Saks Fifth Avenue, offices, hotels, and a number of other impressive clients.

Preservation Hall. 726 St. Peter Street in the French Quarter. One of the few places where one can still hear traditional New Orleans Dixie Land Jazz between the hours of 8 P.M. and 12:30 A.M.

River Road. There are a number of magnificent antebellum plantation homes lining both sides of the Mississippi River along River Road between New Orleans and Baton Rouge that are open to the public. The most famous of these include the San Francisco Plantation House in Reserve, LA; Destrehan Plantation in Destrehan; the Houmas House in Convent; and, Oak Alley in Vacherie. One can either go by automobile or take one of the numerous commercial guided tours.

St. Charles Avenue Streetcar (trolley). A must for any visitor to New Orleans is to catch the streetcar for 60¢ at the corner of Carondelet and Canal streets and take the 5-mile trek through Uptown New Orleans. Next to Bourbon Street perhaps, St. Charles Avenue is the city's most famous thoroughfare. It is lined with elegant homes and mansions dating from the early 1800s to the turn of the century. At the end of the line is Carrollton where you can change cars and return (for an additional 60¢) the same way you came. This time you will see all that you missed the first time. In addition to the fine homes, Audubon Park, Tulane, Loyola and Dominican universities are also located along the "Avenue."

Superdome. Located on Poydras Street near the Central Business District. The Louisiana Superdome, looming over the city's skyline, is the largest indoor sports arena in the world. It seats from 72,800 for regular football games to 100,000-plus during festivals. Inside the dome are four huge ballrooms, a stadium club, two restaurants, five cocktail lounges, eight bars, plus a 166,000 sq. ft. concrete floor. It is truly an engineering marvel. Tours are given daily. Admission charge: adults $3.50; senior citizens $3; children 5–12 years $2.50; children under 5 years free. (504) 587-3645.

The 1984 Louisiana World Exposition—"The World of Rivers: Fresh Water as a Source of Life." Located on the New Orleans riverfront between Julia and the Greater New Orleans Mississippi River Bridge. The Exposition and Louisiana Convention Center have become a natural extension of the development and revitalization of the riverfront. An estimated 11 million people are expected to visit the fair, which will host exhibitions and displays from all over the world.

PRACTICAL INFORMATION FOR NEW ORLEANS

 HOW TO GET THERE. There are, of course, four common ways to get around in the United States: plane, train, bus, and car. Usually, if you plan to travel long distances, it is cheaper to go by plane than by rail. But for distances under 300 miles, the train is cheaper and may be faster too, because the station is often in the middle of town and you won't have to take a long ride to and from the airport. Another benefit of rail travel is seeing the scenery, which can't be seen when flying.

For short trips between cities, buses offer the same sightseeing advantage as trains but are usually cheaper and may provide more frequent service.

By bus. *Continental Trailways* and *Greyhound* bus routes provide a vast array of scheduled trips, allowing travelers from all U.S. areas to come closer to their vacation destinations and often to reach them directly. Focal points to consider are the same as those for trains. Currently, both offer unlimited travel passes. Greyhound's cost (subject to change): $187—7 days; $240—15 days; $347—30 days. Children from 3 to 11 years old are half fare; children under 3 are free. Continental Trailways travel pass costs about the same, except there are no special rates for children.

Contact your travel agent or a nearby Greyhound or Trailways office for information about special tours to and in the area of New Orleans.

By air. Moisant International Airport, located in Kenner, about 17 miles west of the French Quarter, is New Orleans' main airport for visitors arriving in or leaving the city. Among major airlines serving the airport are *American, Delta, Eastern, Republic,* and *Southwest.* Some international airlines serving the New Orleans area are *Aeromexico, Continental, Jet America, Lacsa, Northwest Orient, Pan American, Sahsa, Taca International, USAir,* and *Trans World.* Also serving New Orleans area are regional airlines, which offer many scheduled flights from other Southern and Midwestern cities. They include *Ozark, Coastal,* and *Texas International.*

Discounts are usually available to members of the family who are traveling together. Thirty-day excursion fares, youth fares for college students, and special low fares for senior citizens as well as for members of the armed forces are also offered by many airlines that may also offer standby reduced rate fares. All special fares are subject to restrictions requiring the traveler to make the trip when the airlines are least busy, usually midweek. Savings can range from 15 to 50 percent over regular coach fares, but since discounts change frequently, it is best to consult your travel agent for the most recent fares.

To accommodate those travelers who require transportation to and from the airport, there are several methods. The municipal bus system runs a bus to and from the airport and the Central Business District. One-way bus fare is 65 cents.

The ride is over an hour long and the bus makes regular stops to pick up passengers along the route. *Orleans Transportation* has limousines that run to and from CBD hotels and the airport ($6 one-way). Taxicabs also make the trip: $18 for one to three persons, $6 for each additional person. There also are a number of car rental companies located at the airport.

By train. *Amtrak* has three major lines that connect New Orleans with the Pacific, Atlantic and north central states. The silver *Crescent* makes daily runs from New York to New Orleans by way of Washington, D.C. The *City of New Orleans* runs daily between New Orleans and Chicago. The *Sunset Limited* makes the two-day trip between New Orleans and Los Angeles. It departs New Orleans on Monday, Wednesday, and Sunday, and leaves Los Angeles on Saturday, Wednesday, and Friday.

Foreign visitors are eligible to purchase the U.S. Rail Pass. So check with your travel agent before traveling to the U.S. Although residents of the U.S. are not eligible for the U.S. Rail Pass, Amtrak does offer several flat-rate excursion fares to them. Fares change periodically. Check with Amtrak or your travel agent for up-to-date costs.

For Amtrak information and reservations, call (toll free) 1–800–874–2800. The Union Passenger Terminal, 1001 Loyola Ave., in the heart of the Central Business District, is the city's only train station (528–1600).

TELEPHONES. The area code for all of the New Orleans area is 504. If you are calling within the New Orleans area, you need not use the area code number. For information within the New Orleans area, dial 1 + 411. For information (directory assistance) outside of New Orleans but within southeastern Louisiana, dial 1 + 555–1212. When direct-dialing a long-distance number from anywhere in New Orleans, you must dial the number "1" before dialing the area code and the number itself. An operator will assist you on person-to-person, credit-card and collect calls if you dial "0" (zero) first. Pay telephones are still 10 cents with no time limit. See *Facts at Your Fingertips* for emergency telephone numbers.

HOTELS AND MOTELS. New Orleans offers almost any kind of accommodation, from simple motel rooms to posh hotels in the French Quarter.

The best known hotels in New Orleans—the Hilton, Hyatt, Royal Orleans, Marriott, Fairmont, Pontchartrain, Monteleone—are fashionable and in the center of the city and generally high-priced, providing a variety of restaurants and services to their guests.

European-style hotels are beginning to prosper here; they provide personal attention, rooms that are often minisuites, and a concierge to perform services. These hotels are usually small and gracious and often present you with baskets of fruit or bottles of wine. The rooms are often decorated with original art works and antiques. The Soniat House in the French Quarter is an example of this type of accommodation. The types of amenities differ from place to place, of course.

Most of the larger and more expensive hotels in the French Quarter and Central Business District offer weekend and holiday packages that include special rates, tours, live entertainment, meals, and other services. Check with your travel agent, or call the hotel using its toll free number.

Rates are generally priced for double occupancy, that is, two persons. You can expect that there will be more rooms available at the higher end of the range of prices listed.

The hotels below are listed and categorized according to location, style, and distinction of accommodations.

As a general rule, the *deluxe* category refers to the top hotels in New Orleans. The *expensive* category often caters to business travelers and includes many of the convention-oriented, "brand name" hotels that are perfectly suitable for tourists. All hotels in this range provide the full spectrum of services you'd expect to find away from home.

Moderate hotels provide fewer services but are priced to reflect the sacrifice in comfort; *inexpensive* hotels in the guide are just that: inexpensive. They are clean, responsible properties that are modest but pleasant; they are especially appreciated by young travelers and travelers on a budget.

Note: Prices listed below may vary by season and inflate during special events like Mardi Gras and the World's Fair. Also, most of the prices do not include the additional 10 percent tax. Check with individual hotels for current prices.

Abbreviations:

Special rates
FP—Family Plan
S—Summer Rates
M—Military Rates
G—Government Rates
C—Commercial Rates

CC: Credit Cards
AE—American Express
CB—Carte Blanche
D—Diner's Club
V—Visa
MC—Master Card

Languages
S—Spanish
F—French
G—German
I—Italian
Da—Danish

Nw—Norwegian
P—Portuguese
C—Chinese
Gr—Greek
Ar—Arabic

V—Vietnamese
J—Japanese
H—Hebrew
T—Turkish

CENTRAL BUSINESS DISTRICT

Deluxe ($98–$145)

Fairmont Hotel. Located one-half block of Canal St. at University Pl. 70140; 529–7111; (800)527–4727. Formerly the Roosevelt Hotel, the Fairmont offers old-fashioned grace and charm with all of the modern conveniences. For dining and entertainment there are several restaurants serving breakfast, lunch and dinner. The restaurants include the famous *Sazerac Restaurant* and the *Blue Room* with big name live entertainment. There are also a number of in-house bars, an outdoor heated swimming pool, two tennis courts, babysitting service, valet service, barber and beauty shops, exhibition hall and meeting rooms. Parking available. *LANG:* S,F,G,Da,V. *CC:* AE,MC,D,CB,V. 750 rooms plus suites. $100–$130.

Hyatt Regency. 500 Poydras Plaza, 70140; 561–1234; (800) 288–9000. The Hyatt offers several restaurants and cocktail lounges as well as free parking, babysitting services, heated outdoor pool, valet service, in-house movies, barber and beauty shops, convention and meeting rooms and halls, and handicapped facilities. It also is adjacent to the Louisiana Super Dome. *LANG:* S,F,G,I,P,C, Sign Language. *CC:* AE,CB,D,V,MC. *Special Rates:* S,M,G,C. 1,195 rooms. $99–$119.

Inter-Continental Hotel New Orleans. 444 St. Charles Ave. 70130; 525–5514; (800) 327–0200. Opened in late 1983. This hotel will have a number of facilities to add to the visitor's comfort, including gourmet and conventional restaurants, 24-hour room service, parking, cocktail lounges, health club and spa, barber and beauty shops, handicapped facilities, and more convention facilities. *LANG:* S,F,I,G. *CC:* All major. 504 rooms plus 44 suites. $125–$145.

New Orleans Hilton & Towers Hotel. Poydras St. at the Mississippi River 70140; 561–0500. The Hilton, with a splendid view of the Mississippi River, has all of the trappings of a fine hotel. In addition to the usual restaurants and lounges, the hotel offers special luxury accommodations in the Towers, saunas, and health club, outdoor pool, outdoor and indoor tennis and racquetball, valet service, shops and parking. *LANG:* S,F,G,I. *CC:* AE,CB,D,V,MC. *Special Rates:* FP,S,M,G. 1,146 rooms plus suites. $100–$128.

Sheraton New Orleans Hotel. 500 Canal St. 70130; 525–2500. The Sheraton, still in the process of expanding, offers six restaurants and lounges, 24-hour room service, free parking, heated outdoor pool, meeting and convention facilities, babysitting service, valet, and concierge service, laundry, gift shops. *LANG:* S,F,G,I. *CC:* All major. 1,200 rooms plus and 84 suites. $98–$124.

Expensive ($70–$115)

Best Western Rault Center Hotel. 1111 Gravier St. 70112; 586–1100; (800) 535–9092. Restaurants and lounges, laundry, babysitting, parking, meeting rooms, valet service, complimentary morning paper. *LANG:* S. *CC:* AE,MC,D. *Special Rates:* FP,G,C. 176 rooms. $74.

Downtown Howard Johnson's Motel. 330 Loyola Ave. 70112; 581–1600; (800) 535–7830. Restaurant, free parking, outdoor heated pool, meeting and exhibit rooms, handicapped facilities, valet service, babysitting, free in-house movies, courtyard, and balconies. *LANG:* S,F,I. *CC:* AE,CB,D,V,MC. *Special Rates:* FP. 300 rooms. $73.

International Hotel. 300 Canal St. near the Mississippi 70140; 581–1300; (800) 535–7783. Restaurants, paid parking, lounge, pool, meeting rooms, two ballrooms, babysitting, handicapped facilities, sauna, valet service, laundry machine, barber and beauty shop, gift shop. About 1½ miles from French Quarter and Super Dome. *LANG:* S,F,I,G. *CC:* All major. *Special Rates:* FP,S,M,G,C. 375 rooms plus suites. $95–$115.

Le Pavillon Hotel. Baronne and Poydras Sts. 70112; 581–3111; (800) 535–9095. Plush old-fashioned hotel with renovated sparkle. Restaurant and lounge, paid parking, pool, meeting and exhibit rooms, valet service, gift shop. *LANG:* S,F,G,I. *CC:* AE,CB,D,V,MC. *Special Rates:* S.C. 226 rooms. $72–$76.

Ramada Hotel New Orleans. 1732 Canal St. 70112; 525–7714. Restaurants and lounges, valet parking and valet service, in-room movies, barber and beauty shops, gift shop, rooms with wet bars or kitchenettes. A short bus ride to French Quarter and Superdome. *LANG:* S,F,G. *CC:* All major. 1,036 rooms. $73.

The Warwick Hotel. 1315 Gravier St. 70112; 586–0100; (800) 535–9141. Restaurant, lounge, in-room movies, complimentary cocktails, morning newspaper, free local calls, sauna, valet service, meeting rooms. *LANG:* S,F. *CC:* AE,CB,D,V,MC. *Special Rates:* FP,G,C. 171 rooms. $70–$90.

Moderate ($34–$65)

Ambassador TraveLodge. 3800 Tulane Ave. 70119; 488–2661. Free parking, restaurant-lounge, pool, kitchenette with sink. About 1½ miles to French Quarter and Super Dome. *CC:* All major. $39.

Best Western Patio Motel. 2820 Tulane Ave. 70119; 822–0200. Pool, free parking, washerteria. About 1 mile from French Quarter and Super Dome on bus route. *LANG:* F. *CC:* AE,CB,D,V,MC, Exxon, Sohio. 76 rooms. $38.50–$43.50.

Fountain Bay Club Hotel. 4040 Tulane Ave. 70119; 486–6111; (800) 327–3384. Restaurant, lounge, live entertainment and dancing nightly, pool, babysitting, meeting and exhibit rooms, free parking, handicapped facilities, valet service, courtyard, barber and beauty shop, gift shop. About 1½ miles from French Quarter and Super Dome on bus route. *LANG:* S,F,G,I. *CC:* AE,CB,D,V,MC. *Special Rates:* FP,M,G,C. 454 rooms. $48–$61.

LaSalle Hotel. 1113 Canal St. 70112; 523–5831. Complimentary coffee, babysitting, valet service, laundry machines. *LANG:* S,F, *CC:* AE,CB,D,V,MC. *Special Rates:* S,C. 60 rooms. $34.

Quality Inn Midtown. 1725 Tulane Ave. 70119; 486–5541. Restaurant, lounge with live entertainment, free parking, meeting rooms, steambaths, laundry room and service, handicapped service. About 1½ miles to French Quarter and Super Dome on busline. *CC:* AE,CB,D,V,MC. 102 rooms. $52.

Rodeway Inn Downtown. 1725 Tulane Ave. 70112; 529–5411. Restaurant, lounge, pool, free parking, babysitting, valet service. A short bus ride to French Quarter. *LANG:* S,F,G. *CC:* AE,CB,D,V,MC. 150 rooms. $55.

TraveLodge at Downtown New Orleans. 1630 Canal St. 70112; 586–0110; (800) 255–3050. Restaurant, lounge, pool, free parking, meeting rooms, valet service, handicapped facilities. *CC:* AE,CB,D,V,MC. *Special Rates:* FP,M,G,C. 216 rooms. $58–$65.

Inexpensive (from $22)

Canal Guest House. 2743 Canal St. 70119; 821–9743. House built in early 1900s, private and semiprivate baths, parking, patio, daily and weekly rates. *LANG:* S,P,I. $28 and up.

Crescent Motel. 3522 Tulane Ave. 70119; 486–5736. Restaurant, lounge, free parking, pool. About 1½ miles from French Quarter and Super Dome on bus route. *CC:* All major. 20 rooms. $22.

International Center YMCA. 936 St. Charles Ave. 70130; 586–9622. Restaurant, indoor pool, health club, male and female accommodations. 225 rooms. $24–$31.

FRENCH QUARTER
Deluxe ($70–$170)

The Iberville at Canal Place. 365 Canal St. 70130; 525–2536. Scheduled to open in May 1984. This Trusthouse Forte deluxe hotel will feature a number of services for their guests, including an elegant gourmet dining room with an additional casual 24-hour restaurant, lounge, 24-hour room service, full service health club, concierge service, executive conference rooms, and a ballroom. *LANG:* F,S,G. *CC:* All major. 440 luxury guestrooms and 44 suites. $140–$170.

The Monteleone Hotel. 214 Royal St. 70140; 523–3341. Old-fashioned New Orleans hotel with charm. Features restaurants, lounges, pool, paid parking, babysitting, meeting and exhibit rooms, valet service, barber and beauty shops, gift shop. *LANG:* S,F,G,I. *CC:* AE,CB,D,V,MC. *Special Rates:* FP,G,C. 600 rooms. $85–$95.

The Royal Orleans Hotel. 621 St. Louis St. 70140; 529–5333; (800) 535–7968. A recreation of New Orleans' old St. Louis hotel, the Royal Orleans offers restaurants, lounges, pool, babysitting, transportation desk, meeting rooms, valet service, florist, balconies, jewelry store, gift shop, barber shop. *LANG:* S,F,G,I,Ar,V. *CC:* AE,V,MC. *Special rates:* FP. 356 rooms. $125–$140.

Royal Sonesta Hotel. 300 Bourbon St. 70140; 586–0300; (800) 343–7170. Located on the French Quarter's most popular night-life street, the Royal Sonesta has restaurants, lounges with live entertainment, oyster bars, foreign currency exchange, pool, transportation desk, meeting rooms. Note: you may want to ask for a room that doesn't face Bourbon Street unless you enjoy sitting on the gallery and watching—and hearing—revelers on the street. *LANG:* S,F,I,Nw,P,Gr,Ar,V. *CC:* AE,CB,D,V,MC. *Packages and Special Rates:* S,C. 500 rooms plus suites. $95–$155.

The Soniat House. 1133 Chartres St. 70116; 522–0570. A small European-style hotel offering graceful old-world elegance. Rooms and suites furnished with period antiques. Complimentary continental breakfast, 24-hour room service, valet and laundry service, jacuzzi bathtubs in many rooms. *CC:* All major. 24 rooms including suites. From $70.

Expensive ($65–$140)

Best Western French Market Inn. 501 Decatur St. 70130; 561–5621; (800) 528–1234. Two blocks from Jackson Square. Complimentary coffee and morning newspaper, courtyard, babysitting service. *CC:* AE,CB,D,V,MC. *Special Rates:* M,G,C. 53 rooms. $76.50.

Bienville House Hotel. 320 Decatur St. 70130; 529–2345; (800) 535–7838. Restaurant, lounge, pool, babysitting, meeting rooms, exhibit hall, free local calls, valet service, courtyard. *LANG:* G. *CC:* AE,CB,D,V,MC. *Special Rates:* M,G,C. 82 rooms. $75.

Dauphine Orleans Hotel. 415 Dauphine St. 70112; 586–1800; (800) 327–9073. Complimentary continental breakfast and cocktail, morning paper, lounge, pool, babysitting, in-house movies, laundry service, courtyard, meeting and exhibit room. *CC:* AE,CB,D,V,MC. *Special Rates:* FP,S,M,G,C. 110 rooms. $79–$89.

The De La Poste Motor Hotel. 316 Chartres St. 70130; 581–1200. Restaurant, lounge, pool babysitting, indoor valet parking, valet service, courtyard, meeting and banquet rooms. *CC:* AE,CB,D,V,MC. *Special Rates:* FP,C. 100 rooms. $90–$99.

Holiday Inn Chateau LeMoyne. 1130 Chartres St. 70112; 581–1303; (800) 238–5400. Restaurant, lounge with live entertainment, pool, valet service, baby-sitting, meeting rooms, courtyard, slave quarter suites. *LANG:* S,F,G. *CC:* AE,D,V,MC. *Special Rates:* FP,C,G,S. 170 rooms. $77.

Holiday Inn—French Quarter. 124 Royal St. 70130; 529–7211; (800) 238–8000. Restaurant, lounge, indoor pool, free parking, handicapped facilities, laundry machine, tour desk, valet service, babysitting. *LANG:* F,S,G,Da. *CC:* AE,MC,D,CB,V. 252 rooms. $67–$74.

Hotel Maison De Ville. 727 Toulouse St. 70130; 561–5858. Complimentary continental breakfast, pool, valet service, babysitting, concierge. *LANG:* S,F. *CC:* No credit cards. 21 rooms plus suites and cottages. $100–$115.

Maison Chartres Hotel. 508 Chartres St. 70130; 529–2172. Complimentary continental breakfast, pool, valet service, courtyard, paid parking. *LANG:* S,F. *CC:* All major. 16 rooms. $65–$85.

Maison Dupuy Hotel. 1001 Toulouse St. 70112; 586–8000; (800) 535–9177. Restaurant, lounge, pool babysitting, valet service, free local calls, meeting rooms, courtyard, gift shop. *LANG:* Ar,F,G,Gr,H,I,J,S,T. 196 rooms. $85–$130.

Marie Antoinette Hotel. 827 Toulouse St. 70112; 525–2300; (800) 535–9111. Restaurant, lounge, meeting rooms, babysitting, paid parking, courtyard, pool, daily newspaper, complimentary shoeshine, 24-hour room service. *LANG:* S,F,G,I. *CC:* AE,CB,D,V,MC. *Special rates:* S,C. 93 rooms. $75–$115.

New Orleans Marriott Hotel. 555 Canal St. 70140; 581–1000. Restaurants, lounges, meeting and convention rooms, handicapped facilities, pool, babysitting, valet service, barber and beauty shops, gift shop. *LANG:* S,F,G,I. *CC:* AE,CB,D,V,MC. *Special Rates:* FP,M,G,C. $115–$135.

Quality Inn on Bourbon St. 541 Bourbon 70130; 524–7611. Restaurant, lounge, pool, parking, valet service, gift shop tour desk, courtyard and balcony rooms. Bourbon St. can get noisy on weekends, holidays and for special events so you may prefer to face the courtyard if you're a light sleeper. *CC:* AE,CB,D,V,MC. 186 rooms. $86.

Saint Ann Hotel. 717 Conti St. 70130; 581–1881; (800) 535–9730. Restaurant, lounge, paid parking, babysitting, valet service, meeting rooms, pool, courtyard, balcony. *LANG:* S,F. *CC:* AE,D,V,MC. *Special Rates:* S,C. 59 rooms. $85–$120.

St. Louis Hotel. 730 Bienville St. 70130; 581–7300; (800) 535–9741. Restaurant, lounge, babysitting, complimentary continental breakfast, paid parking, meeting rooms, valet service, courtyard, balcony. *LANG:* S,F. *CC:* AE,D,V,MC. 66 rooms. $110–$140.

Moderate ($40–$125)

A Hotel . . . The Frenchmen. 417 Frenchmen St. 70116; 948–2166. Guesthouse with hotel amenities, period furnishings, ceiling fans, pool, spa, balconies, courtyard, continental breakfast, cocktails, valet service. *CC:* AE,CB,D,V,MC. 25 rooms. $60–$80.

Burgundy Inn. 911 Burgundy St. 70116; 524–4401; (800) 535–7785. Off-street parking, private bath. 67 rooms. $55.

Chateau Motor Hotel. 1001 Chartres St. 70116; 524–9636. Sidewalk cafe, lounge, pool, babysitting, valet service, courtyard, free parking. *CC:* AE,CB,D,V,MC. 42 rooms. $50–$55.

Cornstalk Hotel. 915 Royal St. 70116; 523–1515. Located in turn-of-the-century building with high ceilings. Complimentary continental breakfast, antique furnishings, babysitting, parking, balcony. *LANG:* I,F. *CC:* AE,V,MC. 14 rooms. $60–$80.

Lafitte Guest House. 1003 Bourbon St. 70116; 581–2678. High ceilings, antique furnishings, paid parking, free local calls, and complimentary continental breakfast. Since it's pretty far up Bourbon St., it doesn't receive as much noise as hotels farther down. *CC:* AE,V,MC. 14 rooms. $63–$87.

LaMothe House. 621 Esplanade Ave. 70116; 947–1161, 947–1162. Restored mansion with antique furnishings, courtyard, free parking, free local calls, complimentary continental breakfast, valet service, tours arranged. *CC:* AE,V,MC. 20 rooms plus suites. $65–$75.

Landmark French Quarter. 920 N. Rampart St. 70140; 524–3333. *Jazz Garden* lounge and restaurant. 100 rooms. $58.50–$65.

LeRichelieu Motor Hotel. 1234 Chartres St. 70116; 529–2492; (800) 535–9653. Restaurant, lounge, free parking, pool, kitchenettes, babysitting, valet service, courtyard, balcony. *LANG:* F. *CC:* AE,CB,D,V,MC. 86 rooms. $65–$75.

Nine-O-Five Royal Hotel. 905 Royal St. 70116; 523–4068. Kitchenettes, babysitting, courtyard. 7 rooms. $40.

Noble Arms Inn, Hotel and Guest House. 1006 Royal St. 70116; 524–2222. Spacious rooms in small hotel with balconies, courtyard, paid parking, kitchenettes. *CC:* AE,D,V,MC. 16 rooms. $51–$73.

Place D'Armes Hotel. 625 St. Ann St. 70116; 524–4531. Lounge, pool, babysitting, complimentary continental breakfast, paid parking, meeting room, courtyard. *LANG:* S. *CC:* AE,D,V,MC. 72 rooms. $65.

Prince Conti Hotel. 830 Conti St. 70112; 529–4172; (800) 535–7908. Complimentary continental breakfast, free parking, babysitting, lounge, meeting room. *LANG:* S,F. *CC:* AE,CB,D,V,MC. 58 rooms. $60–$100.

Provincial Motor Hotel. 1024 Chartres St. 70116; 581–4995; (800) 535–7908. Restaurant, lounge, pool, babysitting, free local calls, free parking, courtyard. *CC:* AE,CB,V,MC,D. 96 rooms. $65–$70.

St. Peter Guest House. 1005 St. Peter St. 70116; 524–9232; (800) 535–9741. Restored townhouse with courtyard and slave quarters. Private bath, television, telephone, restaurant serving breakfast only. *LANG:* S. *CC:* AE,CB,D,V,MC. *Special Rates:* M,G,C. $49–$89.

623 Ursulines—A Guest House. 623 Ursuline St. 70116; 529–5489. Courtyard, balcony, free local calls, paid parking. 7 rooms. $44–$46.

Villa Convento Hotel. 616 Ursuline St. 70116; 522–1793. Complimentary continental breakfast, patio, balconies, valet service. *CC:* V,MC,AE. 24 rooms. $40–$125.

Inexpensive ($36–$42)

French Quarter Maisonettes. 1130 Chartres St. 70116; 524–9918. Patio, paid parking, courtyard. 7 rooms. $36–$42.

UPTOWN

Deluxe ($85–$155)

The Pontchartrain Hotel. 2031 St. Charles Ave. 70140; 524–0581; (800) 323–7500. Located along fashionable St. Charles Ave. in Uptown New Orleans. The Pontchartrain has the old-fashioned charm and grace of some of the country's better hotels. It's dining room, the *Caribbean Room,* is known internationally. The Pontchartrain also offers other dining rooms, oyster bars, meeting rooms, valet service, free local calls, paid parking, babysitting. *LANG:* S,F,I. *CC:* AE,CB,C,V,MC. 100 rooms and petit suites. $85–$155.

Moderate ($55–$61)

St. Charles Hotel. 2203 St. Charles Ave. 70140; 529–4261; (800) 535–9676. Restaurant, lounge, meeting rooms, valet service, free parking. *LANG:* S,F. *CC:* AE,CB,D,V,MC. *Special Rates:* G,C. 130 rooms. $55.

St. Charles Inn. 3636 St. Charles Ave. 70115; 899–8888. Restaurant, lounge, complimentary continental breakfast and newspaper, valet service, babysitting. *LANG:* S,F. *CC:* AE,CB,D,V,MC. *Special Rates:* M,G,C, Senior Citizens. 40 rooms. $61.

Inexpensive ($30–$75)

Columns Hotel. 3811 St. Charles Ave. 70115; 899–9308. Small restaurant, charming old Uptown hotel, free coffee, private and shared baths. *LANG:* F,G, Indonesian, Malay. 18 rooms. $35–$75.

Old World Inn. 1330 Prytania St. 70130; 566–1330. European-style guesthouse, complimentary continental breakfast. *CC:* AE. *Special Rates:* Student rates for dormitory beds. 15 rooms. $30–$35.

Parkview Guest House. 7004 St. Charles Ave. 70118; 866–5580 or 865–9100. Old Victorian guesthouse furnished with period antiques, continental breakfast, maid service, community refrigerator, weekly and monthly rates available. 25 rooms. $38–$55.

St. Charles Guest House. 1748 Prytania St. 70130; 523–6556. Pool, patio, carriage baths, some rooms share baths. *CC:* AE,V,MC. 25 rooms. $35.

Uptown Inn. 1550 Foucher St. 70115; 899–1000. Off-street parking, complimentary coffee in A.M. *LANG:* F,S. *CC:* AE,CB,D,V,MC. 32 rooms. $38–$43.

EAST NEW ORLEANS

Moderate ($36–$50)

Holiday Inn I–10 East Hirise Hotel. 6324 Chef Menteur Hwy. 70126; 241–2900; (800) 238–5400. Restaurant, lounge, pool, free transportation to airport and French Quarter, meeting and exhibit rooms, babysitting, handicapped facilities. *Special Rates:* FP. 207 rooms. $47.

Howard Johnson's Motor Lodge East. 4200 Old Gentilly Rd. 70126; 944–0151; (800) 654–2000. Restaurant, lounge, courtesy lakefront transportation, babysitting, valet service, meeting and exhibit rooms, pool. *CC:* AE,CB,V,MC,D. Special Rates: FP,S,M,G,C. 160 rooms. $43–$50.

Quality Inn Bel-Air Motel. 4104 Chef Menteur Hwy. 70126; 944–4531; (800) 228–5151. Pool, gift shop, free parking. CC: AE,CB,D,V,MC. 53 rooms. $36.

Ramada Inn Lake Forest. 10100 I–10 Service Rd. 70127; 246–6000; (800) 255–3050. Restaurant, lounge, pool, babysitting, meeting rooms, handicapped facilities, free local calls, tennis, valet service, free parking. *LANG:* S,F,G,I. *CC:* AE,CB,D,V,MC. *Special Rates:* FP,S,M,G,C. 175 rooms. $43.

Inexpensive ($24–$29)

Del Mar Motel. 8542 Chef Menteur Hwy. 70127; 242–2770. Free parking, kitchenette. *CC:* V,MC. 18 rooms. $24.

Park Plaza Motel. 4460 Chef Menteur Hwy. 70126; 949–8301. Restaurant, pool, babysitting, free parking, courtesy lakefront airport transportation. *CC:* AE,CB,D,V,MC. 58 rooms. $26–$29.

Royal Palms Motel. 7800 Chef Menteur Hwy. 70126; 241–1577. Pool, free parking, city tours available, daily and weekly rates. *CC:* MC,V. $24.

Webber's Motel. 9300 Chef Menteur Hwy. 70127; 242–5150. Free parking, color television. *CC:* V,MC. 50 rooms. $28.

JEFFERSON PARISH: WEST BANK

Expensive ($100)

NEL Apartments. 221 Friedrichs Rd., Gretna 70053; 367–6078 or 368–8816. Townhouse apartments with two bedrooms, dining-living combo, furnished or unfurnished. Short drive across Mississippi River to New Orleans Central Business District. Daily and weekly rates. $100.

Moderate ($68–$85)

Sheraton Westbank Motor Inn Hotel. 100 Westbank Expressway, Gretna 70053; 366–8531; (800) 325–3535. Lounge, meeting rooms, valet service, free parking, free local calls, heliport on property, in-house movies. *LANG:* S. *CC:* AE,CB,D,V,MC. *Special Rates:* FP,M,G. 168 rooms. $68–$85.

JEFFERSON PARISH: METAIRIE

Moderate ($41–$75)

Best Western Gateway Hotel. 2261 N. Causeway Blvd., Metairie 70001; 833–8211; (800) 528–1234. Restaurant, lounge, pool, babysitting, meeting rooms, free parking, free transportation to airport. *LANG:* S,F. *CC:* AE,CB,D,V,MC, Exxon. *Special Rates:* M,G,C. 206 rooms. $57–$70.

Lakeside Inn. 3800 Hessmer St., Metairie 70002; 455–6110. Complimentary continental breakfast, free transportation to and from airport, pool, meeting rooms, rental cars, valet service. *CC:* AE,V,CB,MC,D. *Special Rates:* M,G,C. 38 rooms. $41–$51.

Landmark Motor Hotel. 2601 Severn Ave., Metairie 70001; 888–9500; (800) 535–8840. Restaurant, lounge, pool, babysitting, free transportation to airport, meeting rooms. *LANG:* S. *CC:* AE,CB,D,V,MC. *Special Rates:* M,G,C. 207 rooms. $52–$75.

Ramada Inn Causeway. 2713 N. Causeway Blvd., Metairie 70002; 835–4141; (800) 228–2828. Free airport transportation, restaurant, lounge, pool, meeting rooms, handicapped facilities, valet service, free parking. *CC:* AE,CB,D,V,MC. *Special Rates:* FP,M,G,C. 128 rooms. $49–$52.

Inexpensive ($27–$33)

Keystone Motel. 8825 Airline Highway, Metairie 70003; 467–5501. 29 rooms. $26.75–$32.10.

AIRPORT AREA

Moderate ($35–$97)

Airport Sheraton Inn—New Orleans. 2150 Veterans Blvd., Kenner 70062; 467–3111; (800) 325–3535. Restaurant, lounge, free airport transportation, oyster bar, pool, babysitting, tennis, meeting rooms, free parking. *CC:* AE,D,V,MC. *Special Rates:* FP,M,G,C. 250 rooms. $71.

Best Western International. 2610 Willimas Blvd., Kenner 70062; 466–1401; (800) 528–1234. Restaurant, lounge, free airport transportation, meeting rooms, valet service, cable TV, pool. *LANG:* S,I. *CC:* AE,D,V,MC,CB. 200 rooms. $55–$60.

Days Inn—Airport. 1300 Veterans Blvd., Kenner 70062; 469–2531. Restaurant, pool, suites with kitchen, gift shop. 371 rooms. $35–$88.

Holiday Inn Airport Holidome. I–10 and Williams Blvd., Kenner 70062; 467–5611; (800) 238–8000. Restaurant, lounge, free airport transportation, babysitting, meeting and exhibit rooms, handicapped facilities, free local calls, pool, sauna, health club, valet service. *LANG:* S,F,Da., Gr. *CC:* AE,D,V,MC. *Special Rates:* C. 306 rooms. $48–$97.

New Orleans Airport Hilton. 901 Airline Hwy., Kenner 70062; 469–5000. Restaurant, lounge, free airport transportation, babysitting, meeting and exhibit rooms, tennis, valet service, in-house movies. *LANG:* S,F,I. *CC:* AE,D,V,CB,MC. *Special Rates:* FP,M,C. 284 rooms. $65–$90.

Quality Inn Airport. 2125 Veterans Blvd., Kenner 70062; 464–6464. Restaurant, lounge, game room, meeting room, free parking, pool, jacuzzi. *CC:* All major. 128 rooms. $56–$60.

Ramada Inn Airport Hotel. 1021 Airline Hwy., Kenner 70062; 467–1381; (800) 228–2828. Restaurant, lounge, free airport transportation, pool, meeting and exhibit rooms, handicapped facilities, valet service, free parking. *LANG:* S,F. *CC:* AE,CB,D,V,MC. *Special Rates:* FP,M,G,C. 166 rooms. $66.34.

TraveLodge Airport. 2240 Veterans Blvd., Kenner 70062; 469–7341; (800) 255–3050. Restaurant, lounge, pool, free airport transportation, babysitting, meeting and exhibit rooms, handicapped facilities, free parking, valet service. *LANG:* S. *CC:* AE,CB,D,V,MC. *Special Rates:* FP,M,G,C. 103 rooms. $45.

 BED AND BREAKFAST. Bed & Breakfast Inc. 1236 Decatur St., New Orleans 70116; 525–4640. Listing of areawide homes offering B&B accommodations. Prices unavailable.

New Orleans Bed & Breakfast. P.O. Box 8163, New Orleans 70182; 949–6705. Extensive listing of areawide homes offering B&B accommodations as well as private homes and apartments for rent. Tours available. $20 and up.

 TRAILER PARKS. New Orleans Travel Park. 7323 Chef Menteur Highway (US Hwy. 90 East); 242–7795. Daily tours (free tour for 3-day stay), bus service to and from French Quarter, laundry, gameroom, showers, swimming pools, full hookups. $15.

Riverboat Travel Park. 6323 Chef Menteur Highway (US Highway 90 East); 246–2628. Free transportation to and from French Quarter, pool, gameroom, laundry, showers, propane, tours. $16.

 HOSTELS. For those on tight budgets, New Orleans hostels offer clean accommodations, a communal atmosphere, and reasonable rates. The two main hostels in New Orleans are located in the heart of the city and within walking distance or a short bus ride to most of the city's attractions.

Marquette House International Hostel. 2253 Carondelet St. not far from the Central Business District. 523–3014. Member of the International Youth Hostel Association. TV lounge, user's kitchen, dining area, garden, patio. *LANG:* S,F. $18 members and $22 for nonmembers.

Hostel on Burgundy. 895–9087 or 581–4607 (call ahead for reservations). Kitchen, linens and towels provided. Weekly or nightly rates. You must pick up the key at 1114 Royal St. before going to the hostel. $10.

HOW TO GET AROUND. From the airport. To get to the French Quarter and Central Business District from Moisant International Airport by cab costs $18 for the first three people plus $6 for each additional passenger. The *Jefferson Parish Transit* system also runs a bus from the airport to the Central Business District. The fare is 65 cents one way, but the ride is long—at least an hour—and tedious because the bus makes regular stops to pick up passengers along the way. In the CBD, the airport bus can be caught at the corner of Tulane Avenue and Elks Place across from the New Orleans Public Library. Call the Jefferson Parish Transit at 737–9611 for schedules, stops and busfare information. Limousine service to and from downtown hotels and the airport also is available through *Orleans Transportation* (464–0611) for $6 per person.

By bus. The *Regional Transit Authority* operates the public transportation system in the city. For the most part, it is a good system with interconnecting lines throughout the city. The buses generally are clean and on time. Busfare is 60 cents plus 5 cents for transfer tickets. For bus route information, call 569–2600.

By streetcar. RTA also operates the *St. Charles Ave. Streetcar* that makes the 5-mile trek from the CBD to Carrollton along picturesque St. Charles Ave. A 24-hour pass to the St. Charles Ave. streetcar and the Broadway bus (to Audubon Zoo), costs $4.50 per person and is good from midnight to midnight. It entitles the bearer to as many trips back and forth within that period as desired. The pass is available only at the Streetcar Store, 111 St. Charles Ave. Busfare 60 cents.

By taxi. Rates are fairly high in the city, though most rides are relatively short. Cabs are metered: 90 cents minimum plus 80 cents per mile. Cabs can be secured by telephone, hailed from the sidewalk, or found at the numerous hotel cab stands in the Central Business District and French Quarter. The larger taxi companies include *Morrison's* (891–5818), *United* (522–9771), and *Yellow-Checker* (943–2411).

On foot. The best way to see parts of New Orleans is on foot. Many of the historic districts are easy walks or available by public transit. However, as mentioned earlier in *Facts at Your Fingertips,* there are certain neighborhoods that either should be avoided during certain hours or altogether. The *Exploring New Orleans* chapter of this guide provides specific recommendations where one should go or avoid, and the best time of the day to visit certain sections of the city. For example, certain sections of the French Quarter and Central Business District and the area around the Superdome should be avoided at night. Also, it is wise to travel in groups when visiting the old St. Louis cemeteries, Faubourg Marigny and the warehouse district; and even the Garden District at times. Discretion will make your visit to New Orleans a much more pleasurable experience.

By car. If driving to and in New Orleans, get a road map of the city in advance and study it carefully. Most of the city's streets are very narrow, and locals drive through them fast and often with abandon. If possible, avoid using a car in the French Quarter and Central Business District and during rush hour (roughly between 5:00 and 6:30 P.M.). On certain streets, parking is forbidden during rush hours. Look for the warning signs. Illegally parked cars are towed away. There's nothing more frustrating than having to bail your car out of the local police auto pound. A parking violation can cost you anywhere from $20 to $65. Parking lots are expensive, usually quite busy with normal daily traffic. Parking metered spaces are available, but offer limited time use. Most hotels provide parking for their guests. Curbs painted yellow designate no parking or stopping.

Rental cars. Most major car rental agencies, including *Agency, Avis, American, Budget, Dollar, Econo-Car, Hertz, National, Payless, Sears, Thrifty,* are located at the airport. Many rent vans as well. Check your local telephone directory for toll-free reservations. It is often cheaper to rent at the airport. Also ask your travel agent to check the rates of small, locally owned car rental companies such as *Lamarque Ford* (443–2500); *American Rent-All* (837–9500); and *Toyota Car and Truck Rental* (837–0623). Rates are often cheaper than the larger companies.

By boat. You can catch the free Canal St. ferry at the foot of Canal St. and the Mississippi River. The half-mile trip from Canal St. to Algiers Point is the best bargain in the city. It gives you a great view of the river, Central Business District, French Quarter, docks, shipping on the river, and other great sights. The ferry casts off every 12 minutes and the round trip takes about 24 minutes. For longer excursions on the river and connection waterways there are several riverboat companies that offer tours lasting from two to five hours. The *Delta Queen* and *Mississippi Queen* offer trips that last from one day to several weeks (586–0631). The *Steamboat Natchez,* the *Riverboat President, Cotton Blossom,* and the *Bayou Jean Lafitte* offer trips that last no more than one or two hours as well as half-day and full-day excursions (524–9787, 525–6311). The *Natchez* moors at the foot of St. Peter St. and the river in the French Quarter, and the others tie up at the foot of Canal St. The *Cotton Blossom* also offers the "Zoo Cruise" from Canal St. upriver to the Audubon Park Zoo. For schedules and fares, call 586–8777. (For more details on these riverboats, see Tours section.)

 TOURIST INFORMATION. The *Greater New Orleans Tourist and Convention Commission* and the *Louisiana Tourist Development Commission,* 334 Royal St. (566–5011), publish a number of booklets, brochures and maps on New Orleans and the surrounding area. In addition, it distributes scores of informational brochures about hotels, sightseeing companies, tours, plantations, shops, and restaurants. The *Visitor Information Center,* located in the Tourist Commission headquarters at 334 Royal in the French Quarter, should be the first stop for visitors to the New Orleans area. The commission also has Visitors Information desk at the New Orleans International Airport near the Customs Office. Both places have bilingual staffs. Open 9 A.M. to 5 P.M. daily. Written requests for information should be addressed to the commission's office: 334 Royal St., New Orleans, LA 70130.

When visiting a city like New Orleans, there are several telephone numbers good to have at your fingertips. For weather forecasts, call 525–8831; marine recreational forecasts, 522–2686; Passport Agency, 589–6728.

For daily information about arts and entertainment, call 566–5047 or 522–ARTS.

There are a number of publications in New Orleans that offer extensive up-to-date information and listings about restaurants, museums, shopping, children's activities, theater events, films, dance, art, and music. These publications include *Louisiana Life Magazine, New Orleans Magazine, Go Magazine, Menu, Out and About Magazine, Where Magazine, Welcome Magazine,* and *This Week in New Orleans.* Most of these magazines can be obtained at minimal or at no cost in hotel lobbies. Others can be purchased at newsstands.

The city's largest newspaper, *The Times-Picayune/The States-Item,* has daily listings of things to do and see in its calendar of events and in its weekly (Friday) entertainment tabloid, *Lagniappe.*

 RECOMMENDED READING. The New Orleans Tourist and Convention Commission publishes a number of helpful informational brochures and pamphlets about New Orleans and its environs. Free copies can be obtained at the commission's office on Royal St. in the French Quarter or by writing ahead to 334 Royal St., New Orleans, La. 70130.

Architecture. For those visitors interested in the history of New Orleans architecture, the Friends of the Cabildo's prize winning series of volumns is highly recommended. Each volume in the *New Orleans Architecture* series explores the architectural history of a particular section of the city, such as the Central Business District, the Lower Garden District, and Creole Faubourgs, and Esplanade Avenue. Other volumes are scheduled. These books can be obtained at most New Orleans bookstores, or by writing to the Friends of the Cabildo, 751 Chartres, New Orleans, LA 70116, or to the publisher, Pelican Publishing Company, 1101 Monroe St., Gretna, LA 70053. They cost about $25 each. Perhaps a more affordable resource to the visitor is the pocket-sized *A Guide to New Orleans Architecture* by the New Orleans chapter of the American Institute of Architects. This well-illustrated paperback guide is available in most bookstores for $8.95.

History. For an in-depth look at the city's history, pick up *New Orleans: An Illustrated History* by John R. Kemp. Published by Windsor Publications of Woodland Hills, CA, it is available in most New Orleans bookstores or by writing directly to the publisher at 21220 Erwin St., Box 1500, Woodland Hills, CA 91365. The book costs $24.95 plus shipping cost. It is beautifully illustrated and contains essays on the history of New Orleans architecture and restoration by noted New Orleans writers. *A Short History of New Orleans* by Mel Leavitt is a more anecdotal look at the city's history. Published by Lexikos, 703 Market St., San Francisco, CA 94103; however, it is available in most New Orleans area bookstores. Another good general survey of New Orleans history can be found in Charles "Pie" Dufour's *Ten Flags in the Wind,* published by Harper and

Row. It sells for about $12 or $13 and can be found in New Orleans bookstores. For an interesting and well-written history of the city—written through an explanation of New Orleans street names—is John Chase's *Frenchmen Desire Good Children*. Originally published by Robert L. Crager of New Orleans, this book is now available in paperback for less than $10 in all area bookstores. By the way, the title of the book is made up of New Orleans street names. Another inexpensive but well-written history of the city is Herbert Asbury's 1936 *The French Quarter: An Informal History of the New Orleans Underworld*. It has been re-released by Ballantine Books in paperback and sells for less than $5 in all bookstores in the area.

Music. For jazz enthusiasts Al Rose and Edmund Souchon's *New Orleans Jazz: A Family Album*, published by Louisiana State University Press, has become a classic. It is in hardcover only and sells for about $25. It does not contain a complete history of jazz but biographies of hundreds of individual New Orleans jazz musicians. Al Rose's *Storyville*, published by the University of Alabama Press, is now in softcover and sells in New Orleans area bookstores for about $10. This book gives a good account of the origins of jazz and New Orleans' once infamous red-light district, Storyville.

Mardi Gras. Visitors and Mardi Gras fans will enjoy Errol Laborde's *Mardi Gras! A Celebration*, published by Picayune Press Ltd., 326 Picayune Pl., New Orleans, LA 70130. Almost all bookstores have it, and it sells for about $16.

Literature. To get a flavor for the New Orleans people once immortalized in Tennessee Williams *A Streetcar Named Desire*, anyone visiting the city first should read John Kennedy Toole's Pulitzer Prize-winning *A Confederacy of Dunces*, published by Louisiana State University Press, Baton Rouge, LA 70803. Although the hardback copy sells for about $15, it is out in paperback in local bookstores and sells for about $7. It is a brilliant satire on the human comedy, but more important it brilliantly captures the Brooklynese accent, or downtownese as it is called locally, of many New Orleanians.

 **SEASONAL EVENTS.** New Orleans has long enjoyed its reputation as a city that enjoys a good party and parade. As a general rule, most outdoor functions, such as fairs, festivals and parades, are free. Some, however, charge admission fees.

Special Note: From May 12 to November 11, 1984, New Orleans will be hosting the 1984 Louisiana World Exposition. See special insert for details.

January. New Orleans starts off the new year on January 1 with the famous *Sugar Bowl Classic* football game between top-ranked US college football teams. The Sugar Bowl game, one of the oldest in the country, is held at the Louisiana Superdome. Call 525–8573. Several days before and after the football game there are a number of other sporting events tied to the Sugar Bowl Classic, including a basketball game, tennis tournament, and sailing regatta at the Southern Yacht Club. Thousands of visitors flock to the city during this time to root for the home team. The French Quarter, especially Bourbon Street, resembles Mardi Gras day.

On January 8, *Chalmette National Historical Park,* located a few miles down-river from the city, holds its annual re-enactment of the 1815 Battle of New Orleans. Call 271–2412.

February. Usually, this is the month for the biggest free show on earth—*Mardi Gras.* However, in 1984 it falls on March 6. Over 60 parades roll day and night in and around the city during the two weeks before Mardi Gras Day. The balls, attendance by invitation only, outnumber the parades. The three best known parades are Bacchus, Rex and Comus. Bacchus, which parades the Sunday night before Mardi Gras Day, is one of the newest and clearly most elaborate of the parades. Rex and Comus, the oldest and grandest, parade Mardi Gras Day (Comus is the last parade).

March. As New Orleans is predominantly Catholic and the month of March is Lenten season, few official functions take place. But on March 17 Irish New Orleanians hold their annual *St. Patrick's Day Parade* in the Irish Channel. It is fun, but it is by no means on the same scale as the St. Patrick's Day Parade in New York. Two days later New Orleanians of Sicilian descent celebrate *St. Joseph's Day.* This is a carry-over celebration from the Middle Ages when, as the story goes, a prayer to St. Joseph saved Sicily from a devastating famine. St. Joseph Day in New Orleans is celebrated in private homes and churches (especially St. Joseph's on Tulane Ave.) with St. Joseph Altars stacked high with magnificent Italian and Sicilian pastry. Anyone who has prayed to St. Joseph for a favor and gotten it, erects an altar the next year in his honor. There also is a parade in the French Quarter that night. This is the one celebration during Lent when almost anything goes. The *New Orleans PGA Open* golf tournament also is held this month. The dates are March 19–25 in 1984 at the Lakewood Country Club, General DeGaulle Dr., Algiers. This year, *Mardi Gras* falls on March 6 (see February for Mardi Gras details).

April. After Easter, the festivities start up again. *Jefferson Downs* horse racing begins its season that continues to November. Call 466–8521. April in New Orleans has become synonymous with the *Spring Fiesta* and the *Jazz and Heritage Festival.* Spring Fiesta begins the first Friday after Easter (April 28–May 15 in 1984) and continues for 19 days with tours of French Quarter and Garden District homes, plantations, patios by candlelight, and—yes—a parade, "A Night in New Orleans." Call 581–1367 or write: Spring Fiesta, 529 St. Ann St., New Orleans, LA 70116. The Jazz and Heritage Festival, held in late April and early May, has become world famous for its music (jazz, gospel, folk, popular), performers, and Louisiana food. It takes place at the Fairgrounds Race Track, 1751 Gentilly Blvd. Call 522–4786 or write: New Orleans Jazz and Heritage Festival, 1205 North Rampart St., New Orleans, LA 70119. Anything you have heard in the way of New Orleans music is found here from traditional New Orleans jazz and gospel to early rhythm and blues, rock 'n roll and bluegrass.

May. May is a quiet month in New Orleans although the Spring Festival and Jazz and Heritage Festival carry over from April.

June. The little town of Lafitte, south of New Orleans on La. 45, holds its annual *World Championship Pirogue Races* on Bayou Barataria in late June. Both the town and bayou are associated with Louisiana's infamous buccaneer,

Jean Lafitte. The races are preceded by a full day of merriment, boat parades, and the naming of a queen. Call 347–1846.

July. *La Fete* and *New Orleans Food Festival* are two rather new festivals in the city scene. They were created in the late 1970s to attract visitors to the city during the hot summer months. The city bills La Fete as an annual family summer festival, featuring special events in the French Market, fireworks display on the River on July 4, culminating with festivities on Bastille Day (July 14). The best part of La Fete is the Food Festival (July 2–3), where for the price of admission one gets to sample the best Creole and Cajun food prepared by the best Creole and Cajun chefs. Call 522–6500. Fishermen will enjoy the *International Grand Isle Tarpon Rodeo* at Grand Isle, located about 60 miles southwest of New Orleans on La. 1. The rodeo is billed as the oldest competitive fishing contest in America. Third week in July. Call 525–6525.

August. The town of Lafitte holds its annual *Seafood Festival* in the second week of August. It comes complete with a jambalaya contest (a delicious southern Louisiana dish made from rice, seafood, fowl, sausage, herbs, etc., with strong Spanish influence), talent show and seafood dinner. Call 341–1930.

September. The *New Orleans Philharmonic Orchestra* season begins this month and runs through May. The symphony now performs at its new home, the Orpheum Theatre, in the Central Business District. Call 524–0404.

October. During the second week of this month the little town of Bridge City across the Mississippi River from New Orleans holds its annual *Gumbo Festival* in a carnival atmosphere. In addition to the popular gumbo dish, jambalaya, oysters, and red beans and rice also are served. Call 436–4881. Later in the month, the town of Laplace, west of New Orleans on US 61 holds its *Andouille Festival,* featuring the popular and delectable Cajun sausage, andouille. Carnival atmosphere with rides and lively entertainment. Call 652–2065 or 652–6098. New Orleans' relatively new *Festa d'Italia,* sponsored by the American Italian Federation of the Southeast, is held on Columbus Day (2nd Monday). Parade, good Italian food, art, music. Held at the Piazza d'Italia on Poydras and Tchoupitoulas streets. Call 891–1904.

November. The small town of Gretna across the river from New Orleans has its *Mississippi River Fair and Trade Exposition* with arts and crafts, midway entertainment, during the first week of the month. On the second weekend of the month, the Destrehan Plantation upriver from New Orleans holds its annual *Destrehan Autumn Festival.* Call 568–5661. The two-day event features food prepared by famous New Orleans restaurants, crafts and musical entertainment. Both fairs charge admission. Call 746–9315. The New Orleans *Fair Grounds* opens its horseracing season Thanksgiving Day and it continues until the end of March. Call 944–5515.

December. The *Plaquemines Parish Fair and Orange Festival* is in the heart of the state's citrus and commercial fishing country about 60 miles downriver from New Orleans at Fort Jackson. Held in the early part of the month, the festival is famous for its salty oysters. In addition, it has all of the flavor of a typical south Louisiana festival complete with seafood, live entertainment and the ubiquitous carnival rides. Call 656–7752. Each Christmas Eve residents on both sides of the river in St. James Parish above New Orleans carry on the old French custom of lighting *bonfires on the Mississippi River levees* to light the way for Papa Noel. They begin gathering wood for these huge pyres on Thanksgiving. On the Sunday evening prior to Christmas Day, there is *Christmas carolling* at Jackson Square.

 FREE EVENTS. New Orleans is in itself a free event. The city's unique architecture and neighborhoods have delighted visitors for generations. The French Quarter is known worldwide. On weekends, especially during summer months, the Quarter is alive with street musicians, and scores of artists can be found at work around Jackson Square. Also, ambling through the farmer's market and flea market at the lower end of the French Market is a pleasant way to spend a warm weekend afternoon.

Unquestionably, the biggest free show on earth is *Mardi Gras.* During the two weeks building up to Mardi Gras, over 60 parades roll through the streets in one part of town or another. On Mardi Gras, the delightful and abandoned madness lasts the full 24 hours with over a score of carnival clubs and marching groups parading through the streets. The French Quarter, and especially Bourbon St., is packed shoulder to shoulder with revelers, and one will see and experience things there that you probably have never seen before and may never see again. Among the best known parades are Bacchus, Zulu, Rex, and Comus. Bacchus parades the Sunday night before Shrove Tuesday, and the other three roll on Mardi Gras. For information about Mardi Gras schedules, contact the Greater New Orleans Tourist and Convention Commission. Also get a copy of Arthur Hardy's annual *New Orleans Mardi Gras Guide.*

Parades are a big part of the city's history. New Orleanians look for any excuse to hold a parade. The descendants of Erin hold their annual St. Patrick's Day parade on March 17 in the Irish Channel. A few weeks later in April, the Spring Fiesta holds its "A Night in New Orleans" parade.

In recent years, festivals have become increasingly popular in New Orleans and nearby communities. Usually there is no admission charge, but you are expected to buy food, refreshments and other items during your visit. For a more detailed listing, see *Seasonal Events.*

For day-to-day listings of free events and activities in the city, check the New Orleans' *The Times-Picayune/The States-Item's* daily calendar of events section, or call 566–5047 or 522–ARTS.

The *New Orleans Recreation Department* sponsors free concerts at various times of the year, including Christmas. Call 586–5275.

The *New Orleans Museum of Art* in City Park has a free admission day every Thursday. If antiquities are your pleasure, antique shop-browsing along Royal St. and Magazine St. can be fascinating. Also, it doesn't cost anything to look. Several other New Orleans area museums also are free at all times. They are *Middle American Research Institute's* exhibits on pre-Colombian South and Central American culture, Dinwiddie Hall, Tulane University (865–4511); *Cabrini Doll Museum and Art Center,* 1218 Burgundy St. (586–5204); *Chalmette*

National Historical Park, or Chalmette Battlefield, below New Orleans in the town of Chalmette, where the Battle of New Orleans took place in 1815.

TOURS. Tourism is one of New Orleans' major industries, and, as a result, practically every type of touring service conceivable has popped up. There are bus tours, walking tours, steamboat tours. There are tours of restaurants and bars, plantations, the French Quarter, the Mississippi River, museums, houses, and graveyards.

River and Bayou Cruises. For those who want overnight journeys on the river lasting two or three days, or even weeks, contact the *Delta Queen Steamboat Company* for reservations on the *Delta Queen* or *Mississippi Queen* steamboats, 2 Canal St., Suite 2020, International Trade Mart Building, 586–0631. For one-day or half-day excursions on the Mississippi and connecting waterways, the *New Orleans Steamboat Company* has the *Steamboat Natchez* (about as authentic a steamboat as one can get), the *Riverboat President* (with moonlight cruises and dance bands), the *Bayou Jean Lafitte* (travels the Mississippi to Bayou Barataria, once the stronghold of the infamous pirate, Jean Lafitte), and the sternwheeler *Cotton Blossom.* The *Natchez* is moored at the foot of St. Peter and the river in French Quarter. The *President, Bayou Jean Lafitte,* and the *Cotton Blossom,* are moored at the foot of Canal St. and the river. For information, call 524–9787 or 525–6311. The *Cotton Blossom* also offers a "Zoo Cruise" round trip from Canal St. upriver to the Audubon Park Zoo. Sailing time each way is about one hour. Round trip with zoo admission, it's $9.50 for adults, $4.75 for children 3–15 years. One way with Zoo admission is $7.50 for adults, $3.75 for children 3–15 years. The round-trip cruise only is $6.50 for adults; $3.25 for children 3–15 years. One way cruise only, $.50 for adults, $2.25 for children 3–15 years. Children under 3 years may travel free for all cruises. For further information, call 586–8777. The riverboat *The Voyageur* plies the Mississippi from the foot of Canal St., where it docks, to the Chalmette Battlefield below New Orleans. It also tours connecting bayous and waterways. For reservations and charters, call 523–5555. *Cajun Bayou Cruise* provides a look at the wilds of the Cajun bayous from a small open bateau (small French boat used in the bayou country). Tours are conducted by a multilingual guide. This company is a small operation, and one local newspaper described it as neither "slick or well-ordered" but beautiful and fascinating. For reservations call 529–1669 or 891–8132. *AAA Tours* also offers tours of the Cajun country and bayous. 467–1734. *Jacco Tours,* 728 Dumaine, 568–0141, has minibus tours of the bayou country.

City and Plantation Tours. Several of the larger sightseeing companies offer a variety of bus tours in New Orleans and to the plantation houses up and down the Mississippi River. *Gray Line Tours of New Orleans* offers two daytime tours of the city, including a riverboat ride, the French Quarter, Garden District, cemeteries, lakefront, and St. Charles Ave. It also offers a tour of plantation houses along the old River Road and five after-dark tours of the city's night life. The daytime tours begin between 9:30 A.M. and 11:00 A.M. and last from three hours on. The tours depart from several of the leading hotels. For reservations, check with the hotel desk or call 525–0138. Several other large sightseeing companies offer similar tours. Sometimes the choice comes down to convenience and price. Others include *Southern Tours Inc.* of New Orleans, 486–0604, *Dixieland Tours,* 283–7318, and *New Orleans Tours Inc.* (American Sightseeing International), 246–1991 or 1–800–535–8632. These companies also offer charter rates for large groups.

Other tours. The yellow pages of the New Orleans telephone directory and the New Orleans Tourist and Convention Commission office at 334 Royal St. list a number of smaller sightseeing companies offering a variety of tours, such as group and personal tours, night life and dining in New Orleans, carriage tours of the French Quarter, and multilingual tours of the city and environs. Examples of these are *Louisiana Tours Inc.,* 525–8052; *Fantasia Tours Inc.* (Spanish), 865–9979; *Heritage Tours* (personal tours in French, Spanish, German and Arabic), 522–8285 or 949–9805; *Pacheco Tours* (city and plantations Spanish), 488–3654; *Pan American Travel, Inc.* (Spanish), 443–4701; *Gay 90s Carriage Tours* (horse-drawn carriage tour of the French Quarter). Tours available at Jackson Square and other French Quarter locations, 482–7013.

Walking Tours. *French Quarter. Friends of the Cabildo,* a nonprofit, volunteer affiliate of the Louisiana State Museum system in the French Quarter offers a tour of the Quarter that comes highly recommended. 9:30 A.M. and 1:30 P.M. daily, except Sunday, Monday, and holidays. The $5 charge is tax deductible. Children under 12 are free when accompanied by an adult, 13 to 20 years old, half price. No reservations needed. Tours begin at the Presbytere on Jackson Square. For further details, call 523–3939. *National Park Service* guides give free walking tours of the French Quarter at 10:30 A.M., 11:30 A.M. and 3:00 P.M. daily, except New Year's Day, Mardi Gras and Christmas. They also give daily tours of St. Louis Cemetery No. 1. The tour begins at 1:00 P.M. Reservations required for the cemetery tour. All tours begin at the National Park Service Information Center, 527 St. Ann St. on Jackson Square. 589–2636. *Mardi Gras Tours* also gives walking tours of the *Vieux Carré.* Tours leave daily from the New Orleans Tourist and Convention Center, 334 Royal St., 10:00 A.M., except Sunday. Reservations suggested. 822–8973 or 522–7565. Also check with the *Spring Fiesta* office at 529 St. Ann for their spring tour schedule. In the month of April the Spring Fiesta offers, in conjunction with its annual festival, a number of walking and candlelight tours of the French Quarter, New Orleans homes, and plantations. 581–1367.

Central Business District. The Preservation Resource Center, 604 Julia St., 581–7032, is dedicated to the preservation of old New Orleans. Throughout the year the PRC offers a series of walking tours of New Orleans neighborhoods. The tours are given irregularly during the year, so check with the center for prices and schedules.

Garden District. All of the larger and smaller sightseeing companies offer tours of the Garden District along with their tours of other parts of the city. The smaller companies also offer stylized tours of the district or any other part of the city a visitor might want to see. The *Preservation Resource Center* offers a walking tour of the district as does *McGehee Garden District Tours,* 2343 Prytania St., 561–1224. McGehee Tours is sponsored by the parents league of the Louise S. McGehee School, a fashionable Uptown girls' school and offers group walking and bus tours by appointment. Prices range from $8 to $33 a person with a $500 group minimum.

Superdome. Guided tours of the world's largest building of its kind are given from 9:30 A.M. to 4:00 P.M. daily. Adults, $3.50; senior citizens, $3; children (5–12 years), $2.50; infants (4 years and under), free. Group tours also can be arranged, 587–3006.

Air Tours. Seeing New Orleans and the surrounding marshland by air can be especially rewarding. There are two companies offering sightseeing tours by air: *Aviation Associates* (241–9321) which flies small fixed-wing planes accommodating two–three passengers and *Louisiana Helicopters Inc.* (362–4500).

 PARKS, ZOOS, BOTANICAL GARDENS. Audubon Park and Zoological Garden is one of the most beautiful urban parks in the nation. It encompasses 400-acres in the fashionable Uptown New Orleans area on St. Charles Ave. across from Tulane and Loyola universities. The land making up the park originally was the Foucher and Boré plantations. The city bought the land from speculators in 1871 and created Upper City Park. The park was renamed Audubon Park for naturalist John James Audubon around the turn of the century and redesigned partially from plans drawn up by famed landscape architect Frederick Law Olmsted and Sons who designed New York's Central Park. It was the site of the 1884–1885 World's Industrial and Cotton Centennial Exhibition—New Orleans' first world's fair—and featured a 31-acre main exhibition hall. The last remnant from the fair is a large chunk of iron ore in the middle of the park's golf course. Several generations of New Orleanians have grown up calling it a meteorite.

Aside from the golf course, Audubon Park also offers horseback riding, a public swimming pool, tennis courts, bicycle rentals, picnicking throughout the park and jogging paths. There is also a mile-and-three-quarter jogging path with exercise stations along the way. The park is closed to automobile traffic on weekends. There is plenty of parking throughout the park.

The 58-acre zoo is in a state of ongoing expansion. The main entrance to the zoo is off Magazine St. near the river. There is ample free parking there, also at the main entrance is an information office and gift shop. Visitors can stroll through the picturesque setting at their leisure to see over a thousand animals kept in natural-like settings, or take the Mombasa Railway ($1) for a guided tour of the zoo. You catch the train inside the zoo. The zoo is divided into five main sections and several subsections. Each of the main sections—Asian Domain, World of Primates, African Savannah, North American Grasslands, and South American Pampas—features animals native to those sections of the world. In addition, the zoo also has a sea lion pool, bird house and sanctuary, reptiles, aquarium, elephant rides ($1), a children's petting zoo, restaurants and gift

AUDUBON
PARK ZOO

Entrance

Points of Interest

1) African Savannah
2) Animal Holding Areas
3) Aquarium
4) Asian Domain
5) Beer Garden
6) Bird House
7) Bird Sanctuary
8) Education Bldg.
9) Elephant Rides
10) Flight Cage
11) Future Australian Exhibit
12) Future Reptile House
13) Giraffe Areas
14) Hospital
15) Louisiana Swamp Exhibit
16) Monkey Hill
17) North American Grasslands
18) Picnic Areas
19) Reflection Plaza
20) Safari Tram Station
21) Sea Lion Pool
22) South African Pampas
23) Wissner Children's Zoo
24) World of Primates

shops. Scheduled for completion by mid-decade are the Louisiana Swamp and Australian exhibits.

The zoo is open from 9:30 A.M. to 4:30 P.M., Monday through Friday; 9:30 A.M. to 5:30 P.M. (during daylight savings time); 9:30 A.M. to 4:30 P.M., Saturdays, Sundays, and holidays. Adults $3; Children (3–15 years), $1.50; Senior citizens and children (under 3 years), free. How to get there: If driving from the CBD or French Quarter, follow St. Charles Ave. to the main entrance to Audubon Park and then drive through the park to the zoo entrance on Magazine St. Or drive up Magazine St. from Canal St. to the zoo. If using public transportation, take the Magazine St. bus from Canal St. to the zoo. Or take the St. Charles Ave. streetcar to Broadway (about three blocks above Audubon Park), transfer to the Broadway bus, which will take you to within a block of the zoo entrance. Be sure to tell the bus driver where you are going before getting on the bus. You want to make sure you're going in the right direction. If the weather is pretty and you want to walk, take the streetcar to the St. Charles entrance to Audubon Park and walk the ten blocks through the park to the zoo's Magazine St. entrance. For zoo information, call 861–2537.

A great way to get to the zoo from the Central Business District is to catch the *Cotton Blossom* sternwheeler at the foot of Canal St. and cruise up the Mississippi to the zoo landing. For cruise information call 586–8777 (and for more details, see the Tours section of this chapter).

City Park was once the sugar plantation of Louis Allard. Today the 1500-acre park is the fifth largest urban park in the nation. The grounds with their magnificent live oaks and network of man-made lagoons, are well worth seeing. Much of the land making up City Park was acquired by the city in 1854. However, the first improvements were not made until the 1890s. Located in City Park is the New Orleans Museum of Art. On the south side of the museum are the majestic 19th-century dueling oaks where many scores were settled and honors upheld. Behind the museum is a beautiful rose garden. Much of the park was built or improved under the aegis of the Works Progress Administration during the Depression of the 1930s. Evident everywhere are signs left by the WPA including the Beaux Arts-style pavilion that stands near the Casino (1914). The Casino has an information office, concessions, and bicycle and boat rentals. It is located on Dreyfous Drive to the left of the New Orleans Museum of Art. The bronze equestrian statue of New Orleans-born Confederate General P. G. T. Beauregard stands at the main entrance to the Park. It was dedicated in 1915 by the general's granddaughter. (Beauregard's forces fired the first shot opening the Civil War at Fort Sumter, South Carolina.)

City Park also features three 18-hole golf courses, tennis courts, canoes and paddle boats, picnic grounds, horseback riding, fishing, an amusement park, a beautiful carousel (built in 1904), a petting zoo and storyland for children, and a miniature train.

Longue Vue House and Gardens once was the 8-acre private estate of Edith Rosenwald Stern and Edgar B. Stern. It is now open to the public. The 45-room house and five surrounding English and Spanish gardens are exquisite. The formal English gardens complement the great country house while the Spanish

Points of Interest

1) Amusement rides and
   Storyland
2) Boating
3) Camellia Garden and
   Duelling Oak
4) Casino Restaurant
5) Golf Courses
6) Golf Driving Range
7) New Orleans Botanical
   Garden
8) New Orleans Museum
   of Art
9) Old Driving Range
   Recreation Area
10) Pan American Stadium
11) Popps Fountain
12) Riding Stables
13) Tennis Courts
14) Tad Gormley Stadium

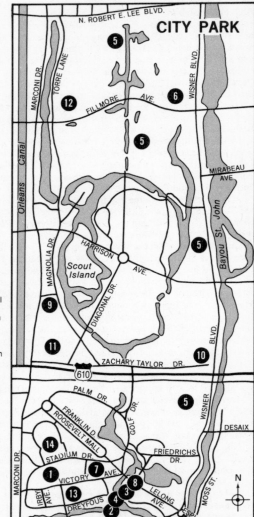

"water" gardens, with their 25 fountains are a soothing treat for eye and ear. The house was erected in the late 1930s in the Classical style. Longue Vue House and Gardens are administered by the Longue Vue Foundation. In addition to tours of the house and gardens, Longue Vue offers lectures and workshops on horticulture, architecture, decorative arts, and landscape gardening. For information, call (504) 488–1875 or 488–5488. Admission to the house and garden: adults, $5; children and students, $3. Gardens only, $2 and $1. The estate is located at 7 Bamboo Rd. off Metairie Rd. Open 10:00 A.M. to 4:30 P.M., Tuesday through Friday; 1:00 to 5:00 P.M., Saturday and Sunday. Closed Mondays and holidays.

Louisiana Nature Center, located in eastern New Orleans, 11000 Lake Forest Blvd., is an 86-acre wilderness park in the middle of suburban New Orleans. The center is a nonprofit, private institution dedicated to preserving what little is left of the natural environs that once surrounded the city. The main building at the center contains exhibitions on south Louisiana flora and wildlife, a media center, lecture hall, and gift shop. The center also offers woodland trails and birdwatching classes, nighttime canoe trips through swamplands, craft workshops and field trips. For information, call (504) 246–9381. Adults, $2; senior citizens (over 65), $1; children (14–17), $1; children (under 3) free. Open 9:00 A.M. to 5:00 P.M., Tuesday–Friday; Noon to 5:00 P.M., Saturday and Sunday. Closed Mondays.

PARTICIPANT SPORTS. Swimming. A public swimming pool in New Orleans is located at *Audubon Park* (2 pools), 524–8829, open from late May to the first week of August from 10:00 A.M. to 6:00 P.M., Tuesday through Sunday. Admission $1. Swimming in Lake Pontchartrain is permitted at *Sand Beach,* Lakeshore Dr. and Franklin Ave.; and *Old Beach,* Lakeshore Dr. and Bayou St. John. A word of caution to swimming in the lake: the state Board of Health has issued a notice that swimming in Lake Pontchartrain poses a risk to health due to high pollution levels.

Tennis. *The Hilton Tennis and Racquetball Club* at the New Orleans Hilton, Poydras Street, offers indoor and outdoor tennis, racquetball, gym, saunas and whirlpools. Guest membership is $5.50 per day for those registered at New Orleans hotels, plus rates for facility used.

Public tennis courts in New Orleans include:

Wisner Tennis Center, City Park, one block off City Park Ave. on Dreyfus, 48 courts, open 7:00 A.M.–10:00 P.M., Monday through Thursdays; 7:00 A.M.–7:00 P.M., Friday through Sunday. Rates $2–$3.60 per hour. Reservations in person (482–2230).

Stern Tennis Center, 4025 Saratoga. Seven courts. 8:00 A.M.–8:00 P.M., Monday through Friday; 8:00 A.M.–6:00 P.M., Saturday and Sunday. $2.75 per hour weekdays, $3.75 per hour weekends. 891–0627.

Joe Brown Park, Read Blvd. 10 courts. 9:00 A.M.–10:00 P.M. $2.50 per hour before 5:00 P.M.; $3.50 after 5:00 P.M.

Audubon Park, off Magazine St. 9:00 A.M.–5:00 P.M., $3 per hour. 865–7445.

Golf. Four 18-hole public golf courses are at *City Park,* 1046 Filmore (283–3458). Green fees $5–$5.75. After 3:00 P.M., $3. *Audubon Park,* 473 Walnut, has one 18-hole course (861–9513). Green fees: $4.35 weekdays; $6.80 weekends.

Other 18-hole public courses in the New Orleans area include *Pretty Acres Golf Club* in Covington, just north of the Lake Pontchartrain Causeway on US 190 (892–9260) and *Royal Golf Club* off Airport Road in Slidell (643–3000).

Sailing. Sailing on Lake Pontchartrain is a popular year-round sport. There are no boat rental houses.

Jogging: Popular places to jog in New Orleans are *City Park* in midtown and *Audubon Park* in uptown. Audubon Park is probably the most popular city spot for jogging. The front section of the park is closed to traffic, and a 2-mile jogging path winds around the golf course and its scenic lagoons. Paralleling the jogging trail are exercise stations as well as bicycling paths. The park is accessible from downtown by the St. Charles trolley and the Magazine St. bus. The Mississippi River levee is another, though less popular option, for the jogger seeking a quiet run.

Bicycling. Bicycling rentals and a bike riding path are available at *Audubon Park* (861–2537). For the bike enthusiast seeking longer trips, the miles of rural roads north of Lake Pontchartrain offer an endless variety of scenic routes. St. Tammany, Washington, Tangipahoa, St. Helena, and Livingston parishes north of New Orleans are popular areas. Detailed maps of these parishes can be obtained for $1 each from the *Louisiana Department of Transportation,* P.O. Box 44254, Capitol Station, Baton Rouge, LA 70804. The *Sierra Club*'s Guide to the Delta Country details many of the area's most popular routes. The telephone number for the Sierra Club in New Orleans is 455–0882. The *Crescent City Cyclists* (947–5083) offer weekend tours of southern Louisiana and Mississippi.

Horseback riding. *City Park* (486–0704) has a public stable.

Canoeing. *Audubon Park* (861–2537) and *City Park* (486–0704) offer canoe and boat rentals. City Park's 1,500 acres has a network of semitropical lagoons running lazily through it. Outside New Orleans, but within a two-hour drive of the city, are numerous streams, rivers and swamps for canoeing. The *Canoe and Trail Shop* (488–8525) and *Wilderness Outfitters* (835–1932) frequently sponsor trips into areas like Honey Island Swamp, north of Slidell, and the Tangipahoa and Bogue Chitto Rivers. Campgrounds along these rivers also offer canoe rentals (see Camping section in *Facts at Your Fingertips*). Other rental firms along the Tangipahoa River, which runs adjacent to Interstate 55 in Tangipahoa Parish, include *Beaver Creek Canoe Rentals,* Box 163, Tangipahoa, LA (Tel. 504–229–4392) and *Riverside Canoe Rentals,* Route 2, Box 1-C, Amite, LA (Tel. 504–748–4878).

Tubing. Tubing down scenic rivers in an inner tube is a popular summer sport on the Tangipahoa and Bogue Chitto Rivers, north of Lake Pontchartrain. Campgrounds in the area offer tube rentals (see Camping section of *Facts at Your Fingertips*).

Hiking. The *Canoe and Trail Shop* (488–8528), *Delta Wilderness Outfitters* (835–1933), the local *Sierra Club* (455–0832) and the *Louisiana Nature Center*

(241–9606) frequently sponsor excursions into the prime backpacking and hiking areas around New Orleans such as the Bogue Chitto National Wildlife Refuge and Honey Island Swamp in eastern St. Tammany Parish.

The New Orleans Sierra Club has published a book, *Trail Guide to the Delta Country* ($7.50 plus 75¢ mailing charge), that gives valuable information about camping, canoeing, hiking, tubing, cycling, and bird watching in Louisiana and Mississippi. To get a copy, send cash, check or money order to Sierra Club Trail Guide, 111 S. Hennessey St., New Orleans, LA 70119.

See *Facts at Your Fingertips* for information on hunting and fishing.

 SPECTATOR SPORTS. Baseball. Although New Orleans has no major or minor league teams, top-flight collegiate baseball is played by Tulane University and the University of New Orleans in the spring.

Basketball. Tulane University and the University of New Orleans both play NCAA Division I competition. Tulane plays in the rugged Metro Conference, which features national powers like Louisville and Memphis State, while UNO is an independent. Dillard, Xavier, Southern University-New Orleans, and Delgado Junior College also field teams. All play home games at gyms and field houses on their respective campuses. Tulane and UNO occasionally play a game in the Louisiana Superdome. The Superdome is also the site of the annual *Sugar Bowl Basketball Tournament,* played the week preceding the annual football classic.

Football. The New Orleans Saints of the National Football League play home games on Sunday in the Louisiana Superdome. Tulane University plays the home games of its independent major college schedule in the Superdome, usually on Saturday afternoons. Tickets for Saints (587–3664) and Tulane (865–5507 or 587–3768) games are usually available on game day. The exception is the LSU–Tulane game played in odd years in the Superdome. That game is usually a sell-out. Grambling and Southern Universities renew their annual rivalry in late November in the *Bayou Classic,* also in the Superdome. The Superdome is also the site of the *Sugar Bowl Game,* played New Year's Day or night.

Golf. The nation's top professional golfers compete annually in the *Greater New Orleans Open* at Lakewood Country Club (4801 General De Gaulle Dr, 393–2610), usually in mid-spring.

Horseracing. Flat racing action is available virtually year-round. *The Fairgrounds* (1751 Gentilly Blvd.; 943–2200), the nation's third oldest racetrack, is open from Thanksgiving to early April, with afternoon cards, Wednesday through Sunday. The big races of the season are the New Orleans Handicap for older horses and the Louisiana Derby for three-year-holds, a major prep for the Kentucky Derby. Both races are run in March. From April to November, night racing is held, Wednesday through Saturday, at *Jefferson Downs,* Williams Blvd and Lakefront, Kenner (466–8251), about 20 minutes from downtown New Orleans. Both tracks offer clubhouse dining.

Running. *The Mardi Gras Marathon* is held annually on a Sunday preceding Mardi Gras Day. Thousands of runners from across the country participate in the 26.2-mile race, 24 miles of it over a span of the Lake Pontchartrain Causeway. For information on the race, call the New Orleans Track Club, 246–0001.

Tournaments. In addition to the football game and basketball tournament, other activities associated with the annual Sugar Bowl Classic (611 Gravier St.) include a sailing regatta, road race, a flag football tournament and a tennis tournament. All are held prior to the New Year's Day football game. For general information call 525–8573; for ticket information call 525–8603.

 BABYSITTING SERVICES. Don't be reluctant to bring the children to New Orleans. Daytime activities are plentiful, and for those evenings when parents want to be out on the town, most of the city's major hotels offer babysitting services; call to check.

 CHILDREN'S ACTIVITIES. The pleasures of New Orleans generally appeal to adults and children alike. However, there are a number of activities and places that are especially recommended for children.

RIDES

Steamboat rides on the Mississippi hold a particular fascination. Aside from the view of the city and the water lapping at the sides of the boat, kids love to watch the big sternwheel turning. The mighty *Natchez* with its off-key steam calliope blasting out tunes, and the *Cotton Blossom* with its hour-long trip upriver to the Audubon Zoo are great fun. Catch the *Natchez* at the foot of St. Peter St. at the river in the French Quarter (524–9787) and the *Cotton Blossom* at the foot of Canal St. in the CBD (586–8777). The *St. Charles Ave. streetcar* is always a favorite. For 60 cents per person, you can take a 5-mile trip from Canal St. to the front entrance of Audubon Park in Uptown New Orleans. The streetcar, a throwback to a more leisurely paced New Orleans, slowly rambles along its tracks, jostling its passengers from side to side. It's a great ride and an excellent, inexpensive way to see the beautiful homes along famous St. Charles Ave.

SNACKS

For a real challenge, go to the Cafe du Monde in the French Quarter for beignets (French doughnuts). The trick is to try eating them without sprinkling or blowing powdered sugar all over the place.

MUSEUMS

The major historical and art museums have exhibits for children.

Of particular interest to children is the *Musée Conti Wax Museum,* 917 Conti St. in the French Quarter. It has a number of exhibits with full life-size wax figures of Jean Lafitte, the Louisiana pirate, Andrew Jackson and the Battle of

New Orleans, Marie Laveau, the Voodoo Queen, as well as popular fictional characters like Dracula, the Hunchback of Notre Dame, the Wolf Man, and Mad Scientist. Open 10:00 A.M. to 5:30 P.M. daily. Children of all ages will enjoy the historical toy exhibit in the Louisiana State Museum's *Presbytere* (751 Chartres) and the Mardi Gras exhibit in the *Old U.S. Mint Building* (400 Esplanade Ave. at the River). Young girls especially will enjoy the *Cabrini Doll Museum and Art Center* at 1218 Burgundy St. in the French Quarter. It has over 500 dolls from all over the world with some dating back to the 1870s. The museum has been closed for many months, but is scheduled to reopen in January 1984. Hours are from 1:30 P.M. to 6:00 P.M., Monday through Friday. Admission is free. The museum is owned and operated by the city. Also popular with children is the *Pontalba Historical Puppetorium* facing Jackson Square in the French Quarter. It has twelve stage settings, depicting various aspects of New Orleans history. Performances are given only for groups of 20 or more with advance notice (522–0344), 9:30 A.M. to 6:00 P.M. daily. $1.50 adults, $1 for children.

PARKS

Aubudon Park has a number of swing sets in various parts of the park, but more importantly, the *Audubon Zoo* has become one of the best medium-sized zoos in the country. It has animals from all over the world, including Africa, the Orient, South America, and Australia. Its open from 9:30 A.M. to 4:30 P.M., Monday through Friday, and from 9:30 A.M. to 5:30 P.M., weekends and holidays. Adults, $3; children 3–15 years, $1.50; children under 3 and senior citizens, free. Another great park for children is *City Park*, the fifth largest urban park in the nation. The park's main entrance is located at Esplanade and North Carrollton avenues about three miles from the French Quarter. The park has a number of playgrounds, a small amusement park and carousel, petting zoo, miniature train, canoe and paddle boat rides.

OTHER ACTIVITIES

Kids especially love Mardi Gras and its two weeks of "throw me somethin' mister!" They can scramble on the ground with natives and fellow visitors for the coveted toys and trinkets thrown from the floats.

Watching ships of all types ply up and down the Mississippi River is exciting for children. The best place to view them is from Jackson Square's Moon Walk. Jackson Square also hosts a number of diversions for children with its carnival of street musicians, clowns, mimes, and sidewalk artists.

Young boys and girls will enjoy a visit to Chalmette Battlefield below New Orleans in St. Bernard Parish where General Andrew Jackson, with the help of Jean Lafitte the pirate, defeated the British in the Battle of New Orleans in 1815.

A more comprehensive source of information on weekly children's events is *The Times-Picayune/The States-Item's Lagniappe* magazine in Friday's issue or the Sunday Calendar section. Both supplements include announcements of special events oriented toward children plus museum hours, exhibitions, and other current events that would be of interest to the entire family.

 HISTORIC HOUSES AND BUILDINGS. The Gallier House. 1118–1132 Royal St., in the French Quarter, is one of the finest historic houses in the city. It was built around 1858 by James Gallier, Jr., and has been lovingly restored to the time when the notable architect lived there. This house shows how the wealthy lived in mid-19th-century New Orleans. Visitors are served complimentary coffee and light refreshments on the upper gallery overlooking Royal St. Adults, $2.50; children, $1; students-senior citizens, $2. Group rates available. Docent tours. Open 10:00 A.M. to 4:30 P.M., Monday through Saturday. (504) 523–6722.

Historic Hermann-Grima House and Courtyard. 820 St. Louis St., in the French Quarter, is the local headquarters of the Christian Woman's Exchange. It was built in 1831 for wealthy merchant Samuel Hermann, Sr., then sold to Felix Grima, a prominent attorney, in 1844. The historic house contains a gift shop, Creole kitchen and courtyard *par-terre*. The courtyard, one of the largest in the French Quarter, has been replanted in the early 19th-century style. Adults, $2; children, $1. Group rates available. Docent tours. Open weekdays and Saturday from 10:00 A.M. to 3:30 P.M.; Sundays from 1:00 P.M. to 4:30 P.M. Closed Wednesday. (504) 525–5661.

Le Carpentier or **Beauregard-Keyes House.** 1113 Chartres St., was built by New Orleans autioneer Joseph Le Carpentier in 1827. During the winter of 1866–67 Civil War General P. G. T. Beauregard rented a room here then lived here after the war. The house later became the residence of novelist, Frances Parkinson Keyes who wrote many books about the region. The historic house boasts lovely French Quarter gardens. Adults, $2.50; children (under 12), 75 cents. Docent tours. Open from 10:00 A.M. to 4:30 P.M., Monday through Saturday. (Last tour begins at 3:00 P.M.) (504) 523–7257.

Ursuline Convent. 1112 Chartres St., in the French Quarter, is the oldest French colonial building in the lower Mississippi Valley. French Ursuline nuns moved into the building in 1749. It became Louisiana's first convent and first Catholic school and was used until the nuns moved to another location in 1824. From 1831–34, it housed the Louisiana State Legislature. Restored. Adults, $2.50; students-senior citizens, $1.50; children (under 12), $1. Group tours arranged through Memorial Tours, (504) 561–0008. Individual tours of church and old convent given on Fridays at 1:00 P.M., 2:00 P.M. and 3:00 P.M.

New Orleans Spring Fiesta Mid-19th-Century Townhouse. 826 St. Ann St., in the French Quarter, is furnished with early 19th-century and Victorian pieces and *objets d'art*. $1.50. Group tours arranged. Docent guides. Open 11:00 A.M. to 4:00 P.M., Monday through Thursday. (504) 581–1367.

St. Louis Cathedral (Cathedral of St. Louis King of France). On Jackson Square, is the oldest active Roman Catholic cathedral in the US (1793). The present cathedral (built in 1790s and remodeled in the 1850s) is the third church to occupy this site since New Orleans was founded in 1718. The remodeled cathedral was done to the specifications of noted architect J. N. B. de Pouilly. The cathedral was named for Louis IX of France. Free guided tours daily Monday through Saturday from 9:00 A.M. to 5:00 P.M.; Sundays, 1:00 P.M. to 5:00 P.M.

Lafitte's Blacksmith Shop. 941 Bourbon St., in the French Quarter. Although this is now a bar, it is also one of the oldest buildings in New Orleans. The oldest record of ownership dates it to 1772. Legend has it that it was once a blacksmith shop run by the pirate Jean Lafitte and his brother.

The Cornstalk Fence. 915 Royal St., in the French Quarter and 1448 Fourth St., in the Garden District. These fences, the only two of their kind, were cast in Philadelphia in the early part of the 19th century. The picturesque wrought-iron fence intertwines corn stalks with ears of corn, morning glories, vines and blossoms. The one in the Quarter is painted yellow and green to resemble corn—a bit garish.

1850 House (part of the Louisiana State Museum complex). 523 St. Ann St., on Jackson Square, recreates the living style of upper middle class New Orleanians during the 1850s. It is a beautifully restored 3-story section of one of the two Pontalba buildings, containing authentic furniture of the period. Adults, $1; students, 50 cents. Open 9:00 A.M. to 5:00 P.M., Tuesday through Sunday. (504) 568–6968.

Pitot House. 1440 Moss St., on Bayou St. John, is an excellent example of colonial plantation architecture in Louisiana with its definite West Indian flavor. It was built around 1880 for the Ducayet family and later owned by James Pitot, the second Mayor of New Orleans. Furnished in the Federal period with many Louisiana-made furnishings. Operated by the Louisiana Landmarks Society. Open on Thursdays only from 11:00 A.M. to 4:00 P.M. Group tours arranged by appointment. Docent tours. $1.50. (504) 482–0312.

Women's Opera Guild Home. 2504 Prytania St., in the Garden District, is a splendid pre-Civil War Garden District mansion of Greek revival and Italianate architecture. House has early 19th-century period furnishings and Victorian *objets d'art.* The Guild inherited the mansion and its many fine paintings from the Seebold family. $2. Group tours arranged. Open 1:00 P.M. to 4:00 P.M., Monday through Friday. (504) 899–1945.

Jackson Square. In the heart of the French Quarter, was first established in 1721 as a drill field for soldiers. Known first as the Place d'Armes under the French and then the Plaza de Armas under the Spanish, the square was renamed in honor of General Andrew Jackson in 1851. The park's focal point is a statue of Jackson on horseback. It is the world's first bronze equestrian statue with more than one hoof unsupported. The statue was cast in 1853 and is the work of sculptor Clark Mills. The trees, bushes, and flowers in the square are all indigenous to the area. During the warmer months, band concerts are held in the park on Saturday afternoons, featuring jazz bands as well as other forms of music. The concerts are sponsored by the New Orleans Recreation Dept. but do not have a fixed annual schedule. For information, call 587–1999, or check local newspapers for weekend events. The park is open to the public from sunup to sundown.

Louisiana State Museum Complex. Located on Jackson Square, in the French Quarter, LSM consists of eight historical buildings: Cabildo, Presbytere, Arsenal, Jackson and Creole houses, the Lower Pontalba, Madame John's Legacy, and the Old U.S. Mint. (For detailed descriptions of each building and its exhibitions, see listing for the Louisiana State Museum in the Museum section.) The museum has a number of permanent historical exhibitions as well as regularly changing exhibits on the various facets of Louisiana's history. For the most part, the museum concentrates on the city's and state's colonial history. Other exhibits include an exquisite display of Mardi Gras costumes, steamboats on the Mississippi, jazz, the 1850 House, early 19th-century portraits, colonial Louisiana furniture, 19th-century clothing, the Newcomb (College) style of art, colonial maps and documents. A favorite is the death mask of Napoleon made by one of his attending physicians, Dr. Francesco Antommarchi. Antommarchi made the mold at St. Helena forty hours after Napoleon's death in 1821. The physician presented the city of New Orleans with one of the bronze casts made from the mold in 1834. It is on view in the Cabildo. On display in the Cabildo, from April 29–November 18, 1984, is the magnificent "Louis XIV, Sun King" exhibition from France. The exhibit occupies the entire Cabildo. During this period, other exhibits have been removed from the building. The exhibitions are just a small tip of the museum's vast collections of decorative arts, textiles, paintings, historical photographs, prints, furniture, weapons, jazz, Mardi Gras costumes and accoutrements, and buildings. Hours for all eight buildings are 9:00 A.M. to 5:00 P.M., Tuesday through Sunday. Adults, $1; students, 50 cents; senior citizens and children under 12, free. Note: this is the admission fee to each separate building. Docent tours by the Friends of the Cabildo, (504) 523–3939.

St. Louis Cemeteries No. 1 and No. 2. St. Louis No. 1 is located on Basin and St. Louis streets, and No. 2 can be found between St. Louis and Iberville streets along North Claiborne Ave. Both are located behind the French Quarter in Faubourg Trémé. Established in 1796, St. Louis Cemetery No. 1 is the oldest extant graveyard in the city. The cemetery, like others in the city, are famous for their ornate aboveground tombs. They have been called cities of the dead. Local legend has it that New Orleans cemeteries are built aboveground because some parts of the city are just at or below sea level and to dig into the ground would mean coming up with water. It's a nice story, but the city's Mediterranean and southern European heritage probably had more to do with the custom of aboveground tombs. St. Louis No. 2 dates from the 1820s, and it was laid out in the same general style as its predecessor. New Orleanians from all walks of life were buried here during the 19th century—white, black, slave, and free, from the city's most prominent citizens to the lowliest. Some of those buried in these two cemeteries are Voodoo Queen Marie Laveau (St. Louis No. 1), notice the gris gris "X's" marked on her tomb, Paul Morphy (renowned 19th-century world chess champion from New Orleans), Etienne Boré (St. Louis No. 1) who revolutionized the sugar industry on his plantation at what is now Audubon Park, and Homer Plessy who described himself as "seven-eighths caucasian and one-eighth African blood" in his 1892 challenge of Louisiana's Jim Crow segregation laws (which resulted in the famous 1896 U.S. Supreme

Court decision *Plessy vs. Ferguson,* that set up over a half-century of "separate but equal" segregation laws throughout the South). A word of caution: the best and safest way to visit these cemeteries is by guided tour and in large numbers. The cemeteries are located next to a federal housing project and an exceptionally high crime area.

MUSEUMS. Like most large cities, New Orleans has its share of museums. Because of the city's preoccupation with its past, most of the museums are historical in nature and are located in the French Quarter or close by. In recent years New Orleans' two largest museums—the Louisiana State Museum and the New Orleans Museum of Art—have gained impressive national reputations. The New Orleans Museum of Art hosted the *King Tut* and *Alexander* exhibits during their tours in this country as well as other major international exhibitions. The Louisiana State Museum, one of the largest historical museums in the country, also has participated in several exhibit exchange programs with France and Spain. Like the New Orleans orchestra and Mardi Gras, the Louisiana State Museum and the New Orleans Museum of Art form the nucleus of the city's cultural life. They are both first-rate museums that have made considerable strides in the last decade.

Louisiana State Museum. Located on Jackson Square, in the French Quarter, LSM consists of eight historical buildings: Cabildo, Presbytere, Arsenal, Jackson and Creole houses, the Lower Pontalba, Madame John's Legacy, and the old U.S. Mint. The museum has a number of changing and permanent exhibitions on the history of New Orleans and Louisiana from colonial times to the late 19th century. Exhibits include an exquisite display of Mardi Gras costumes, jazz, Louisiana paintings and furniture, decorative arts, fashion, historical maps and documents, and Mississippi River memorabilia. By far the most exciting exhibit scheduled for the museum from April 29–November 18, 1984, is "Louis XIV, the Sun King." It has been described as the most important historical exhibit ever to have been sent from France to the U.S. The Louisiana State Museum is the only place in the U.S. where the exhibition will appear. The LSM buildings are open from 9:00 A.M. to 5:00 P.M., Tuesday through Sunday. Closed Mondays and legal holidays. Adults, $1; students, 50 cents; senior citizens and children under 12, free. Docent tours for large groups also available (504) 523–3939. Listed below is a detailed description of each building:

The Presbytere. Jackson Square. The first structure on this site, a small Capuchin monastery built shortly after the French colonized the area, was destroyed by the fire of 1788. In 1791 Don Andres Almonester y Roxas began construction on a new structure. The Presbytere was planned as a residence for clergy serving the parish. Building had hardly begun, however, when the fire of 1794 swept through the city and damaged the new structure. After the U.S. took over Louisiana in 1803, the Presbytere was finally completed (in 1813) but it was never used as a clerical residence. In 1853 the Presbytere was purchased by the city from the wardens of the cathedral and served as a courthouse. It is now part of the Louisiana State Museum. Among the exhibits inside are antique toys and 19th-century portraits. There are changing exhibits on display as well.

The Cabildo. Chartres St., facing Jackson Square. A lot of New Orleans history has taken place here. During the Spanish colonial period, the structure on this site housed the governing council of the colony but burned in 1788. Don Andres Almonester y Roxas contributed funds for the replacement building which you see before you (built between 1795 and 1799). A small portion of the 1753 structure can still be seen in one of the ground-floor rooms of the current Cabildo. The wrought-iron railing on the balcony is considered to be the finest work of its kind from the Spanish colonial period. From this building, France, Spain, the United States and the Confederate states have governed. The Sala Capitular on the second floor is the room in which the ceremony of transferring Louisiana from France to the U.S. took in place in 1803 (the Louisiana Purchase). Today the Cabildo is part of the Louisiana State Museum complex. The building will be closed until April. From April 29 to November 18, 1984, the exhibition "Louis XIV, the Sun King" will occupy all three stories of the Cabildo. It is the largest and most spectacular historical exhibition ever to be sent from France to the U.S. and was planned to coincide with the 1984 Louisiana World Exposition. It consists of priceless paintings, documents, furniture, decorative arts and other magnificent 17th- and 18th-century treasures on loan to the museum by the French government. When the exhibit closes in November, the Cabildo will be refitted with a number of historical exhibits depicting Louisiana's colonial experience. Same admission hours and charges as the Presbytere and other LSM buildings.

The Arsenal. Standing to the rear of the Cabildo on St. Peter Street is the old arsenal. It was built in 1839 on the site of the 1769 Spanish Arsenal. During the Sun King exhibition, the Arsenal will be used as a gift shop and bookstore for the exhibit. After the show closes and returns to France, the Arsenal's galleries will house special exhibits on the history of paintings and photographs. The Arsenal will be closed to the public until the Sun King exhibit opens in April. Hours are the same as other buildings in LSM system.

Jackson and Creole houses. Located to the rear of the Arsenal, facing St. Peter St. Located within the Jackson House is the Louisiana Folk Art collection, which has been described as the finest of its kind in the country. The collection includes portraits, landscapes, sculptures, and other forms of folk art. The Jackson House was named for General and later President Andrew Jackson, the hero of the 1815 Battle of New Orleans. This building was reconstructed in 1936 by the Works Progress Administration, and the original building on this site dates back to 1842. Hours and admission same as other LSM buildings. The Creole House, built in 1842 on the site of a colonial prison, is not open to the public. It is the headquarters for the Friends of the Cabildo, the museum's volunteer organization that provides tours of the museum and French Quarter. The organization publishes books on New Orleans history, and raises money for museum projects.

Pontalba Buildings and 1850 House. Fronting both sides of Jackson Square on St. Ann and St. Peter streets. Work on the planned luxury apartments was commissioned by Baroness Micaela Almonester de Pontalba and began on the 16 row houses facing St. Peter St. in 1849. It was completed in 1850. The identical row on St. Ann was finished in 1850. The building on St. Peter is owned by the City of New Orleans while the one on St. Ann is part of the Louisiana State Museum system. The second and third levels in both buildings are private residences while shops and restaurants occupy the ground floor. Only the 1850 House, 523 St. Ann, is open to the public. It is a beautifully restored, three-story section of one of the two Pontalba buildings, containing authentic furniture of the period. The museum has recreated the living style of upper-middle-class New Orleanians during the 1850s. Hours and admission same as other LSM buildings.

Madame John's Legacy. 632 Dumaine St. (part of the Louisiana State Museum), in the French Quarter. It is an excellent example of French colonial architecture in Louisiana. The cottage was built in 1788 shortly after the Good Friday fire of that same year, which destroyed most of the city. It was constructed for Manuel de Lanzos by Robert Jones. The house got its name from one of the characters in George Washington Cable's fictional story, "Tite Poulette." According to the story Madame John was a quadroon who inherited the house but sold her "legacy" and later became very poor. On display in the house is a fine collection of colonial and early 19th-century Louisiana furniture. 581–4321. Hours and admission same as other LSM buildings.

The Old U.S. Mint. 400 Esplanade Ave. near the Mississippi River, in the French Quarter. The mint was designed by William Strickland (designer of the Philadelphia Mint) and construction began in 1835, during the presidency of Andrew Jackson. It was the first branch U.S. Mint, operating from 1838 to 1861. In the early 1850s the building was renovated by Army engineer P. G. T. Beauregard, later of Civil War fame. Beauregard replaced most of the wooden superstructure with brick and cast iron and plastered and painted the outside a reddish brown to simulate brownstone, a popular Victorian color. During the Civil War, it served as the Confederacy's only mint for a few months in 1861. After the war, it continued to operate as a U.S. mint from the mid-1870s to 1909. In the 1930s, the building was temporarily used as a federal detention center and Coast Guard warehouse. The mint was restored to its present condition in the late 1970s. For public enjoyment, there are three floors of historical exhibits. The Mint Museum is located on the ground floor. It gives a history of the building. On the second floor are the Jazz and Mardi Gras exhibits. The Mardi Gras collection is the largest of its type in the world. With costumes, photographs, artifacts, and other historical documents it illustrates the history and mystique of this unique institution. The Jazz exhibit traces the history of New Orleans music from the 1790s to the early 20th century ragtime and jazz as it is known today through a narrated slide show, musical instruments, photographs, paintings, posters, sheet music, and other items. Located on the third floor is the Louisiana Historical Center and the Amistad Research Center. The Louisiana Historical Center has a vast collection of books and historical documents pertaining to the colonial and 19th-century history of Louisiana. It is open to researchers by application, which can be obtained at the center. The

Amistad Research Center is one of the nation's most important centers for studying the history of black Americans. Hours and admission same as other LSM buildings.

New Orleans Museum of Art. Located in City Park, NOMA has a representative permanent collection of art ranging from pre-Colombian and Far Eastern work to European, American, and African. The building was constructed with funds donated by sugar planter and philanthropist Isaac Delgado in 1911 and named in his honor until 1971 when it was changed to the New Orleans Museum of Art with the opening of three new wings. The original neo-Classical building was designed by Chicago architect Samuel Marx. The three newer wings are the Wisner Education Wing of rotating exhibits and educational programs for visiting schoolchildren, the Stern Auditorium used for art lectures and films, and the City Wing which contains galleries for the permanent collection and the Ella West Freeman Gallery for special exhibitions.

Donations of individual works and private collections have served to enrich the outstanding NOMA collection. Special collections include the Samuel H. Kress Collection of Italian Painting from the 13th through 18th centuries; the Chapman H. Hyams Collection of 19th-century French Art; the Morgan Whitney Collection of Chinese Jades; the Melvin Billups Glass Collection; the Latter-Schlesinger Collection of Portrait Miniatures; and the Victor K. Kiam Bequest of 20th-century European and American Painting and Sculpture. There are also collections of African and Oceanic Art acquired from the Kiam estate. NOMA also features a very strong photography collection with works by such notables as Laszlo Moholy-Nagy, Walker Evans, Alfred Stieglitz, and James Van Der Zee.

In the late 1960s NOMA began building a special collection devoted to the Arts of the Americas—North, Central and South—spanning works from pre-Colombian to present times. North American paintings include works by such artists as John Singleton Copley, Charles Willson Peale, Gilbert Stuart, and John Singer Sargent. NOMA's collection of Latin Colonial painting and sculpture is the largest in the U.S. and its works from the pre-Colombian Indian civilizations are outstanding.

In recent years, NOMA has presented several major international traveling exhibitions such as "The Treasures of Tutankhamun," "Peru's Golden Treasures," "The Search for Alexander," and "Honore Daumier 1801–1879, from the Armand Hammer Collection."

Among the exhibits scheduled for 1984 are Korean folk paintings; Leonardo da Vinci's Codex Hammer (sponsored by the Armand Hammer Foundation); Waters of America, 19th Century American paintings of rivers, streams, lakes, and waterfalls (planned to coincide with the 1984 Louisiana World Exposition); masterpieces of the American West; Spanish Colonial Painting and Sculpture; traditional art of the Plains Indians, and ancient Chinese Bronzes. The fabulous Faberge Egg Collection, once owned by the Czars of Russia, will be exhibited on the second floor of the City Wing for the next five years. Check *Lagniappe* in Friday's *The Times-Picayune/The States-Item* for current films, lectures, and exhibitions. Museum hours are 10:00 A.M. to 5:00 P.M., Tuesdays, Wednesdays,

Fridays, Saturdays, and Sundays; 1:00 P.M. to 9:00 P.M., Thursdays. Closed Mondays. Adults $1; children (6–17), and senior citizens (over 65), 50¢. Thursdays admission is free for all. The museum also contains a bookshop. (504) 488–2631.

The Historic New Orleans Collection. Located at 533 Royal St. (Merieult House), in the French Quarter, the Historic New Orleans Collection is a definite must during any visit to the *Vieux Carré.* It is housed in the 1792 house built by Jean Francois Merieult. The collection includes ten permanent exhibition galleries featuring the colonial and antebellum history of New Orelans in a complex of connecting 18th-century houses. Each gallery describes a phase of New Orleans history through historical maps, paintings, documents, decorative arts, and other items. One of the galleries includes the Williams' residence, which houses fine antiques from various parts of the world. The residence is part of the tour. The buildings and collections were once the private residence and collection of the late General and Mrs. L. Kemper Williams who set up the Kemper Williams' Foundation that administers the Historic New Orleans Collection. The main gallery on Royal St. has changing exhibits on the social and cultural history of the city. It is the only gallery in the complex that is free to the public. In addition, the collection has two historic museum residences, a research center for the study of New Orleans and Louisiana history, and a gift shop. The hours are 10:00 A.M. to 5:00 P.M., Tuesdays through Saturdays. First-floor gallery, free; guided tours, $2. Docent tours available. (504) 523–7146.

SPECIAL INTEREST MUSEUMS

Confederate Memorial Museum. 929 Camp St. near Lee Circle. Contains the largest collection in this part of the country of rare weapons, uniforms, and memorabilia from the Civil War. The collection, filling one large hall and two smaller side wings, deals exclusively with the Confederacy. It also contains a large collection of Confederate President Jefferson Davis memorabilia, which was donated by his widow. Also on display are a series of prints describing events leading to Louisiana's secession from the United States, its joining the Confederate States, and the fall of New Orleans to the Union army and navy. The museum is owned by the Louisiana Historical Association. Hours: 10:00 A.M. to 4:00 P.M., Monday through Saturday. Admission: Adults, $1; students and senior citizens, 50¢; children under 12 years, 25¢. For group reservations call (504) 523–4522.

Louisiana Maritime Museum. 31st floor of the International Trade Mart Building, at the foot of Canal St. Great view of the Mississippi River and French Quarter. Extensive collection of historical artifacts pertaining to the maritime history of New Orleans and life along the Mississippi. Among the pieces to note are the ornate furniture made in Paris that once furnished the *Steamboat J. M. White*—one of the grandest from the steamboat era—and the beautifully carved polychrome figurehead from a ship that sailed the South Pacific in the 1870s. Other items displayed include ship models, maps, seafaring tools, and a cypress

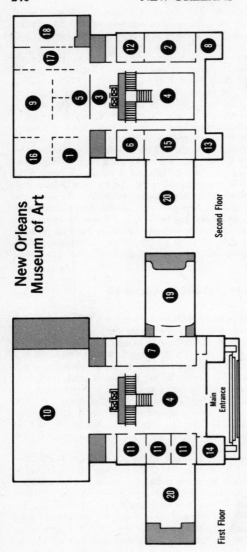

New Orleans
Museum of Art

Second Floor

First Floor

Main
Entrance

Points of Interest

1) African Art
2) American Decorative Art
3) Billups Glass Collection
4) City Wings
5) Contemporary European
   and American Art
6) Degas and the
   Impressionists

7) Downman Gallery
8) Dutch Paintings
9) Early 20th Century
   European and
   American Art
10) Freeman Gallery
11) Kress Collection
12) Kuntz Collection
13) Miniature Collection
14) Museum Shop

15) 19th Century French Art
16) Oriental Art
17) Pre-Columbian Art
18) Restaurant
19) Stern Auditorium
20) Wisner Education Wing

pirogue (canoe). Hours: 9:00 A.M. to 4:00 P.M., Mondays through Saturdays. Adults, $2.50; children, $1.50; discount for senior citizens. (504) 581–1874.

Pharmacy Museum. 514 Chartres St., in the French Quarter. "La Pharmacie Francaise" resembles a 19th-century apothecary with shelves, jars, and cabinets filled with medicinal herbs, cures, and instruments dating to the early 19th century. Hours: 10:00 A.M. to 5:00 P.M., Tuesdays through Saturdays. Admission: 25¢. 524–9077.

Middle American Research Institute. 4th Floor, Dinwiddie Hall, Tulane University, facing St. Charles Ave. Exhibits and collections pertaining to pre-Colombian, South and Central American culture. Established in 1924, the institute has an extensive collection of pre-Colombian Mayan artifacts mainly from northern Central America and central and southern Mexico. The institute also has the largest collection of Guatemalan textiles (dating from the 1920s and 1930s) in the nation. Many artifacts, including jewelry, pottery, and costumes, are on display in the 35 glass cases that line the single long gallery. Hours: 8:30 A.M. to 5:00 P.M., Monday through Friday. No admission charge. (504) 865–5110.

Musee Conti Wax Museum. 917 Conti St. Commercial museum featuring numerous historical settings using expertly fashioned wax figures. It has 144 life size, costumed figures in 31 settings such as the 1815 Battle of New Orleans, the Louisiana Purchase of 1803, Voodoo Queen Marie Laveau, Madame Lalaurie's haunted house, Jean Lafitte the pirate, frontiersman Jim Bowie, and author Mark Twain. Another section of the museum, called "The Haunted Dungeon," contains well-executed scenes (pardon the pun) from stories by Edgar Allan Poe, Robert Louis Stevenson, and Victor Hugo, among others. You'll find creatures such as Dracula, Frankenstein, the Hunchback of Notre Dame, the Wolf Man, and the like. A fun museum for children. Admission: Adults, $3.50; children, $1.25; senior citizens, $3. Group rates available. Hours: 10:00 A.M. to 5:30 P.M. daily. Tours available in French and Spanish. 525–2605.

Voodoo Museum. 636 St. Ann St., in the French Quarter. Combination commercial museum and store featuring voodoo paraphernalia and supplies. Exhibits include gris gris potions, voodoo altar, and a boa constrictor. The gift shop sells potions, ceremonial candles, dolls, books on voodoo, psychic readings. Special group tour rates for schools and conventions. Voodoo entertainment and dances can be arranged. Walking tour available. Hours: 10:00 A.M. to midnight. Admission: adults, $2; students, $1; children under 7 years, free. 523–2906.

Cabrini Doll Museum and Art Center. 1218 Burgundy St., in the French Quarter. Small doll museum operated by the city. The collection of 500 dolls from all over the world includes dolls from Latvia, China, Japan, Russia, Spain, Italy, England, France, and Germany. Of particular interest is a collection of Japanese Tea Ceremony dolls. The oldest in the collection is a French fashion doll dating to the 1870s. Hours: 1:30 P.M. to 6:00 P.M., Monday through Friday. No admission charge. The museum also offers free art classes for children aged 8 to 15—call in advance. 524–9919.

ART GALLERIES. Art galleries, because they deal in a commodity that too often is considered a luxury, sadly count among the very first commercial ventures to be affected by the nation's economy. For this reason, certain of the galleries listed below may have closed by the time this volume appears in print. On the other hand, new worthwhile art galleries may have opened.

Visitors interested in New Orleans galleries should consult listings in the local press or call the Arts Council for up-to-date information.

French Quarter. *Gasperi Folk Art Gallery,* 831 St. Peter St., handles international and regional folk art, including works by Louisiana primitives Chief Wiley, Clementine Hunter, and Sister Gertrude Morgan.

Nahan Galleries, 540 Royal St., is a relatively large, two-story operation with something for every taste; the outstanding items here are limited edition prints by top-flight international artists, including Picasso, Chagall, Miro, and Agam. Similar to Nahan, but smaller and more select, is the *927 Gallery,* at 906 Royal St.

Reinike Gallery, 300 Dauphine St., features nicely executed figurative paintings, frequently landscapes, by local and national artists.

The Sandra Zahn Oreck Gallery, 529 Wilkinson Row, is more of a gift boutique than an exhibition facility, although original paintings and prints are always on view; the gallery is located on a charming and easy-to-overlook side street, closed to vehicular traffic and lined with renovated former warehouses, today containing chic shops.

Tahir Gallery, 823 Chartres St., specializes in 20th-century American prints.

The Tilden-Foley Gallery, 933 Royal St., carries 19th- and 20th-century art, including works by interesting local and regional artists.

Vincent Mann Galleries, 900 Royal St., handles paintings by lesser-known French Impressionists of the 19th and early 20th centuries; fascinating shows are quite often staged here.

Galerie Jules Laforgue, at 2119 Frenchmen St., is located a short distance from the French Quarter and is well worth a look; the gallery deals in first-rate figurative art by local artists.

Posters, which are available in shops all over the Quarter, are the specialty at *Lorenzo Bergen Galleries,* 610 and 730 Royal St. At these locations, visitors will find the biggest, most comprehensive collection of posters in town.

Uptown. *Aaron-Hastings,* 1130 St. Charles Ave. Small and unassuming, it handles quality contemporary art by local artists.

The St. Charles Gallery, 1720 St. Charles Ave., distinctly patrician, specializes in British watercolors from the 18th and 19th centuries.

The Fine Arts Gallery of New Orleans, 1820 St. Charles Ave., handles museum-quality marine genre and landscape paintings from the 17th through the 20th centuries.

The Bienville Gallery is located at 1800 Hastings Pl., which intersects Magazine St.; this offbeat establishment frequently features art dealing with sex and/or death.

Optima Studio, at 2025 Magazine St., is an artists' cooperative with a store-front gallery; works by member artists are regularly exhibited here.

Galerie Simonne Stern is located at 2727 Prytania St., which runs parallel to Magazine St., four blocks in the direction of Lake Pontchartrain. The most prestigious New Orleans gallery handling local contemporary art, Simonne Stern occupies space in an unusual converted building, originally a turn-of-the-century skating rink. Housed in the same building is the *Oriental Collectables* gallery, which deals in high quality oriental art and *objets.*

The Arthur Roger Gallery, New Orleans' liveliest and most stylish commercial facility, is located in slick quarters at 3005 Magazine St.; the exhibitions here showcase some of the finest art produced in New Orleans, along with contemporary paintings and sculptures imported from New York.

The Mario Villa Gallery, 3908 Magazine St., in a large, tastefully appointed gallery representing some of Lousiana's most imaginative contemporary artists, frequently from area universities.

The Davis Gallery, at 3964 Magazine St., has for sale magnificent examples of African art, which the gallery's owners import regularly (and legally) into the U.S.

The Academy Gallery, housed in a restored Victorian residence at 5256 Magazine St., is affiliated with a private art school, the New Orleans Academy of Fine Arts. Exhibitions include works by both faculty members and unaffiliated local artists.

A Gallery for Fine Photography, at 5423 Magazine, deals in historical and contemporary photography by many of the most important names associated with that field.

The Contemporary Arts Center, 900 Camp St. (523–1216), on the fringes of the Central Business District. Exhibitions and theme shows feature works by local artists in addition to special exhibits of traveling shows. CAC also hold concerts, films theatrical and dance performances in addition to art-related workshops and seminars. Open Noon to 5:00 P.M., Tuesday through Sunday.

 LIBRARIES. New Orleans has a number of research and general interest libraries throughout the city. Although the city's public library system is adequate, the various research libraries are, in some cases, first rate with notable collections.

The *New Orleans Public Library,* located in the Civic Center, 219 Loyola Ave., in the Central Business District, has the general reading stacks found in most libraries of this nature. In addition, it has special divisions on art and music, business and science, foreign languages, and New Orleans-Louisiana history. Unfortunately, the city's budgetary constraints has forced the library to shorten its hours of operation. Hours: 10:00 A.M. to 6:00 P.M., Tuesday through Saturday. Closed Sunday and Monday. The New Orleans Public Library also has several branch libraries in various parts of the city. (504) 524–7382.

There are also first-rate university libraries in New Orleans that offer the vast resources found in most university libraries. These are research libraries, and the general public can make use of their collections on the premises only. The university libraries have sections on architecture, art, music, medicine, science, business, and U.S., international, and Hispanic-American culture, business and politics. *Tulane University library system,* 7001 Freret St., 865–5604; *Loyola University Library,* 6363 St. Charles Ave., 865–3328; *University of New Orleans Library,* Lake Shore Drive, 286–6353.

New Orleans has a number of special-interest libraries. They are located in museums and universities and run the full gamut from history and art to law and jazz.

Art. *The New Orleans Museum of Art Library.* Located in City Park, 488–2631. A 10,000-volume library emphasizing art and art history. Strong emphasis in pre-Colombian, African, photography, oriental, ancient to modern art. Current art periodicals, exhibition catalog exchange programs with 250 national and international museums. Research only. Recommended call in advance.

History. *Armistad Research Center,* old U.S. Mint Building, 400 Esplanade Ave., 522–0432. Specializes in black history. Extensive library and archival collections, including the papers of the American Missionary Society and local chapters of the National Association for the Advancement of Colored People (NAACP). Special exhibits of paintings, prints and documents are displayed in the library reading room. Research only. The *Louisiana State Museum's Louisiana Historical Center,* located in the old U.S. Mint Building, Esplanade Ave., 568–6968. The center has an extensive research library pertaining to the socio-economic and political history of New Orleans, Louisiana, and the Lower Mississippi Valley. Also extensive genealogical files and reference materials about Louisiana families. The Center also has extensive archival collections from the colonial and pre-Civil War eras, including diaries, letters, maps, and a half-million pages of French and Spanish colonial judicial records. 9:00 A.M. to 5:00 P.M., Monday through Friday. Research only.

Loyola University Library, 6363 St. Charles Ave., 865–3328. Microfilm collections of documents in various French and Spanish archives pertaining to colonial Louisiana. Research only.

New Orleans Public Library Louisiana Division, located in the Civic Center, 219 Loyola Ave., 524–7382. Extensive library and archival collections concerning New Orleans from colonial times to the present. The Louisiana Division also is the city's official archives. 10:00 A.M. to 6:00 P.M., Tuesday through Saturday. Research only.

The *Historic New Orleans Collection library and archives,* 533 Royal St., 523–7146. Extensive library and archives emphasizing the history of New Orleans. Also has the *Vieux Carré Survey* of French Quarter architecture. 10:00 A.M. to 4:30 P.M., Tuesday through Saturday. Research only.

Tulane University Library Special Collections Division, 7001 Freret St., 865–5685. Books, prints, photographs, archives on history of New Orleans, jazz, architecture. 8:30 A.M. to 5:00 P.M., Monday through Friday; 10:00 A.M. to Noon, Saturday. Research only. *Louisiana Division* has extensive collection of rare books about New Orleans and Louisiana and by local writers. Same hours as Special Collections Division, 865–5643. Research only.

The *University of New Orleans Library, Archives and Manuscripts Department,* Lake Shore Dr., 286–6543. Extensive collection of books, manuscripts, photographs, archival collections pertaining to the history of New Orleans. 8:00 A.M. to 4:30 P.M., Monday through Friday; 9:00 A.M. to 1:00 P.M., Saturday. Research only. Recommended call in advance.

Hispanic American. *Tulane University Latin American Library,* 7001 Freret St., 865–5681. Contemporary and historical books, newspapers, magazines, photographs concerning Latin, or Hispanic, America, especially Central America and Mexico. 8:00 A.M. to 12:45 A.M., Monday through Thursday; 8:00 A.M. to 10:45 P.M., Friday; 8:00 A.M. to 5:00 P.M., Saturday; 1:00 P.M. to 12:45 A.M., Sunday. Research only.

Jazz and Music. *Tulane University Library Special Collections Division* (865–5685) and the *Louisiana State Museum's Louisiana Historical Center* (568–6968) have outstanding jazz collections containing hundreds of books, articles, photographs, recordings, vertical files, and musical instruments. The *New Orleans Public Library* (524–7382), Loyola University (865–3328), and Tulane University libraries (865–3328) have extensive music libraries.

Law. The *Louisiana Supreme Court Library,* Civic Center, 301 Loyola Ave., 568–5705.

Tulane University Law School Library, Freret St. Campus, 865–5939.

Loyola University Law School Library, 6363 St. Charles Ave., 865–3426.

Medicine. *Tulane University Matas Medical Library,* Tulane Medical Center, Tulane Ave., 588–5155. *Primate Research Center Library,* Three Rivers Rd., Covington, LA (about 35 miles north of New Orleans), 561–8936 (New Orleans number).

MOVIES. New Orleans' old movie palaces are long gone. Most of them have either been divided up into multicinemas showing second-rate flicks or converted to other uses. The old RKO Orpheum, on University Place in the CBD, is now the permanent home of the New Orleans Philharmonic Symphony Orchestra, and the old Saenger Theatre, on Canal St., is now the Saenger Performing Arts Center, featuring big-name entertainers and Broadway plays. For daily listings of what movies are playing in town, check the *The Times-Picayune/The States-Item* newspaper. Old movies and foreign films are shown at the Prytania Theater, 5339 Prytania St. (895–4513).

MUSIC. In addition to jazz and rhythm and blues— types of music New Orleans made famous (see Night Life)—the city also has a strong symphony orchestra and opera company. The New Orleans Philharmonic Symphony has found a permanent home in the recently restored Orpheum Theatre, 129 University Pl., in the Central Business District. The 65-year-old Beaux Arts Building, erected in 1918, was one of the big stops on the Orpheum circuit when vaudeville was king. The orchestra is under the direction of Philippe Entremont. The season runs from October to May. 524–0404.

New Orleanians have had a long love affair with opera, but unfortunately the city has not had an opera house since the French Opera House was destroyed by fire in 1919. The New Orleans Opera Association now performs at the Theatre of the Performing Arts, 801 N. Rampart St., behind the French Quarter in Louis Armstrong Park. 529–2278 or 529–2279.

The French Market Corporation sponsors jazz concerts every Sunday from 1:00 P.M. to 3:00 P.M. in the French Market at St. Philip and Decatur streets. The New Orleans Recreation Department also sponsors occasional Saturday afternoon concerts in Jackson Square. There is no set schedule, so be sure to check the newspapers.

For performance dates and times, see the New Orleans *Times-Picayune/States-Item's* daily calendar and Friday's *Lagniappe* tabloid. Also see *Go* magazine.

DANCE. Professional dancing is experiencing its bleakest period in recent New Orleans history. *Delta Festival Ballet* is the only major professional dance troup in the city. It has a fall and spring program, and most of its performances take place at the Theater of the Performing Arts, 801 N. Rampart St. (529–2278 or 529–2279). There are, however, several smaller groups that have no set annual schedules. They include the *New Orleans Performing Company*, the *New Orleans Contemporary Dance Theatre*, and the *Crescent City Movin' Company*. Loyola University has *Loyola Ballet* with two or three performances a year, and Tulane University's Center Program brings to town several international dance troups each year. Newcomb College's Physical Education Department has a modern dance group, and it too books a few touring companies. For performance listings, check *The Times-Picayune's* daily calendar of events, or call 566–5047, 522–ARTS.

STAGE. Theater in New Orleans, dating back to the late 18th century, is a tradition almost as old as the city itself. One must keep in mind that theater in New Orleans, although generally good, can't and shouldn't be compared to New York. It is entertaining and reasonably priced. For current productions and performances, call 522–ARTS, and consult the daily calendar in the New Orleans *The Times-Picayune/The State's-Item* newspaper, *Lagniappe* (the TP/SI's Friday entertainment tabloid), and *Go* magazine.

The *Saenger Performing Arts Center,* Canal and N. Rampart streets, is the closest thing New Orleans has to big-time theater. Housed in a recently restored Italianate vaudeville and movie palace dating from the 1920s, the Saenger is on the national theater circuit for Broadway revivals and road shows. Seats are reasonably priced. Reservations needed. 524–0876.

The *Beverly Dinner Playhouse,* 214 Labarre Rd., off River Rd., in neighboring Jefferson Parish, offers a steady menu of Broadway dramas and comedies that feature one or two well-known cinema or television stars supported by a cast of local actors. The plays are usually good; the food is adequate. Reservations needed. 837–4022.

A favorite among many New Orleanians is the *Tulane University Theatre,* which produces the Summer Lyric Theatre, located on the university's Uptown campus. The cast is made up of university students. The theater is especially good in performing standard Broadway musicals. 865–5361.

There are several other popular but smaller theaters in the city that often give credible performances. They include *Le Petit Theatre Du Vieux Carré,* 616 St. Peter, in the French Quarter, 522–2081 or 522–1954 (this is one of the oldest little theaters in the country); *Theatre Marigny,* 616 Frenchmen St., in Faubourg Marigny below the French Quarter, 944–2653 (ask about the dinner and carriage ride package); the *Contemporary Arts Center,* 900 Camp St., in the Central Business District, 523–1216; and, the *Toulouse Theatre,* 615 Toulouse St., in the French Quarter, 522–7852. The *Toulouse Theatre* is the home base for *One Mo' Time,* a long-playing international hit musical about a black vaudeville group in the 1920s. The show features a ragtime band, songs and dances from the 1920s. Most of these theaters require reservations, so call in advance. Also check with *NORD Theatre* (New Orleans Recreation Department), 545 St. Charles Ave., in Gallier Hall, 586–5275; and, the *University of New Orleans Department of Drama and Communications,* at the University's Lakefront campus, 283–0317. Both produce entertaining productions with local talent.

 SHOPPING. Shopping in New Orleans is about the same as in most other major American cities. There are a number of large, sprawling shopping centers in outlying suburbia. Within the city, the better shops and stores concentrate together in various parts of town. The better shopping centers are *Lakeside* on Veterans Highway and Causeway Blvd., and *Clearview Shopping Center* on Veterans and Clearview Ave.—both are located in the western suburb of Jefferson Parish. In eastern New Orleans is *Lake Forest Plaza* on Read Blvd., near I–10. On the West Bank of the River is *Oakwood Shopping Center* on the West Bank Expressway and Holmes Blvd., and *Westside Shopping Center* on the West Bank Expressway and Franklin St. Most of these shopping centers have the same genre of discount and moderately priced department stores and shops.

However, most of the better shops, those carrying designer clothes, etc., are located in older sections of the city. The French Quarter has a number of first-rate clothiers, specialty shops, antique and art galleries, and gift shops. The Central Business District, including Canal St., also has a number of important clothing stores as well as the city's most prestigious jewelry stores. With the explosion of hotel construction in this area during the last decade, more and more high-fashion clothing and specialty shops are springing up in the CBD. *Canal Place* at the foot of Canal St. (construction completed in late 1983) promises to become the ritziest and swankiest shopping mecca in the Deep South. Among the stores featured: Brooks Brothers, Saks Fifth Avenue, F.A.O. Schwarz, Caché, and Custom Shirt Shop, to name a few. A number of top-notch shops also can be found in the Hilton Hotel, Hyatt Regency, and in some of the other big hotels.

Uptown New Orleans has a number of important and fashionable shopping areas. St. Charles Avenue has several fine galleries and several of the city's oldest high-fashion clothing stores, such as *Town and Country.* For antique shoppers, there is no better place than Magazine Street, which starts at Canal St. and parallels the river to Audubon Park. Along this route you will find almost five miles of antique shops, art galleries, clothing shops, restaurants, and almost anything else. Be sure to stop at the New Orleans Tourist and Convention Commission office on Royal St. and pick up a shopper's guide to Magazine St. published by the Magazine St. Merchants Association, or write to the association at P.O. Box 15728, New Orleans, LA 70175.

The Rink at Prytania St. and Washington Ave., in the fashionable Garden District, also has a selection of small shops and boutiques that are popular among Uptown New Orleanians. Within the last decade two other shopping areas in Uptown New Orleans have become *the* place to buy designer and high-fashion clothes. *Uptown Square,* at the foot of Broadway near the River and Audubon Park, and *Riverbend,* where St. Charles and Carrollton avenues meet, probably have more shops and boutiques with internationally known designer names than any other section of the city. They are both centered in delightful old residential areas of the city known for their beautiful oaks, azaleas, and charming Victorian cottages. Both shopping areas are also easily reached by the St. Charles Ave. streetcar.

Special Shopping Notes. Sales on merchandise occur year-round, so if shopping for special items, allow time to shop the daily newspaper first. Store hours vary: major department and retail stores usually open 9:30–10:00 A.M. and close at 5:30 P.M. downtown and 9:00 P.M. in the suburban shopping centers. Some downtown stores are open a few evenings. Phone for current policy. Boutiques and smaller shops/galleries generally are open from 10:00 A.M. to 5:00 P.M. All department and retail stores (except groceries and drugstores) are closed on Sundays.

Major credit cards are used (MasterCard, Visa, Carte Blanche, American Express, and often Diners Club). Personal checks, with proper I.D. (generally two forms of I.D. are necessary) may or may not be accepted. This is also true of traveler's checks.

There are more good shops in New Orleans, and in more categories, than we could fit in a reasonable space in this book. Therefore the shops we list here are a selection of interesting and reputable establishments.

Note: For information on shopping for art, see "Art Galleries" section of *Practical Information for New Orleans.*

DEPARTMENT STORES

New Orleans has only two major department stores: *D. H. Holmes* and *Maison Blanche.* D. H. Holmes, founded in the early 1800s making it the city's oldest department store, is located on Canal St. in the CBD with branches in

Uptown Square, Lake Forest Plaza, and Oakwood shopping centers. Maison Blanche, once D. H. Holmes' rival on Canal St., closed its CBD store but kept branches in the Clearview, Lake Forest Plaza, and Westside shopping centers. Both have full lines of good merchandise, including clothing and accessories for men, women, and children, appliances, housewares, garden equipment, and anything else one would expect to find in department stores. They also include specialty sections and high-fashion designer clothing and accessories.

MEN'S AND WOMEN'S CLOTHING

High fashion for New Orleans men and women is generally in keeping with the culture and attitudes of the local people: conservative and traditional but elegant. Some boutiques cater to the trendy, but most know the demands of the local market.

In the French Quarter, *Weinstein's,* 715 Bienville, carries European fashions for men and, more recently, for women running the gamut from sportswear to formal evening attire with accessories. Featured are such designer names as Chester Barrie, Cerrutti, Pinky and Diane for Private Label, Alpha Cubic, Byblos, Issey Miyoke, and Marcasiano. *Lilly Pulitzer of New Orleans,* 530 Wilkinson Row, has Lilly originals in sportswear for men, women, and children.

Across Canal St. in the Canal Business District, *Terry and Juden Co., Ltd.,* 135 Carondelet St., features custom shirtmaking as well as stylish and traditional clothing for men and women from Southwick, H. Freeman and Norman Hilton. *Godchaux's,* 828 Canal St., is a New Orleans clothing institution dating back to the last century. It carries a full line of moderately priced to expensive quality clothing and accessories for men and women and has a number of suburban branches. *Saks Fifth Avenue,* which needs no explanation, is located in Canal Place.

Women's Shopping. Fashion clothing shops and boutiques for women have been popping up in New Orleans in recent years at an incredible rate. Most of them, not surprisingly, are concentrated in the fashionable Uptown-University area.

Uptown Square, at the foot of Broadway, has an impressive selection of such establishments. *Bare Facts* carries a full line of fine lingerie by Christian Dior, Olga, Lily of France, Eve Stillman and others. *Ambiance* has accessories for fashion-conscious women, including art deco fabrics and leather goods, by such designers as Judith Leiber, Barbara Bolan, Halston, and Susan Gail. *Bagatelle* stocks day dresses, evening gowns, separates and suits by Perry Ellis, Albert Nipon, Helene Sidel, Albert Capraro, and Robert Haik. *Things, Inc.* carries traditional clothing, summer and winter wear, cocktail dresses, and ball gowns by Lady Thompson, David Brooks, Crazy Horse, LaCoste, de Lanthe, and Esprit. *Poppy's* features classical women's clothing, sports and resort wear, and a full line of accessories, including shoes and handbags. *Kreeger's* is a locally owned store carrying conventional and designer clothes for women and juniors.

Moving on to the Riverbend area, *Collection III,* 8209 Hampson St., carries designer apparel for women, including sportswear, day and evening clothes, lingerie, and accessories. *Hampson House,* 8126 Hampson St., has casual and after-five fashions. Down the block at *Yvonne's You Boutique,* 8131 Hampson, the shopper will enjoy the custom-designed fashions and accessories, shoes and Italian leather included, and French lingerie. *The Rose and The Ring,* a block away at 733 Dante, carries everything from designer sportswear to evening gowns. *The Front Room,* 8211 Hampson St., is a designer boutique with a full line of women's clothes from day and sportswear to evening gowns. While in the neighborhood, don't miss *Mignon Faget, Ltd.,* 710 Dublin St. Mignon Faget is known throughout the area for her own magnificent, custom-designed jewelry. She also carries clothing accessories and toiletries.

Heading back to the downtown area, *Carrywells,* in The Rink at Prytania and Washington, stocks designer handbags and accessories. *Town and Country,* 1432 St. Charles Ave., carries complete lines of designer clothing and accessories, except shoes, for women of all ages. *Roger Johns Ltd.,* in the Hyatt Regency Hotel, carries the top fashion names in day and evening wear and accessories. Canal Place, so far has lined up *Saks Fifth Avenue* and *Kreeger's.* In addition to branches in Canal Place and Uptown Square, Kreeger's also has a store at Lakeside Shopping Center in nearby Jefferson Parish. *Gus Mayer,* Canal and Carondelet, carries high-quality traditional and classical clothing and accessories for all occasions.

Men's Clothing. Men's clothing shops have not multiplied at the same pace as those for women. But like women's fashions in New Orleans, men dress relatively conservatively. This is still a Deep South conservative city. Most of the best men's shops are located in the French Quarter and Central Business District.

In the busy world of the Central Business District, conservative types go to *Brooks Brothers* and the *Custom Shirt Shop* in Canal Place or *Porter-Stevens* at Carondelet and Gravier streets. Porter-Stevens, which carries such names as Hart Schaffner & Marx, Christian Dior and Pierre Cardin, also has branches in the Oakwood, Lakeside, and Lake Forest Plaza shopping centers. For fashion-conscious men, *Rubenstein Brothers,* 102 St. Charles St., is a first-rate men's clothier featuring top fashion names as Yves St. Laurent, Tiger of Sweden, Ermengildo Zegna, Pierre Cardin, Giorgio Armani, and others.

Top Drawer, 1212 St. Charles Ave., *Gentry,* Uptown Square, and *Perlis,* 6070 Magazine St., have served several generations of Uptown preppies. They all carry similar labels—Corbin, Linett, Gant, Sero.

CHILDREN'S CLOTHING

D. H. Holmes, Godchaux's, and *Maison Blanche* have extensive departments for the younger folk. Many of the stores and shops listed in this book for men and women also carry clothes for children.

SHOES

Feet First, 518 Chartres, has an exciting selection of designer shoes for women at discounts from 25%–50%. It also has branch stores at 7775 Maple St., in

Uptown New Orleans, and at 3750 Veterans Memorial Highway, in neighboring Jefferson Parish. Also in the French Quarter, *Bergeron's,* 315 Royal St., features Vaneli pumps, and *Krischel's,* 316 Royal St., has a great selection of shoes and accessories. *Imperial Shoe Store* on Canal St., has been a long-time favorite with New Orleans women.

Uptown Square offers several shoe stores for women that carry *Saint Germain, Galleria Shoe Boutique,* and *Godchaux's.*

DISCOUNT/OUTLETS

Everyone always enjoys a bargain. There are several discount stores and outlets that offer quality merchandise at lower than retail prices. *Uptown Izzy's,* 833 Conti, in the French Quarter, carries designer clothes for women at discounts of 30%–60% off retail prices. Izzy's also has stores at 8219 Oak St., Uptown, and 3750 Veterans Highway. In the French Quarter is the *Dansk Factory Outlet,* 541 Royal, that offers 30%–60% discounts on Dansk wine glasses, teakwood salad bowls, crystal, porcelain dinnerware, stainless steel cookware and kitchen utensils.

Deansgate—The Factory Store, 960 Poeyfarre, sells suits, sportscoats, etc., at factory prices. Another popular factory outlet for men's clothing is *Haspel,* 3515 19th St., in Metairie, and on the West Bank at 3767 Gen. DeGaulle Dr. in the Cypress Plaza Shopping Center. In addition to traditional clothing, Haspel features the locally favorite cord and seersucker suits. For children's clothing, *William B. Coleman Outlet Shop,* 4001 Earhart Blvd., and *Lynley Designs,* 2628 Jefferson Highway, offer great buys.

COSMETICS, PERFUMES, AND TOILETRIES

Almost all of the women's shops and boutiques described in the *Clothing* section of this book carry full lines of cosmetics, perfumes, and toiletries. However, there are two perfume companies in the French Quarter worth noting. *Bourbon French Perfume Co.,* 318 Royal, and *Hove Parfumeur Ltd.,* 824 Royal, both manufacture fine fragrances for men and women.

TOBACCO AND PIPE SHOPS

The Epitome in Fine Tobacco, 729 St. Louis, next door to Antoine's Restaurant, is one of the best tobacco shops in the city. According to its owner, he decided to open the shop one night when, after dining at Antoine's, he couldn't find a good after-dinner cigar anywhere in the Quarter.

LEATHER AND LUGGAGE

Le Sac, 637 Royal St., and in the Hyatt Regency Hotel, carries high fashion leather goods for men and women, including French and Italian shoes, handbags, luggage, clothing, and accessories. *Rapp's Luggage and Gifts,* 604 Canal

St., stocks major lines of luggage and leather goods. Rapp's also has branch stores at Lake Forest Plaza, Uptown Square, and Oakwood shopping centers.

JEWELRY

Coleman E. Adler & Sons, Inc., 722 Canal St., has been an institution among New Orleanians for generations. It carries top-of-the-line jewelry, watches, flat silver and holloware, crystal, china, Boehm and Royal Worcester porcelains. Other good jewelry stores in the business district include *Hausmann's Jewelry Co.,* 732 Canal, *Leo Miller Co.,* 129 Baronne St., and *Pailet & Penedo,* 152 Baronne St.

For antique and modern jewelry, two shops in the French Quarter offer interesting selections: *New Orleans Silversmiths,* 600 Chartres, and *Nancy Kittay,* 518 Chartres.

In the Uptown Riverbend area, there are several shops and boutiques worth visiting: *Donna Browne,* Dante Village, *Parker & Sloss, Inc.,* 701 Dante St., and *Simply Gold, Inc.,* 7623 Maple St. One definitely should not miss *Mignon Faget, Ltd.,* 710 Dublin St. Faget designs and makes the most magnificent gold jewelry.

ANTIQUES

New Orleans has an excellent selection of antique shops, ranging from the pricey shops on Royal St. to the moderately priced and bargain-hunting spots on Magazine St.

The outdoor flea market is held each weekend in the lower French Market near Esplanade Ave. It is a hodgepodge of furniture, bric-a-brac, clothes, appliances, and you-name-it. The outdoor flea market is held on Saturdays and Sundays, from 7:00 A.M. to 7:00 P.M. Sunday is the better day to go as many more booths are in operation and the nearby shops are open for business as well.

Moreover, in the vicinity of the big outdoor flea market, at addresses in the 1100 to 1300 blocks of Decatur St., are a number of smaller indoor flea markets, and shops with interesting second-hand merchandise.

French and English Antiques. *French Antique Shop,* 225 Royal, *Henry Stern Antiques,* 329 Royal, *Manheim Galleries,* 403–409 Royal, *M.S. Rau, Inc.,* 630 Royal, *Rothschild's, Inc.,* 241 and 321 Royal, *Royal Antiques, Ltd.,* 309 Royal, *Stan Levy Imports, Inc.,* 1028 Louisiana Ave., *Waldhorn Company, Inc.,* 343 Royal, and *Morton's Auction Exchange,* 643 Magazine St.

Antique Weapons. *James H. Cohen & Sons, Inc.,* 437 Royal.

Nautical Antiques. *Ye Olde Ship Store,* 831 Decatur St., in the French Quarter. *The Mariner, Inc.,* 519 Wilkinson Row, in the Quarter.

Coins and Stamps. *James H. Cohen & Sons, Inc.,* 437 Royal, and *Southern Coins and Stamps, Ltd.,* 422 Chartres.

Books. *A Collector's Book Shop,* 3119 Magazine St.

Clothing. *Second Hand Rose,* 3110 Magazine St., features clothes for men and women dating from 1850 to 1950. *BeBe L'Unique,* 3115 Magazine, and *The Two Thereas,* 3646 Magazine St., both offer antique apparel and accessories. Two particularly worthwhile shops are *Mathilda's,* dealing in antique clothing, and

One of Those Things, specializing in Art Deco paraphernalia; these shops are located at 1222 and 1228 Decatur St., respectively. Somewhat farther afield is the city's best Deco outlet, *The Dumaine Nostalgia Shop,* at 607 Dumaine St.

Rugs: *The Galleria Persian Arts,* 309 Chartres, carries Persian and oriental carpets, some are new and some antique.

Magazine St. should be of particular interest to the budget-conscious antique shopper. Scores of antique shops lie along this 5-mile stretch. They range from elegant French and English furnishings to moderately priced "junque." There are all kinds of shops here—photo galleries, antique clothes, import houses, antique books, and about anything else one can imagine. Of particular note is *Morton's Auction Exchange,* 643 Magazine St., it is a virtual department store of imported English and European furniture and bric-a-brac. For more information about shopping on Magazine St., pick up the brochure published by the Magazine St. Merchants Association at the Tourist and Convention Commission office or write to P.O. Box 15728, 70175.

BOOKS

The following downtown and French Quarter bookstores are recommended for very good to excellent stocks of books in general, and especially about New Orleans and Louisiana. *B. Dalton Bookseller,* 714 Canal St., *Doubleday Book Shop,* 633 Canal, and *Dolphen Book Shops,* 823 Royal and Uptown Square. For the best selection of used books, check *Beckham's Bookshop,* 228 Decatur. Beckham has two other branches in the Quarter: *Librarie Bookshop,* 829 Royal, and *Old Books,* 1309 Decatur.

The best Uptown bookshops are *Maple Street Book Shop,* 7523 Maple St., *Little Professor Book Center,* 1000 S. Carrollton Ave., and the *Dolphin Book Shop* in Uptown Square.

TOYS

F. A. O. Schwarz, one of the world's finest toymakers, is scheduled to open a store in Canal Pl., at the foot of Canal St., sometime in late 1983. *Le Petit Soldier Shop,* 528 Royal St., in the French Quarter, has an excellent collection of miniature soldiers, books, etc. *Kid's Stuff, Ltd.,* 8200 Hampson St., in the Riverbend area, is a first-rate toy store featuring imported and domestic playthings. *D. H. Holmes Department Store* on Canal St. also has a well appointed toy department.

RECORDS

A vast array of records and tapes are available all over the New Orleans area. Rock, blues, soul, Dixieland jazz, progressive jazz, country, classical, pop, comedy are standards in better record shops. Check the yellow pages of the telephone directory for a more extensive listing. *Werlein's For Music,* 605 Canal St., has records, tapes and cassettes to suit most music tastes. *Leisure Landing Records and Tapes,* 5500 Magazine St., is an outstanding record shop and has one of the best selections in town. *The Mushroom,* 1037 Broadway in the Uptown University Section, also has a terrific selection. *Smith's,* 2019 St. Charles, ranks with the best, especially for classical music and older pop recordings that the newer and trendier shops don't carry.

FOOD

Visitors to New Orleans almost immediately fall in love with the area's fabulous seafood. Several area retailers will pack and ship Louisiana seafood and other Creole cuisine food baskets almost anywhere in the U.S. They also will pack these local delicacies so that you can take them home with you aboard the airplane. Providing these services are *Battistella's Sea Foods,* Inc., 910 Touro (949–2724), *Creole Kitchens,* 518 Julia St. (566–0140), and *Seafood Connection,* 1800 9th St. Kenner (466–7355).

 DINING OUT. The listing of restaurants that follows is almost—but not quite—a collection of the best places in town. There is some question as to whether the ninth best French Creole place should be left out in favor of the second-best sandwich house, but if we seem to do it anyway it is in order to provide a variety of dining venues. The restaurants are grouped first by style of cooking and then by price range.

In considering price, we figure the amount of an average meal per person excluding drinks, wine, tips, and tax. Tax in the City of New Orleans proper is 8 percent; in the surrounding parishes it ranges from 5 to 7 percent. The standard tip is 15 percent, given for acceptable service with only minor flaws. Polished or special service can be rewarded with 20 percent and up. Regardless of what you've read or thought previously, waiters in New Orleans expect tips to be figured on the total bill *including* tax, drinks, and wine—even very expensive wine.

A restaurant noted as *Deluxe* will involve a food expenditure of $30 or more. *Expensive* restaurants will serve a dinner from $20 to $30. *Moderate* places will be in the neighborhood of $15, and *Inexpensive* restaurants permit spending $10 or less.

Reservations at all the major restaurants are recommended, and urged well in advance for weekends. Some places, such as Le Ruth's and breakfast at Brennan's, book out months in advance, especially in the peak season between Christmas and Mardi Gras. While on the phone, ask about credit card acceptance (which has a way of changing) and dress code. Most of the more pricey places require jackets for men, and a few insist on a tie also.

Most restaurants in New Orleans accept credit cards, although a few (Galatoire's and Mosca's among them) brook no plastic of any kind. Credit card information is in the listings as follows: AE—American Express; CB—Carte Blanche; DC—Diners Club; MC—Master Card; V—Visa. The notation "All major credit cards" indicates acceptance of all five of these.

The listings indicate which meals the restaurant serves as follows: B—Breakfast; L—Lunch; D—Dinner. Usual lunch hours are from 11:30 A.M. till 2:30 P.M. Dinner is most often 6:00 P.M. till 10:00 P.M., although quite a few places close at 9:00 P.M. Some restaurants stay open between lunch and dinner—this is, for example, a good time to go to Galatoire's and avoid the line.

CREOLE FRENCH

Deluxe

Antoine's. 713 St. Louis, French Quarter; 581–4422. This is the oldest restaurant under continuous family ownership in America, and a venerable relic of the oldest styles of Creole cooking. The restaurant is enormous; the preferred room is the cavernous, Germanic Red Room, with its thousands of testimonials and framed clippings. The menu is all in French, but rather than translate it the waiter will instead try to recommend his favorite dishes, which are not necessarily the best in the house. About three quarters of the food at Antoine's, including almost all of the seafood entrees, are pretty forgettable. The specialties are first courses: oysters Foch, the original oysters Rockefeller, crawfish cardinale, alligator soup. The chicken dishes are the most consistent and are unusual to boot. The tournedos marchand de vin is a local classic, but stay away from the same steak with bearnaise. The French bread is marvelous, as are the puffed-up soufflee potatoes. Finish it all off with the grand baked Alaska and the fine, strong coffee and then tour the rest of the place. You'll see the giant wine cellar (which contains some 25,000 bottles) among other things. Antoine's is a tricky restaurant for visitors; it's best to have an experienced regular diner with you when going there. L, D; Monday—Friday. AE, DC, MC, V.

Jonathan. 714 N. Rampart, French Quarter; 586–1930. This is a stunning art deco palace with elegant appointments and service and an extremely creative chef. While Creole food is present on the menu, you are as likely to find anything from Mexican to Indian food as well. The plats du jour are amazing at times, and the desserts are superb. L Monday–Friday; D seven days. All major credit cards.

La Provence. US 190, Lacombe (35 miles from downtown New Orleans, across Lake Pontchartrain); 626–7662. A country inn surrounded by tall pines, this is the staging area for chef-owner Chris Kerageorgiou's fascinating French-Greek-Creole culinary masterpieces. There's always something new here, served with style and tasting of excitement. La Provence is generally agreed to be one of the five or so best places to eat in the area. Try the charcuterie on Sunday, the rack of lamb, and the duck dishes. D Wednesday–Saturday; L, D Sunday. MC, V.

LeRuth's. 636 Franklin, Gretna; 362–4914. A converted modest house is one of the most controversial places in town, particularly since founder Warren LeRuth turned it over to sons Lee and Larry. However, the food here remains a vigorous collection of modern Creole cuisine. Specialties are crabmeat St. Francis, artichoke and oyster soup, stuffed smoked duck, soft shell crab with crab and herbs, and elemental sherbets. Service is of the rather casual Creole style, and paintings overcrowd the walls. Tough to get a reservation here; call a month or two ahead. D Tuesday–Saturday. MC, V.

Rib Room. In the Royal Orleans Hotel, 621 St. Louis, French Quarter; 529–7045. This is a lovely, large room with some continental overtones but a basically Creole menu. Especially good are the crabmeat appetizers, the soups, and the prime rib, which is a specialty. You can also get some imaginatively prepared seafood entrees and good pastries for dessert. L, D, seven days. All major credit cards.

Expensive

Arnaud's. 813 Bienville, French Quarter; 523–5433. This is an old-line Creole restaurant which had degenerated to a sad state until the present owners took over in 1978. Now the restaurant is lovely, bright, and still distinctively Arnaud's, with its tile floors and wall of beveled glass. Start with the shrimp Arnaud (the best version of shrimp remoulade in town) and soup. There are good seafood creations: pompano en croute, trout meuniere, redfish with hollandaise, plus a good Cornish hen stuffed with a smokey paté. Interesting beef dishes. For dessert, the bread pudding is the best version of a ubiquitous local classic. Also fine are the bananas Foster. L Monday–Friday; D seven days; Brunch Sunday. All major credit cards.

Broussard's. 819 Conti, French Quarter; 581–3866. This is another restored relic, with three overadorned rooms surrounding a lovely courtyard. The food is basically Creole with Italian touches. Especially good are the various game birds, the veal Oscar, and shrimp Chandeleur. Service is polished and solicitous. D seven days. All major credit cards.

Caribbean Room. In the Pontchartrain Hotel, 2031 St. Charles Ave., Uptown; 524–0581. This is a lovely, very comfortable room with a splashing fountain in the middle. The C-Room is a favorite of Uptown families, serving Creole dishes which were rather light before lightness became fashionable. The specialty is trout Veronique, with its glazed hollandaise sauce and green grapes. But they also roast a fine sirloin here, as well as prepare a variety of offbeat local seafood entrees and first courses. The dessert is an overkill of ice cream and chocolate sauce called mile-high pie. L Monday–Friday; D seven days; Brunch Sunday. AE, DC, MC, V.

Christian's. 3835 Iberville, Mid-City; 482-4924. This restaurant was called Christian's (after the owner) years before it moved into its present premises: a small church, pews used as banquettes. The tables are too close together, but the food is good. Start with the two good oyster casseroles, then move to the seafood, which is the restaurant's best shot. Also good are the sweetbreads in a gelatinous demi-glacé. Expremely popular. L, D Tuesday–Saturday. AE, DC, MC, V.

Commander's Palace. 1403 Washington Ave., Garden District; 899–8221. Operated by the elder branch of the Brennan family, this is a much better place than Brennan's itself. The property is uncommonly lovely, with a tree-covered courtyard and an airy room upstairs overlooking it. The food is a lighter version of traditional Creole: not much roux is used. Start with the soups; the turtle soup is by far the best in town, but all soups are good. Entree specialties include trout with pecans, grilled redfish, pannee veal with fettucine, and tournedos demi-glace, but the range is broad. For dessert, try the bananas Foster (not on the menu, but always available) or the Celebration, a mound of chocolate-covered ice cream with Melba sauce. Commander's is a lot of fun, and it has the best California wine list in New Orleans. L, D seven days. All major credit cards.

Frank Occhipanti's. 2712 N. Arnoult, Metairie; 888–1131. A very large and popular suburban French-Italian-Creole place, probably the best restaurant in Metairie. Start with oysters Diablo, the fine artichoke soup, and the memorable house dressing on the salad. The steaks are prime and broiled with excitement; the veal dishes are many in number and use excellent white veal. Good seafood and chicken dishes as well. Occhipanti's has a little bit of everything and good service. L Monday–Friday; D Monday–Saturday. All major credit cards.

K-Paul's Louisiana Kitchen. 525 Chartres, French Quarter; 524–0420. No reservations. In just a few years' time, chef Paul Prudhomme has transformed an old Quarter bar (it still shows many signs of its past) into one of the most-discussed restaurants in America. K-Paul's is really the only Cajun restaurant in New Orleans proper, but beyond that it is the most experimental as well. One can expect to see just about any fresh foodstuff arranged by the most original hybrid of cooking styles. Much of it is spicy and robust, some of it to a fault. The most consistent dishes are the etouffees and gumbos, the blackened redfish, trout czarina, and the enchiladas (!). Good duck, rabbit, chicken, and guinea fowl dishes are prepared using animals grown on the restaurant's own farm. Upstairs are vended a variety of patés and sausages and poor-boy sandwiches. K-Paul's makes much of the casualness of its operations, but the prices do not match. "Cajun-style seating" means that couples share tables with other couples. For most meals, a wait in line is unavoidable. D Monday–Friday. No credit cards.

Maison Andre. Village Aurora Mall, Gretna; 392–0000. This is a relatively new but very original and deft restaurant whose food makes you forget you're in a shopping center. There is a weird but good chicken bouillabaisse, a marvelous crabmeat fettucine, eminently edible essays on local fresh seafoods, a fine smokey, hammy chicken Pontalba, and a few nice veal and beef dishes. For dessert, get the parfait versions of bananas Foster or cherries Jubilee. L Tuesday–Friday; D Tuesday–Saturday. AE, CB, DC, MC, V.

Maurice's Bistro. 1763 Stumpf Blvd., Gretna; 361–9000. Another unique Creole menu assembled by the brother of the owner of Maison Andre; the two used to run a place together, and their styles are somewhat similar. What you get here is a basket of terrific fried parsley with an unusual bread. Follow that with the mixed seafood appetizer, containing unusual approaches to oysters, shrimp, crab, and catfish in separate sections. The best dish is veal Normandy, a fine rendering of the French classic with sour cream and Calvados. The steaks are crustily broiled, and the seafood fresh and sharpened with a very good meuniere sauce of the old-fashioned brown style. An engaging restaurant with an enthusiastic local following. L Monday–Friday; D Monday–Saturday. All major credit cards.

Moderate

Berdou's. 300 Monroe Street, Gretna; 368–2401. A very good Creole restaurant populated by West Bank families who eat, at very low prices, polished old-style food somewhat like that at Galatoire's. Start with shrimp remoulade or the garlicky crabmeat Berdou. The best entree is also the best pompano en papillote in town, a flavorful fish poached in a white sauce in a paper bag which is opened at the table. Also good is trout Marguery, the fried and broiled seafood in general, and the lamb chops. It is possible to have an entire meal for less than ten dollars here. The management is stodgy about things like jeans and dining late. L, D Tuesday–Saturday; closes at 7:30 P.M., but open all afternoon. No credit cards.

Cafe Savanna. 8324 Oak, Uptown; 866–3223. A small, casual cafe serving an assortment of very good seafood specialties, particularly fried catfish. Also good are the daily specials and the sandwiches. There is an assortment of fried vegetables dusted with a unique, spicy coating that makes a good side course. L, D Tuesday–Saturday. No credit cards.

Cafe Sbisa. 1011 Decatur, French Quarter; 561–8354. An interesting-looking place on two levels, hewn out of the remains of an ancient Quarter joint. The specialty is grilled seafood, and this is excellent whatever the seafood. Sbisa's is the only place in town with swordfish on a consistent basis. Also good is the roast duck. D seven days and Sunday brunch. AE, DC, MC, V.

Delmonico. 1300 St. Charles Ave., Uptown; 525–4937. One of the older restaurants in town, founded before the turn of the century, Delmonico still purveys a consistently good and broad selection of old-style Creole cooking in a comfortable, antique-filled, very New Orleans setting. Start with shrimp remoulade and seafood gumbo, both among the best in town. The better part of the entree list involves seafood; the best of this is catfish meuniere, served with a couple of fat, tasty stuffed shrimp. Also good are the stuffed red snapper and the seafood brochette. A variety of good things are made with baby beef, chicken, and liver. The desserts are small but good. L, D seven days. AE, MC, V.

Dooky Chase. 2301 Orleans Ave., Downtown; 822–9506. For years this has been the dining-out bastion of the black community, as well as one of the most consistently good Creole restaurants in the city. The seafood is fresh and prepared to order; the best single item is stuffed shrimp, but all of the fish and shellfish are broiled and fried with deftness. Excellent fried and broiled chicken and, at lunch, some good pot food. Extensive children's menu. Near Theatre of the Performing Arts and French Quarter, and popular among persons of all races. L, D seven days. AE, MC, V.

Feelings Cafe. 2600 Chartres, Downtown; 945–2222. A very pleasant, small restaurant with a lush courtyard in an old building in the increasingly popular Bywater section. Feelings has an abbreviated list of table d'hote dinners at very reasonable prices. The food is modest but well prepared and imaginative; chicken is a specialty, as are the French silk pie and peanut butter pie for dessert. D Thursday–Saturday; Sunday brunch. AE, MC, V.

Flamingos Cafe. 1625 St. Charles Ave., Uptown; 523–6141. A nutty-looking, gaudy place with gay overtones but a mixed clientele, Flamingos has a 16-page menu that's more hilarious than the cutesy ones you see at chain places—and better food, too. The specialty is quiche, very heavy with eggs and well prepared, using imaginative ingredients. Also good are the soups, particularly the cold ones. There are lots of salads, omelettes, and crepes, but these are not as consistent as the quiches. Good drinks. Fun place. L, D seven days. All major credit cards.

Galatoire's. 209 Bourbon, French Quarter; 525–2021. No reservations. Of the old-line New Orleans restaurants, Galatoire's has the best food at the lowest prices and, not surprisingly, is the most difficult to get a table in. The line forms at around 11:45 A.M. for lunch and 6:00 P.M. for dinner; it can be avoided by coming between 1:30 P.M. and 5:30 P.M., during which time the place is only half-full instead of packed to the rafters. It's a surprisingly modest one room, with mirrors all around and ceiling fans overhead—a classic look. The specialty is definitely seafood, although the lengthy menu promises almost everything else. Start with shrimp remoulade, oysters Rockefeller, or oysters en brochette. The house entree recommendation is for trout Marguery, with its thick white sauce of shrimp and mushrooms, but trout amandine is better (or, if you want the sauce, order *shrimp* Marguery). When pompano is in season they do some wonderful things broiling it; ditto for the crawfish, which come as etouffee. Two good crabmeat dishes: Yvonne and maison. Steak and lamb dishes are popular but not quite as good as the fish. For dessert, get crepes maison and the very strong, addictive coffee. Galatoire's is a must for the gourmet even on the briefest stop in New Orleans. L, D Tuesday–Sunday. No credit cards.

Garden Cafe. 2727 Prytania, Garden District; 899–3900. This pretty little cafe is very convenient to those taking walking tours of the Garden District, in which it is central. There are good standard breakfasts and imaginatively prepared lighter lunches, with a scattering of continental food among the Creole specialties. The best food is the daily lunch special, although the sandwiches and en croute dishes are also nice. A pleasant oasis, popular with the Uptown crowd. B, L, D Tuesday–Saturday; Sunday brunch. MC, V.

Marti's. 1041 Dumaine, French Quarter; 524–6060. An engaging Creole bistro across the street from the Theatre of the Performing Arts, and habituated both by the Theatre's patrons as well as by Quarterites, most of whom complain about the food and the prices. The truth is that this sort of stuff—red beans and rice, grilled andouille, boiled brisket, fried chicken, panneed veal, etc., is rarely seen in a comfortable setting at prices over $5, which is the very thing that makes this restaurant so valuable. The aforementioned are all good choices, as are the capon stuffed with pecans, the cold soups, the sauteed redfish, and the specials on the blackboard. The service is erratic but not annoying. L Monday–Friday; D Monday–Saturday. AE, DC, MC, V.

Maylie's. 1009 Poydras, Central Business District; 525–9547. The second-oldest restaurant in town, founded in 1876 to serve the workers in a market that's no longer there. Now they serve deviled eggs remoulade, turtle soup, gumbo, boiled beef, fried seafood, and bread pudding at very low prices. At times, all of this is exemplary, but the kitchen and service are extremely inconsistent. Don't come here if you're in a hurry. A charming old antique restaurant with a nice patio. L, D Monday–Friday. AE, DC, MC, V.

Mr. B's. 201 Royal, French Quarter; 523–2078. This is the informal restaurant of the Brennans of Commander's Palace fame—a group talented enough to be a few steps ahead of the marketplace, which they certainly are here. You know you're near the restaurant when you smell hickory smoke. Over hickory logs and a couple of other woods they broil redfish, steaks, and prime ribs. The first is a superb specialty. Also good are shrimp Chippewa, a successful variant on the elusive barbecue shrimp recipe. There is a variety of other seafood and meat, and a pasta bar which whips up an interesting, rich assortment of dishes to order. Good, very rich desserts and a nice bar. L, D seven days. AE, CB, DC, MC, V.

Inexpensive

Buster Holmes. 921 Burgundy, French Quarter; 561–9375. Everyone's image of a soul food restaurant, Buster's turns out a large variety of predictable pot foods (beans, stews, etc.) and fried platters (fish, oysters, chicken, etc.) at very low prices in a minimum of atmosphere. Unfortunately, none of it is as good as it used to be but it's a real institution. L, D seven days. No credit cards.

Eddie's. 2119 Law, Gentilly; 945–2207; Bill Cosby, on the *Tonight Show,* once told a hilarious anecdote about looking for this place, which is almost impossible to find because it's on a terribly potholed street and it doesn't have a sign. However, the search is worthwhile because here are some great versions of red beans with sausage, fried chicken, fried seafood, gumbo, and the rest of the everyday Creole basics, served with courtesy to a mixed clientele. The neighborhood is not bad. To get to the restaurant, bear in mind that Law St. does not cross any major thoroughfares—it passes under their bridges. The best way to get there is to head toward the lake on Elysian Fields, make a U-turn under the bridge at the I–10 junction, double back and turn right on Law. It's four blocks west on the right-hand side of the street. L, D Monday–Saturday. No credit cards.

Gautreau's. 1728 Soniat, Uptown; 899–7397. A new restaurant, very popular with Uptown ladies, serving polite but tasty versions of Creole classics at surprisingly low prices. There are gumbos, bisques, salads, and entrees which change daily; if you happen to come on the right day (and there's no pattern to it), try the crab bisque and the crab au gratin. The tiled floor and tin ceiling make for a loud ambience. L Monday–Friday. No credit cards.

Hummingbird Grill. 804 St. Charles, Central Business District; 523–9165. This is a rather scruffy place in the heart of skidrow; however, civilization is preserved by the cops who seem always to be eating there. The food, especially the daily specials, use better ingredients and more care in the cooking than many a restaurant with four times these prices. Most raw materials are fresh, and the spread for your delicious, fresh cornbread is butter. At peak hours, service is good. No credit cards.

Wise Cafeteria. 909 S. Jefferson Davis Parkway, Mid-City; 488–7811. Unlike other cafeterias, at Wise's little emphasis is put on decor and loads and loads of it on cooking. In that long steam table is a matchless assortment of Creole-style food, homely but wonderful. From the shrimp remoulade (a great one, by the way) at the beginning to the bran muffins at the end, everything is first class. Specialties: broiled fish, boiled beef, desserts, and vegetables. L, D Sunday–Friday. No credit cards.

STEAK HOUSES

Expensive

Butcher Shop. 3322 N. Turnbull, Metairie; 454–2666. This is by far the most atmospheric of the major steak houses, and one of the best, too. The beef seems to be aged a bit longer than in most places, and the broiling—complete with the ubiquitous New Orleans butter sauce—is skillful. There is also a selection of local seafood, lamb, and chicken, as well as a superb salad. You can buy fresh steaks to take home, too. L Monday–Friday. D Monday–Saturday. All major credit cards.

Crescent City Steak House. 1001 N. Broad, Mid City; 821–3271. This restaurant is the originator of what has come to be thought of as the New Orleans-style of steak cookery. The pool of butter sauce is a variation of a common Eastern European theme: herb butter cooked with a steak to help flavor and tenderize it. The milder butter sauce here works wonderfully with the excellent prime aged beef. The best steak is the strip; the other cuts are greatly inferior. The best side dish is lyonnaise potatoes. Because of the portions and the usual deserted nature of the restaurant, one is more likely to feel ripped off here than at the other steak houses, although the prices are actually a little lower. L, D Tuesday–Sunday. All major credit cards.

Ruth's Chris Steak House. 711 N. Broad, Mid-City; 482–9278. 3633 Veterans Blvd., Metairie; 888–3600. Also locations in Gretna and Baton Rouge. Ruth's is the leading purveyor of the New Orleans-style steak: excellent prime beef broiled and served with a sizzling butter sauce. The quality and aging of the beef here cannot be denied, although the cooking provides varying levels of excitement. There's a good house salad but the other side dishes are ho-hum. As everything is a la carte, one can spend quite a few dollars here. L, D seven days. All major credit cards.

Moderate

Charlie's Steak House. 4510 Dryades, Uptown; 895–9705. The pedigree of the beef and the prices are lower at Charlie's, but there are no flaws in the cooking. The steaks are brought out sizzling on metal plates in their butter sauce, and, in the case of the T-bones and strips, are gargantuan. Side dishes are great: the Roquefort dressing for the salad is one of the strongest anywhere, made on the premises. And the onion rings are thin, lightly fried, and irresistible. The waiters are amusing characters. L, D. Monday–Saturday. All major credit cards.

Del Frisco's. 14 West Bank Expressway, Gretna; 368–2222. This relatively new place has combined the New Orleans butter-sauce idea with the exterior charring of a great New York steak to produce the best steak in New Orleans. The beef is cut to order and is of superb quality and aging. The side dishes—the fried calamari, onion rings, potatoes au gratin—soups, and salads are all first rate. Some of the above come with the steak, so the tab is kept within control. Good wine list and very attentive service. L Monday–Friday; D Monday–Saturday. All major credit cards.

SEAFOOD

Moderate

Bozo's. 3117 21st, Metairie; 831–8666. The best seafood house in the area, Bozo's has a more limited menu than most; but the upshot is that they serve only those items which are consistently available, fresh, in high quality. The list includes small fillets of catfish, big butterflied shrimp, claw crabmeat made into a stuffing, and oysters—superb both raw on the half-shell or fried. When the rest of the town has poor oysters, Bozo's manages to still have great ones. Everything is cooked to order and comes out crackly, hot, and well seasoned. There's also a good chicken-andouille gumbo and, in season, boiled or marinated crawfish. L, D Tuesday–Saturday. All major credit cards.

Bruning's. West End Park; 282–9395. Bruning's is the best of a lot of sadly declining restaurants in what should be New Orleans' best seafood area. West End Park is shore-to-shore seafood places, most of them looking out over the lake and serving carelessly prepared food. If you must take in West End, come here for the fried catfish and cross your fingers. L, D Thursday–Tuesday. DC, MC, V.

Casamento's. 4330 Magazine, Uptown; 895–9761. Casamento's specializes in oysters: raw at the bar or fried to order on a platter or in a sandwich. They are very good at this, as they are at frying whatever other seafood they may happen to have that day. The two rooms sparkle from floor to ceiling; with all the tile, they somewhat resemble giant shower stalls. An Uptown favorite and very consistent. L, D Tuesday–Sunday. Closed throughout the summer months. No credit cards.

Compagno's Fern Restaurant. 7839 St. Charles Ave., Uptown; 866–9313. A small neighborhood place with a menu of good seafood, fried to order, and acceptable Italian dishes. L, D Wednesday–Sunday. No credit cards.

Drago's. 3232 N. Arnoult, Metairie; 887–9611. The Yugoslavians were the original Louisiana seafood dealers, so it's no surprise that one of the best seafood places in town is also the best Yugoslavian place. The oysters are very good here, and the variety of seafood available at any given moment is staggering. Drago's does more broiling than most places and has interesting specials. (Also see entry under "Yugoslavian" in this section.) L, D Monday–Saturday. All major credit cards.

Felix's. 739 Iberville, French Quarter; 522–4440. The best thing about Felix's is their oyster bar, where there is no waiting and the shuckers are accomplished. At the tables, you are served seafood from a very long, comprehensive menu; the food ranges from very good to ho-hum, but the place is always packed, mostly with visitors. Service is indifferent. L, D. Monday–Saturday. Open till 2 A.M. No credit cards.

Joe Petrossi's. 901 Louisiana Ave., Uptown; 895–3504. A small, popular little family seafood place, with very good boiled crabs and a well-rounded menu of fried seafood as well. L, D Wednesday–Sunday. No credit cards.

Lakeview Seafood. 7400 Hayne Blvd., New Orleans East; 242–2819. An old, dumpy-looking shack where, at the long tables, large families devour larger platters of good boiled seafood and then pit their appetites against the shrimp or oyster "boat." That is a loaf of bread, hollowed out, buttered, toasted, and filled with the fried seafood of your choice. Not as good as in its glory years, but still very interesting. L, D Monday–Saturday. No credit cards.

Middendorf's. Interstate 55, Manchac; about 40 miles from New Orleans; 1–386–6666. This is the restaurant Orleanians think of when they want catfish. There are two varieties: the thin fish is the better, being a big platter of small, crisp tidbits. The raw oysters are also superb and there is a full menu of other types of seafood. L, D Tuesday–Sunday. MC, V.

Roussel's. 30 miles west of New Orleans on Airline Highway (U.S. 61 North) at US 51, Laplace; 1–652–9910. This is another distant mecca for local eaters. Roussel's is a distinctly Cajun-style restaurant, serving the best oyster-andouille gumbo anywhere (Laplace is the home of andouille, a thick, garlicky ham sausage), as well as good crawfish dishes in and out of season. There are also large daily dinners at prices that seem like misprints on the low side. L, D seven days. All major credit cards.

Inexpensive

Acme Oyster House. 724 Iberville, French Quarter; 523–8928. The grand-daddy of local oyster bars, the Acme has a big old marble counter at which you stand and eat dozen after dozen of oysters which have been opened before your eyes by old pros. Next to that is another bar where you get your beer, the preferred drink with oysters. And in the back there are sandwiches. You can also eat oysters at a table, but that's strictly for the tired or uninformed. L, D Monday–Saturday. Closes at 7:00 P.M. No credit cards.

Alonso & Son. 587 Central Ave., Jefferson; 733–2796. A very crowded neighborhood place, not much to look at, serving some of the best fried seafood in the city at very low prices. Alonso's also does good daily plates and poor-boy sandwiches. The clientele provides a fine taste of local color. L, D Monday–Saturday. No credit cards.

Barrow's Shady Inn, 2714 Mistletoe, Uptown; 482–9427. All they serve here is fried catfish, and it's the best in the city; very light, fried to order with a thin, crunchy layer of seasoned corn meal on fresh, tender fish. It comes with potato salad of some merit. Barrow's has been around since the forties, but as it's off the thoroughfare hardly anybody knows about it, despite the fact that it's repeatedly received national press. L Thursday–Sunday; D Tuesday–Sunday. No credit cards.

SANDWICHES AND FAST FOOD

Inexpensive

Bud's Broiler. 2338 Banks, Mid-City; 821–3022. Other locations around town. Bud's broils its hamburgers over charcoal and serves them on a toasted bun with other good ingredients like grated cheddar and hickory smoke sauce. The premises are a little seedy but the service is fast. L, D seven days. No credit cards.

Camellia Grill. 626 S. Carrollton Ave., Uptown; 866–9573. The class act among lunch counters, with linen napkins and a maitre d'. The hamburgers are legendary, as are the deli sandwiches, breakfasts, pecan pie, and cheesecake. Open 9:00 A.M.–1:30 A.M. seven days. No credit cards.

Central Grocery. 923 Decatur, French Quarter; 523–1620. Strictly a take-out place, the Central Grocery is of special note as the originator and still greatest practitioner of the muffuletta, a giant Italian sandwich. The place is also a wonderland of imported delicacies and smells great. Open 9:00 A.M.–5:00 P.M. Monday–Saturday. No credit cards.

Jonah's Deli. In the Marketplace, 1015 Decatur, French Quarter; 528–9086. A comfortable loft in a collection of boutiques, Jonah's serves very good lox and an assortment of other deli specialties, along with Dr. Brown's soft drinks, a rarity in New Orleans. Open 10:00 A.M.–5:00 P.M. seven days. No credit cards.

Napolean House. 500 Chartres St., French Quarter; 524–9752. This ancient bar which made a major concession to the 20th century recently by adding air conditioning, also serves a variety of sandwiches, most of them in an Italian vein. Those include great muffuletta, and a good Italian sausage poor boy. Open from 11:00 A.M. to midnight Monday–Thursday; 11:00 A.M. to 2 A.M. Friday and Saturday; noon–midnight Sunday. AE.

Mama Rosa's Little Slice of Italy. 828 N. Rampart, French Quarter; 523–5546. Written up as one of the ten best pizza places in America in *People*, Mama Rosa's has pretty good thick-crust pizza. But even better are its sandwiches, made on a marvelous home-baked, heavy-crusted bread. Open 11:30 A.M.–12:30 A.M. Tuesday–Saturday. No credit cards.

Martin Deli. 3827 Baronne, Uptown; 899–7411. The closest thing in town to a New York deli, with a large assortment of very good sandwiches thick with meat. You dine at the counter standing up. You get a free sandwich when you buy four and a glass of wine costs a quarter. Martin's is also the city's biggest wine store, worth a browse. Open 10:00 A.M.–7:00 P.M. Monday–Saturday; 10:00 A.M.–1:00 P.M. Sunday. MC, V.

Maspero's. 601 Decatur, French Quarter; 523–8414. Maspero's is the Quarter's most popular sandwich place, and at most times there is a line for the many tables and the sandwiches served at them. They are served on a tasty hard French roll, and are stuffed with good ham, pastrami, corned beef, roast beef, etc. Low prices. Mediocre hamburgers. Open 11:00 A.M.–midnight seven days. No credit cards.

Mother's. 401 Poydras, Central Business District; 523–9658. Mother's is the great poor-boy restaurant, serving sandwiches the length of your lower arm on fresh, delicious French bread. They roast all their own meats; the ham is a special treat, but the roast beef, turkey, and other combinations are marvelous. Mother's also has good breakfasts and wonderful, rib-sticking plate lunches. On Tuesday, the feature is some of the best red beans and rice around. Open 6:00 A.M.–3:00 P.M. Tuesday–Saturday. No credit cards.

Parasol's. 2533 Constance, Garden District; 899–2054. Parasol's is head-quarters for the Irish Channel, always full of fine local characters. They also serve great poor-boys, the roast beef being arguably the best in town and the seafood poor-boys right up there. You'll be here awhile because it always takes them a half-hour to make your sandwich. L, D. Monday and Wednesday–Saturday. No credit cards.

Pavone's. In Lakeside Shopping Center, the Plaza in Lake Forest, and at 9065 Judge Perez Dr., Chalmette. In the two shopping centers Pavone's is a mere window from which issue forth great slices of New York-style pizza, along with stromboli, sausage rolls, and other related specialties. L, D Monday–Saturday. No credit cards.

Popeyes. Various locations around town. Popeyes is a home-grown, fried chicken, fast food place which has gone nationwide on the merits of its very spicy chicken. On the side you get "dirty rice" dressing and some delicious freshly baked buttermilk biscuits. The chicken can be very good but it's inconsistent. B, L, D. No credit cards.

Port of Call. 838 Esplanade, French Quarter; 523–0120. This is a dark bar with a ship theme and the best hamburgers in New Orleans, made from freshly ground steak and broiled over charcoal, served with a baked potato. They also have pizza and steaks in a rear dining room. L, D seven days. AE, MC, V.

R&O Pizza Place. 300 Metairie-Hammond Highway, Bucktown; 831–1248. In the old lakefront fishing community of Bucktown is this restaurant, serving in minimal surroundings good pizza as well as some of the best poor-boy sandwiches in town. They use an unusual Italian bread for their sandwiches, to good effect. L, D daily except Tuesdays. No credit cards.

Uglesich's. 1238 Baronne, Uptown; 523–8547. This place has the very seedy look of a great New Orleans neighborhood poor-boy place, of which it's a textbook example. Best sandwiches are fried seafood: soft-shell crab, shrimp, trout, and oysters. The oysters are opened to order and the French fries are freshly cut. L Monday–Friday. No credit cards.

Mrs. Wheat's Kitchen. 3840 Veterans Blvd., Metairie; 888–5618. The spe-cialty here is the Natchitoches meat pie, a spicy Central Louisiana staple that's something like a Mexican empanada. They're delicious and habit-forming. L, D seven days. No credit cards.

HEALTH FOOD/VEGETARIAN
Inexpensive

Back To The Garden. 207 Dauphine, French Quarter; 524–6915. A small cafe serving a large assortment of salads, juices, meatless sandwiches, and other vegetarian specialties. There is actually some taste in the stuff and everything is fresh. L, D Monday–Saturday. No credit cards.

Schan's. Independence Mall, 4241 Veterans Blvd., Metairie; 456–9666. A good little kitchen adjacent to a health food store prepares beguilingly good meatless dishes, as well as salads and sandwiches. L Monday–Friday. No credit cards.

CUISINES BY NATIONALITY

CHINESE
Expensive

Trey Yuen. Causeway Blvd., Mandeville (about 30 miles from downtown New Orleans); 1–626–4476. The biggest, best-looking Chinese restaurant in the area, Trey Yuen lines them up outside with a menu of pretty average to pretty good Chinese food mostly Cantonese, but a little of everything. However, some of the specials, particularly those involving seafood, are remarkable, as is the Chinese feast for eight or more that you have to book well in advance. L Sunday; D seven days. All major credit cards.

Inexpensive

Asia Gardens. 530 Bourbon, French Quarter; 525–4149. At the end of an alleyway flanked by typical Bourbon St. sleaze is a very good little place, quiet and comfortable, serving decent Cantonese dishes with a few items from other parts of China. D, seven days. AE, MC, V.

China Doll. 830 Manhattan Blvd., across the Norvio in Harvey. 366–8203. A rather nice-looking place in a shopping center, this restaurant serves lots of the usual Cantonese stuff with a sprinkling of more exotic fare like shark's fin soup and soft-shell crabs with Cantonese sauce. Good service, low prices. L Monday–Friday; D Monday–Saturday. AE, MC, V.

Gin's Mee Hong. 739 Conti, French Quarter; 523–8471. Gin's is one of the oldest Chinese places in town, and while there is nothing new here, they do a reasonably good job of preparing things like moo goo gai pan and ginger beef. Lots of regulars have never gone to any other oriental place, nor do they want to. D Tuesday–Sunday. No credit cards.

Golden Dragon. 4417 Veterans Blvd., Metairie; 887–6081. A pleasant place on the second floor (there's another restaurant downstairs), this place has the most varied Chinese menu in town, with samples of Cantonese, Szechuan, Hunan, and Mandarin cooking, all of it prepared with deftness. Especially good are the hot and sour soup and the River Shang pork. D Tuesday–Saturday. MC, V.

Peking. 6600 Morrison Rd., New Orleans East; 241–3321. The Peking has, relatively speaking, an abbrieviated menu, but everything is a specialty. The shrimp toast, fried dumplings, and moo shu pork are the best in town, and the chef has a few tricks of his own with chicken. Rather modest, but consistently good. L, D, Tuesday–Saturday. AE, MC, V.

FRENCH

Deluxe

L'Escale. 730 Bienville, French Quarter; 524–3022; By far the most expensive restaurant in town and one of the dearest in the country, this place was opened in 1982 by the Louis XVI people who wanted to see if Parisian (or is it New York?) French food and service would fly in a city which never had it before. The hope was also to attract some oil money from Houston for some good old-fashioned conspicuous consumption. Every dish is breathtaking in appearance, and most of the time it even comes out hot and tastes good, too. The best food is conveniently assembled into a $95 dinner, ten courses long, including such things as an assortment of marinated and smoked fish on an ice floe with statuettes of arctic fauna; warmed foie gras on lettuce flown in from Italy; a seafood bisque with the large pieces of seafood artfully arranged at the bottom of the plate; salmon in a perfectly round pool of Champagne sauce, decorated with drawings in glacé de viand; quail in a sauce of Chateau d'Yquem, with fried potatoes carved into odd boxes that look like refugees from an M. C. Escher print and green beans flown in from France. The waiters wear white tie and tails and white gloves and spend much of the evening (but you have the table the whole night) explaining the menu. When everything is right, the meal is memorable, but at these prices one tends to notice even the slightest glitch, and chances are that a slight one or two will show itself. D Monday–Saturday. All major credit cards.

Louis XVI. 829 Toulouse, French Quarter; 581–7000. This is the first successful, full French service restaurant in the city, and it's still one of the best places to have an elegant meal. There are a few Creole items here and there, but for the most part the fare is continental: racks of lamb in pastry, beef Wellington, steak Diane, duck with peppercorns, steak au poivre, etc. There are some marvelous soufles, one (the Rockefeller) an especial treat. Attentive and very polite service. Things are calm here but not boring. D seven days. All major credit cards.

Sazerac. In the Fairmont Hotel, University Place; Central Business District; 524–8904. A large, expensively (but somewhat cornily) furnished room providing rather inconsistent food served with much fanfare. Specialties are, however, good bets and include oysters Pierre, lobster bisque, and rack of lamb bouquetiere. At lunchtime a reliably exciting, memorable steak tartare is served, prepared tableside. The pastry department is very good and provides lots of interesting desserts. Other fillips include a strolling accordionist, a sommelier who does drawings, and a singer who does caricatures. The wine list is very extensive, with especially large California possibilities. At certain times of year (Christmas being one of them), the Sazerac puts on very good theme dinners at somewhat relaxed prices. L, D seven days. All major credit cards.

Versailles. 2100 St. Charles Ave., Uptown; 524–2535. Chef-owner Gunter Preuss has a hotel restaurant without the hotel. There is much polish in the food, and the kitchen is capable of preparing almost everything if you have ideas. Start with snails en croute or the crabmeat appetizer. The best entrees are poultry: a startlingly successful pair of quail dishes, and a roast duck in port sauce. They do some nice things with beef and veal; for the latter meat, the chef's German origins comes out in a couple of dishes. Good desserts, particularly during the winter, when the chef gets ambitious. The wine list is one of the better ones, with an especially good selection of German wines. D Monday–Saturday. All major credit cards.

Winston's. In the New Orleans Hilton at the foot of Poydras in the Central Business District; 561–0500. This is an imitation of the Hilton's very successful Atlanta restaurant but with a vague English theme. You are served by a butler and a maid, or by both, or sometimes by neither. They recite the menu, then recite it again until you can remember it. Some of the food is good or even very good, but the restaurant is not consistent in any course except soup, where some nice bisques are often prepared. The meal is a prix fixe affair and includes all the standard courses. D seven days. All major credit cards.

Expensive

Crozier's. 7033 Read Lane, New Orleans East; 241–8220. In the minds of many local diners, this small bistro serves the best food in New Orleans. The chef is indeed talented, and his ambitions are limited to a dozen or so dishes which he does better than anyone else in New Orleans: sweetbreads meuniere, steak au poivre, tournedos with a cream sauce and shrimp and foie gras, an incredible coq au vin. Gerard Crozier doesn't care much for ceremony and so there is little of it; the service is efficient and straightforward. D Tuesday–Saturday. MC, V.

Moderate

Savoir-Faire. 2203 St. Charles Ave., Uptown; 529–4261. Here is a good new bistro with an interior that looks like a cross between Galatoire's and the Morning Call, but there's almost nothing New Orleans about the menu. The food has uncommon polish, considering the prices; the ingredients are fresh and the preparations imaginative. Best bets are the crudites, the garlic soup, the platter of cold seafoods, sweetbreads with butter and capers, bouillabaisse, shrimp ragout, and the daily specials. Not much for dessert; coffee is wonderful and comes in giant cups. Original. L, D Monday–Saturday. All major credit cards.

GERMAN
Moderate

Kolb's. 125 St. Charles Ave., Central Business District; 522–8278. For decades Kolb's (pronounced "kobs") was the only German restaurant in town, and it's still the most aggressively Teutonic place: lots of corny stuff, from beer steins to a German automaton "cranking" the belt-connected ceiling fans. The menu is lengthy and has all the classics of the cuisine, but you will be hard-pressed to assemble a decent meal here. It's popular among businessmen for lunch. L, D Monday–Saturday. AE, MC, V.

Willy Coln's. 2505 Whitney Ave., Gretna; 361–3860. A small, good-looking chef-owned restaurant, Willy Coln's serves a mixed menu of German, Creole, Caribbean, and French food, mainly because the chef spent time in all those places and took ideas from them. There is a very German Oktoberfest and Mai-Winefest, when the restaurant takes on a boisterous character; otherwise, it's strictly for gourmets. Start with the Bahamian seafood chowder, and order ahead for the roast veal shank for two, tender meat falling from the bone with fresh vegetables. Good versions of weiner schnitzel, jeager schnitzel, steak au poivre, and roast duck with peppercorns. Airy Black Forest cake and, occasionally, strudels for dessert. Good service and a general joie de vivre prevail. D Tuesday–Saturday. All major credit cards.

INDIAN
Moderate

Taj Mahal. 1521 N. Causeway Blvd., Metairie; 833–3456. New Orleans' first Indian place did not open until 1982, but it's a good one, with authentic tandoori clay ovens and spices imported from India. Especially good are the tandoori meats, the vindaloos, and the large assortment of vegetarian dishes. L Monday, Tuesday, Thursday, Friday; D Thursday–Tuesday. All major credit cards.

ITALIAN

Expensive

La Riviera. 4506 Shores Dr., Metairie; 888–6238. A very good restaurant with a creative chef-owner whose dishes are more Northern Italian than is ordinarily seen in seemingly all-Sicilian New Orleans. Especially good is the appetizer of crabmeat ravioli; the veal and trout entrees and steak pizzaiola are the best entrees. D Monday–Saturday. AE, DC, MC, V.

Pascal's Manale. 1838 Napoleon Ave., Uptown; 895–4877. It looks like a neighborhood restaurant, which it once was, but people come from all over to eat the barbecued shrimp, an incredible local classic created here. Unfortunately, the consistency has been lacking in recent years. When the shrimp are good, they're large and spicy and messy but wonderful. Other times, they look right but taste wrong. The rest of the menu consists of southern Italian classics in Creole form, and the track record is erratic there too. However, the place remains crowded all the time; even with a reservation, waits of an hour or more are not uncommon. The oysters in the bar are quite good. L, D Monday–Saturday; no L Saturday. All major credit cards.

Moderate

Broadway Cafe. Uptown Square, Broadway at the river, Uptown; 861–1455. The shopping center location makes the decor and food a real surprise, since both are very modern and creatively conceived. The place is in the shape of the city, with aisles and overhead struts following the course of the river and the radiating streets. The menu is a very light northern Italian which almost doesn't seem Italian. The pasta dishes are excellent, with few red sauces seen. The veal is beautiful—white, with the piccata being the best but an excellent vitello tonnato available as well. L, D Monday–Saturday. All major credit cards.

Mosca's. US 90, Waggaman; about 15 miles from downtown New Orleans; 436–8942. A roadside shack literally on the edge of a swamp, Mosca's serves what is generally agreed to be among the most unusual Italian food in the nation. It is the embodiment of the Creole-Italian style, using lots of seafood and robust, oily, garlicky sauces in simple preparations. All courses are designed to be split at least two ways. Start with the marinated crab salad. The best entrees are Italian oysters, breaded and broiled in a big pan. The Italian shrimp are also broiled, this time with an unabashed assortment of herbs. Equally good and oily is the chicken a la grandee, the homemade Italian sausage with roasted potato. Be sure to have the homemade spaghetti bordelaise as a side dish. Very hearty and unique eating. There is an aggressive disregard for amenities, with wine served in tumblers and service country-style. D Tuesday–Saturday. Reservations a must for Friday, not available for Saturday.

Sclafani's. 1315 N. Causeway Blvd., Metairie; 835–1718. A big old place with intolerably slow service and a gigantic menu combining local versions of Sicilian specialties and lots of straightforward Creole food. The fried and broiled seafood is very good. L, D Monday–Friday; D seven days. AE, MC, V.

Tony Angello's. 6262 Fleur de Lis Dr., Lakeview; 488–0888. The best purveyor of the most common style of Italian cooking in New Orleans: Sicilian, with lots of red sauces a bit on the sweet side, breaded veal, redfish with crabmeat on top, oyster artichoke soup, eggplant, rolls, cannelloni, and manicotti. All of this is quite good. The restaurant is extremely popular. D Tuesday–Saturday. AE, MC, V.

Tortorici's. 441 Royal, French Quarter; 522–4295. An old, somewhat grand place which relies a bit too heavily on the tourist trade, Tortorici's can be very good but is also occasionally a bit boring. Good shrimp scampi and Italian seafood in general lead the menu possibilities; there is also a good table d'hote dinner. L, D Monday–Saturday. AE, MC, V.

Inexpensive

Eva's Spot. 337 Dauphine, French Quarter; 523–8534. A little hole in the wall close enough to downtown to get heavy lunch trade, Eva's serves arguably the best lasagne in town: very cheesey, not too sweet, or oily, firm and flavorful. There are also other Italian specialties of no great note and good, very cheap lunch specials and sandwiches. L Monday–Saturday. No credit cards.

Napoli. 1917 Ridgelake Dr., Metairie; 837–8463. This is the lunch version of Tony Angello's, operated by one of his former managers and serving similar food along with good versions of New Orleans lunchtime staples. L Monday–Friday. AE, MC, V.

Old Italy. 2800 Tulane Ave., Mid-City; 821–4751. A small lunch place serving the nearby Criminal Courts complex with fascinating, unique food. The orancini (fried rice and cheese balls) and pasta with tuna are best, but all the food is good. L Monday–Friday. No credit cards.

Toney's Spaghetti House. 212 Bourbon, French Quarter; 561–9253. The neon signs which proclaim Toney the Spaghetti King are accurate. You can get the pasta with just about anything here, and all of the variations are delicious. At lunch you can get some great special platters of other kinds of food; at dinner there is good pizza. For breakfast, the best biscuits in New Orleans. B, L, D served continuously 7:00 A.M.–1:00 A.M. Monday–Saturday. No credit cards.

JAPANESE

Moderate

Mount Fuji. 3042 Gen. Collins Ave., Algiers; 393–2920. A nice-looking place with two menus. The one they give most customers contains pretty good versions of tempura and teriyaki. The real Japanese menu, however, reveals an outstanding assortment of sashimi, sushi, shabu-shabu, sukiyaki, and an eight-course kaiseki of incomparable fascination. Some of this may not be available unless you call a day ahead. D seven days. AE, DC, MC, V.

Shogun. 1414 Veterans Blvd., Metairie; 833–7477. A small, modern, pretty little restaurant in three sections. One is a set of stools around an authentic sushi bar, where the chef makes beautiful items of the raw, rice-stuffed fish of your choice. The second is another bunch of stools around the teppan-yaki tables, where meats are skewered, grilled, and fried. And there are standard tables and an extensive menu of good Japanese fare. L, D Monday and Wednesday–Saturday. AE, MC, V

KOREAN
Moderate

Genghis Khan. 4053 Tulane, Mid City; 482–4044. A fascinating restaurant run by the first violinist of the New Orleans Symphony, with a good selection of such Korean dishes as bulgoki, kimchee, and whole steamed fish. Also good is the peppery chicken Imperial. Live classical music some nights. D Monday–Saturday; hours change frequently. AE, MC, V.

MEXICAN
Inexpensive

Castillo's. 620 Conti, French Quarter; 581–9602. Everything is authentic here, right down to the somewhat slack hygiene and the slow service. But the food is delicious, from the oniony guacamole to the chicken with mole, enchiladas de res, chilmole de puerco, and even a Mexican chicken soup. L, D seven days. MC, V.

El Patio. 3244 Georgia Ave., Kenner; 443–1188. A very pretty little place operated by a Mexican family, El Patio serves the usual Mexican fare for the suburban crowd as well as some adventuresome dishes for the adventurous. There is an especially good selection of Mexican seafood dishes, with the stuffed squid being remarkable. They also do a large variety of soups and delicious nachos. A strolling guitarist-singer provides the "Cielito Lindo." D Monday–Saturday. AE. MC, V.

MIDDLE EASTERN
Inexpensive

Hagi Baba. 733 St. Peter, French Quarter; 525–9127. A small, dark restaurant with an adjoining gift shop with remarkable Lebanese and Syrian foods. Especially good are the gyros, baba ghanoooj, hoummos, and the kebabs. The menu is lengthy and the chef cares. L, D seven days. MC, V.

St. George's Bakery. 3226 Williams Blvd., Kenner; 443–1888. A small place in a strip shopping center, St. George's bakes all its own breads and prepares with it some unique, delightful sandwiches of marinated lamb and beef, as well as sausages of the same meats, dressed with a beguiling combination of herbs. Also good is the baba ghanooj and hoummos, as well as the large selection of Armenian pastries. L, D Monday–Saturday. No credit cards.

SPANISH
Moderate

Espana. 2705 Jefferson Highway, Jefferson; 835–1502. A small dining room with a dark bar that occasionally features live flamenco, the Espana has a menu of Iberian Spanish food including arroz con calamares of special note. Also a decent paella, bacalao, arroz con pollo, and the like. Strangely enough, they also have a large Italian menu and this is rather good. The flan is among the creamiest and richest around. D Monday–Saturday. MC, V.

YUGOSLAVIAN

Moderate

Drago's. 3232 N. Arnoult, Metairie; 887–9611. What started out as a straight seafood restaurant has remained that while evolving into a very talented Yugoslavian kitchen, serving, among other things, many different varieties of squid, a great spinach soup, muckalica, musaka, sarma (stuffed cabbage rolls), and more. You can get a variety of things on the Yugoslavian platter. (Also see entry under Seafood in this section.) L, D Monday–Saturday. All major credit cards.

FAMOUS, BUT . . .

Brennan's. *Deluxe.* 417 Royal, French Quarter; 525–9711. A big, stunningly good-looking restaurant in the classic *Vieux Carré*-style, complete with courtyard, Brennan's invented the Creole breakfast decades ago and the meal has become an institution. The prices for it are at levels you would consider appropriate for dinner, and lunch and dinner prices are even higher. With luck, you can have a good or even great French-Creole meal at Brennan's, but chances are you'll only be a number in the production line in the kitchen instead. The restaurant does have one of the best and best-priced French wine cellars in the city. B, L, D seven days. All major credit cards.

Corinne Dunbar's. *Expensive.* 1617 St. Charles Ave., Uptown; 525–2957. The reputation is that you are served an elaborate, wonderful Creole meal in a lavish mansion as if you were a house guest. The realities are ordinary food in a modest house with standard restaurant service. D Tuesday–Saturday. No credit cards.

Court of Two Sisters. *Expensive.* 613 Royal, French Quarter; 522–7261. This is another pretty courtyard with a French-Creole restaurant surrounding it, but that's the best that can be said. The place is infamous among locals for having all the appearances but none of the substance of a great New Orleans restaurant. The food is marginal, the service atrocious and the din annoying. There is a brunch buffet daily with a jazz band. Brunch and dinner seven days. All major credit cards.

 DESSERT. With the exception of the oriental restaurants, most New Orleans eateries have serious dessert menus. One of the most popular items is bread pudding, which is very unlike the item served elsewhere under that name. New Orleans bread pudding is usually custardy, raisiny, and moistened with this or that version of whiskey or rum sauce. Fancier but also a local staple is bananas Foster, made by flaming bananas in brandy and banana liqueur with cinnamon and butter and sugar and dumping all of that over ice cream.

Pralines—the classic New Orleans candy of caramelized sugar and nuts—are available just about everywhere and in the French Quarter in particular. However, there are some specialists in the confection. Two of them—*Evans'* and *Aunt Sally's*—are near one another in the French Market (800 block of Decatur), and you can watch the actual manufacture of pralines in progress. Also good are *Leah's* (714 St. Louis) and *Laura's* (115 Royal). Despite the fact that all these places are extremely touristy, their pralines are first rate.

With desserts like that and more, there is little call for a strictly dessert place, although there are some popular ice cream stands. *Haagen-Dazs* has three locations: Uptown, Metairie, and in the French Quarter. *Baskin-Robbins* has many outlets around town; see the phone book.

There is one local ice cream parlor which has become an institution, however. *Angelo Brocato's* (214 N. Carrollton Ave., Mid-City; 488–1465.) An authentic Italian gelati, manufacturing all its own ice creams. Best are spumone, cassata, terrancino (with a sort of cinnamon flavor), and the lemon and strawberry ices, but the assortment of flavors is complete. They also make cannoli (a ricotta-stuffed confection), and a wide variety of Italian cookies and candies. Open 11:00 A.M.–9:00 P.M., seven days. No credit cards.

Then, of course, there are the coffeehouses, which are considered in the next section.

 CAFES/COFFEEHOUSES. New Orleans' weather generally goes directly from requiring air conditioning to requiring heating; the humidity makes al fresco dining uncomfortable on all but a very few lucky days a year. Outdoor cafes are few. However, there is one tradition of long standing here, that of finishing off the evening at one of the two French Market coffeehouses—one of which, ironically, is no longer within ten miles of the French Market.

Café Du Monde is still where it's always been, at the uptown extremity of the market (Decatur at St. Ann), with a small dining room and a large canvas-covered outside section. The coffee is *café au lait,* the famous New Orleans dark-roasted coffee and chicory blend, far too strong to be drunk without the hot milk poured in the cup at same time the coffee is. The doughnuts are beignets, leaden little fried squares of sourdough, served three to the order, dusted with powdered sugar which will probably wind up dusting you, too. (Don't laugh while you're eating one.) The same items are served in slightly better and more consistent form in the much less atmospheric circumstances of the *Morning Call* (3325 Severn, Metairie), where the 60-year-old furnishings of the old French Quarter premises were moved some years ago into a stark space in an antiseptic suburban strip shopping center. Both places are extremely well patronized 24 hours a day, seven days a week.

Just off Jackson Square is *La Marquise* (525 Chartres, French Quarter; 524–0420; open 9:00 A.M.–5:00 P.M., Thursday–Tuesday), a fine little French pastry shop run by two very talented French chefs. There are a few tables inside and on the patio, and there is much coffee-drinking done here, too.

NIGHT LIFE AND BARS. It has been said that if one drops dead of cirrhosis of the liver in New Orleans, it's considered a death by natural causes. Drinking accompanies almost every recreational activity hereabouts, particularly those which take place after dark. And some major events like Mardi Gras or the Jazz Festival take on truly bacchanalian proportions with regard to imbibing.

The city's enthusiastic interest in dining also brings with it opportunities for the clinking of glasses. In fact, it removes a lot of nightclubbing from the streets; Orleanians tend to think of a dinner out as an entire evening's activity, rather than the beginning or end of it.

In any case, if you want to have a social drink, you can get one here no matter what time of what day it is. Blue laws prevent you from getting a screwdriver in a store on Sundays, but the orange-juice-and-vodka version of the same thing is readily available. The bars never close—not even on Election Day. Things *do* slow down considerably as Mardi Gras becomes Ash Wednesday, but that only happens once a year.

The live music or the array of characters, not the quality of mixology, is the determining factor in the liveliness (and livelihood) of a club. However, there are some local drink specialties you should know about. Up and down Bourbon St. you will see many places touting the Hurricane. This is a creation of Pat O'Brien's and really should be had only there; it's four and a half ounces of dark rum with a variety of fruit juices in a tall, curved glass. The mint julep, you will be told by many bartenders, is *not* a good drink; they say this when they're out of mint. In reality, the drink can be very refreshing, and has an old-timey kind of flavor of bourbon, mint, and quinine.

The best of the local drink specialties is the Ramos gin fizz, invented at the Sazerac Bar but now done best in the Royal Orleans' Esplanade Lounge. It's gin with cream, egg white, orange flower water, and soda. Not as rich as it sounds, it makes a nice before-dinner cocktail and is refreshing in the summer. Finally, there is the Sazerac itself which, it is claimed by the Sazerac Bar, is the original cocktail. It's a bit of bourbon and bitters in a glass coated with absinthe substitute by being thrown whirling in the air. It's not for those who dislike potent drinks.

Of course, the main attraction in the way of night life for anyone visiting New Orleans is live music. There is plenty of it, ranging from the very oldest and most authentic Dixieland jazz to New Wave rock and modern jazz. The best places tend to be rather old, slightly rundown, and crowded; clubs offering comfortable amenities, like prompt drink service and comfortable seating, are few and far between. Dancing space is also at a premium, but the music seems to move those inclined to discover enough for their heart's content.

Everyone winds up on Bourbon Street sooner or later. While there is a little bit of everything and much of interest, the street is dominated at present by all manner of seedy operations: T-shirt stores, porn theaters, bad fast food places, etc. The strip joints continue in operation; even though the Sexual Revolution has turned them into a tawdry curiosity at best, the barkers will still try to get you inside for a peek. There are also a few shows of female impersonators, which can be interesting in their way.

Six blocks from Canal Street, at about the point where Bourbon becomes more residential, the block between St. Ann and Dumaine features the densest cruising traffic of gays in the city. The masses are moving from the populous gay bars at either end of the block. For a long time, this was where most of the gay action was concentrated, although now there are more bars along North Rampart in the Armstrong Park area and in the Marigny section just east of the Quarter.

The only other concentration of clubs in the area is in a section of the sprawling Metairie suburb called Fat City. There's a mall to the south and hundreds of apartments to the north, so the emphasis tends to be on youth and the single state. However, stability is not the strong suit and there is constant change in ownerships and entertainment policies among these places.

All bars in the New Orleans area are allowed unlimited hours. In the French Quarter, closing is rarely earlier than 2:00 A.M., with a great many places open (and busy) 24 hours, seven days. Credit card acceptance in bars and clubs is rare; if they do take plastic, this fact is usually displayed prominently.

Prices range from around $4 a drink in the best hotels down to $1.50 or even less in the neighborhood bars. In the jazz clubs, it is customary to have a two-drink minimum; annoyingly, some require that you order both drinks at once. Few Quarter clubs have a cover charge; in other parts of the city there is a preference for a cover to a minimum.

For up-to-date information on performers at clubs, the best places to look are the *Lagniappe* section in the Friday *The Times-Picayune/The States-Item,* or in *Gambit,* a weekly newspaper.

MOSTLY JAZZ

Blue Angel. 225 Bourbon, French Quarter; 522–0301. The house band here is a quartet called the Chosen Few under the direction of cornetist George Finola. Also featured is Connie Jones' Crescent City Jazz Band. It's a big, comfortable place, not as well-worn as most of the other old-line Bourbon Street jazz houses. They also serve food. Jazz comes on in 30-minutes sets continuously from noon till 3:00 A.M.

Duke's Place. In the Monteleone Hotel, 214 Royal, French Quarter; 581–1567. The current generation of the Dukes of Dixieland plays a real toe-tapper of a show of straight-ahead Dixieland jazz in comfortable surroundings in the penthouse. Monday–Saturday, 9:30 P.M.–12:30 A.M.

The Famous Door. 339 Bourbon, French Quarter; 522–7626. This is one of the three or four old places in the Quarter where the last of the original breed of Dixieland bands perform on a rotating basis, Roy Liberto's Bourbon St. Five and Leroy Jones and His Jazz Band are among them. Very solidly traditional in sound and appearance. Friday–Tuesday, 8:00 P.M.–2:00 A.M., Wednesday and Thursday, 9:00 P.M.–2:00 A.M.

Snug Harbor. 630 Frenchmen Street, Marigny; 944–0100. On Fridays and Saturdays only, this club, which adjoins a restaurant, has some of the best of the local contemporary and avant-garde jazz groups. There is enough talent working in that mode these days that one can hear some pretty exciting experimental stuff, and no place features as much of it as the Snug Harbor does. From 11:00 P.M. till, Friday and Saturday.

Maison Bourbon. 641 Bourbon, French Quarter; 522–8818. A large, open-air (at least during the warmer months) lounge with a rotation of very good original Dixieland bands. The advantage to this place is that you can sample the music, which is quite loud, from the street before deciding whether to enter. Wednesday–Monday, 11:00 A.M.–4:00 P.M.; Friday–Wednesday, 9:00 P.M.–2:00 A.M.

Maple Leaf Bar. 8316 Oak, Uptown. 866–9359. While there is a goodly amount of live jazz here played in an assortment of styles you are just as likely to hear Cajun music, bluegrass, blues, or ragtime. A very engaging place, popular with the postgraduate crowd. This homey establishment also houses a laundromat. Open seven days; music from 10:00 P.M. till, Monday–Saturday; from 8:00 P.M., Sunday.

Marriott Hotel's Lobby Bar, 555 Canal, Downtown; 581–1000. Every weekday afternoon save Monday, Alvin Alcorn and his trio hold forth from 4:00 till 7:00 P.M. with their very traditional—and very good—Dixieland jazz. Alcorn, who plays trumpet, is one of the old-timers who is best known in recent years for his Sunday Jazz Brunch at Commander's Palace; he plays the same stuff here to those who have purchased the one-drink minimum. No cover.

Pete Fountain's. In the New Orleans Hilton, Poydras at the river; 561–0500. The famed New Orleans clarinetist packs the house and rewards those in attendance with energetic shows of traditional and not-so-traditional jazz. Reservations are sometimes difficult to get, so call ahead well in advance. A well-appointed club. Tuesday–Saturday, 10 P.M. till.

Preservation Hall. 726 St. Peter, French Quarter; 523–8939. You'll have to line up to pay your pittance to get into this old place, where jazz aficionados from all over the world flock in to grab one of the few small chairs in the unair-conditioned room and listen to the best of the old-line groups in unamplified splendor. Those in the know get there at least a half-hour before the music starts to beat the line. All the Dixieland you'll hear here is the genuine article; probably the most exciting is Kid Thomas and his Algiers Stompers, a/k/a The Preservation Hall Jazz Band, featuring the startling virtuosity of banjo player Emanuel Sayles. Nightly from 8:00 P.M.

Tipitina's. 501 Napoleon, Uptown; 899–9114. This is general headquarters for the devotees of the loosely defined "New Orleans Sound." Acts which perform in this rickety, minimally appointed place range from modern jazz through blues and rock and even reggae. The name is a referemnce to a song by the late Professor Longhair; the club was instituted to provide a place for him and his ilk to perform regularly. Tends to get crowded in a hurry. There is also a pretty good menu of New Orleans culinary specialties—poor boys, red beans and rice, and the like. Open daily from around noon, with music starting at around 9:30 P.M.

Tyler's Beer Garden. 5234 Magazine, Uptown; 891–4989. Modern jazz, with more or less of a pop-rock leaning, performed by some of the better younger practitioners of the art. The place is rather crowded all the time, and not designed especially well for comfort or good sight lines. However, the camaraderie is high and the music great. Boiled and fried seafood and oysters on the half shell are served, along with a long list of available beers. Open nightly from around noon; music starts at about 10:00 P.M.

SUPPER CLUBS

Blue Room. Fairmont Hotel, University Place, Central Business District; 529–5744. One of the last of the big, gilded rooms outside Las Vegas, the Blue Room offers up a continually varying lineup of big-name acts, performing with the room's standing orchestra. Said combo plays between and before acts for dancing. Cover charge; reservations necessary. The dinner served is ambitious but not always entirely perfect; it might be a better idea to dine in the lavish Sazerac Room down the lobby and come back here for the show and dessert. Drink prices are high. Shows Monday–Saturday at 9:00 and 11:00 P.M.

PIANO BARS

Arnaud's Grill Room. 813 Bienville, French Quarter; 523–5433. A lovely antique bar just off the main dining room of the old restaurant, this place serves inexpensive plate lunches to the tune of a big old upright piano which is sometimes manned by a pianist and sometimes not. Inexpensive drinks. Open 11:30 A.M. till, Monday–Friday.

Fairmont Court. In the Fairmont Hotel, University Place, Central Business District; 529–7111. This is a very comfortable little club next door to the Blue Room. There is a pianist (who usually sings and sometimes has a couple of accompanists) who starts playing around 9:00 P.M. in hour-long sets.

Gazebo Cafe. In the French Market, 1018 Decatur, French Quarter; 522–0862. This outdoor cafe features a pianist during most of the hours from 11:00 A.M. till 10:00 P.M. Monday–Friday; 6:00 P.M. till 10:00 P.M. Saturday.

Jonathan. 714 N. Rampart, French Quarter. 586–1930. The most interesting-looking room in this striking art deco restaurant is in fact the lounge, where a pianist holds forth every night but Sunday. Great cappuccino.

Pontchartrain Bayou Bar. In the Pontchartrain Hotel, 2031 St. Charles Ave., Uptown; 524–0581. An intimate piano bar featuring one of the local greats: "Tuts" Washington, a timeless practitioner of blues and traditional jazz, and teller of fascinating stories if you can get him started. Jacket and tie required.

Good bar snacks. Open daily except Sunday; music 5:00 till 8:30 P.M., Monday–Wednesday; 5:00 till 12:30 A.M., Thursday and Friday; 8:30 P.M.–12:30 A.M., Saturday.

R & B ROCK AND NEW WAVE

Bobby's Place. 520 E. St. Bernard Hwy., Chalmette; 271–0137. A popular suburban club whose specialty is oldies but goodies, performed by the eponymous Bobby as well as other acts. The emphasis is on New Orleans R&B of the late fifties and early sixties. Music Thursday–Saturday from 10:00 P.M.

Dixie's Music Bar. 701 Bourbon, French Quarter; 566–7445. A rather loud club with a good program of music, mostly in the soul and R&B bags, but occasionally contemporary rock and New Wave. Music Friday and Saturday from 8:00 P.M.; Sunday–Thursday from 9:00 P.M.

544 Club. 544 Bourbon, French Quarter; 523–8611. Another popular spot on a heavily trafficked corner of the Bourbon Street Strip, this club features soul, rhythm and blues, and a bit of jazz. Music daily from 3:00 P.M. till.

Jimmy's. 8200 Willow, Uptown; 866–9549. A very popular club among the college audience. Jimmy's brings in an assortment of nationally known rock acts, interspersed with the best of the local talent. Gets very crowded very fast. Music Wednesday–Saturday from 9:00 P.M.

Lucky Pierre's. 735 Bourbon, French Quarter; 525–9377. This is a popular all-night spot serving food for Quarterites and others. In the front room, Frankie Ford performs his oldies hits like "Sea Cruise" as well as his current collection of ballads at the piano. Nightly from 9:00 P.M.

Luther Kent's Rising Sun. 400 Dauphine, French Quarter; 523–8239. Mr. Kent is the leader of an excellent New Orleans-style jazz/rock band called Trick Bag, which you can expect to see in this two-level, comfortable club Thursday–Sunday from 11:30 P.M. till 3:30 A.M.

Mason's Las Vegas Strip. 2309 S. Claiborne, Center City; 529–7681. At Mason's Motel. Most nights, all three clubs in this complex are jumping with everything from jazz to soul, all performed by the leading artists from the black community, for which this place is the entertainment mecca. The audiences, however, are quite mixed and the music is unfettered nightly from 9:00 P.M.

Old Absinthe Bar. 400 Bourbon, French Quarter; 561–9231. This is an ancient place which shows its age in a collection of business cards stuck to every surface, some of them dating to the 1930s. The music, however, is of a more modern nature, being mostly rock groups who play at volumes less than ear-splitting. Good drinks and a congenial collection of people. Music nightly from 10:00 P.M.

Riverboat President. Canal Street Wharf; 586–8777. This is a lovely old art-deco sidewheeler which is no longer under steam but still, by way of diesel power, cruises the river on weekends with touring rock groups performing on one of its four large decks. There are occasional weekday concerts as well. The acoustics are better than you'd think possible on a boat, and the *joie de vivre* runs high. Call for details of concerts, which change from week to week.

Richie's 3-d. 3501 Chateau Blvd., Kenner; 466–3333. A large, Vegas-style club featuring nationally known rock and country bands. Tickets are sometimes a necessity well in advance of the date. Thursday–Saturday from 8:00 P.M., with occasional weekday shows.

Tupelo's Tavern. 8301 Oak, Uptown; 866–3658. This is a minimally decorated club which at times gets to the standing-room-only state, the people being mostly of college age. The music mix is very good, featuring the best of the up-and-coming local bands playing rock, New Wave, and reggae. Music Tuesday–Saturday from 10:00 P.M.

FOLK AND COUNTRY-AND-WESTERN

Penny Post Coffee House. 5110 Danneel, Uptown; This is the only place in the city that schedules folk music on any kind of a regular schedule. Bluegrass sometimes gets on the bill as well. The club is populated by the chess-and-backgammon set, who also smoke cigarettes and generally act Bohemian. Music Wednesday–Sunday, 8:00 P.M.–midnight.

DISCO

Augie's Del Lago. 1930 West End Park, Lakefront; 282–8647. This is a two-level place which is very crowded on weekends. The surroundings are great: Lake Pontchartrain, over which you can gaze while the rock and oldies play on for dancing. Good drinks. More or less a singles place. There is live music from 10:00 P.M., and Friday & Saturday; Sunday from 4:00 P.M., but the place is open daily from around noon.

Forty-One-Forty-One. 4139 St. Charles Ave., 891–8973. A well-designed, comfortable disco frequented by the Uptown jacket-and-tie folks, many of whom are well past 30. Music nightly for dancing from 8:00 P.M.

SPECIAL HANGOUTS

Columns Hotel. 3811 St. Charles Ave., Uptown; 899–9308. This is an old mansion on St. Charles Ave. which has been converted into a small guesthouse hotel. However, the scene in the lounge, which tends to spill over into the lobby and into the small but good restaurant, is strictly provided by locals. The place is currently chic as an after-work place for young professionals. Open daily from about noon.

Fat Harry's. 4330 St. Charles Ave., Uptown; 895–9582. Always popping, Fat Harry's population can, on any given evening, back up onto the sidewalk in front of the streetcar tracks. Strictly a horsing-around kind of place, Fat Harry's is popular with the fraternity gang, both pre- and postgraduate. Open daily.

Napoleon House. 500 Chartres, French Quarter; 524–9752. The doors are wide-open onto the Quarter corner; there's no air conditioning, but little is needed within these ancient, crumbling walls. The building is so named because it was offered to Napoleon as a refuge from exile. Some of the bartenders look old enough to perhaps be able to recall the exact circumstances. The music is classical, played by a stereo in a rear room; you can select your own scratched record and play it. There's a pleasant patio in the rear. The drinks are pretty bad, but the prices are very low. Some good sandwiches are also served. The Napoleon House is a time warp, which is why everyone likes it. Open Monday–Saturday, 11:00 A.M. till 2:00 A.M.

Nick's Big Train Bar. 505 S. Tonti, Center City; 822–9981. This tumbling-down old white shack, across from the city's last independent brewery, is generally conceded to be the home of the best purveyor of specialty drinks in New Orleans. Nick himself was a much-decorated mixologist, especially famed for pousse-cafes of thirty or more layers. His successors are still doing things like that, as well as creating extremely unusual and usually delicious drinks on the spot to your tastes. The crowd is mostly on the young side, from Tulane University; however, Nick's is a legend in the minds of anyone who's been there. Open daily, 4:00 P.M. till.

Pat O'Brien's. 718 St. Peter, French Quarter. 525–4823. It's always a mob scene in this best-known of New Orleans lounges. There are several large rooms and a larger courtyard; in each, there are different drink specialties, different prices (most pretty low), and different entertainment. No one segment of the population has been able to stake a claim on Pat O's; you're liable to meet just about anyone here. The house drink is the Hurricane, served in a large glass (which you get to keep) and full of fruit juices and dark rum. There are over four ounces of booze in one of these, so one drink should do it. It's quite interesting to spend an entire night here, moving from one part to another; the atmosphere is sort of year-round Mardi Gras. Open daily from 11:00 A.M.

Que Sera. 3636 St. Charles Ave., Uptown; 897–2598. A big bar with a patio in front facing the streetcar tracks, Que Sera is very popular among the medical professionals at the several nearby hospitals, and with other Uptowners as well. Much serious talk, at least until about 11:00 P.M., by which time everyone is loose enough to let go a little. Open daily.

Top of the Mart. International Trade Mart, 2 Canal Street, Downtown; 522–9795. This is a revolving lounge atop one of the taller buildings downtown. The view is made even better by the fact that the building is right on the river front; you can watch the fascinating choreography of the tugboats, barges, sea-going ships, and ferries in the busiest part of the second-busiest port in the nation. When the thing turns to the other direction, you can look across the whole city and into Lake Pontchartrain. The lounge is comfortable, the service fast and friendly, and there is occasionally a jazz trio playing. Open daily.

EXCURSIONS OUTSIDE NEW ORLEANS

Plantations, Cajun Country and the Gulf

by
Jeanie Blake

Jeanie Blake, a former art critic and general assignment reporter for
The Times-Picayune/The State's-Item, *is currently a feature writer for
the newspaper's Lifestyle section. She has been recipient of several jour-
nalism awards bestowed by her peers.*

Tourists to New Orleans are frequently so captured by her charms
they never break away from her tight embrace. But there is much more

288

to Louisiana than New Orleans; and if you have the time and are adventurous, other wonderous sites, unique to Louisiana, are nearby and ready to cast a spell. There's Natchitoches, which has been called New Orleans in the wilds, Lafayette and its Cajun cuisine and music, the Mississippi Gulf Coast and its sunny beaches, and, of course, the plantations.

Plantations Along River Road

Visiting the plantations is usually one of the priorities for visitors to Louisiana. Time has seen the destruction of many of the River Road Plantations (Belle Grove, Uncle Sam, Mount Airey, to name a few), but some of the most elegant plantation homes in the state can still be visited along the east and west bank of the Mississippi River, between Baton Rouge and New Orleans.

The River Road mimicks the path of the winding Mississippi River, once the major "highway" of this area, and weaves its way through Louisiana's rich agricultural past and its industrial present. At various places its official name changes—to Highway 44, Highway 75, Highway 18—but to locals, it simply remains the River Road.

A good place to start your tour is Destrehan Plantation, the closest east-bank plantation to New Orleans, located eight miles west of the New Orleans International Airport on the River Road. Although only minimally restored and with sparse furnishings, Destrehan is the oldest plantation home left intact in the lower Mississippi Valley.

Robert de Logny began the three-year construction of his plantation home in 1781. In 1800 Jean Noel d'Estrehan inherited the home, which still bears his name. Destrehan Plantation was built in the West Indies style, which was popular among early south Louisiana homes, and was remodeled in the Greek Revival style in 1840. The house, which is composed of hand-hewn heart-of-cypress timbers and bousillage construction, is open daily (except major holidays) from 10:00 A.M. to 4:00 P.M. Admission is $3 for adults and $2 for children. After the nakedness of Destrehan Plantation, the grandeur of San Francisco Plantation, which has been meticulously restored, is almost mind boggling. It is located about 20 minutes from Destrehan, west along the River Road.

Built in 1854, San Francisco Plantation is known for its bold, Bavarian use of color, its fanciful ceiling frescos and its ornate millwork. Originally it was called "San Frusquin" (one's all). While San Franciso's "Steamboat Gothic" exteriors is something of a curiosity, its interior follows the traditional format of Creole lifestyle with the main living rooms and bedrooms on the second floor and only a dining room and services rooms on the ground level.

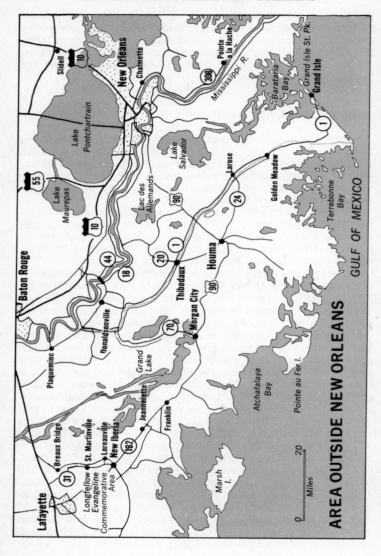

AREA OUTSIDE NEW ORLEANS

The house is open daily 10:00 A.M. to 4:00 P.M. Admission is $4.25 for adults; $3 for visitors 12–17 years old; and $2 for children 6–11.

Back on the River Road, you will pass Manresa, built in 1831 as a college for the sons of wealthy Louisiana planters, and Texcuco Plantation.

If you are ready for a respite from touring or want something to eat, one nice place to stop is the Cabin Restaurant, located at the corner of Highways 22 and 44 in Burnside. The 145-year-old cabin, once one of the original slave dwellings of the Monroe Plantation, is now a reasonably priced restaurant.

The next River Road plantation is only a few minutes from the Cabin and it is a classic! Built on land once occupied by the Houmas Indians, Houmas House is really two structures in one. Alexandre Latil, who purchased the property from the Indians, constructed his four-room, two-story house in the last quarter of the 18th century. Then, in 1840, John Smith Preston built his Greek Revival mansion directly in front of the smaller rear structure. In time, the two houses were connected by an arched carriageway.

In 1940 Dr. George Crozat of New Orleans bought Houmas House and completely restored it. Houmas House, which was the setting for the movie "Hush, Hush, Sweet Charlotte," is open daily February through October from 10:00 A.M. to 5:00 P.M. and November through January from 10:00 A.M. to 4:00 P.M. The house is closed Thanksgiving, Christmas and New Year's Day. Admission: Adults, $4; children 6–12 years, $1.50; 13–18 years, $2.50.

The River Road after Houmas House becomes a rustic gravel path. On your way toward Carville, you will pass two plantations that were built by Marius Pons Bringier as wedding presents for his children: Bocage, located two miles above Burnside, and the Hermitage, one mile below Darrow. Both homes are private, but can be seen from the River Road.

The last house on the east bank before the tour crosses the river is Ashland-Belle Helene, located about six miles above Darrow. Belle Helene was designed by famed New Orleans architect James Gallier, Sr., and was once the grandest plantation in the area. Now, it is fighting for survival. Its once elegant formal gardens are overgrown with weeds; its fine wooden floors are reduced to dirt and its paint is chipped away.

Belle Helene is open to the public from 10:00 A.M. to 4:00 P.M., but it might be a good idea to skip this once beautiful lady. It is situated in an isolated location and there is only one caretaker who reluctantly gives visitors a tour for a $2 admission fee.

At Carville (which has the only hospital in the continental U.S. that cares for victims of Hansen's Disease [leprosy]) take the free ferry ride over the Mississippi River to White Castle, home of Nottoway, the

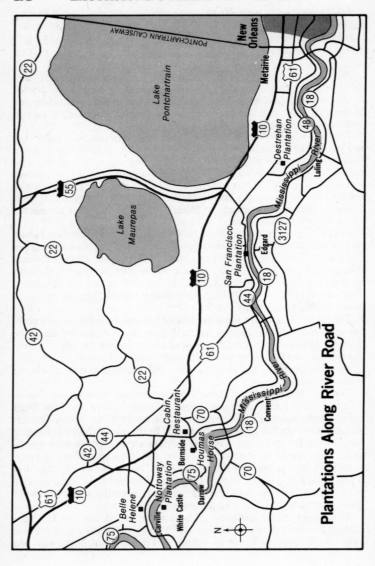

Plantations Along River Road

South's largest plantation. With its 64 rooms and more than 53,000 sq. ft., Nottoway has been called an American castle; and indeed it is. It is also a dream palace as few plantations have been restored as grandly as this one.

Nottoway was designed by Henry Howard, a popular 19th-century architect who also designed Madewood Plantation, for John Hamden Randolph. In 1980 Arlin Dease, who previously restored The Myrtles, Mount Hope and Milbank Manor, bought Nottoway and began an extensive renovation.

Nottoway is open daily (except Christmas) from 9:00 A.M. to 5:00 P.M. Admission is $4 for adults and $2 for children 12 years of age or younger. This is also the last stop and end of a very busy plantation-filled day.

Cajun Country

The Creoles of New Orleans have a country cousin—the Cajuns, a diverse group of people whose ancestors came to Louisiana in the late 18th century from Nova Scotia, then the Canadian province of Acadia.

In the early 18th century French colonists settled in Acadia, which —to their displeasure—soon became a British possession. In 1755, the British told the Acadians to make a choice: either swear allegiance to the King of England and renounce their Roman Catholic faith or leave the territory. They decided to leave, and many relocated in Louisiana along the Mississippi River, Bayou Teche, and Bayou Lafourche. The term "Cajun" derived from the name "Acadias." What is today called Cajun country consists of 22 parishes, the center of which is Lafayette. Three of Acadiana's most charming tourist towns are St. Martinville, New Iberia and Loreauville.

To start your tour of Cajun country, take I–10 west from New Orleans toward Baton Rouge. From New Orleans it takes about one hour and 40 minutes to reach the Breaux Bridge Exit 109, which is located 10 miles before the Lafayette turnoff. From Breaux Bridge, take Louisiana 347 and turn onto Junction 350. The trip to St. Martinville takes about three hours from New Orleans. The Longfellow-Evangeline State Commemorative Area, named in honor of Henry Wadsworth Longfellow and the heroine of his famous poem, is located north of town, on Highway 31. The Acadian House Museum is here and contains furnishings and memorabilia depicting the life of the early Acadian settlers. It is open from 9:30 A.M. to 4:30 P.M., Monday through Saturday, and from 1:00 to 4 P.M. on Sunday. The charge is 25 cents per person.

One spot where tourists always visit is the Evangeline Oak where the real Evangeline (Emmeline Labiche) waited for her lover on the banks of the Bayou Teche. Her grave is in the tiny cemetery next to the historic St. Martin de Tours Church. Other spots worth a visit include St. Michael's Cemetery, which dates back to the 1840s; St. Martin's Courthouse, an antebellum structure built in the classic Greek Revival style; and the Old Castille Hotel, which was built around 1790 and is located next to the Evangeline Oak.

Loreauville is only ten miles away, heading south on Highway 86. The big attraction here is the Loreauville Heritage Village Museum, at 403 Main Street (La. 86) in Loreauville, which is "one woman's tribute to the people of Acadiana." This outdoor museum is arranged like a village and depicts four centuries of life along Bayou Teche. It was established by Mae Barros, who wanted a museum that the working people could identify with. It is open daily from dawn to dusk. Admission is $1 for adults, 50 cents for students.

Continuing south, less than five miles away on Highway 31, is New Iberia, Louisiana's sugar cane capitol and home of one of the state's finest plantation houses, Shadows-on-the-Teche, located at the intersection of Center Street and Main Street. This plantation, a property of the National Trust for Historic Preservation, was built in the 1830s for David Weeks, a wealthy planter. It is open daily from 9:00 A.M. to 4:30 P.M., except Christmas and Thanksgiving. Admission is $2 for adults; $1 for students and senior citizens.

Other sites worth visiting on Main Street include the Gebert Oak, a registered specimen of the Live Oak Society located at 541 Main Street, and the statue of Hadrian, a 7-foot monument built in A.D. 130 in Rome.

If you have any questions while visiting New Iberia, the people at the Acadiana Regional Tourist Information Center will be glad to help you. Located at the junction of Highway 90 and Highway 14, it is open 9:00 A.M. to 5:00 P.M., Wednesday through Sunday (318) 365–1540.

The Gulf Coast

The Mississippi Gulf Coast with its white sandy beaches and stately white mansions has long been a favorite vacation retreat for Orleanians anxious to leave the hectic pace of the city. In its heyday, the Gulf Coast was a fashionable resort community for wealthy Northerners and Southerners. And while hurricanes have destroyed many of its fine old homes, the Gulf Coast—in particular Pass Christian (called "The Pass")—still retains an undeniable grandeur.

Most visitors make Pass Christian or Biloxi their destination, but if you continue your drive to Ocean Springs, you'll find a quaint, relatively unexplored community, perfect for a one-day excursion away from New Orleans.

Located only 90 miles from New Orleans by way of I–10 East, Ocean Springs began when Pierre LeMoyne d'Iberville stepped onto its beaches. He called his new settlement "Biloxey" after the friendly Indians who welcomes his expedition to their shores.

When the settlement finally relocated across the bay, the original community became known as Old Biloxi and continued on as a small Indian trading post. Permanent settlers began moving into the territory after the Louisiana Purchase of 1803. In 1854, its name was changed to Ocean Springs in tribute to the area's springs which the Indians maintained had curative powers.

Ocean Springs is a small community with a population of 14,420, according to its 1980 census. It has a year-round mild climate and uncrowded beaches that overlook Biloxi Bay and Deer Island, one of the barrier islands in the Mississippi Sound.

Before starting a tour of the area, you may want to visit the Chamber of Commerce, located in the old railroad depot on Washington Avenue and Robinson Street. Free tour maps of the town can be obtained here. St. John's Episcopal Church on Porter Avenue is a recommended stop for anyone interested in architecture. This elegant small church was designed in 1892 by Louis Sullivan, "the father of American architecture."

Sullivan, the pioneer of the skyscraper, summered in Ocean Springs, which he called "the land of my inspiration and dreams." His one-story shingle house is situated at the corner of Holcomb Boulevard and Shearwater Drive. It is not open to the public.

Back on Shearwater Drive, you will pass Shearwater Pottery, which has been an Ocean Springs tradition since 1927. Shearwater Pottery is one family's dedication to craft and a visit here is highly recommended. This was also the home of famed watercolorist Walter Anderson, who died in 1965. Anderson's cottage, which is now a mini-museum, can be viewed from 1:00 to 5:30 P.M. on Thursdays. The showroom, which features pottery by the Anderson family, is open Monday through Saturday, 9:00 A.M. to 5:30 P.M., and on Sundays from 1:00 to 5:30 P.M.

Ocean Springs, once a health resort, is now a community filled with artists and craftsmen. Another popular place for crafts is Neil Ballard's shop on Government Street, three blocks from U.S. Highway 90. Ballard's specialty is pewter jewelry. His shop is open from 9:00 A.M. to 5:00 P.M., Tuesday through Saturday. Or you might want to try Josie Gautier's Singing River Ceramics and Hobby Shop in Gautier, 12 miles east of Ocean Springs on Highway 90. Her shop is open 9:00 A.M. to 5:00 P.M., Tuesday through Saturday, and from 1:00 to 5:00 P.M. on Sundays.

On your way back to New Orleans, go U.S. Highway 90 from Ocean Springs, heading west. Biloxi, which is only three miles across the

Biloxi-Ocean Springs Bridge, is the site of Beauvoir, the last home of Jefferson Davis, the president of the Confederacy. It is open daily.

The 22-mile strip on Highway 90 between Ocean Springs and Bay St. Louis is called the Scenic Route, and it lives up to its name. On one side of the highway is the Gulf of Mexico and on the other are lovely old homes. This stretch is more time-consuming than the interstate, but you will definitely consider it time well spent.

PRACTICAL INFORMATION FOR

THE OUTER AREAS

HOW TO GET THERE. By air. *Delta, Royale* and *Republic* airlines service cities within the state. Aircraft charter and rental services, including helicopter, are available.

By car. I–55 will take you from Kentwood to Hammond. I–20, in the north, runs west from Monroe, Ruston to Shreveport. On I–10, you can go west from Slidell through New Orleans, Baton Rouge, Lafayette, Jennings to Lake Charles. I–10 East will take you from New Orleans to the Mississippi Gulf Coast.

Car rental. You can rent an *Avis, Hertz, Budget* or *National* car in Baton Route, Lafayette, New Orleans, and Shreveport.

By bus. *Greyhound* and *Trailways* serve cities within the state as well as the Mississippi Gulf Coast.

By ferry. The Mississippi River may be crossed by ferry at New Orleans, Plaquemine, White Castle, Reserve, Luling, Belle Chase, St. Francisville, and Lutcher.

HOTELS AND MOTELS located outside of New Orleans are less expensive than those in the Crescent City. The price category in this section, for double occupancy, without meals, will average as follows: *Deluxe,* $60 and up; *Expensive,* $45–$60; *Moderate,* $30–$45; *Inexpensive,* less than $30.

For a more complete description of the hotel and motel categories see *Facts at Your Fingertips* at the front of this volume.

ALEXANDRIA

Holiday Inn. *Moderate.* 2300 MacArthur Dr.; (318) 443–7331 or (800) 238–8000. Pool, lounge, restaurant, playground, Sgt. Major's Pub.

Rodeway Inn. *Moderate.* 742 MacArthur Dr.; (318) 448–1611 or (800) 228–2000. Pool, 24-hour restaurant.

TraveLodge. *Moderate.* 1116 MacArthur Dr.; (318) 448–1841 or (800) 225–3050. Pool, restaurant.

BATON ROUGE

Hilton Hotel. *Deluxe.* I–10 at Corporate Square; (504) 924–5000. Pool, tennis and health club, penthouse suites, 24-hour room service, Captain French's Dining Room.

Holiday Inn South. *Expensive.* 9940 Airline Hwy.; (504) 924–7021 or (800) 238–8000. Gameroom, lounge, pool, restaurant.

Prince Murate Motor Inn. *Expensive.* 1480 Nicholson Dr.; (504) 387–111. Pool, restaurant, lounge.

Howard Johnson Motor Lodge. *Moderate.* 2365 College Dr.; (504) 925–2451 or (800) 654–2000. Pool, restaurant next to building.

LAFAYETTE

Sheraton Acadiana. *Deluxe.* 1801 Penhook Rd.; (318) 233–8120 or (800) 325–3535. Restaurant, two lounges, pool.

Sheraton Town House. *Expensive.* 1020 Penhook Rd.; (318) 234–7471 or (800) 325–3535. Pool, restaurant.

Best Western Evangeline Inn. *Moderate.* Hwy. 167 North; (318) 233–2090 or (800) 528–1234. Restaurant, coffee shop, lounge, pool. Located 5 miles from Evangeline Downs.

NATCHITOCHES

Holiday Inn. *Moderate.* Hwy. 1 South By-pass; (318) 357–8281 or (800) 238–8000. Pool, restaurant, lounge.

SHREVEPORT/BOSSIER CITY

Hilton Inn. *Deluxe.* I–20 and Airline Dr.; Bossier City; (318) 747–2400. Lillian's Discotheque, Yesterday's Restaurant, swimming pool.

Ramada Inn. *Expensive.* 5116 Monkhouse Dr.; (318) 635–7531 or (800) 228–2828. Pool, 24-hour restaurant, lounge.

 ANTEBELLUM ACCOMMODATIONS. Once only the privileged few could enjoy the luxury of spending the night in a plantation home. But times have changed—and so has the economy—and a growing number of plantations are opening their doors not only to visitors but to overnight guests. There are no televisions or telephones in these antebellum accommodations, but there is an elegance that transcends 20th-century invention. Space is limited and reservations are a must. Prices quoted are for double occupancy; and it should be noted that not all rooms have private baths.

Madewood Plantation House, Hwy. 308, in Napoleonville has four rooms in the main house. A $125 charge includes dinner, a plantation breakfast, drinks and a tour of the house. (504) 524–1988.

Nottoway Plantation, north of White Castle, on La. 1, has nine rooms in the main house. A $100 charge includes a complimentary bottle of champange, morning coffee served in your room, breakfast, a tour of the plantation and use of the swimming pool. (504) 545–2730.

The Myrtles, U.S. Hwy 61, near St. Francisville, has six rooms in the main house and four in a new building. The rate ranges from $38 to $45, which includes breakfast and a tour. (504) 635–6277.

The Cottage, U.S. Hwy. 61 at Cottage Lane, 6 miles north of St. Francisville, has six rooms in the main house, which is surrounded by 360 acres with formal gardens. A tour and breakfast are included in the $40 fee. (504) 635–3674.

Wakefield, U.S. 61, 8 miles north of St. Francisville, has three rooms in the main house. The $35 charge includes a continental breakfast and tour of the house. (504) 635–3988.

Propinquity, 523 Royal St., St. Francisville, has two rooms in the main house that are rented. A continental breakfast and tour is included in the $35 charge. (504) 635–6855.

Mount Hope Plantation, 8151 Highland Rd., in Baton Rouge, has two rooms in the main house. The $53 charge includes breakfast and a tour. (504) 766–8600.

Mintmere Plantation, 1400 Main St., in Mintmere, only rents one two-room suite. The $100 charge includes breakfast and a tour. (318) 364–6210.

Albania, La. 182, Bayou Teche, just south of Jeanerette, rents one cottage, which has a living room, bedroom and kitchen. The cost is $45. (318) 276–4816.

Oak Alley Plantation, River Road, near Vacherie, rents one cottage that has a living room, two bedrooms and a kitchen. The fee is $50. (504) 265–2151.

Brame-Bennett House, 227 South Baton Rouge St., Clinton, has two rooms in the main house. A $60 charge includes breakfast and tour. (504) 683–5241.

Milbank, Bank St., one block off La. 10 in Jackson, has one room in the main house. The $50 fee includes breakfast and a tour. (504) 634–7273.

Glencoe, La. 68, 4½ miles north of La. 10 intersection near Jackson, has rooms in the main house. Prices range from $60 to $75, which includes tour, breakfast and use of the swimming pool and tennis courts. (504) 629–5387.

Asphodel, La. 68 south of La. 10 and north of U.S. 61 near Jackson, has ten rooms in a new building. Prices range from $40 to $45, which includes plantation breakfast. (504) 654–6868.

 TOURIST INFORMATION SERVICES. *Louisiana Office of Tourism,* 666 N. Foster Blvd., Baton Rouge, has information about all Louisiana events and tourist attractions. It is open from 8:00 A.M.–4:00 P.M., Monday through Friday. (504) 925–3860.

Baton Rouge Tourist Center, Old State Capitol, River Road at North Boulevard, Baton Rouge, is open from 9:30 A.M.–5:00 P.M.. Monday through Friday;

from 10:00 A.M.–5:00 P.M., Saturday; and from 1:00–5:00 P.M., Sunday. (504) 383–1825.

Natchitoches Tourist Center, 781 Front St., Natchitoches, is open from 8:00 A.M.–5:00 P.M., Monday through Friday. (318) 352–4411.

Lafayette Tourist Center, U.S. Hwy. 90 at 16th St., Lafayette, is open from 8:30 A.M.–5:00 P.M., Monday through Friday; and from 9:00 A.M.–5:00 P.M. on weekends. (318) 232–3737.

Alexandria-Pineville Tourist Center, 214 Jackson St., Alexandria, is open 8:30 A.M.–4:30 P.M., Monday through Friday. (318) 442–6671.

Shreveport-Bossier Tourist Center, 629 Spring St., Shreveport, is open from 8:00 A.M.–5:00 P.M., Monday through Friday. (318) 222–9391.

Lake Charles Tourist Center, Lakeshore Dr. at I-10, is open from 8:00 A.M.–4:30 P.M., Monday through Friday. (318) 436–9588.

 SEASONAL EVENTS. In Louisiana, festivals and fairs are favorite ways to—as they say in Cajun Country—"pass a good time." Most towns and cities have at least one event that celebrates a season (spring, summer, the harvest, Christmas), a group of people (the Cajuns, Italians, Germans), a crop (watermelon, strawberry, peaches) or a creature (usually the crawfish, crab, oyster or catfish). In other words, festivals celebrate life in Louisiana—the good life, that is.

The most spectacular event of all is, of course, Mardi Gras, which is always held the Tuesday before Ash Wednesday and culminates two weeks of parades and parties. But Louisiana has approximately 230 fairs and festivals; and while none are as lavish as Mardi Gras in New Orleans, each one has a spirit and a flair all its own. For the exact dates of the events write the Louisiana Office of Tourism, P.O. Box 44291, Baton Rouge, LA 70804 or call (504) 925–3860.

January. Commemoration celebration of the *Battle of New Orleans* is held every year at the Chalmette National Historical Park, located east of New Orleans on State 46. During the ceremonies the last battle of the War of 1812 is re-enacted.

February. This is usually the month is which *Mardi Gras* is celebrated in New Orleans, Lafayette, Eunice, Houma and Mamou.

March. Springtime is when the azaleas are in bloom and the time to visit beautiful old homes that are private the rest of the year. Antebellum homes are on display during the *Audubon Pilgrimage* in St. Francisville, the *Dogwood Tour of Homes* in Bogalusa, and the *Tour of Homes* in Franklin. The *Amite Oyster Day* is a good time to taste oysters at their seasonal best.

April. *Holiday in Dixie* is a 10-day festival that celebrates the Louisiana Purchase and is held every year in Shreveport. *The Madewood Arts Festival* is a fun-filled weekend of music and crafts exhibit at Madewood Plantation House in Napoleonville.

May. *Contraband Day* in Lake Charles is a popular festival that marks the beginning of the water sports season and commemorates Jean Lafitte's visit to Calcasieu Parish. As the legend goes, the pirate used his contraband to buy food from the early settlers there. Lafitte then became a regular visitor to the area and, some say, his buried treasure is still hidden somewhere in Calcasieu Parish. *The Crawfish Festival* in Breaux Bridge is held on the shores of the Bayou Teche in the heart of the "Crawfish Capital of the World." The festival features a fais-do-do (a dance where the children are put to sleep to the sound of the old French and Cajun lullabies), a crawfish eating contest and a crawfish cooking contest. *The Poke Salad Festival* in Blanchard is a weekend of fiddling contests and square dancing. There's plenty of good food at this festival, which specializes in—what else?—poke salad, a wild plant resembling spinach. *The Sawmill Days* "tells it like it was" in Fisher during the late 19th century. In 1979, the Village of Fisher, the last of the Louisiana sawmill towns built during the lumbering heyday, was designated a Louisiana Landmark and placed on the National Register of Historic Districts. The festival features a logging contest, music and crafts.

June. *The Corney Creek Festival* in Bernice began as a fun way to get people interested in preserving the scenic little stream. The festival features a turtle race and a spitting contest. (The record is 18.1 feet.) *The Melrose Arts and Crafts Festival* is a large exhibit held at beautiful Melrose Plantation, a National Historic Landmark. *The Jambalaya Festival* in Gonzales, "the Jambalaya Capital of the World," has three different stages of music plus an arts and crafts exhibit. *The World's Champion Pirogue Races* in Lafitte begins with a series of four races. The last event is for the "World's Championship."

July. *Louisiana Legend Heritage Festival* in Monroe features a food fair and an outdoor drama, which is shown every Saturday night during July in Kiroli Park. There is also an "Old South Showboat" voyage along the Ouachita River. *The Louisiana Catfish Festival* is held in Des Allemands, the "Catfish Capital of the Universe," and features the World Championship Skinning contest. *The Oyster Festival in Galliano* consists of continuous (well, almost) music for three days.

August. *The Greenwood Pioneer Days* in Greenwood begins with a watermelon supper and a concert in the town square. On Saturday, there is a tour of the historical homes in the area.

September. *Festival Acadiens* in Lafayette celebrates the contributions made by the Cajuns in Louisiana. *Louisiana Shrimp and Petroleum Festival* held Labor Day weekend in Morgan City joins together two very strange bedfellows. *Sauce Piquante and Music Festival* is a four-day event in Kinder.

October. *French Food Festival* in LaRose is held the last full weekend of October and features French and Cajun cusine. *The Louisiana State Fair,* an annual event since 1906, is held in Shreveport. The 10-day fair features a livestock/agriculture show, top entertainment, educational and commercial exhibits and a giant midway. Another popular annual event held in Shreveport is the *Red River Revel.* Every year more than 200,000 people enjoy the food, music and crafts at this outdoor festival. *The Washington Parish Free Fair,* which prides itself on being the "second largest free fair in the U.S.A.," is held in Franklin and features a rodeo, community exhibits and entertainment. *The Louisiana Swine Festival* (yes, you read it right) is held in Basile. *The Interna-*

tional Rice Festival is held in Crowley, the heart of rice country in Louisiana. *The Natchitoches Historic Tour of Homes* is held the second weekend in Natchitoches.

November. *The Pecan Festival* in Colfax honors Louisiana's favorite nut. *Destrehan Plantation* has a fall festival the second weekend in November.

December. On the first Saturday in December more than 100,000 visitors come to the small French-Spanish town of Natchitoches to see the oldest permanent community in the Louisiana Purchase turn into a city of lights. This town's annual *Christmas Festival,* a tradition since 1927, has been billed as the "Mardi Gras" of northern Louisiana, and it is. The celebration begins with fireworks, followed by a moment of darkness, then the city becomes ablaze when 175,000 tiny colored lights transform the town into a fairyland. The Christmas lights remain on view from 5:30 to 11:00 P.M., daily through New Year's Day. On *Christmas Eve,* giant bonfires are lighted on the MIssissippi River levees in St. James Parish. The bonfires, legend says, were started by the early settlers to help Santa.Claus find his way to their new homes.

 TOURS. Note: Tour prices quoted below are subject to change so be sure to call ahead for latest prices. *Abbott Tours,* 2609 Canal St., New Orleans, 827–5920 or 1–800 –535–8550, has a "Natchez Rendevous" package, which is an overnight trip to Natchez, MS, that includes one night at the newly renovated Eola Hotel, two meals (breakfast and dinner) and a tour of three plantation homes. The bus trip, which takes approximately three hours, leaves New Orleans every Saturday and costs $99 per person, double occupancy, or $129 per person, single occupancy.

Dixieland Sightseeing Tours, 4861 Chef Menteur Hwy., New Orleans, 245–1702, has a daily River Road plantation tour from 9:00 A.M. to 4:00 P.M. The trip features a visit to Houmas House and San Francisco Plantation and costs $25 per person.

Jacco Tours, 728 Dumain St., New Orleans, 568–0140, has a six-hour Cajun country, bayou, and plantation tour that includes a ride through the swamp and a visit to Destrehan Plantation. The cost is $33 for adults and $15 for children under 15 years of age.

Orleans Transportation Service, 1793 Julia St., New Orleans, 525–0138, has a daily River Road plantation tour that lasts 6½ hours, visits Oak Alley Plantation and Houmas House and costs $26.

Southern Tours, 500 Poydras Plaza Blvd., New Orleans, 486–0604 or 1–800–535–7160, has a daily plantation tour that visits San Francisco Plantation and Houmas House. The tour lasts 7 hours and costs $25 for adults and $12.50 for children 6 to 12 years of age. Children under six years go free.

New Orleans Steamboat Company, 2340 ITM Building, New Orleans, 586–8777, has a daily, non stop bayou cruise that takes 5 hours. It costs $11.50 for adults and $5.75 for children ages 6 to 12. Children under six years of age go free.

Bayou Canoe Tours, Route 1, Box 481NA, Sulphur, 1–318–527–9613, has guided canoe trips along the Calcasieu River, into Beckwith Bayou and Beaver Creek. The trip costs $25, which includes lunch.

Passe Partout Touring Co., 329 Beverly Dr., Lafayette, 318–235–1891, has custom bus, boat and helicopter tours of Acadiana, including Lafayette, New Iberia, Opelousas, Loreauville, Abbeville, St. Martinville, Franklin, and Baton Rouge.

Boat Tours of the Atchafalya Basin, "Louisiana's great swampland wilderness," leave McGee's Landing in Henderson. The cost is $7.50 for adults and $4 for children under 12 years of age. For further information call (318) 228–8523.

Annie Miller's Swamp Tours in Houma are given by—who else?—Mrs. Miller, the lady who talks to alligators. Her tour is given twice daily and lasts approximately 3 hours. The cost is $30 per person. For more information call 879–3934.

SPORTS. Horseracing has been a popular pastime in Louisiana since its antebellum days when New Orleans alone had five fine tracks. Metairie Cemetery, in fact, was once the location for the famous Metairie Race Course, which closed its doors in 1872.

But horseracing is alive and well in Louisiana where there are five tracks located throughout the state. As they say in Acadiana, *"Ils sont partis!"* (They're off!)

The Fair Grounds in New Orleans is the oldest track in the South. The season for the 110-year-old landmark begins on Thanksgiving Day and continues until March.

Jefferson Downs in Kenner has evening racing from April to mid-November.

Evangeline Downs in Lafayette has evening races Thursday through Saturday and afternoon races on Sunday, Memorial Day, and Labor Day. The track is open from April through September.

Louisiana Downs in Shreveport-Bossier City has two tracks that are used during its May to October season, the highlight of which is the $200,000 Louisiana Downs Handicap.

Delta Downs in Vinton has two different kinds of racing: quarter horses race from April through July and thoroughbreds race from September to March. Evening races are held Thursday through Saturday and at 1:00 P.M. on Sunday.

HISTORIC SITES. Louisiana has more than sixty plantation homes that are open to the public. These homes are usually located on or near waterways, such as the Mississippi River, the Red River or Bayou Teche, since the rivers and bayous were the major source of transportation for the planters and, more importantly, their sugar cane and cotton crops. Most of these homes are privately owned and have an admission charge, usually from $3 to $4.50. It also should be noted that these homes are usually closed for major holidays.

Chalmette: *Beauregard House,* a small but traditional antebellum home built in 1832, now serves as a visitors' center for the Chalmette National Historical Park, located 8 miles east of New Orleans on State 46. This is also the site of the Battle of New Orleans. There is no admission fee. Open daily from 8:00 A.M. to 5:00 P.M., closed Christmas, Mardi Gras, New Year's Day.

Vacherie: *Oak Alley Plantation.* This classical antebellum home, on the River Road, is a National Historic Landmark, and is also famous for its magnificent alley of twenty-eight evenly spaced live oak trees that form a quarter-mile archway to the house. Open daily from 9:00 A.M. to 5:30 P.M. (504) 523–4351.

Napoleonville: *Madewood Plantation.* Hwy. 308. This beautiful Greek-Revival mansion was built by Col. Thomas Pugh, who died of yellow fever before it was completed in 1848. It is now owned by Keith Marshall of New Orleans. Open daily, except major holidays, from 10:00 A.M. to 5:00 P.M. (504) 524–1988.

Mintmere: *Mintmere Plantation.* 1400 Main St. A Greek Revival, raised cottage built in 1857. The Armand Broussard House, an 18th-century, mud-and-moss plantation house, is also located on the grounds. Open daily. (318) 364–6210.

Franklin: *Frances Plantation.* U.S. 90, 4 miles east of Franklin. This 165-year-old home is now an antique and interior design shop. Open 9:00 A.M. to 5:00 P.M. , closed Sundays and Mondays. (318) 828–5472.

Arlington Plantation. U.S. 90, 1 mile east of Franklin on Bayou Teche. This antebellum home was built by Euphrazie Carlin, a wealthy planter who owned approximately 2,000 slaves. Open 10:00 A.M.–4:00 P.M., Tuesday through Saturday. (318) 828–2644.

Oaklawn Manor. Irish Bend Road (Parish Road 28), 5 miles north of Franklin. This grand Greek Colonial Manor House has been beautifully restored. Its grounds are filled with magnificent live oaks believed to be growing at Oaklawn when Columbus discovered America. Open 9:30 A.M.–5:30 P.M., daily, March through September, and from 9:30 A.M.–4:30 P.M., October to February. (318) 828–0434.

St. Francisville. *The Myrtles.* U.S. Hwy. 61. This 186-year-old home features a unique 110-foot grapevine grillwork gallery and, according to local legend, a ghost. Open 9:00 A.M.–5:00 P.M. daily (504) 635–6277.

Rosedown. 2 miles east of St. Francisville on Hwy. 10 and U.S. 61. This 1835 plantation home and its Versailles-inspired gardens give visitors an authentic view of the antebellum lifestyle of Southern planters. Open daily, 9:00 A.M.–5:00 P.M. (504) 524–8407.

Wakefield Plantation. U.S. 61, 8 miles north of St. Francisville. This Greek-Revival structure, completed in 1836, is missing its third story, which was removed in 1877 and then transferred to another location. Open 9:00 A.M. to 5:00 P.M., Wednesday through Friday. (504) 635–3988.

Catalpa. North of St. Francisville on U.S. 61. This Victorian-type cottage, built in 1885, features a double horseshoe alley of live oaks and beautiful antique furnishings. Open daily 9:00 A.M. to 5:00 P.M., closed the months of December and January. (504) 635–3372.

Cottage. U.S. Hwy. 61 at Cottage Lane. One of the few remaining complete antebellum plantations in the South built in the period 1795 to 1850. Open daily, 9:00 A.M. to 5:00 P.M. (504) 635–3674.

Jackson: *Milbank Manor.* Bank Street, one block off La. 10. This classical Greek structure was built in 1836 and has been used over the years as a hotel, bank, city hall, and apartment house. Open 10:00 A.M.–4:00 P.M., Tuesday through Saturday. (504) 634–7273.

Glencoe Plantation. La. 68, 4½ miles north of Jackson. Considered Louisiana's finest example of Queen Anne style, Victorian Gothic architecture. Open 10:00 A.M. to 4:00 P.M., Monday through Saturday, and from 12:30 P.M.–4:00 P.M., Sunday. (504) 629–5387.

Baton Rouge: *Magnolia Mound Plantation.* 2161 Nicholson Dr. Situated on a high natural ridge, overlooking the Mississippi River, this 18th-century structure was once the home of Prince Achille Murate, great nephew of Napoleon Bonaparte. Open 10:00 A.M. to 4:00 P.M., Tuesday through Saturday, and from 1:00 to 4:00 P.M., Sunday. (504) 343–4955.

Mount Hope Plantation. 8151 Highland Rd. Build in 1817 and furnished in the Federal Sheraton and Empire periods. Open daily, 9:00 A.M. to 5:00 P.M. (504) 766–8600.

Old State Capitol. River Road at North Boulevard. This Gothic castle, a National Historic Landmark, was built in 1849 and was the capitol of the state until 1932. Open 9:30 A.M.–5:00 P.M., Monday through Friday; 10:00 A.M.–5:00 P.M., Saturday; and 1:00–5:00 P.M., Sunday. (504) 383–1825.

Melrose: *Melrose Plantation.* 2 miles east of La. 1 via La. 493. This complex of antebellum structures, a National Historic Landmark, includes Melrose Plantation (built in 1833), Yucca House (the original home, 1796) and the African House. Open 2:00–4:30 P.M., daily except Monday and Wednesday.

Thibodaux: *Edward Douglass White State Commemorative Area.* Hwy 1, 5 miles north of Thibodaux. Restored white-frame 130-year-old homestead of the former statesman and Chief Justice of the U.S. Supreme Court. Open 9:00 A.M.–5:00 P.M., Monday through Saturday, and from 1:00–5:00 P.M., Sunday. (504) 446–8486.

Lafayette: *Acadian Village and Gardens.* Mouton Road. Restored bayou town, which shows the 19th-century life of the French Acadians. Open daily, 10:00 A.M.–5:00 P.M. (318) 981–2364. Lafayette Museum. 1122 Lafayette St. Listed in the National Register of Historic Places, this museum, which features antiques and historic documents, is located in the home of Alexandre Mouton, the first democratic governor of Louisiana. Open 9:00 A.M.–noon and from 2:00–5:00 P.M., Tuesday through Saturday, and 3:00–5:00 P.M., Sunday. (318) 234–2208.

MUSEUMS. Baton Rouge: *Louisiana State University Rural Life Museum.* Burden Research Plantation, 4560 Essen Lane at I–10. Depicts life on a 19th-century Louisiana plantation. Open 8:30 A.M.–4 P.M., Monday through Friday. (504) 766–8241.

Anglo-American Art Museum. Memorial Tower on the LSU campus. This charming, albeit small, museum features a portrait collection and rooms furnished from various eras in American history. Open 8 A.M.–4:30 P.M., Monday through Friday; 9 A.M.–noon and 1–4 P.M., Saturday; and from 1–4:30 P.M., Sunday. (504) 388–8451.

The Old Governor's Mansion Museum. 502 North Blvd. Built in 1940, it is filled with memorabilia of Louisiana governors. Open 10 A.M.–5 P.M., Tuesday through Saturday; and 1–5 P.M., Sunday. (504) 344–9463.

Houma: *Southdown Plantation and Terrebone Museum.* Hwy. 311. The second story of this structure, which was built in 1856, was added in 1856. Open daily 10:00 A.M.–4:00 P.M. (504) 868–2732.

St. Francisville: *Oakley Plantation.* Located in the Audubon State Commemorative Area, Hwy. 965, east of St. Francisville. This plantation, now restored as a museum featuring works of naturalist John James Audubon, was occupied by Audubon and was the setting for many of his "Birds of America" paintings. Open 9:00 A.M. to 5:00 P.M., Monday through Saturday, and from 1:00 to 5:00 P.M., Sunday. (504) 635–3739.

Epps: *Poverty Point Museum.* La. 134. This museum, located in a state park, features hundred of artifacts of the Poverty Point Indians, who lived in this area more than 2,700 years ago. Open 9:00 A.M.–5:00 P.M., Tuesday through Saturday, and from 1:00–5:00 P.M., Sunday. (318) 926–5492.

Patterson: *Wedell-Williams Aviation Museum.* Off U.S. 90 on La. 182. This old airstrip is where Jimmy Wedell and Harry Williams made aviation history in the early 1930s. Open noon–5:00 P.M., Tuesday through Sunday. (504) 395–7067.

Cloutierville: *Bayou Folk Museum.* Main Street. In this raised Louisiana cottage, built in the early 1800s and now owned by Northwestern State University, there is a museum showing the history of the people in the Cane River area as well as a section devoted to author Kate Chopin, who once lived in this house. Open 1:30–5:30 P.M., Saturday and Sunday, March through May and September and November; and from 10:00 A.M.–5:00 P.M., Tuesday through Friday, and 1:30–5:30 P.M., Saturday and Sunday, June through August. Closed December through February. (318) 379–2321.

 DINING OUT. Restaurants in Louisiana offer a unique selection of food, much of which reflects the French heritage of the state. Some favorite local dishes that you should seek out are jambalaya, gumbo, boudin, couchon du lait, crawfish etouffee, crawfish or crabmeat bisque, soft-shell crab, turtle sauce piquante, boiled seafood and oysters on the half shell.

Price categories and ranges for a complete dinner are as follows: *Expensive,* $15 and up; *Moderate,* $7–$15; *Inexpensive,* under $7. Not included are drinks, tax, and tip. For a more complete explanation of restaurant categories see *Facts at Your Fingertips* at the front of this volume.

SHREVEPORT

Ernest's Supper Club. *Expensive.* 612 Commerce St., (318) 221–0234. Good atmosphere and great seafood.

Sansone's. *Expensive.* 701 East King's Hwy.; (318) 865–5146. Steak, Italian and seafood dishes are the specialities. An enjoyable restaurant with entertainment.

DONALDSONVILLE

Lafitte's Landing Restaurant. *Moderate.* (504) 473–1232. La. 18 at the foot of the Sunshine Bridge. Delightful restaurant with an ambitious menu, located in a raised cottage once frequented by the pirate Jean Lafitte.

LAKE CHARLES

Plantation House. *Expensive.* 903 Broad St. (318) 439–5692. Seafood is the specialty.

ALEXANDRIA

Herbie K's. *Moderate.* 3515 Lee Rd. (318) 442–1821. Known for its seafood. Good homemade raspberry sherbert.

LAFAYETTE

Chez Marcelle. *Expensive.* 102 North St. Julien Rd. in Broussard. (318) 837–3100. This elegant restaurant has some of the finest Creole food around.

Chez Pastor. *Expensive.* 1211 Pinhook Rd. (318) 234–5189. Cajun and Creole cuisine.

BATON ROUGE

The Chalet Brandt. *Expensive.* 7655 Old Hammond Hwy. (504) 927–6040. French cuisine and great pastries.

Giamanco's Restaurant. *Moderate.* 4624 Government St. (503) 928–5045. Italian food is the specialty. Family-owned restaurant.

INDEX

INDEX